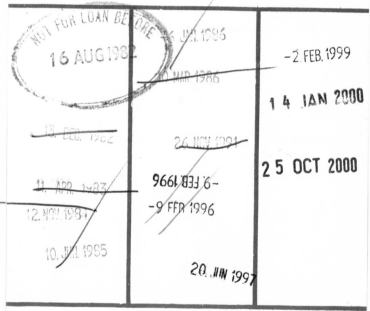

Parent-Child Interaction

The Socialization Process Observed in Twin and Singleton Families

Hugh Lytton

The University of Calgary
Canada

PLENUM PRESS • NEW YORK AND LONDON

Library of Congress Cataloging in Publication Data

Lytton, Hugh.
  Parent-child interaction.

  Includes bibliographical references and index.
  1. Parent and child. 2. Socialization. 3. Twins—Psychology. I. Title.
[DNLM: 1. Parent-child relations. 2. Socialization twins—Psychology.
3. Child behavior. WS105.5.F2 L998p]
BF723.P25L97   155.4'18   80-18285
ISBN 0-306-40521-0

© 1980 Plenum Press, New York
A Division of Plenum Publishing Corporation
227 West 17th Street, New York, N.Y. 10011

Printed in the United States of America

To my family

Preface

This work is largely based on what has been a mammoth—one person called it a "heroic"—research project. Both fieldwork and data analyses were laborious and time-consuming, and the work could not have come to fruition without the cooperation of many people. Above all, I owe a debt of gratitude to the mothers and fathers who recognized the importance of such an investigation in building a secure knowledge base concerning human development and who kindly allowed us to come into their homes. The children, at 2½, did not have such an appreciation, but naturally I am very grateful to them for the star roles they played in the work. I have to thank all my collaborators for their help in various aspects of the research: Walter Zwirner was statistical consultant to the project, and Pat Olsen and Arlene Grineau were the chief research assistants—I owe particular thanks to them. Others who helped generously with data collection or data analysis (including program writing) were Pat Bachor, Valerie Becker, Rob Black, Doreen Darby, Judy Eser, Con Ferris, Susan Horsley, "Jagan," Ann Johnson, Wayne Miller, Sambhu Nath, Deanna Piwowar, Bruce Roe, Ken Ryba, Laurel Saville, Cecilia Schnurr, Terry Taerum, Debbie Twaddle, and John Wrenshall. Sherry Pitcher kindly prepared the index.

Dorice Conway and Reginald Sauvé collaborated in the analysis of identical–fraternal twin differences (Chapter 4); Nicholas Martin and Lindon Eaves were chiefly responsible for the biometric–genetic analysis of the data (Chapter 9). Marie Ellement of the hematology laboratory of the Foothills Hospital carried out the blood-typing of the twins.

I am very grateful also to the people who read drafts of one or more chapters of this book and who are responsible for many improvements (I am accountable for any defects that remain): Monica Baehr, Robert B. Cairns, Philip E. Vernon, Denise Watts, and my wife, Cornelia.

My thanks are also due to Pat Dalgetty, Linda Culshaw, and Betty Reimer, who patiently and efficiently typed and retyped the manuscript.

The research was funded by Canada Council grants No. S70-1679,

S71-1770, and S74-1620. First, a half-sabbatical and a Canada Council
Leave Fellowship and, later, a Killam Resident Fellowship of the University
of Calgary provided me with the freedom of mind necessary to write the
book. I am deeply appreciative of the help afforded me by these institutions.

The overall project of examining parent–child relations and twin
development has not yet come to an end, however. With the help of Denise
Watts, I am now engaged in looking at twins in longitudinal perspective and
am carrying out a follow-up study of the twins at school and at home, now
that they are 8–10 years old. Hopefully, this work will see the light of day in
the not-too-distant future.

A note to the reader: The reader not interested in the details of findings, methodology, or analysis can read Chapter 1, the summary and discussion sections of Chapters 3–9, and then Chapter 10. This last chapter
draws together what, in my subjective view, are the most important points
of the book and places them in the context of their implications for human
development. One hardly dares as yet write of a "theory of human development," because we have not yet got such a theory. What the large variety
and abundance of research in developmental psychology has accomplished
is to trace some patterns in the development of behavior—some of which
are becoming quite well established. This book will, I hope, make a small
contribution toward furthering this process.

HUGH LYTTON

Contents

List of Tables

List of Figures

CHAPTER 1

Introduction and Basic Concepts

THE FORGOTTEN ASPECT OF SOCIALIZATION

Living in groups imposes its own necessities and patterns of existence. With many animals, these are transmitted by genes or by physiological influences. In the case of social insects, such as bees, for instance, the quality of food given to larvae determines their behavior as either queens or workers. As we ascend the phylogenetic scale, however, the role of learning in the acquisition of social acts assumes greater importance with increasing brain size and complexity, and the young depend more on their parents to transmit these patterns by action and gesture. This process has been called *socialization* and it exists in one form or another in mammals but has been studied particularly in primates (see Wilson, 1975, for an account). The capacity for verbal communication in humans adds a special dimension of elaboration and intensity to the process and increases the learning component manifoldly.

While the socialization process has, no doubt, been part and parcel of the human condition for the last million years, it has come under scientific, empirical scrutiny (as distinct from literary or diary accounts) only over the last 40 years or so. For research purposes, the more traditional formulation has construed socialization essentially as the effects of parental child-rearing practices (nowadays called *parenting*) on children's characteristics. Such research was often sired by psychoanalytic theory—hence the preoccupation with conscience and dependency—and brought to birth by social learning theory, which supplied the notion of the environment's molding the child and also prompted the empirical method. Parental practices and attitudes (the *antecedents*) were almost always ascertained by interview and con-

1

sequent ratings (e.g., Burton, Maccoby, & Allinsmith, 1961; Schaffer & Emerson, 1964; Sears, Maccoby, & Levin, 1957; Yarrow, Campbell, & Burton, 1968). The child's characteristics were sometimes assessed by the same interview (e.g., Sears et al., 1957; Yarrow et al., 1968), but sometimes also by means of experimental probes (e.g., Burton et al., 1961; Sears, Rau, & Alpert, 1965) or a verbal test (Hoffman & Saltzstein, 1967).

The metatheoretical view that underlay this whole approach implied that the child was a passive being who was being molded by parental influences, a theory that we can trace back at least to the 17th century and Locke's view of the child as a "tabula rasa." In more recent times, however, the view of socialization as a unidirectional influence process has come under attack, as ignoring the child's impact on the parents.

The idea that the child is an active organism who comes into the world equipped with certain capabilities and who is motivated to solve problems and to influence and master his environment has gained general acceptance over the last decade or two, fostered by the cognitive school of psychology and supported by new experimental approaches and evidence (cf. Bower, 1974; Kalnins & Bruner, 1973). In the specific context of parent–child relations, the position that this active child affects adults, too, has been most vigorously propounded by Bell (1968), who has more recently extended it and underpinned it with supporting evidence (Bell, 1977). An important piece of evidence, which the theory positing a unidirectional parent-to-child influence has difficulty accommodating, is, for instance, the finding that a foster mother displayed different attitudes to two infants of the same sex and age assigned at the same time (Yarrow, 1963). Moreover, as Bell points out, even the most helpless newborn exerts a powerful influence on his parents. His very arrival completely transforms their lives. His cry is an irresistible force that brings his parents to his side, and in the extreme case, if his crying is prolonged and irritating, it may provoke them into battering him. Also, while parents' actions will bring about changes in the child's behavior, these very changes will, in turn, affect and modify their approach to him. There is evidence, too, that certain congenital[1] characteristics, such as physical abnormalities (Bell, 1977) or "primary reaction patterns," (Thomas, Chess, & Birch, 1968) contribute to the child's behavior and to parental reactions to him. As Bell (1977) puts it:

> Just as the (physical) experimenter's behavior is shaped and controlled by the nature of the particles, the nature of the child's behavior must require an adjustment of some sort by the parent, and, at this very basic level, there is a reciprocal relation despite the inequality of maturity. (p. 63)

That child behavior can, indeed, affect adult or parent behavior has, in fact, been shown experimentally for various psychological areas, for instance, as regards nurturance or the promotion of independence (Osofsky

---

[1] Congenital means "present at birth," not necessarily "hereditary."

& O'Connell, 1972; Yarrow, Waxler, & Scott, 1971). It should be emphasized that Bell (1977) claims only that the findings of socialization research *can* be reinterpreted, not that they must be and that he notes himself that in many cases his explanation for the correlational findings does not assign an exclusive role to child-effects (p. 81).

Indeed, the emphasis on child effects inevitably implied and brought in its train a further shift in perspective, namely, a new emphasis on the reciprocal interactions (sometimes called *transactions* in this sense) between parents and child. Any relationship is, after all, a two-way process in which, as in a tennis game, the actions of each partner are in part determined and modified by those of the other. Socialization must also be interpreted as a reciprocal process: not only do parents do things to the child, but the child does things to parents, too. Not only do parents socialize the child, but the child socializes the parents, at least to some extent.

Reciprocal influences have been demonstrated empirically in a few studies. Some recent microanalytic investigations have, for instance, shown reciprocal phasing and turn taking, particularly in vocalization and gazing, within parent–infant dyads (Brazelton, Koslowski, & Main, 1974; Schaffer, 1974; Stern, 1974). Even triadic reciprocal effects over time have been identified in the area of child competence, with the direction of influence going from mother to child to father to mother (Clarke-Stewart, 1978). However, in general, in empirical research the reciprocal nature of socialization has hitherto been its most neglected aspect, and it is, in fact, also the most difficult to analyze and specify.

Socialization may be interpreted to mean simply the transmission of the cultural values and rules of a society in all its uniqueness and particularity, something for which Margaret Mead (1963) has suggested the term enculturation. However, bearing in mind the bidirectional influence processes at work, we are led to a broader perspective, and we can think of socialization as "the integration of a child into his social world" (Richards, 1974)—a world that shapes him but that he also helps to shape.

Readers not interested in methodological issues should proceed straight to the section "About This Book" at the end of the chapter.

DIFFERENT STRATEGIES IN THE STUDY OF PARENT–CHILD INTERACTION

The armamentarium of investigators of socialization has changed and expanded over the years. Interviews and self-reports have continued in use, but there has been a considerable shift in emphasis toward experimental investigation of a parent–child relations over the last two decades, bringing with it greater contact with the behavior being studied and more rigorous control of the variables. A more recent development has been the appearance of naturalistic observation studies of parents and children that have burgeoned over the last 5–10 years, though many more deal with infants (e.g., Bell & Ainsworth, 1972; Clarke-Stewart, 1973; Lamb, 1977; Lewis, 1972) than with children over 2 years of age (e.g., Clarke-Stewart, 1978; Minton, Kagan, & Levine, 1971; Patterson & Cobb, 1973).

While a variety of influences can be cited for this development, the most important stimulus has, no doubt, come from ethology[2] whose interests, methods, and personnel have spilled over from the study of animals to the study of children (e.g., Blurton-Jones, 1972; Hinde, 1976). In addition, the recognition that interaction is the central concept of social development also instigated a natural trend toward studying it directly by means of naturalistic observation in the home.

Three core types of method for studying parent–child interaction can be distinguished, namely, naturalistic observation, laboratory experimentation, and interview. In its "pure form," I would define *naturalistic observation* as *observation of unconstrained behavior in a setting and in situations to which the conclusions are meant to apply;* a school, a store, or the home can be settings for naturalistic studies, each for its own purpose. *Laboratory experimentation* in its pure form implies, at a minimum, *the experimental control of the stimuli—that is, the independent variable(s)—in a laboratory setting.* The interview hardly needs defining here. A stark contrast between the three methods, while useful for discussion, is, however, itself an oversimplification, since (1) the conditions defining the pure form of each of them consist of several dimensions that are sometimes treated as inextricably fused, but that can, in fact, be varied independently; and (2) various combinations and permutations of whole methods are possible.

Just as there are many ways of factoring a psychological domain, so one can identify many different "dimensions of naturalness" as marking the distinction between field and laboratory research, as shown by the discussions by Parke (1979) and Tunnell (1977). I would regard as the main dimensions *setting* and *control*, and these dimensions can, in fact, be combined to varying degrees in different types of investigation.

"Naturalness" is important because it determines the "ecological validity" of an investigation, a term that has come into use in recent years (cf. the critique by Bronfenbrenner, 1977). It refers to the generalizability of research results to real-life situations. I would define *ecological validity* in general and formal terms as *the extent to which a procedure assesses behavior or identifies relationships as they occur in the subjects' life situations to which the conclusions are meant to apply.* In the case of socializa-

---

[2] *Ethology* has been defined as "the biological study of behavior" (Tinbergen, 1963). Careful observation in a natural habitat has been its methodological characteristic, and an evolutionary perspective its theoretical hallmark.

tion research, this means the degree to which the data are representative of normal parent–child interaction. Ecological validity is obviously one crucial yardstick by which the appropriateness and usefulness of any particular method of investigation must be measured.

Combining Dimensions in Different Ways

Although "field investigation" has popularly been identified with lack of control or less rigorous control and "laboratory experiment" with strict control, the setting of an investigation or observation can vary independently of the degree of control that the investigator exercises over the stimuli and background variables. Various possible combinations of different settings and degrees of control over stimuli and responses are illustrated in Table 1. Jointly these dimensions create a continuum of naturalness, the two poles of which are exemplified by observations in completely unstructured situations in the home (e.g., Baldwin *et al.*, 1949; Barker & Wright, 1955; Bell & Ainsworth, 1972) and by structured cooperation tasks or structured teaching tasks in the laboratory (e.g., Hess & Shipman, 1967; Shapira & Madsen, 1969), in which the social behavior of both partners is under experimenter control. These two types of investigation mark extremes on the continuum of naturalness, but there are many intermediate positions on this scale. Which exact position on the continuum should be occupied by each of the combinations is a matter of judgment,

Table 1. Dimensions of Naturalness[a]

Type of investigation	Setting	Control Independent variable	Control Dependent variable
Naturalistic home observation	Field (including home)	Low	Low
Natural experiment (Natural event)	Field	Low	Low
Observation of unstructured interaction	Lab	Low	Low
Field experiment	Field	High	Low
Controlled field experiment	Field	High	High
Controlled lab experiment	Lab	High	High

[a] These are only illustrations of the many combinations possible. The first and last type of investigation are clearly the end poles of the continuum, but the positions of the intermediate investigations are more a matter of judgment.

depending on the relative importance one attaches to setting or degrees of control.

Different Strategies Compared

Let us now briefly consider the differing aims, the advantages and drawbacks, and the problems inherent in each of the core types of method. For the purposes of this examination I will discuss the "pure forms" of laboratory experiment, home observation, and interview. Fuller treatments can be found in Cairns (1979a), Lytton (1971), Parke (1979), and Tunnell (1977).

Experimental Situation in Laboratory Playroom

The experimental situation has the obvious advantage that certain stimuli can be isolated and manipulated, other external conditions can be held reasonably constant, and the subjects' responses can be constrained within a behavior category, thus permitting the (fairly) unequivocal identification of cause and effect and the easy comparison between crystallized situations or groups. but the rigor of control of stimuli in this situation may only provide an illusory advantage, since what must be in doubt is the generalizability of the data from the strictly defined laboratory conditions to the natural situation in which the child's socialization experiences normally take place. Such generalization must be in doubt because the experimental analog of socialization differs in essential and systematic respects from its real-life equivalent, the most important differences being that (1) the experimenter–child interaction lacks normal reciprocity, the experimenter having maximum control over his own behavior in this situation; and (2) the child does not have a history of enduring, complex, emotionally charged relationships with the experimenter as he has with his parents.

The experimental situation may be a particularly poor analog of moral development, as Hoffman (1970) notes, since this development depends on long-range, cumulative interactions, inevitably absent in the laboratory. Matters are made worse if the experimental interaction has an artificial character, unrepresentative of the behaviors to which the experimenter wants to conclude, as sometimes happens. An unrepresentative task is, however, not necessarily confined to the laboratory setting: the lack of ecological validity would remain the same, if such a task was arranged in the home.

In general, when discrepant results have arisen from a laboratory experiment compared with a parallel investigation under more natural conditions, the phenomena have involved interpersonal relations. An example is the study of imitation, where an investigation by Yarrow and Scott (1972) suggests that sustained warm relationships with parents, etc., do enhance imitative behavior in children, whereas short laboratory warmth-manipulations with strange experimenters often fail to do so (see Hetherington & McIntyre, 1975). Gump and Sutton-Smith (1955) also provide an example from peer play where an experimentally arranged analog led to misleading results.

However, there no doubt are research aims for which the experimental laboratory design, with its rigorous control of stimuli, is appropriate and ecologically valid, though these lie outside the area of socialization. Generalizability may be in little doubt when classes of behavior are under investigation whose response mode is not altered significantly by setting and controlled techniques, and I would count among these learning tasks, for example, perceptual discrimination tasks, or Piagetian concept formation experiments. Perhaps I may enunciate a general principle, for which complete empirical validation is lacking as yet, though scattered strands of evidence exist: *Experimental laboratory designs are appropriate where the hypotheses to be tested and the phenomena under study do not involve relationships with others.* When the effects of human interaction (e.g., social reinforcement) on learning-task behaviors are at issue, a modified experimental design may be more appropriate, that is, one that will rigidly control the immediate stimuli but leave the setting natural—home or school—and employ as experimenter a person familiar to the child, for example, a parent or a teacher.

Naturalistic Observation in the Home

The strong point of naturalistic observation is the immediacy and first-hand nature of the data. Moreover, the process of recording and counting naturally occurring acts, carefully defined, possesses a high degree of objectivity. Recording concrete behavior of parents and children in sequence in natural settings permits us to see such behavior along a time line; it opens up the possibility of analyzing the to-and-fro of the interchanges and of demonstrating how some parental acts function as stimuli controlling certain child behavior, and how some child acts control certain parental behavior. In this way, we can identify separately effects due to children and those due to parents, as well as their reciprocal interaction.

The most evident drawback of the naturalistic observation is that it precludes us from manipulating and isolating the treatment, or independent, variables and thus to test their effects in the most direct manner (but see below on the question of hypothesis testing in naturalistic studies). Further, obtaining reliable data in the welter of fast-flowing actions that make up unconstrained family interchanges is, admittedly, difficult, and the method is extremely time-consuming and therefore costly.

The chief objection from the point of view of ecological validity, however, is the argument that the data thus obtained are no longer representative of what normally occurs between parents and children, since the presence of the observer affects and changes the relationship. Nevertheless, observed behavior in the home is likely to be closer to "normal parent–child interaction" than is behavior arranged and observed in the laboratory. The criterion of "normal interaction" is, strictly speaking, beyond the reach of the objective outside observer and accessible only to those involved in it, and such persons are *ipso facto* subjectively biased observers. The validity of different methods of studying parent–child interaction is therefore difficult to assess empirically, though in this the topic does not differ from many other psychological constructs that lack a criterion that can be defined and measured by consensually agreed on procedures.

It must be remembered that data arising from experiment or psychometric test are similarly affected by the presence and the characteristics of the observer–experimenter. Interview data, too, are notoriously liable to distortion. Indeed, the predominant source of distortion, attributable to the subjects, in both observation and interview is the same human propensity: a "social desirability" set. Investigators in the area of parent–child interaction who have decided that this distortion is the price they are willing to accept for the benefits to be gained from the naturalistic method (1) have reduced the distortion to the minimum possible and (2) have accepted that their data reflect "interaction-in-the-presence-of-observer." Baumrind (1967), for instance, observed both spankings and hugs and assumed that "fewer instances of such extreme behavior occurred with an observer present than would otherwise have occurred." What would affect research results more seriously would be differential observer effects in different homes, as these would alter in unknown ways the comparison between, say, lower- and middle-class families. There is some evidence, though rather weak, that this may, in fact, happen (cf. Randall, 1975, discussed in Chapter 2).

The presence of an observer has often been felt to have more restrictive and distorting effects with children older than about 4 or 5. For such children, the complete naturalistic method would appear to have been employed only in studies using specimen records (e.g., Barker & Wright, 1955) and in researches in the behaviorist tradition that sought baseline data for the purpose of behavior modification (e.g., Patterson & Cobb, 1973). The reason for the rarity of this method in the case of older children lies, no doubt, in the somewhat strained behavior that the awareness of being observed produces in them, as well as in the difficulty of observing their more wide-ranging activities, and in the lower density of critical incidents. The effect of the observer's presence on the subjects' behavior and hence on the validity of the data will be discussed in greater detail, in the context of the available evidence, in Chapter 2.

Given the research aim of demonstrating regularities in the contingencies of behavior that parents and children offer each other in the home, most investigators would claim that the irreducible amount of distortion attendant on this method must be allowed for, but that it is not sufficient to invalidate the data—at least, for younger children.

What is the effect on mother–child interaction of a simply moving the locale of the investigation into the laboratory playroom, a setting that presents unusual and novel features to both mother and child, while keeping the demand characteristics of the situation (i.e., the degree of control) the same? Schalock (1956) and Belsky (1977) found that mothers attended more to their children in a free-play situation in the laboratory than they did at home. O'Rourke (1963) discovered a shift in maternal and paternal roles in family discussions between home and laboratory. Watts (1978) and Yuzwak (1979) also noted some differences between home and laboratory in maternal and child behaviors in a free-play situation, though these were not overwhelming. We would conclude that the setting alone can easily affect the normative level of mother and child behavior or their interactions, although it will not necessarily change the rank orders substantially.

Hypothesis Testing in Naturalistic Observation Studies

It is often thought that observation of completely unconstrained interactions of parents and children (or other interactants) precludes the testing of hypotheses. However, in a sense, the testing of hypotheses about *normal* interactions in *natural* settings can be done *only* where these conditions apply. It is true that in a naturalistic observation one cannot hold constant all variables save the one to be manipulated (nor can one do this, it should be added, in any strict sense in the laboratory experiment with humans). However, in a sequence analysis, one notes the sequence of behavior along a time line, and one can infer that the direction of effects flows from antecedent to consequent in time; that is, if antecedent A over a time span is regularly followed by response R, more than the ordinary occurrence of R in the record (the base rate) would warrant, one can conclude that A facilitates R, that is, is at least one of the causes of R. The researcher detects the effects of A above the noise of all the other behaviors that go on at the same time, in this way statistically controlling for the other variables. Thus, Patterson (1979) could test the hypothesis that parents' punishing behavior suppresses an aggressive child's hostile and aggressive behavior—it did not, though it did have this effect with nonproblem children. Hinde (1974) could test the hypothesis that rhesus monkey mothers take the initiative in separating themselves physically from their infants rather than the other way round—they did do this.

Observations at two points in time that are separated by an interval of some weeks or months further allow the researcher to test hypotheses concerning cause–effect relationships by means of time-lag analysis, based on the logical assumption that earlier events can influence later ones, but not the other way round, though it is sometimes difficult to disentangle certain competing hypotheses (cf. Rozelle & Campbell, 1969). In this way, Clarke-Stewart (1973), for instance, showed that the child's smiling and vocalizing at one age tended to increase mother's responsiveness and sociability some months later.

Further, naturalistic observation can also be employed in the service of a "natural experiment" that investigates "the progressive accommodation between the growing human organism and its environment through a systematic contrast between two or more environmental systems" (Bronfenbrenner, 1977, p. 517). It then provides the opportunity for testing hypotheses about differences between groups, for example, between divorced and intact families, or between twin and singleton families.

Interview

While the interview lacks both the control and the immediacy of the other two modes of attack, it has convenience and cheapness to recommend it. A further considerable advantage is that the range of behavior that can be sampled via interview and report—though at one remove—covers the whole gamut of interactions between parents and children.

But with this method above all others, there have been cogent objections to accepting, at face value, the resulting data. M. R. Yarrow (1963, p. 217), for instance, writes, "Mothers' interview responses represent self-description by extremely ego-involved reporters." Over the last two decades, however, definite efforts have been made to reduce the sources of distortion in the interview by focusing on recent events and concrete facts that mothers could report fairly accurately, for example, time spent on play or basic care. Such efforts seem to have been fairly successful (Rutter & Brown, 1966; Douglas, Lawson, & Cooper, 1968). Smith (1958), too, found that most mothers' reports on their own behavior tally pretty well with the behavior observed, though she also noted that some "defensive" mothers in the interview gave answers that were probably biased toward normality.

With the modifications introduced in some of these studies, which mean that the information input is more strictly controlled, the interview has shown reasonable agreement with other data and will have a useful role to play, particularly in obtaining data that are inaccessible to direct observation and for information about internal cues. While uncorroborated reports must be treated with caution, verbal reports by parents that are supplemented by, and checked against, observational measures, or each other, will inspire greater confidence in their veracity and validity.

Combining Process with Trait Analysis

A whole range of possibilities is open to the investigator, not only by way of combining the dimensions of setting and control to varying degrees, as discussed earlier, but also by combining several core methods of investigation in a "multistep strategy" (Parke, 1979). The investigator will thus offset their respective disadvantages and gain the benefit of a comparative viewpoint. A heuristically useful tactic, which has been employed in this investigation, for instance, is to combine a contingent analysis of behavior sequences (process analysis) with a correlational trait analysis.

The process analysis identifies immediate contingencies and effects of parents on child and vice versa, analyzes the mechanisms by which social behavior patterns arise and are maintained and eliminated, and shows how behavioral changes are a function of interactional–contextual factors. It is a microanalysis at a molecular level. The trait analysis examines the long-term effects of parent characteristics on child characteristics (or vice versa), assessed by summary behavior counts or ratings on a more molar level.

In discussing trait ratings, we must bear in mind their nature and limitations as put succinctly by White (1970):

> . . . a dispositional statement in psychology usually states some probabilistic consistency in a subject that depends upon a situation for its manifestation and . . . it usually alludes to some characteristic which he shows relatively more frequently than others. (p. 681)

A rating, applied to a carefully defined trait thus understood, is essentially an abstraction from observed behavior, summarized and interpreted through the conceptual system of the trait definition as well as that of the rater. Since he is able to give weight to subtle or unique clues, he will be able to transcend the fragmentation inherent in behavior counts and may bring to light a quality and unity in the subject's behavior undetectable by the simple summing of counts, A rating reflects a cohesive view of an individual, because it summarizes tendencies existing over a long time-span or over a variety of situations, and it takes account of internal cues and behavior inaccessible to an outside observer. It does not ignore particular contingencies or contextual factors but selectively takes account of those where the disposition can and does manifest itself (see White's definition above). That it sums over such contingencies is its limitation, as well as its strength. These considerations will go some way toward explaining the overall effectiveness of ratings (see also Chapter 2). The fact that the weighting the rater gives to various pieces of evidence is complex and difficult to specify—even where the evidential base is made explicit—may introduce some unreliability, but it does not destroy the ratings' heuristic usefulness.

Ratings assess outcomes rather than processes, and they may fruitfully be used to predict individual differences in the stable characteristics of children. Summary behavior counts (formed by summing instances of actions) are situation-bound, but if variations in context and relationships are held constant, they can be used like ratings to measure generalized response tendencies within the given context or relationship (cf. Cairns & Green, 1979). The important thing, to ensure that a measure—be it count or rating—and the results deriving from it are intelligible and interpretable, is that it should be based on clearly defined behavior.

A good example of the combined use of process and trait analysis is the study by Yarrow *et al.* (1971), who investigated the effects that children's immediate behavior, seen in sequence, as well as their characteristics, arrived at by summary behavior counts, had on the nurturant–nonnurturant responses of nursery-school teachers. The author's comments sum up the advantages of this combination:

> The combined use of two research approaches in the present study has pointed up the direct effect and the generalized effect of child characteristics on the adult. Both effects are important. by using both approaches we have seen how the adult's behavior towards the child is governed not solely by the child's immediate responding, but as well by the images and expectations that the adult develops about the child. (p. 311)

In fact, there simply is not one single "best" approach. A truism that still bears repeating is that in the final analysis, a decision on research design is dictated by the nature of the research question and by the research practicalities.

ABOUT THIS BOOK

Examining Parent–Child Interaction

This book presents a research program that took a close look at the socialization process, as it manifests itself in the ordinary day-to-day interactions between parents and young children. The investigation examined the social development of 2- to 3-year-old boys within the context of what Bronfenbrenner (1977) has called the "microsystem" in which they grow up—in this case, the home, It paid particular attention to the development of attachment, compliance, and speech, which it viewed as parts of the interactive matrix of relationships between parent and child, and it examined in more summary fashion other domains of interaction, namely, positively and negatively toned actions in general, autonomy, and activity level. The book places this empirical study in the context of the literature and the theory as they concern these characteristics and the socialization process in general.

The research used a broad plan of attack that deployed three strategies simultaneously: naturalistic observation, interview, and experiment.

The advantages of naturalistic observation over research relying on secondhand reports and experiments were set out in earlier sections of this chapter. In this research program, such observation was considered essential, as it alone can provide us with the details of interactions, that is, with a verbatim record (in code) of actual interchanges and happenings between parents and children. The record obtained affords us a view of family interactions such as Bronfenbrenner (1977) or Feiring and Lewis (1978), among others, are asking for: "If what we profess to study is the dynamics in addition to the statics of a family system, it is necessary to view family interaction as an influence or change process that involves social interchange in sequences over time" (Feiring & Lewis, 1978, p. 280). The ecological validity of such data is limited only by the effects exerted by the observer (see Chapter 2 for an evaluation), and the consequent distortion is, I would suggest, at any rate less than that inherent in other methods.

In view of the sometimes disappointing results obtained with interviews (see also M. R. Yarrow's cautionary remark, p. 10), one tends to be wary of this procedure. However, I did not want to forgo the potentialities that lie in overall impressions nor to lose all information that was not obtainable from direct observation, since only a fraction of parent–child interaction can be observed in two 3-hour observation periods. Hence, interviews were the second prong of the research plan. There is some reassurance in the fact that is seems, when mothers know there are other sources of information available, their reports in interviews become more veridical than would otherwise be the case (Kohn & Carroll, 1960). It was expected that observation would have this corrective effect in our case. Data from the interviews were used mainly as evidence auxiliary to that derived from direct observation in establishing ratings for various child and parent characteristics (see Chapter 2 for details). My decision to include ratings was influenced also by evidence from a number of studies (e.g., Blunden, Spring, & Greenberg, 1974) showing that trait ratings tend to predict other characteristics (e.g., "problem child") better than observation-based measures do.

The third methodological approach was an experimental situation in a laboratory playroom. The purpose was to elicit, under controlled conditions, the same child characteristics that were under study in the home observation in order to see how these would relate to the parallel home observation variables. In this situation, the external conditions were held constant, and the stimuli to which the child had to react were under experimental control. However, it was found that this approach could not be integrated very closely with the other two methods, and its relative usefulness will be discussed in Chapter 2.

The three central objectives of the research program were realized by analyses at three interrelated levels, based on the first two approaches discussed above:

1.   The first objective was to produce a firsthand descriptive, normative account of unconstrained parent–child interactions and of child-rearing approaches employed in North American society at this time—behaviors that make up the socialization experiences of the 2-year-old child. This was done by means of straight behavior counts.

2.   The second objective was to analyze the reciprocal effects of contingencies that parents and children set up for each other, as they operate both immediately and over a medium time-span. Direct observation permits the analysis of behavior sequences and thus, as noted above, provides evidence for specifying the major direction of influence—be it unidirectional or bidirectional—between parents and children. The identification of these contingencies and the direction of influence in the ongoing family interaction has rarely been attempted for this age group. But such an analysis is the first step in building a theory of parent–child interaction, based on the actual incidence and relationships of different kinds of behavior in the natural habitat. The questions asked for attachment and compliance behavior were: (1) What pattern of parental behavior is associated sequentially with child behavior? (2) How do the contingencies provided by the child in these areas affect parental actions?

As regards parent–child communication the questions asked were: (1) How is amount of speech distributed over different family members? (2) Who in the family is mainly responsible for initiating dialogues, and hence for the level of communication in the family? (3) What degree of verbal responsiveness do different family members display?

The identification of the direction of influence over a medium time-span was possible, in some cases, by carrying out a cross-lagged correlational analysis of parents' and children's behavior counts between the first and second observation sessions.

3.   The third objective was to identify the interrelationships of parents' and children's enduring response tendencies (traits) and to assess the power of parental behavior tendencies to predict the child characteristics of compliance, attachment, speech, etc. This was the "trait analysis," based on summary behavior counts and ratings. Placing the parent variables in the position of predictors that "explain" the child variables (the criteria) was an assumption made here for heuristic purposes only, and possible reversals of the direction of effects will be discussed.

The process analysis of observational measures and the trait analysis of summary behavior counts and ratings were designed to complement and illuminate each other and to enable us to reach a better understanding of the nature of the relationships involved. Like Yarrow *et al.* (1971), I found that this procedure bore fruit.

Genetic Analysis

Effects by children on parents have come to be accepted and recognized by many workers as an important aspect of parent–child interchanges. Bell (1977) points out that demonstrating their reality does not require that we trace the effects to their ultimate origins. Nevertheless, the question of their origin naturally imposes itself on the curious mind. To what extent are we dealing with organismic "givens" that are—at least, in part—genetically determined? This question has hardly begun to be studied in the area of young children's social interactive behavior; and rarely has a genetic analysis been employed as a direct way of providing evidence for child effects. Proponents of the theory of sociobiology (e.g., Wilson, 1975) make it their central tenet that social behavior has biological roots and an evolutionary history. But for support of this theory, they rely more on analogy from subhuman organisms than on direct proof (see Chapter 9 for a further discussion).

Because the possibility of a genetic contribution to variation in social behavior was here taken seriously, I attempted to determine whether it actually played a significant role in our variables by means of a twin analysis, one of the direct ways of examining genetic factors in humans. For this reason, twins were sought out as the main part of the sample.

Twins are a special group. Having twins, as well as singletons, in the sample also provided an opportunity to examine their socialization experiences to see how far they differ from those of singletons, in other words, to discover whether having two children of the same age in the family makes a difference. This proved to be a fruitful field of inquiry.

In sum, the work has five distinctive features: (1) the examination of the reciprocal nature of parent–child influences from direct observation; (2) the dual analysis of social behavior viewed as both a process and a trait; (3) the inclusion of fathers in the investigation; (4) the search for a genetic explanation; and (5) the analysis of differences in parent–child relations between twins and singletons and the effects these have on the socialization process.

CHAPTER 2

Design and Methods

DESIGN

The effects of parents' child-rearing practices on children's behavior, and children's reciprocal effects on parents, were studied via three approaches: naturalistic observation in the home, interviews and overall ratings, and experiment in the laboratory playroom. Primary emphasis was placed on objective recording of detailed behavior in an unstructured situation. We also conducted two interviews with the mother and obtained a 24-hour record of events (a "diary") from her, we summed up the evidence from the direct observation as well as from these probes by means of global ratings of child and parent characteristics. In addition, as a complementary approach, we constructed experimental tasks that elicited the same child characteristics that were under study in the home observation. How useful this procedure was will be discussed below.

The order of investigative procedures was as follows:

1. Introductory interview with mother.
2. Two 3-hour observation sessions, usually in successive weeks.
3. A 24-hour diary completed by mother before the second observation.
4. A second interview with mother immediately following the second observation, conducted by an extra observer, present during this observation.
5. An experimental playroom session; two separate sessions were arranged for twins, with mother present for both. The Peabody Picture Vocabulary Test was administered during this session.
6. For twins: blood typing at the hematology laboratory of the university-affiliated hospital after the completion of the psychological investigation.

The child variables of compliance, attachment, independence, speech, and activity level were selected *a priori* as target variables for this study since they represent important social characteristics of the growing individual. Which parent behavior exerted significant influence on a given child behavior was determined in two ways, the first one being a computerized "sequence analysis." This identified the parent antecedents that preceded a given child response at above-chance level and that therefore acted as "facilitators" for this child behavior (see Chapters 5 and 6 for details). The significant parent antecedents thus were not predetermined but searched for by computer. The apparently atheoretical nature of this search is, however, deceptive, since the author's theoretical assumptions affected the selection of the behavior to be recorded and coded. For example, the theoretical notion (derived from cognitive developmental theory and literature) that mother's use of reasoning may have a bearing on the child's compliance led to a separate code for "reasoning." The reciprocal effects of the child on his parents were examined by reversing the search; that is, the child's behavior was treated as the antecedent and the parent's responses that occurred with above-chance frequency were looked for.

The second way in which determinants of child behavior were indentified was by means of regression or "trait" analysis, at outlined in Chapter 1. The parent variables in this analysis were those that past research and theory in the area had indicated as important (see below). Both ratings and summary behavior counts were the measures used.

The decision to concentrate on 2- to 3-year olds was prompted by three main considerations. First, very few studies have reported observations of the interactions of parents with children of this age (see Chapter 1). Second, this is the age at which the first serious demands are made that the child's social behavior conform to his parents' or society's norms, that is, when the essential business of socialization gets under way. And third the child's speech becomes, for the most part, intelligible, and genuine two-way verbal communication between parent and child, both of an informative and of an exhortatory–affective nature, becomes possible.

I decided to confine the investigation to one sex only, as the likelihood of the existence of sex differences in social characteristics (cf. Sears, Rau, & Alpert, 1965) meant separate analyses for the two sexes, and therefore, double the sample size would have been necessary to achieve the same degree of power to detect significant relationships. As will be seen later, this approach would have been economically prohibitive. A sample of males, rather than females, was chosen because it was thought that the potential for conflict with less docile and more physically active boys would provide greater opportunities for observing the socialization process, with its stresses and strains. Twins were originally included in the sample because we intended to assess the importance of a genetic contribution to these social characteristics, but their inclusion also provided the opportunity of comparing the differing socialization experiences that singletons and twins are exposed to—an important extra bonus (see Chapter 4).

Fieldwork for the main study was carried out over two years, from 1971 to 1973. the main investigation was preceded by a year's pilot study, during which we experimented with observation and recording procedures, laid down decision rules for coding, refined the code so as to make it more adapted to our purpose, and established preliminary interobserver reliabilities. The interview format and the procedures for the experimental playroom tasks were also evolved at that time. When the frequencies of certain crucial types of behavior for the 30 subjects of the pilot sample (1 set of triplets, 9 sets of twins, 9 singletons, all 2 to 3-year-old boys) were compared with those for the main sample, it was found that there were systematic and significant differences between the two groups that preluded carrying out my original intention of pooling the data from the two samples. This monograph is therefore based on data from the main sample. However, most of the correlation and regression analyses carried out on the main sample were also carried out on the pilot sample, and these analyses therefore provide useful replications on an independent sample. The results will be drawn on from time to time to corroborate, or to show the limitations of, conclusions based on the main sample.

Subjects

The sample of the main study consisted of 46 sets of same-sex male twins (17 monozygotic [MZ] and 29 dizygotic [DZ]) and 44 male singletons, a total of 136 boys, all white. Mean age was 32.4 months, range 25–35 months. Mean ages of the three groups were (in months): MZ, 32.0; DZ, 32.4; and singletons, 33.4.

Singletons were included in the sample only if they came from a two-parent family and if they had a sibling within three years of themselves in age, in order to reproduce the "twoness" of the twin situation to some extent. Families where the mother worked full time were also excluded. The singleton families were obtained through the local child health clinics, which are attended by more than 65% of the Calgary child population, both middle and working class, for immunization purposes. Apart from the above limitations, the subjects were selected only on the basis of their parents' willingness to participate on being asked and on the basis of the need to match the social-class distribution of the twins. The sample is therefore not self-selected in the sense that the parents volunteered in response to an advertisement.

Twins were located through the birth registers of the local hospitals. The expectation is that after the first year of life, surviving same-sex twin pairs represent 0.64% of the population, and therefore 0.32% will be same-sex male pairs (Allen, 1955). This statistic provides an expectation of 25.6 same-sex male pairs per year, given approximately 8,000 births per year in Calgary. We ascertained 25 born in 1969 and 26 born in 1970; therefore, our ascertainment approximates the theoretical expectation very closely. Of these pairs, 14 were not included in the investigation: in 3 pairs, one partner had died; 6 families had left the city; 2 families did not speak English in the home; 1 could not be traced; and 2 refused to participate. While no data are available to compare those not included with those participating, the sample represents a very large proportion of the total male twin populations born during those years, and there is no reason to suspect that the sample differs from the total pupulation to any significant extent. Nine of the twin sets came from nearby towns. All available twins were seen, even if the mother was the only parent in the home (five families).

The basis for the assignment of social class was the father's occupation determined by Blishen's scale of socioeconomic status (Blishen, 1967). Scale score 52 and above was counted as middle class, score 47 and below, as working class. For borderline cases, years of father's education were also taken into account in deciding social-class status. The social-class distribution of the twins dictated that of the singletons for matching purposes, so that both groups contained one-third middle-class and two-thirds working-class families (all white). The sample is thus reasonably representative of white North American families from the point of view of social class, but it contains a preponderance of twins.

Since social class, as indexed by father's occupation, was associated with only a few child and parent characteristics, a breakdown by mother's education was carried out at a later stage. This breakdown is shown in Table 2. While we meticulously matched the social-class distribution of the twins among the singleton sample, it can be seen that a bias crept in, in that

Table 2. Breakdown of Sample by Mother's Education and Twinship

Mother's education group	MZ pairs	DZ pairs	All twin pairs	Single-tons	N of families	N of children
1. Not completed high school	9	9	18	11	29	47
2. High school graduate	5	10	15	16	31	46
3. Some college	3	9	12	13	25	37
4. College graduate	0	1	1	4	5	6
Total	17	29	46	44	90	136

Twins: Singletons $\chi^2(3) = 5.20$ N.S.
MZ: DZ $\chi^2(3) = 5.44$ N.S.

the lower education groups were represented somewhat more heavily among twin families compared with singleton families and among MZ compared with DZ families. Neither difference, however, is significant when tested by chi-square.

ETHOLOGICAL APPROACH: NATURALISTIC OBSERVATION

Observations and Observers

The observers were two female psychologist research assistants, who organized and supervised the fieldwork, and two women with no particular professional background. The latter, who carried out most of the observations on a part-time basis, were particularly acceptable to the families, because they were themselves mothers who knew "what it was like" and because of their warm manner toward parents and children. (The latter characteristic was shared by the psychologists!) It was found quite possible to train them to record reasonably reliably (see "Training Procedures" below), and in addition, the accuracy of their coding was monitored from time to time by the psychologist research assistants.

The observer visited the home on two afternoons in successive weeks, observing completely unstructured interaction for the three hours preceding the child's bedtime (roughly 5–8 P.M.), a time that usually included the family supper. This period was chosen because by the end of the day, with young children around and mother's nerves being frayed, there is a greater likelihood of being able to observe less well-controlled and more stressful parent–child interaction than during, say, the quiet morning hours. The two visits were deliberately arranged for the same time in order to increase the trustworthiness of the data for that time of day, although generalization to other times of the day must therefore remain in doubt. More probes would ideally be desirable but were ruled out because of cost and the extra strain on the families' hospitality. The only restriction placed on the family was that the child (or both twins) and at least one parent should, for the most part, remain in the living-room area. If a child left the area for any length of time, recording was interrupted. Where there was a father, we made sure that he would be present for at least part of the observations, if at all possible. We have records for the fathers of 120 children. In the case of singletons, another sibling was almost always present, and with twins, a third child was often there.

Behavior Record and Code

In adopting naturalistic observation—an essentially ethological approach—as my principal method of investigation, I was concerned to observe carefully and to record in quantifiable form the actual functioning of child and parents in their moment-to-moment behavior.

It was first hoped that by leaving a videotape camera with the family and removing the observer, the embarrassment felt by the family in the presence of a silent observer would be reduced and a less biased and yet complete record of interaction would be obtained. This method was tried out in several families, and all mothers reported that they were more conscious of, and felt more constrained by, the presence of the camera than they were in the presence of human observers. Moreover, if the observer was absent, the camera was also relatively fixed in its field of vision (though mothers were instructed to turn it on the child if the child was too long out of view, but this would only be done from time to time). Therefore, much of the action was lost visually, though some of it could be reconstructed subsequently with lesser confidence by means of speech and other noises, only some of them intelligible, that were recorded on the tape.

For these reasons, we abandoned videotaping as a regular recording procedure after the first three or four cases. Videotaping was retained, however, for the special purposes of facilitating interobserver reliability checks and obtaining material for training observers (see below).

The form of behavior record chosen was a code that serves as a kind of shorthand and is also quantifiable (see below for details). Its essential aspect is that it can be directly converted to a count of specified types of behavior by hand or by computer analysis. At first, this code was written down by the observer on the spot, because it was thought that dictating a running commentary into a microphone, even at a very low volume, would constitute an additional and unwelcome intrusion in an ordinary living room. The verbal interaction of the family was recorded on tape and this audio record was used later to supplement and correct the observer's written record. After some trials, however, it was found that speaking the code into a microphone, in a low murmur, did not represent a significantly greater intrusion than did the presence of the observer by itself, and it was not objected to by parents. We therefore soon adopted the practice of speaking the code into one of two microphones of a stereophonic tape recorder. The family's verbal interaction, as well as high-pitched beeps from a timer at 10-sec intervals, was picked up by the second microphone and recorded on the second channel of the same tape.

This method of recording frees the observer's eyes for watching the ongoing action and, above all, ensures that the spoken code can later be accurately identified with any given segment of verbal interaction and is therefore more easily corrected. One very striking effect of the change in procedure was a dramatic increase in the number of statements recorded, a fact that demonstrates that the observer was, in fact, able to see more when she dictated the code.

The code used was based on the APPROACH scheme (Caldwell, 1969), which was originally developed for use in nursery schools. We adapted it to form a Parent–Child Interaction Code (PACIC) and to accommodate the variables of interest in our investigation. (The summary code sheet and an example of a coded piece of interaction are contained in Appendix I). The code, in fact, possesses such basic flexibility that investigators can, by modifying the meaning of some of the symbols, bring into focus and code in detail any particular area of behavior that they are interested in, while leaving in much rougher outline other areas on the fringes of their interest.

In the PACIC each relatively discrete unit of behavior is encoded as a six-place statement by the use of alpha-numerical characters. Caldwell (1969) calls this statement a kind of "behavioral clause" that possesses its own grammatical structure. The letter in the first place indicates the subject of the clause. The second and third place are occupied by a two-digit number representing the predicate. The letter in the fourth place indicates the object; the number in the fifth place provides the possibility of introducing up to nine different adverbs, describing the quality of the action; and the letter in the sixth place gives supplementary information over and above the adverbs in the fifth place. The most important items of supplementary information in this investigation were C, indicating that the action is an instance of compliance, and N, indicating that it is an instance of noncompliance. Statements can and often do contain blank spaces. An example of a statement would be: "Child (C) goes (02) to mother (M) quickly (5), following her request (C)," or "CO2M5C." Lapse of time is marked on the record by a stroke for every 10 sec.

Training Procedures

Gaining fluency in a complex code such as this takes many weeks of training. (We count on about 50–60 hours of training for a new observer.) A further object of training is to achieve uniformity of coding, so that any two observers using the code who note the same behavior will code it in the same way. Videotape is an invaluable aid in training, since any segment of interaction can be viewed again and again until the observer is satisfied with her coding, even though chaos has overtaken the family. In addition, experience in the live situation is, of course, also necessary so that the observer can become habituated to the complexities of real-life interaction when she herself is present.

The coding manual for the APPROACH scheme, kindly made available by Dr. Caldwell, was adapted for PACIC. It lays down the general rules as well as the definition of every symbol. However, to achieve reasonable uniformity of coding, as they came up in practice, many points had to be discussed with the trainees. Decision rules had to be laid down as the occasion arose, for example, how to code a parent ignoring a child's request for help while carrying on with an ongoing action. The establishment of a clear set of rules was part of the initial phase of the investigation when the experimenter and his associate first had to train themselves, and these were then incorporated in the manual. What had to be decided, above all, was not only the exact code for a given item of behavior but which type of behavior to record and which to omit, since in the welter of activity of the normal family, it is neither possible nor desirable to record everything. In fact, this turned out to be the most difficult area in which to lay down decision rules.

Behavior Units and Problems of Recording

The purpose of the investigation will determine the classes of behavior that the observer will concentrate on. Since the purpose of this research was to study a number of social behaviors, including speech and activity level, all actions of the child (or twins) were of interest and were to be recorded, plus those actions by others that impinged on the target child (or twins). We thus recorded actions continuously, as they occurred. However, the code was designed to be more detailed and to present a fine-grained picture in the special areas of interest and a more coarse-grained one in areas of lesser importance. Thus, while we attempted to be very specific about expressions of command, request, or suggestion, and about verbal interaction indicating attachment or hostility, and defined carefully acts of compliance or noncompliance, we were less specific about the actual toy that the child played with (simply recording that he played with some movable object), since this was of no consequence in the context of our investigation. One could, of course, be much more selective in one's recording—for example, concentrating exclusively on control sequences—but one would thereby lose the ongoing interaction and the stream of mutual contingencies obtaining between parent and child.

How do we define the "relatively discrete unit of behavior" to be encoded in a statement? Consider two extremes of a continuum: At one end you have as a unit "going to school," "playing catch," and similar events, extending over some time and comprising a number of subordinate acts; such units are clearly "molar events." At the other end, you have actions dissected into their component parts, as is often done in ethological records; for example, "threatening a person" is divided up into "stares at A, grimaces, lifts right arm, clenches fist, shakes fist," etc. Clearly, this is a molecular description. In addition, there exist actions of intermediate range: gestures, manipulating a toy, and speech, which may occupy only a few seconds. While the extremes of the continuum are thus clearly marked, it is less clear where along the continuum the label *molar* ceases and the label *molecular* begins to apply, since these are qualitative descriptions without generally accepted criteria.

However, it is possible to look for criteria for defining a *discrete unit* in the function of an act. In the present investigation, it was essentially a functional criterion that determined the unit of action. It is this concern for the function and content of an act rather than its minute external definition that marks off the present approach from a purely ethological one. It is the function of an act that formed the criterion for a *behavior unit*. Thus, "plays with toy," "seeks contact," and "threatens" were all considered units, separately coded, but "gets up from chair and walks over to mother," although comprising several distinct muscular activities, was considered a functional entity and given one code only.

Given the multiplicity of events in normal family interaction, it became necessary to reduce the number of separate actions to be noted, within these general rules, in order to avoid overloading the observer. Specific, *ad hoc* rules had to be devised as these problems arose: for example, should smiling and approving be coded separately? When father repeats the same command several times over in very quick succession or when another child in the family plays with father at the same time as the target child, should all these be recorded as separate actions? Even within the decision rules laid down, there is an inevitable variation of interpretation between observers that appears as unreliability, though the disagreement is on nonessentials. Another problem of interpretation—this time in a more important area—arises with the decision whether in certain circumstances the child actually did or did not comply with a parent's request. For example, when the mother says to the child, "Eat properly!" the change in the child's behavior is often so minute that two observers genuinely disagree on whether the child complied with the command.

With our molecular recording system of specific, concrete acts, did we in fact catch variables that have meaning in the context of our research aims? There is always the danger that in recording second-to-second movements and acts, one is led, by following predetermined rules without regard to particular circumstances, into unintended and meaningless distortion of variables or into not catching a variable at all. Thus, when a child played a game with father, father asked him to give him one toy animal after another from his zoo, which the child did. Scoring each of these interchanges as "command" and "comply" would give a misleading picture of the contingencies obtaining in this family, since commands were added up to the general characteristic of "restrictiveness" and complies to "compliance." In another case, a child constantly stayed with his mother and talked to her more than the other twin did. This sign of attachment was not easily picked up by the detailed code, because, first, "talking" was not counted as a sign of attachment, and, second, we found it impossible to include simple proximity in the code and he had no opportunity to walk after his mother, which would have counted as attachment. The observer's impression that this child showed intense attachment to his mother was obviously correct, however. In both cases special steps had to be taken and rules evolved to correct an otherwise misleading behavior count.

Processing the Record

On the day following the observation, the observer listened to the stereotape and transcribed her spoken code onto 80-column data sheets, at the same time inserting a stroke for each 10-sec beep recorded on the track carrying the family's verbal interaction. Often, several actions occur in a 10-sec interval, and on the other hand, one piece of behavior—for example, watching TV—may carry on unchanged over many intervals, in which case the statement would be repeated once for every interval. The 10-sec interval is of a length that an observer can usually cope with; experience showed that with, say, a 5-sec interval, the need to make constant time strokes distracted her from the accurate coding of the interaction. The observer listened to the verbal interaction, too, and went over doubtful passages a second time. This correction stage is most important, as many omissions or coding inaccuracies can be detected at this stage, with the audiotape of the family interaction serving as a reminder of what took place, and the various coding rules can be applied meticulously. The coded statements and the attached time strokes having straightaway been placed in the appropriate columns, the entire record in sequence, plus a code indicating the initiator and terminator of certain interaction sequences, was then transferred to punched cards (and later to tape) for computer processing. A special program was written that analyzed the raw data, summed the occurrences of any specified subject–verb–object combination (e.g., child speaks to mother, or father makes a request of child), and calculated their relative frequencies. It also computed a number of other indices [e.g., the "compliance ratio," i.e., the ratio of compliance instances to compliance plus noncompliance instances—$C/(C + N)$, or the "duration of active behavior"].

Definitions of behavior categories, including derived and superordinate variables, are shown in Table 3.

Interobserver Agreement

We computed interobserver agreement by having two observers observe the same interaction and code it independently, both from videotape recordings and coded on the spot. In the latter case, two observers, sitting in opposite corners of the room, out of earshot of each other, spoke the code in a whisper into two separate microphones. When both observers coded the same subject and predicate within a 30-sec interval, it was counted as an agreement (A); when they coded the same behavior by different codes it was counted as a disagreement (D); when one observer recorded an action that the other observer did not record, it was marked X. These latter instances would arise because an oberver may have overlooked a piece of behavior in the fast-moving scene or because she may have felt that the act in question did not fall within the definition of recordable acts. Agreement was then calculated by the formula: $A/(A + \frac{1}{2}X)$, after adding the Xs from both observers together. A second formula was also used that did not count in the "extra" statements recorded by only one observer: $A/(A + D)$. This second formula is a measure of the extent to which two observers agree on the *coding* of behavior that they both noted and recorded, leaving aside behavior that only one of them either noticed or thought recordable. Agreement was computed for all the subject–predicate combinations summed over 1-hour segments (in one case, .5-hour segment). Table 4 displays the results of four reliability checks for different observer pairs.

As can be seen from the figures relating to the *coding* of behavior (Table 4, right-hand column), the agreement on *coding* is "respectable"; yet, agreement on actual observation was lower than is usually demanded in psychometric investigations. Definitions of the behavioral categories were presented quite precisely in the coding manual, and hence, the difficulty was not the ambiguity of a few broad categories, interpreted differently by different observers. We had 52 verbs referring to concrete behavior in our code in order to allow for possible antecedent parent or child actions, and, in fact, it had been shown (Mash & McElwee, 1974) that interobserver agreement decreases with an increase in the number of categories in the coding system that is, with the complexity of the system (Jones, Reid, & Patterson, 1975). However, since agreement on coding was acceptable and agreement dropped off sharply only when the X actions were taken into account (Table 4), it is clear that the real difficulty lay in agreeing on what to record—a difficulty that seems to have arisen in other observational studies, too (e.g., Jeffree & McConkey, 1976).

In fact, to achieve agreement on recording precisely the same action at the same time in a free-flowing situation with a multitude of activities going on is extremely difficult, and the criterion employed was therefore quite a severe one. (We attained higher levels of agreement for ratings and experimental measures.) In a system of continuous recording such as we employed, the observer may be forced to select one response to record at a time from among several competing pieces of behavior. In one observation, for instance, a child was playing with blocks, his small sister and his mother drifted in and out of the play, and the child and his mother were having a to-and-fro conversation at the same time. While these basic characteristics were noted by both observers, agreement was far from perfect on whether to

Table 3. Definitions of Behavior Categories[a]

Behavioral label	Definition
Number of actions (behavior units)—child	All verbal and nonverbal behavior by child, counting actions continuing over time only once.
Number of actions (behavior units)— mother or father	All mother or father behavior addressed to the child, counting actions continuing over time only once.
Speech acts	All utterances added together, including informational speech, questions, requests, verbal seeking of attention, verbal expression of affection, criticism, etc.
Speech rate—child	Rate of such utterances per minute of observation.
Rate child–mother speech	Rate of such utterances by child addressed to mother, per minute of mother's presence.
Rate mother–child speech	Rate of utterances by mother addressed to child per minute of mother's presence.
Rate mother–child interchange	Sum of rates of child–mother and mother–child speech.
Rate child–father speech Rate father–child speech Rate father–child interchange }	Analogous to speech measures for mother, calculated per minute of father's presence.
Nonverbal attachment rate—child	Approaching, touching, sitting on knee of mother and father per minute of observation.
Verbal attachment rate—child	Seeking attention, seeking help, seeking permission of mother and father per minute of observation.
Attachment rate (narrow)—child	Approaching, touching, seeking attention, seeking help per minute of observation
Attachment behavior (narrow)— percentage—child	Approaching, touching, seeking attention, seeking help of mother and father— percentage of child's actions.
Comply ratio	Instances of compliance/(Instances of compliance + noncompliance).
Rough-and-tumble play	Gross muscle play, e.g., romping with father, throwing ball about, climbing onto furniture, riding a tricycle.
Manipulative play	Play with smaller toys and objects.
Physically active behavior—child	Above two categories plus walking and a few minor ones, e.g., carrying objects, drawing.
Activity shift score—child	Number of times per minute that the child shifted from one activity to another (count of "active behavior")/(minutes spent in "active behavior").
Total activity score—child	Standardized score, combining z-scores of percentage of time spent in active behavior and of activity shift score.

Table 3 (*continued*)

Behavioral label	Definition
Expression of pleasure	Nonverbal positive affect, in particular smiling and laughing.
Expression of displeasure	Nonverbal negative affect, e.g., frowning, whining, crying.
Disruptive, disorganized behavior—child	Behavior that is explosive or designed to give vent to anger or rage, e.g., rolling wildly about the floor, running wildly about the room, throwing toys about.
Love withdrawal—mother	Temporary loss of love, e.g., sending the child to his room or threatening to do so.
Affectionate behavior—mother or father	Superordinate behavioral category—subclass of positive action (parents): showing pleasure, (smiling), approving, expressing affection verbally, holding child in arms, hugging and kissing, taking child on knees.
Twins social interaction ratio	Proportion of time twins spent in common activities out of time spent in active behavior overall.

Main grouped behavior categories

Positive action—child	Superordinate behavioral category, or actions that parents generally welcome (exceptions are noted under "Negative action"): touching mother or father, giving permission, showing pleasure, approving, expressing affection, helping, sitting on parent's knee, stroking, hugging and kissing, playing with parent, offering, any playful activity, and compliance with commands or requests.
Positive action—mother or father	Same actions as for child, plus feeding child.
Negative action—child	Superordinate behavioral category, or actions that parents generally find aversive: ignoring, yelling, refusing, showing displeasure, criticizing, expressing hostility, interfering or restricting, resisting, threatening, hitting, disorganized behavior, and noncompliance; in addition, any child action that was immediately followed by a parent prohibition was empirically classified as a negative action, even if it might otherwise have been classified as a positive action (e.g., "naughty laughter").
Negative action—mother or father	Same actions as for child, except restricting, or physical intervention, hitting, yelling, disorganized behavior.

Continued

Table 3   (*continued*)

Behavioral label	Definition
Physical control—mother or father	Restricting, hitting.
Forms of verbal control:	
Command	Direct imperative, though it may be softened by a "please."
Prohibition	Distinguished from command by the negative form of wording: "Don't be so rough" rather than "Be careful."
Suggestion	Milder form of control, e.g., "Would you like to . . . ?"
Control with reasoning—mother or father	Combining a justification with a command or prohibition just issued, e.g., "Don't put the knife in your mouth—it will hurt."
Neutral action	Superordinate behavioral category: any action not classified as a form of verbal control or a possitive or negative action, e.g., neutral speech, handing something (other than food) to the child, or to the parents, caretaking activities, reasoning not accompanied by a command, etc., would come under this category.

[a] A summary of codes and their labels is shown in Appendix I..The meaning of many code verbs is self-explanatory, for example, child "sitting on father's knee" or mother "helping." Theses meanings are not defined in this table. Where "child" or "mother or father" is shown with a label, the definition applies only to that agent. Otherwise the definition is applicable to all family members.

record speech or child play or mother play at any one moment. Nevertheless, the observers agreed on the basic types of behavior that occupied these 15 minutes, and the categories derived from them will be a faithful reflection of relationships in this family.

In view of these difficulties, it is perhaps not surprising that many ethologists and researches who report observation studies of children do not report interobserver agreement on the actual observation, as opposed to intercoder agreement (e.g., Ainsworth, Bell, & Stayton, 1972; Tracy, Lamb, & Ainsworth, 1976; Baumrind & Black, 1967; Minton, Kagan, & Levine, 1971), or they report reliability coefficients comparable to ours (e.g., Caldwell, 1969, using a very similar code; Lewis, 1972).

Average relative frequencies of some types of behavior important to this research were calculated separately over all the children observed by each observer, and the agreement between observers on these frequencies was investigated. It was found that the two main observers agreed very closely on the seven most important variables ($p = .996$ for the null hypothesis of no difference between them by simultaneous confidence test; cf. Bock & Haggard, 1968).

Table 4. Overall Interobserver Agreement for Behavior Code Subject and Verb Combinations

Method	Duration (min)	N of statements (longer record)	% Jointly observed events	% Agreement A^a $\overline{(A + D + \frac{1}{2}X)}$	% Agreement A^b $\overline{(A + D)}$
1. Videotape	30	328	61.3	68.4	75.1
2. Videotape	60	737	74.5	59.3	75.9
3. Dictated record	60	747	70.3	57.0	77.9
4. Dictated record	60	618	77.7	69.3	85.6
Median				63.9	76.9

[a] Inclues "extra" statements.
[b] Excludes "extra" statements.

Intersituational Stability

The stability of behavior across two observation sessions was first assessed by calculating Spearman's rho coefficients for certain kinds of behavior between the two sessions. The stability coefficients were calculated only on families where dinner was included in both observation sessions, and for father variables only where father was present for both observations. Hence, the N is reduced from the overall N. The data were relative frequencies, that is, frequencies equalized for total number of actions by each agent. The correlations are shown in Table 5.

The results show moderate stability of behavior over the two sessions, with low stability for child toy play, father compliance, and father reasoning, but moderately high stability for child request and activity shift and mother command–prohibition and suggestion and mother–child speech. However, all coefficients are significant. It is, of course, not to be expected that children and parents engage in the same behavior to exactly the same

Table 5.   Intersituation Stability Coefficients (Spearman's Rho)[a]

Child (N = 113)	rho
Attachment rate	.481[d]
Compliance ratio	.443[d]
Toy play percentage time	.206[b]
Rough and tumble play percentage time	.495[d]
Activity shift score	.671[d]
Physically active behavior percentage time	.366[d]
Requests percentage	.641[d]
Rate of child speech	.501[d]
Median	.488

Mother and Father	Mother (N = 113)	Father (N = 82)
Compliance ratio	.452[d]	.214[b]
Command–prohibition percentage	.604[d]	.485[d]
Suggestion percentage	.606[d]	.364[d]
Reasoning percentage	.519[c]	.290[c]
Affectionate behavior percentage	.512[d]	.327[c]
Rate mother(father)–child speech	.787[d]	.483[d]
Median	.562	.346

[a] Percentage = percentage of all actions of a given agent. Rate = rate per minute.
[b] $p < .05$.
[c] $p < .01$.
[d] $p < .001$.

extent on two occasions, as interest in, say, toy play may fluctuate, or the situation may give rise to more or fewer commands differentially for different families. Several probes will average out some of this fluctuation and hence provide a more stable estimate of behavior. It is interesting to note that the child's degree of restlessness (activity shift) and the relative frequency of his requests stay pretty stable and that mother's frequency of commands and her speech to the child also show considerable stability. Father's behavior, on the other hand, shows greater variability, although it is expressed as a proportion of all his actions and therefore takes account of the variable amount of time he was present from one occasion to another. This variability may nevertheless have affected the relative emphasis given to one or the other action.

The stability coefficients indicate the extent to which the rank orders of children, mothers, and fathers for the given actions remain stable from the first to the second observation, but they are not sensitive to differences in mean levels. In order to determine whether any shift in mean level took place between the two observations—either for absolute number of occurrences or for relative frequencies—t tests were carried out for 208 count variables (e.g., "child looks at mother," "mother gives order to child," "father speaks to child"; raw frequencies and relative frequencies were both analyzed). Only 9 of these showed a "significant" shift in mean level ($p < .05$), mainly toward a lower level of occurrence in the second observation. Since this number represents less than 5% of the variables tested, even these differences could have arisen by chance. The mean level of occurrences of the different kinds of actions, therefore, appears to remain quite stable over the two occasions.

Overall, the two kinds of tests together indicate satisfactory stability of behavior over two observation sessions, so that I felt justified in pooling the data from the two observations. The sample of child and parent behavior thus obtained, it can be inferred, is likely to be representative of such behavior *at this particular age and at the specified time.* In similar home observations, Patterson and Cobb (1973) also demonstrated good stability of behavior categories, both in mean level and in ordinal ranking, over several sessions.

Parents' Reactions to Home Observations

It is reasonable to suppose that the introduction of an observer into a home must affect relationships to some extent and produce some distortion of the "normal" interaction. Discussions of this can be found in Weick (1968) and Lytton (1971). Unfortunately, while the existence of distortion is generally recognized, it is difficult to obtain experimental evidence on the degree to which it affects the data, since to do so one must procure as baseline a record unknown to the observed, a difficult feat both practically and ethically. Patterson and his associates (Patterson & Reid, 1969; Harris, 1969) have produced evidence that shows that the presence of an observer increases the variability of social behavior in families and also increases the positive "desirable" responses by parents. However, Lobitz and Johnson (1975) showed that when parents of deviant and nondeviant children were given instructions to present their child as "good," "bad," or "usual" during home observation, all children showed more deviant behavior under the "bad" condition, but their behavior did not shine under the "good" condition. Hughes, Carmichael, Pinkerton, and Tizard (1979) observed mothers with their 4-year-old daughters in the home on four consecutive days. There were no differences in amount or kind of mother–child talk over these four visits. Hence, it would seem that the families were relatively unaffected by the presence of an observer; for example, mothers also slapped their children or swore at them. However, another explanation may be that observer effects were present but did not habituate over the four days.

In line with other investigators (see Moss, 1965; Baumrind, 1967), we took steps to try and minimize the distorting effects that our presence would be likely to have, particularly on parents. While explaining the purpose of the experiment, the observer would stress the child as the focus of interest and would underemphasize the role of the mother as subject. We also avoided being cast in the role of experts in child rearing so as not to give the mother the feeling of being judged. In a preliminary interview, we outlined our procedures (e.g., audiotaping in the home) and explained that, as observers, we could not be involved in the family interaction. We frankly put into words the embarrassment likely to be felt by parents in the presence of observers and asked the mother to act as naturally as possible under the circumstances. We also tried to involve her in the investigation by promising feedback of results. Observers did, in fact, avoid all contact with child or mother during the recording.

What were our experiences in the homes that participated in the study? We certainly had the impression on occasion that parents were being consciously "good parents" in the sense that they played and romped with their children perhaps more than usual for our benefit. Yet, the usual climate of interaction in the home cannot be changed completely over two evenings; for instance, one mother kissed and hugged her children but also yelled at them when she got exasperated (she also mentioned the yelling as a form of control in the interview). While some of the kissing may have been staged, we received the impression that this mother was, indeed, both warm and loving and easily irritated, whether we were there or not. In another working-class home, where father issued many imperious and impatient commands, mother tried to tone down her husband's peremptoriness by emphasizing "please" in her requests to the children. While she probably exaggerated this use because of our presence, there was also no doubt a genuine difference in approach between the parents that was still visible with observers present.

Slapping also occurred in our presence, as a response to misbehavior, though probably with reduced frequency. In this connection, it must be noted that the young child's behavior is almost unaffected by the observer's presence, so that naturally occurring situations will often, willy-nilly, bring out the parents' natural reactions, which they were not able to suppress completely. This is a factor that contributes considerably to a reduction of distortion.

Whereas the 2-year-olds seemed completely unabashed by the presence of the observer or the videotape camera, 6-year-olds were much more conscious of it, and it led them at times not to be "good" but to fool around and clown, particularly in front of the camera.

Investigators have to accept the behavior seen as behavior-in-the-presence-of-an-observer. They are justified in expecting it to deviate universally from normal interaction in one direction, toward social desirability, and thus certain allowances can be made, although one cannot be certain that the amount of deviation is the same from family to family. Randall's (1975) results suggest that in a laboratory, knowledge of being observed affects *working-class* mothers, in that they verbalize *less* to their infants than when they believe themselves to be unobserved, whereas *middle-class* mothers are unaffected by this knowledge. The differences in this study, however, were only marginally significant. Nevertheless, as between direct observation and interview, it would appear that distortion due to a social desirability set is less in the observed interaction, partly because the situation is not completely within the parents' control, whereas interviews largely are.

The following excerpt from an interview with a mother of twins shows some of the effects the observers produced, as well as the habituation effects that seemed to come with the second observation. (Note that behavior frequencies did not differ between the observations, as reported above.)

HL: Did our presence change your behavior a great deal?

MOTHER: Not today.

HL: Not today so much, but the last time we came?

MOTHER: Ian [the husband] said upstairs to me, now that seemed to be a lot smoother tonight than last time. I think it was probably last time that we were all sort of nervous and I was hoping to be perfect—perfect mother, perfect family—and, of course, it's not like that and so you relax the second day.

Maybe you sitting on the floor had something to do with it. It's just that we felt very self-conscious last time eating since my husband and I both have a passion for privacy. We're a very nuclear family. We all have a great deal of privacy and we're very close. We don't really see that much of people. We tend to do things as a family; we go to the zoo, we go tobogganing. We don't entertain a great deal so, when we were eating, I felt very self-conscious and so did Ian, and so, of course, the children started acting up.

HL: . . . I just wondered, what you would have done differently? What happened last time? Could you tell me what you had done differently last time?

MOTHER: Well, I'll tell you what we usually do, which I was quite interested to think. . . . I felt the second time we would play it the way we do usually, which is, I run the house for Ian. . . . So we said tonight, on the phone I told him you'd be here and he said, well, I'll come home and take the boys over, which was just as if we had a dinner party or something, which he would have done anyway.

HL: So that was different. Do you think you reacted differently to the boys because we were here?

MOTHER: No, but I think the boys liked the extra time they got. They'll miss it tomorrow

HL: Did you react to them differently?

MOTHER: No, no, I don't think so. At the table and so, Ian was saying: "Eat up" and so on. We had a live-in help for six months when the twins were born and that helped us learn to be ourselves in front of other people. . . .

HL: Would you have spanked them if we hadn't been here on any occasion?

MOTHER: Probably, I think David probably would have been sent to his room.

HL: Oh, yes.

MOTHER: You know, in about five more minutes. He was shaped up, you see. So yes, I think Ian would have spanked him if you hadn't been here. [Observer's comment: father did give the child a slight slap, in fact.] But, you know, you do feel a little bit awkward when someone else is here.

HL: I suppose, you can't help changing your behavior to some extent.

MOTHER: But not that much for us. But I imagine maybe other people might be, they might feel very awkward.

HL: Well, thank you very much indeed for having us.

INTERVIEW-RATING APPROACH

While the main thrust of our efforts went into the development of feasible, practical, and reliable observation and experimental methods, I did not want to lose all information that was not based on direct observation, as mentioned earlier. I therefore employed interviews and a "diary" completed by the mother as additional probes. It was hoped that the fact that the family was being observed would lead to greater veridicality of the interview responses. One could also not be certain how far the behavior counts would serve to uncover relationships between child and parent variables, and overall ratings were included as a form of insurance. Our data provide an empirical base for deciding how far behavior counts and how far ratings are useful in establishing relationships predicted on theoretical grounds (see below).

Interviews and "Diary"

The initial interview (Interview I, Appendix II), held before the observation sessions, was concerned with obtaining family, demographic, and historical information about the child. The interviewer also informed the mother about what to expect during the various phases of the investigation. The second interview (Interview II, Appendix II) probed into more delicate issues, and it was therefore not conducted until the end of the second observation, by which time mother and investigator were on more familiar and relaxed terms. (The same psychologist interviewed mother on both occasions.) This interview was in large part patterned on the one in the study by Sears, Maccoby, and Levin (1957), and the questions were geared to the areas of concern in the present study. They were intended to elicit the mother's perceptions of the child's characteristics, as well as her own habitual practices and attitudes toward child rearing. The interviewer, who had received special training for this task, adopted a deliberately neutral tone so as not to suggest any particular mode of action as specially desirable. Although there were certain instances of trying to create a good impression, nearly all mothers almost defiantly mentioned some practices that they supposed were not acceptable to advocates of "progressive" child rearing, for instance, spanking. The responses were noted verbatim, and the interview was also tape-recorded for later checking.

Mothers were asked to write a record of all the events and incidents concerning the child over a 24-hour period, writing a segment every hour or so during the day. They were particularly requested to note their own reactions and feelings about the child's doings. In this way we hoped to obtain a very factual record of events and interactions that, since it was written near the time of their happening, would be subject to very little distortion. It was also hoped that since the mother would be expressing her reactions "hot," as it were, the record would provide a fairly accurate reflection of her feelings, which would not have been filtered though too much conscious attitudinizing. Some records were, indeed, very useful and informative accounts of the trials and tribulations of a mother of a young family. One mother, in fact, sent us two accounts because the first one was written on a "bad" day—very vividly portrayed—and she did not want it to stand on its own. Other diaries, on the other hand, were too confined to the trivia of daily life, gave no hint of conflict situations, and suppressed the mother's own feelings and actions so completely that they were of little use. Where there were gaps or obscurities in the diary, these were followed up during the second interview so that we could explore the mother's feelings and reactions further.

Ratings

Ratings were on a 1–5 scale, and the scales were established specifically for this investigation. The child ratings were given by the chief observer, who was present for two observations and who read the diary and the interview protocols. In order to avoid contamination, the mother's ratings were allotted by a second observer, who was present during one observation for this purpose and who conducted both interviews.

Child, mother, and father ratings and their definitions are shown in Table 6. Each rating represents an overall impression and was based on evidence from the observations and the diary as well as on answers to specific questions in Interview II (e.g., answers to questions 1 to 5 formed the basis for the rating of child's compliance, and questions 24, 27, and 30 were used for rating mother's consistency of enforcement). The interview and diary were used only as supplementary sources of evidence, and where they contradicted the evidence of the observer's senses, they were disregarded in the ratings. Because of lack of time, fathers were not interviewed. Toward the end of the investigation, the fathers were given a questionnaire containing the questions from the mother's interview that were appropriate. Twenty-nine fathers (of 15 singletons and 14 twin pairs, that is, of 43 children) completed the questionnaire, and these fathers were allotted ratings similar to the mothers'.

The median interrater reliability for mothers' ratings overall was .80 and for the child ratings was .67. It shoud be noted that it was the child ratings, which were based on the more precisely defined and more fragmented indicators of generalized traits, that showed the lower reliability coefficients.

Table 6. Definitions of Ratings

Rating label	Definition
Child ratings:	
Compliance	Degree to which child complied with parents' requests or commands.
Attachment	Degree of proximity and attention seeking: average of subratings for seeking attention and approval, seeking comfort, seeking to be close to mother or father, reaction to separation from mother.
Instrumental independence	Degree to which child attempted to do things for himself without parents' help: average of subratings for feeding himself, dressing himself, going to the bathroom by himself, dealing with difficulties by himself, and initiating activities.
Maturity of speech	Articulateness of speech, completeness of utterances.
Internalized standards	Degree to which child had internalized and adopted parents' rules without having to be reminded.
Mother and father ratings:	
Reasoning	Degree to which explanations and justifications were used.
Warmth	Degree to which affection was in evidence or reported.
Psychological rewards	Degree to which psychological rewards (e.g., praise and approval) were used.
Material rewards	Use of material privileges (e.g., candy, toys) as rewards.
Verbal–psychological punishment	Use of criticizing, threatening, temporary withdrawal of love.
Physical punishment	Degree to which this was used.
Consistency of enforcement	Consistency with which parents enforced rules.
Restrictiveness	Amount of restrictions imposed, making allowance for their reasonableness.
Play	Amount of play with child.
Encouragement of mature action	Degree to which independence and mature action were encouraged in relation to child's ability.
Support of dependency	Degree to which attachment behavior was encouraged.
Monitoring (mother only)	Degree to which mother kept track of child's doings and whereabouts.

EXPERIMENTAL APPROACH

The experimental approach formed the third leg of the study. The procedures were administered in the university experimental playroom to each child individually in his mother's presence. Twins were normally given the tasks on two separate mornings. The purpose was to obtain measures of the child's social characteristics under study, and therefore, we arranged the experimental situation so as to elict behavior indicative of these traits. The advantages of holding constant the external conditions and of controlling the essential stimuli to which the child is to react need hardly be stressed. Whether the artificial nature of the situation also alters the expression of child behavior so that the experiment may not reflect either the "real" characteristics of the child or the normal relationships is, of course, the crucial question that will be discussed below.

The playroom, approximately 18 feet by 15 feet, contained a table for carrying out the task and tests, chairs, and a number of toys (e.g., telephone, guns, cars, dolls, and a wheeled elephant, as well as a sand tray in which a toy village was built up). The floor was covered with a canvas sheet marked out into numbered three-foot squares. From an adjoining observation room, an observer recorded child and mother behavior through a one-way mirror. Verbal interaction was relayed through a speaker to the observation room and was also tape-recorded.

The procedure consisted essentially of a period of free play, of mother's pretending to leave and then leaving the room, of a form-board task, and of the Peabody Picture Vocabulary Test, administered by the experimenter. Detailed instructions were given to the mother about each part of the procedure, and she was asked to tell here child that he could play with all the toys in the room, except with the sand tray, as the things in it had been built up for some other children.

Measures

The child was given a score on each of the behavior facets that were experimentally elicited. Each score was on a five-point scale, and it was based on the child's action observed within a prescribed number of minutes. Although the format of the scores is identical with that of the ratings based on home observation, interview, etc., they are in fact not overall impressionistic ratings but scores derived in a comparatively precise and objective manner.

The score for *attachment* was the average of subscores based on how often the child returned to mother during the initial exploration of the room and during the free play period and his reaction to mother's pretended leaving and actual leaving.

The score for *instrumental independence* was the average of subscores based on the child's taking off and putting on his coat and on the amount of help he asked of his mother in completing the form-board task.

The score for *compliance* was the average of subscores based on compliance with the prohibition of play in the sand, both in mother's presence and in her absence; willingness to try the form-board task and the tests; and readiness to tidy up the toys when asked.

Activity level was measured by the number of different toys the child picked up and the number of marked floor squares he traversed in 10 minutes' exploratory play.

The child's behavior was allowed and expected to vary within these categories of behavior. Since our instructions, however, constrained the mother's behavior to prescribed classes and modes of action, her behavior could be rated only on the amount of pressure she exerted to secure the child's compliance. The kind of help she provided during the form-board task, was also noted and categorized.

The Peabody Picture Vocabulary Test (PPVT), yielding a vocabulary IQ, was administered at the end of the session (see also Chapter 3). In the case of five children, lack of cooperation during the PPVT in the experimental playroom suggested that the result would be misleading, and the test was therefore repeated in the home a week or two later. We therefore have some information, though based on a very small sample and one of atypical cases, on the reliability of the PPVT. There were both upward and downward changes in IQ score when the test was given at home; they ranged from zero to 13 points, with an average of 5.6 points. The nonsignificance of Kendall's tau between the two occasions for these five cases suggests some instability of PPVT score at this age (judging by the present limited evidence).

For five children, two observers independently allotted scores on the experimental playroom measures. The interobserver reliability coefficients ranged from .76 to .92, and over the five children it was .82. These reliability coefficients are at a level expected in psychometric testing and were achieved with a comparatively small amount of training and effort.

COMMENTS ON THE THREE APPROACHES EMPLOYED

The ease with which a high level of reliability was obtained for the playroom experimental measures, compared with the difficulty with which any similar "respectable" level of reliability was achieved in the home observation behavior count, is an index of the comparative complexity and difficulty of the two situations. In the playroom laboratory, the experimenter has prearranged the stimuli and is in almost complete control of a largely predictable situation. In allotting scores, the investigator abstracts only certain aspects of the immediate multifaceted action, on which he imposes a predetermined category system. In the fast-moving, free-flowing home interaction, on the other hand, the investigator faces a situation that is just the reverse: chaotic, disorderly, unpredictable, and uncertain. To create an orderly, yet faithful and reliable account, consonant in detail with another observer's account, is a task of major proportions.

The difficulty of establishing a high interobserver agreement in such naturalistic observations stands in stark contrast with the validity of the method. Continuous recording during free-flowing interaction results in validity, because it allows one to pick up the natural sequence of interactive behavior that would be lost in sampling behavior only at predetermined time intervals, and it permits one to note unexpectedly significant antecedents that would be lost in sampling only predetermined events—and hence it will yield a close representation of real-life data. It seems that the observation that is most important psychologically and most valid, because it is generalizable to other life situations, may also be the most difficult to capture reliably. Thus, a certain trade-off between validity and reliability may have to be accepted.

Perhaps the conventional insistence on "reliability of measurement" is misplaced in naturalistic observation? I think not, but one should be aware of its limitations. The purposes of trying to achieve high interobserver agreement are (1) to ensure that observers record consistently and (2) to establish that others, working within the same system, would see and record the same thing in the same situation, in other words, that the record obtained is not the result of one observer's idiosyncratic view. However, even if two observers agree very closely, this correlation means only that they have learned, and agreed, to look at things from a common point of view and to work within a common framework of assumptions and methods. It does not follow that one untrained in this system would see and record the same behavior and label it in the same way (cf. Smith & Connolly, 1972).

It cannot be denied that the investigators felt much more competent, and therefore more comfortable, in the experimental than in the home situation. Employing the two approaches side by side helped one to understand psychologists' preference for the experimental laboratory approach.

The interview-rating approach also proved relatively free of problems in its application, and moderate reliabilities between raters were obtained. Its problems are more hidden ones, lying in the area of possible undetected bias and distortion of data. However, first, in view of the demonstrated difficulty of establishing reliable data based on microrecording of behavior units and, second, because of the possibility that some important aspects of the parent–child relationship may slip through the net of behavior counts, the inclusion of ratings in the overall design is no doubt a sensible precaution.

Mention should be made of the time consumed in this kind of research. Taking all interviews, observations, experiments with second observers where necessary, and transcription and correction of records into account, it took about 31 hours to gather and process all the data for a singleton and 36 hours for a twin pair. This does not include punching the data onto cards or later analyses by computer or by hand.

COMPARATIVE YIELD OF DIFFERENT DATA SOURCES

In the present investigation, the three methods were employed in parallel. To the extent that they corroborate each other, the researcher could have increased confidence in the stability of his findings. However, they need not all by equally valuable. An important question is, Which method or data source provides the more meaningful results? Or, in other words, which approach generates variables that exhibit relatively the most stable and theoretically explicable network of relationships linking children's social characteristics to parents' socialization practices? If one type of data source enters into a "nomological net" of relationships expected on theoretical grounds more than another type, it can be claimed that it has shown relatively greater "construct validity." In setting out the concept of construct validity, Cronbach and Meehl (1955) wrote:

> Numerous successful predictions dealing with phenotypically diverse "criteria" give greater weight to the claim of construct validity than do fewer predictions, or predictions involving very similar behavior. (p. 295)

In this investigation, criterion measures for the child characteristics under study were derived from summed behavior counts indicative of these traits, from ratings, and from parallel experimental (playroom) measures. They were submitted to a correlational analysis with summed behavior counts, ratings, and experimental measures relating to other child and parent traits, as well as with the demographic variables: social class (middle or lower), mother's education group, twinship (twin versus singleton), and vocabulary IQ (Peabody Picture Vocabulary Test). The substantive aspect and the theoretical implications of the correlation and regression analyses will be discussed in later chapters.

How do the three data sources used in the investigation fare when they are subjected to a cost–benefit analysis? The cost, in terms of time and manpower, can be only roughly estimated, but overall it was greatest for the behavior counts, somewhat less for ratings (they were based on interviews, 24-hour records, and a lesser amount of observation than the counts), and least for the playroom measures.

The benefits can best be assessed in terms of the useful network of correlations with theoretically related variables that the three types of data sources generated. This means comparing the percentages of significant correlations out of the number of possible correlations that are available from each method. As noted above, this relative payoff can be regarded as an index of the comparative construct validity that each data source is able to attain when used as a method of measuring the variables in question. It should be noted that Cronbach and Meehl's (1955) requirement of numerous predictions to "diverse 'criteria,'" as quoted earlier, is here reversed, since the predictions are from a number of diverse predictors to one criterion at a time. The logic, however, remains the same. For convenience' sake, I have here simply adopted the usual convention of considering the child variables the criteria and the parent variables the predictors, though this direction of causality is by no means immutable.

Table 7 shows the number and percentages of correlations that are significant at the .05 level or better, broken down by criterion categories. In each case, the percentage was computed from the total number of possible correlations with other counts, ratings, experimental measures, or demographic variables, into which the variable in question entered. All intercorrelations among criterion measures with each category have been omitted from this calculation, as have been certain correlations betwen measures that were not experimentally independent and that would have spuriously inflated the number of significant correlations.

Variance due to a common method plays a certain part in these correlations, as can be seen from the correlations within data sources (e.g., count criteria with other counts). These correlations show a higher percentage of significant associations than do the other groupings, except for correlations with the demographic variables. Counts and ratings contribute a far greater number of correlations than do the experimental measures, and therefore, the self-correlations of the former are more heavily weighted when we sum across rows to arrive at the total percentage of significant correlations in the last-but-one column on the right. In order to give equal weighting to each data source in the total, the unweighted means of the percentages in the main rows were calculated and placed in the right-hand column of Table 7.

If we look at the correlations between criterion variables, categorized by data source, and other variables from all data sources (two right-hand columns), we see that count criteria are most productive of significant correlations, followed by ratings, with experimental measures coming in a poor third. This is so even for the unweighted means, although here, counts and ratings are almost on a par. The chief contribution of the experimental criterion measures comes from their within-method correlations, except for the measure for instrumental independence, which produces associations across methods. If we examine the correlations between all criterion variables and other variables, categorized by data sources (bottom line), we note that, leaving aside demographic variables, counts are still highest in the pecking order, but ratings and experimental measures overall tie for second place. Demographic variables show the highest yield of all, both with count and rating criteria and overall. This is not a surprising finding, since variables such as mother's education and twinship are "carrier variables"; that is, they subsume a set of attitudes and practices, the accumulation of which produces stronger effects, and hence associations, than their individual components.

Of the three approaches employed here, behavior counts showed themselves to possess the highest heuristic utility, the criteria entering into a strong network of relationships with other variables, although some of this strong showing seems to represent method variance. In spite of some fragmentation inherent in them, the counts have thus been confirmed in their usefulness as behaviorally anchored indices of the characteristics they defined.

The ratings, though they are the most subjective of the measures, turned out to have good heuristic utility. Another investigation (Emmerich, 1964, 1966), indeed, showed teacher ratings to delineate the dependency construct more coherently, that is, they clustered together more than the observational measures did. The ratings' usefulness may, however, be thought to be due to artifactual reasons. Vernon (1964) wrote:

> Every correlation between traits represents a mixture of (i) genuine overlapping between the types of behavior in the subjects, (ii) common evaluative attitudes of the raters and common cultural theories regarding the interrelations of traits, and (iii) idiosyncratic attitudes and theories in particular raters. (p. 59)

The operation of (ii) and (iii) would, of course, spuriously inflate correlations of ratings. Point (ii) operates when different raters rate a person on the same or different traits, and this would apply to our interrater agreement. However, it applies only to a very limited extent to our correlations among ratings, since the vast majority of them were correlations between child and parent characteristics, for which our design provided separate ratings by different raters precisely in order to avoid halo effect. Nevertheless, it is possible that parent–child correlations were somewhat inflated by stereotypical attitudes about the interrelations of parents' and children's characteristics that are part of psychological folklore held in common by the two raters. However, since each rater concentrated on one target person, this contamination is likely to have been minimal. The possibility of direct halo effect arises only in the smaller number of child–child correlations. Nor will point (iii) influence correlations between parent and child characteristics, since idiosyncratic attitudes, by definition, differ from rater to rater.

Table 7.   Correlations Significant at .05 Level or Better by Criteria

Data sources		Counts			Ratings		
		N poss-ible rs	N sig. rs	%	N poss-ible rs	N sig. rs	%
Counts							
Nonverbal attachment rate		30	7	23.3	28	1	3.6
Verbal attachment rate		30	12	40.0	28	0	0.0
Rate child speech		28	11	39.3	28	10	35.7
Total activity count		30	8	26.7	29	5	17.2
Compliance ratio		31	10	32.3	27	10	37.0
Count criteria overall		149	48	32.2	140	26	18.6
Ratings							
Attachment		30	6	20.0	28	5	17.9
Instrumental independence		32	7	21.9	28	7	25.0
Speech maturity		29	6	20.7	28	7	25.0
Compliance		31	5	16.1	27	8	29.6
Intern. standards		31	4	12.9	27	4	14.8
Rating criteria overall		153	28	18.3	138	31	22.5
Experimental measures							
Attachment	EM[b]	30	0	0.0	28	1	3.6
Instrumental independence	EM	32	5	15.6	28	6	21.4
Total activity	EM	30	0	0.0	29	0	0.0
Compliance	EM	31	4	12.9	27	0	0.0
Experimental criteria overall		123	9	7.3	112	7	6.3
TOTAL		425	85	20.0	390	64	16.4

[a] The sample was reduced for correlations by taking randomly one of each pair of twins.
[b] EM = experimental measure.

The fairly good interrater agreement obtained, particularly for the parent ratings, indicates that the raters were, in fact, agreed on the dimensions that they were rating as well as on the place along them where individuals fell. Their ratings, in other words, were not influenced by idiosyncratic attitudes, as these were largely equalized by the difinitions of the dimensions. It must also not be forgotten that the seeming construct validity of the ratings may to some extent be due to the fact that they were in a large measure based on direct observation.

The rating process, summarizing and abstracting various types of information, thus can yield valid data for ordering subjects and, in the case of the present investigation, apparently has done so. The ratings have

and Data Sources (Pearson Product-Moment. Max. $N = 90$)[a]

Criterion variable with:

Experimental measures			Demographic variables			Total			
N possible rs	N sig. rs	%	N possible rs	N sig. rs	%	N possible rs	N sig. rs	%	Unweighted %
6	2	33.3	4	1	25.0	68	9	13.2	
6	0	0.0	4	1	25.0	68	13	19.1	
7	0	0.0	4	2	50.0	67	23	34.3	
5	0	0.0	4	2	50.0	68	15	22.1	
6	0	0.0	4	1	25.0	68	21	30.1	
30	2	6.7	20	7	35.0	339	83	24.5	23.1
6	0	0.0	4	0	0.0	68	17	25.0	
6	3	50.0	4	1	25.0	70	18	25.7	
7	1	14.3	4	2	50.0	68	16	23.5	
6	0	0.0	4	2	25.0	68	15	22.1	
6	2	33.3	4	1	25.0	68	11	16.2	
31	6	19.4	20	6	30.0	342	71	20.8	22.6
6	0	0.0	4	0	0.0	68	1	1.5	
6	2	33.3	4	2	50.0	70	15	21.4	
5	1	20.0	4	0	0.0	68	1	1.5	
6	3	50.0	4	0	0.0	68	7	10.3	
23	6	26.1	16	2	12.5	274	24	8.8	13.1
84	14	16.7	56	15	26.8	955	178	18.6	20.0

therefore justified themselves from the point of view of the contribution they have made to answering the research questions.

The experimental criterion measures showed the lowest heuristic utility of the three approaches, though experimental measures overall predicted ratings criteria fairly well, particularly instrumental independence. Generally speaking, however, their yield was poor. It seems that the greater precision and reliability of the experimentally obtained playroom measures did not produce high validity. This finding lends weight to the doubts, expressed in Chapter 1, about the generalizability of experimental measures.

A plausible explanation for the poor validity of the measures derived from the experimental situation in the present investigation—as in many others—would be that these young children behaved atypically, being overawed by the strange surroundings, though these were no different from those of an ordinary playroom. We noted, for instance, in the case of a pair of twins, that both were very wild and disobedient at home and much more manageable in the playroom. One of them displayed an unusual degree of anxiety and even cried when shown into the room.

It is also true that the time span of the experiment was relatively brief (three-quarters of an hour), but it was by no means atypical in its length, and many experiments sample much smaller segments of behavior. It is possible that a wider range of experimental situations might increase the utility of this approach, and it is worth exploring what effect repeated exposure to experimental situations with a possible stabilization of responses might have on the resulting correlations. However, in view of the high cost of observation studies, it will be difficult to incorporate repeated experiments together with observation and interview in the same investigation.

Of course, the findings have to be interpreted in the context of the specific measures and approaches employed here. Changes in overall conception or in the details of any method here. Changes in overall conception or in the details of any method might produce different results, which is only to say that the findings of this—and any other investigation—are method-bound. Nevertheless, they are worth bearing in mind in planning investigations, particularly in view of the existing dearth of evidence as regards the relative utility of different data sources.

Summary

Of the three investigative approaches employed here, behavior counts yielded the largest network of significant correlations and therefore had the highest heuristic utility. Criterion ratings also possessed good heuristic utility, with experimental criteria a poor third. Demographic variables, however, generated the highest proportion of significant correlations of all.

CHAPTER 3

Mothers, Fathers, and Young Sons

Incidence, Structure, and Education Level Differences in Their Interactive Behavior

It has been said that, in its haste to step into the twentieth century and to become a respectable science, Psychology skipped the preliminary descriptive stage that other natural sciences had gone through, and so was soon losing touch with the natural phenomena. (Tinbergen, 1963, p. 411)

The task of our time is perhaps to retrace our steps and fill in the descriptive stage in psychology even now. Seeking to explain or predict given phenomena before knowing their nature or their distribution in the natural world may, after all, be to put the cart before the horse and to invite misleading assumptions and conclusions. If this is so, ethological data on the incidence of behavior are of vital interest to students of child development.

Normative data on child and parent interactive behavior have recently begun to appear. Some are reported as necessary base data in the investigation of functional relationships, for example, the duration of crying during the first year of life in Ainsworth, Bell, and Stayton (1972), or the percentage of child compliance and the rate of mother commands for 2-year-olds in Minton, Kagan, and Levine (1971). Patterson and his co-workers have reported the incidence of "noxious behaviors" in 3- to 14-year-old boys in a number of papers (e.g., Patterson & Cobb, 1973). In other papers, the incidence and distribution of various kinds of behavior, of both children and parents, are the main focus of concern (e.g., Escalona, 1973, and Clarke-Stewart, 1973, both dealing with infants). Various accounts in the ethological tradition of very detailed behavior categories, describing the actions of nursery-school children have appeared (e.g., Blurton-Jones, 1972; Smith & Connolly, 1972; McGrew, 1972). Variations in the frequencies of behavior between different social classes or educational groups have also been reported (e.g., Minton *et al.*, 1971; Tulkin & Kagan, 1972).

This chapter is devoted to a normative account of the incidence and structure of child, mother, and father behavior to each other in their own homes and to an analysis of differences between mothers and fathers and between groups based on mother's education. It is therefore keyed to the natural-history phase of a field of study, in which phenomena are described and their distribution in a specified natural setting is examined, and thus, it helps to fill the gap pointed out by Tinbergen. Moreover, it does so for an age group (2-year-olds) for which no data on parent–child interaction, directly observed in a naturalistic situation, seem to be available.

That theoretical assumptions inevitably entered into the relatively atheoretical observation and coding of behavior was pointed out in Chapter 2. The incidence of various types of behavior, to be reported below, must be seen in the light of the main concerns of the project, which were the reciprocal interactions between parents and children that make up the socialization process as it affects compliance, attachment, independence, and speech. Decisions on the behavior to be selected and coded naturally flow from these concerns and were discussed in Chapter 2.

All coded actions by child, mother, and father were summed over all observation sessions. What will be discussed in this chapter will sometimes be the raw frequencies, when these are of interest in their own right, but more often these frequencies are expressed as a percentage of all actions of the agent concerned. The total number of actions varied between individuals in different families; relative frequencies equalize for these differences and indicate what is generally more important, namely, the relative emphasis given to different activities. Certain actions will also be presented as percentages of the time that the agent was present during the observation, or as rates per minute. Raw frequencies can be recovered by the interested reader by reference to the mean numbers of behavior units and mean time present (see Figure 1).

Social class differences as they affect parents' interactions with their children have been the subject of many studies over the years, undertaken in the hope of uncovering the sources of differences in children's later abilities and other characteristics. Bronfenbrenner (1958) summed up earlier work in the area, mainly based on interviews and ratings, by concluding that middle-class parents tend to use more "love-oriented," psychological discipline and are more responsive to the inner states of the child, whereas lower-class parents tend to use more coercive, power-oriented discipline and are more concerned with the child's external behavior.

Recently mother–child interaction has been studied more immediately by measuring the variables via observation either in the home or in the laboratory, and social class differences have been assessed by such more direct methods.[1] (Father has been conspicuous by his absence in investigations concerned with social class differences.) Overall, the results amount to a remarkable confirmation of Bronfenbrenner's generalizations. Middle-class mothers tend to use more flexible, psychological-influence techniques and are more attuned to the child's inner states; this statement subsumes their greater use of suggestions to the child, as well as their greater responsiveness to the child's needs and the greater frequency of positive, rather than negative feedback. Lower-class mothers, on the other hand, tend more toward coercive direction or "power assertion" (including physical punishment) and impose more restrictions on the child's freedom (Brody, 1968; Kamii & Radin, 1967; Kogan & Wimberger, 1969; Minton, Kagan, & Levine, 1971; Streissguth & Bee, 1972; Zegiob & Forehand, 1975; Zussman, 1978). Middle-class mothers generally show a greater degree of involvement with their children's activities and, in particular, enter into more verbal communication with them (Brody, 1968; Greenberg & Formanek, 1974; Kamii & Radin, 1967; Kogan & Wimberger, 1969; Tulkin & Kagan, 1972; Zunich, 1961). The expression of physical affection and contact, where this behavior was kept distinct from the influence techniques of praise and approval, on the other hand, shows no difference between the classes (Tulkin & Kagan, 1972; also Bayley & Schaefer, 1960).

Social class differences in children's interactive behavior with their parents, as opposed to their abilities and learning styles, have been documented more sparsely. Middle-class children tend to vocalize more or to engage more in verbal communication than lower-class children (Greenberg & Formanek, 1974; Messer & Lewis, 1972; Tulkin, 1973). They also are more demanding of mother's attention and company (Kamii & Radin, 1967; Minton *et al.* 1971), but they display attachment behavior to the same extent as lower-class children (Tulkin, 1973). Differences, it seems, are more notable in the cognitive than in the affective area.

The differing control methods and differing use of language and of restrictions by mothers may possibly be due to the cumulative social experiences that different social classes have been exposed to. It has been suggested, for instance, that the lower-class mothers' practices in this respect may be the result of adaptation to the existing social structure, in

---

[1] In this summary of the research I have leaned heavily on a review of the literature by Mrs. Denise Watts.

which they feel controlled by events, without an opportunity of controlling them (Hess, 1970). However, the more directive approach may also be a consequence of the fact that these mothers have less time at their disposal for the niceties of life because they tend to be overwhelmingly preoccupied with procuring its essentials. In any case, there is evidence that such differences have been narrowing over the years (see below).

Since our social class division, based on father's occupation, correlated significantly with only very few variables, frequencies of the various types of behavior were broken down by groups based on mother's education, which is a kind of social class stratification. (Several of the "social class" differences reviewed above were based on grouping by mother's education.) Differences between these education-level groups (see Table 2 for definitions) will be discussed below.

An important topic of discussion will also be differences in interactive behavior between mothers and fathers.

INCIDENCE OF CHILD AND PARENT BEHAVIOR

Figure 1 presents information on the duration of the observations, mother's and father's time present, and the frequency of behavior units, that

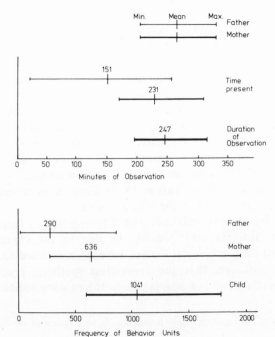

Figure 1. Observation characteristics.

is, the total number of action of each agent.[2] When an action extended over time—and this affected mainly child actions, for example, play with a toy—it was counted only once for the purpose of working out overall means and percentages.

The means of fathers are based on the fathers on the 120 children for whom we have data. These fathers, it will be noted, were present for far less time than the mothers, partly because some were absent for one of the two observations altogether, and partly because they absented themselves more often for part of an observation. They also addressed far fewer actions to the child than mothers did, even when one equalizes for time present. Whether father's presence resulted in different frequencies of mother or child actions, compared with when mother was alone with the children, or vice versa, was investigated for speech, and for control and compliance. These "second-order effects" will be discussed in Chapters 6 and 7.

There were no significant education-level differences in total numbers of actions, but both mothers and fathers (though not the children) of the higher education groups engaged in slightly more actions than did the lower education groups.

Child Actions

Frequencies—percentage of actions and percentage of time—of action counts for child, mother, and father are shown in Figures 2–10. Significant differences between groups based on mother's education level (college-attenders versus non-college-attenders), calculated by independent t tests, are marked on the figures.[3] Child actions have been organized under six headings, partly based on the factor analysis of behavior counts presented below. The meaning of the labels for different actions was explained in Table 3.

Active Play and Movement Behavior

Figure 2 displays the percentage of all actions and the percentage of time that these kinds of activity occupied. That the child should be "physically active" for only 35% of the time on average may cause surprise; however, the larger part of his time would be accounted for by eating

[2] Appendix III lists descriptive statistics for all count variables discussed in this chapter.

[3] T values were calculated from data for all 136 children (or lesser numbers when there were missing cases for certain variables); that is, for every variable, each twin's score was entered separately, including mother and father actions addressed to each twin. However, this is not entirely legitimate in view of the known correlations between twin partners and between parents' actions addressed to each twin. (See Chapter 9 for intrapair correlations.) The probability level for the t tests was therefore based on an adusted number of degrees of freedom, counting each twin family only once (df: 88, for 90 families). Multivariate F tests between the education groups will be reported below.

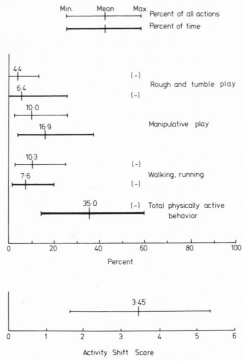

Figure 2. Child's active play and movement behavior. Note: $(+)$ or $(-)$ by the side of the bar in this and all subsequent figures indicates mean of mother's education Groups 3 and 4 higher (lower) than of Groups 1 and 2. For definitions see Chapter 2. $(P < .05)$

(mealtime was usually included in the observation), watching television, looking at books, preparing for bed, etc.

The "Activity Shift Score" indicates the number of times per minute that the child shifted from one activity to another and is essentially an index of the child's restlessness. Such a shift of activity occurred on average three and a half times every minute. It will be noted that children of non-college-educated mothers were significantly more active overall and showed greater restlessness than those of college-educated mothers.

Speech Behavior

Speech acts (number of utterances) make up a considerable proportion of the child's total activity, though other actions occupy more time (see Figure 3). In order to establish how to assess the time that child speech actually occupied, we timed the duration of speech acts of two children in an investigation separate from the usual observation. We found that individual speech acts hardly ever lasted more than one second. The "Rate of speech per minute" can therefore be interpreted as the number of seconds per minute that the children spoke. Thus, the mean rate of 1.80 works out as 3% of the time. While speech acts therefore figure very prominently in the number of separate actions, the proportion of time they occupy is much smaller.

The greater amount of speech produced by children of college-educated mothers is in sharp contrast to their lesser physical activity compared with children of non-college-attenders. Since the code permitted us to record speech while other activities were in progress, this finding is not an artifact of the coding system. Correlations between speech and the various aspects of physical activity are generally negative, and the greater amount of speech and the lesser amount of physical activity seem indeed to be corollaries of mother's higher education.

Demands and Compliance

Instances of demands and requests noted here (Figure 4) do not include demands for attention and help, which are categorized separately (see below). Children of college-attenders produced slightly more demands, both absolutely and relatively, than those of non-college-attenders, though the difference was not significant.

The mean comply ratio (=comply/[comply + noncomply]) of about two-thirds does not take those instances into account when neither comply nor noncomply followed a command. When these instances are considered, the mean ratio of "complies" drops to .56. Children of college-educated mothers had a significantly higher comply ratio, and the absolute number of their "complies" was slightly higher, too (difference nearly significant).

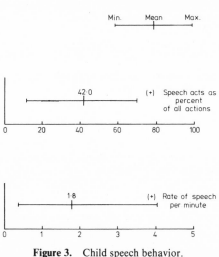

Figure 3.   Child speech behavior.

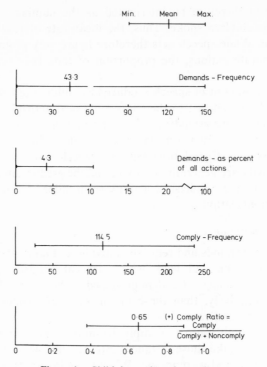

Figure 4.   Child demands and compliance.

Positively and Negatively Toned Behavior

(See Table 3. The definition of these categories will be discussed further in Chapter 8.) The average incidence of all negative actions was higher than of all positive actions (see Figure 5) because a great many actions of 2½-year-old boys in the home seem at least slightly objectionable to parents and therefore change worthy. Many of these actions are outward manifestations of impulses that are indeed not in harmony with the requirements of group living and that the child will eventually learn to moderate, or they are expressions of momentary unpleasant feelings.

Children of college-educated mothers, it will be seen, expressed pleasure less frequently, and they also expressed displeasure less and engaged in slightly fewer negative actions (differences not significant). The higher education of mothers, it seems, imposes greater restraint on the expression of affect and impulse by their children.

Attachment Behavior

Under this heading, I have grouped all aspects of the child's attempts to be close to his mother and father, both physically and psychologically (see Figure 6), actions that generally go under the label of *attachment behavior*. (See Chapter 5 for a further discussion.) Empirically, too, all these actions directed to father cluster together on two factors (see the discussion of factor analysis below). Each category in Figure 6 (except the "Attachment Rates") represents a code verb, and the labels are self-explanatory. The first three actions make up proximal or nonverbal attachment behavior, and the last three distal or verbal attachment behavior. Nonverbal attachment behavior, at the age of 2, occurs more than twice as often as verbal attachment behavior, as can be seen from the rates at the bottom of the figure. It also constitutes more than double the proportion of the child's total actions, but the proportion made up by both types of attachment behavior together is still very modest (4.75%). The action that shows relatively the highest incidence is "Approaching" parents, but at the same time it is psychologically the least significant.

The absence of any significant differences in line with mother's education is an interesting fact in itself. Children of college-attenders tended to engage in slightly more verbal attachment behavior, however, but they sat on father's lap less than did children of non-college-attenders (difference nearly significant).

The "Attachment Rate—Narrow" is based on the number of acts of approaching, touching, seeking attention, and seeking help of mother (or

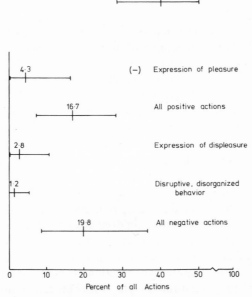

Figure 5. Child positively and negatively toned behavior.

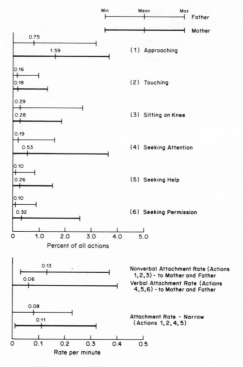

Figure 6.   Child attachment behavior.

father) and thus represents a narrower definition of attachment behavior. The rate was calculated per minute of mother's presence or, for father, per minute of his presence. Even when mother's longer presence has thus been allowed for, she is the more important object of this behavior; the difference is significant at the .001 level (two-tailed t test).

The differences between mother and father for rough-and-tumble play (not shown in the figures) are the reverse of those for attachment behavior. In view of father's lesser availability, the fact that the child engaged in more rough-and-tumble play with him than with mother (.72% versus .45% of child actions, $p < .01$) is all the more remarkable. It looks as if father marks himself out for physical contact games with the boys (he plays "let's be boys," as an observer noted), and there is evidence that he also has more negative physical contact with the children than mother has (Figure 9). It may also be that the children themselves simply sex-type father for romping, but on the other hand, the count of paternal affectionate behavior is also higher than that of maternal affectionate behavior (Figure 9). The greater amount of rough-and-tumble play with him can no doubt partly also be traced to father's having just returned from work and making before and after supper his playtime with the children, while mother, after the whole day with them, retires gratefully to the background. Even under these circumstances, when the child needs closeness, comfort, and attention, he seeks them more with mother than with father.

Mother and Father Actions

Speech Behavior

It is clear that mother tended to speak more to the child than father did, even allowing for differences in time present, and the difference is significant ($p < .001$), as is the difference between the rates of child-to-mother and child-to-father speech (see Figure 7).

College-educated mothers talked significantly more to their children than did non-college-educated mothers, and the differences for fathers were in the same direction but did not reach significance. As partners in this interchange, the children of college-educated mothers also produced a greater amount of speech all round (cf. Figure 3). Thus, a reciprocity system of mutual verbal stimulation and interchange between parents and children is established. (See Chapter 7 for a further discussion.)

Control Behavior and Compliance

It can be seen from Figure 8 that the difference in absolute numbers of commands issued by mother and father is enormous and significant (the average number of commands and prohibitions together for mother is 87.5 and for father 37.4). However, the difference in relative frequency is nonsig-

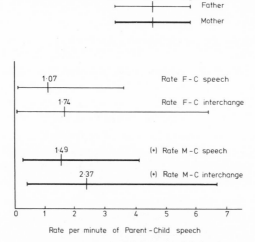

Figure 7. Mother and father speech behavior.

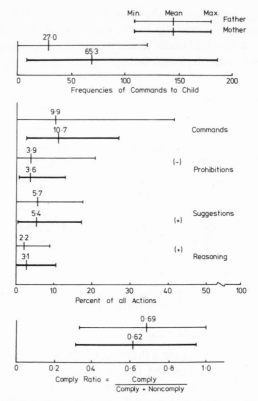

Figure 8. Mother and father control behavior and compliance.

nificant. This discrepancy is partly due to the mother's longer presence during our obsevations, but there remains a large discrepancy if one equalizes for time present: mother's rate of commands and prohibitions per minute of her presence is .38 and father's rate is .25. This difference will reflect the fact that mother feels more responsible for the child's behavior and has a tendency to intervene more—on his behalf, as well as in order to restrain him. An interesting corollary of mother's greater intervention is the fact, to be documented in detail in Chapter 6, that a smaller proportion of her commands, suggestions, etc. than of father's are complied with by the child.

The comply ratio was worked out for mother and father as it was for the child (Figure 4), and it will be seen that its distribution is fairly similar for all three. Nevertheless, father's comply ratio is significantly higher than mother's ($p < .001$), and some fathers, with a comply ration of 1.0, seem to reach a status of saintliness that is not vouchsafed to either mother or child.

Significant differences as a corollary of mother's education are only patchy. However, the differences that do not reach significance are all in a similar direction: college-educated mothers, as well as their husbands, employ fewer prohibitions and use more suggestion and reasoning, as a proportion of all their actions; similarly, they comply more readily with their children's requests. Since this result confirms a similar finding by Minton *et al.* (1971), one can have considerable confidence that this tendency is a stable accompaniment of mother's education.

The figures throw an interesting light on the relative salience of various forms of control used by parents. Commands and prohibitions together occupy a preponderant position among their control statements. Fathers varied very widely in the use of this form of control, and some relied more heavily on it than even the most controlling of mothers. The number of commands must be interpreted in the light of the fact that parents are dealing with 2½-year-old boys. It would be fascinating, though difficult, to obtain a natural history of command giving for varying ages, as well as for girls.

Positively and Negatively Toned Behavior

The entries in Figure 9 are individual coded verbs, except for "Affectionate behavior," All positive action," and "All negative action" (see Table 3 for definitions).

Father displayed significantly more affectionate behavior to the child than mother did ($p < .05$). However, we must remember again that our observation took place at a time when father typically was ready to play with the child and mother was worn out. The time of day is very probably also responsible for the vastly greater proportion of father's actions that were devoted to play with the child compared with mother's (not shown in the figure), most of this play being romping (father's mean percentage: 3.136; mother's: .934, $p < .001$).

The same circumstance may be reflected in the greater proportion of "positive actions" all round ($p < .05$) and the lower proportion of "negative actions" ($p < .001$) that are shown for father as compared with mother. However, for "Hitting" the roles are reversed: father employed this physical form of control more than mother, although the difference is not significant. In view of this reversal, one wonders whether mother's relatively greater use of negative actions is entirely a result of the time of day when we observed. It looks as if mother would in general—perhaps because of her greater involvement with the child—engage in relatively more *verbal* negative actions, including noncompliance with the child's requests (cf. Figure 8), than father. it should be pointed out that all playful negative behavior (e.g., playful threatening and playful hitting) was excluded from these counts. We note also that the incidence of "positive action" for both mother and father was considerably greater than that of "negative action," whereas the child displayed more negative than positive actions (Figure 5).

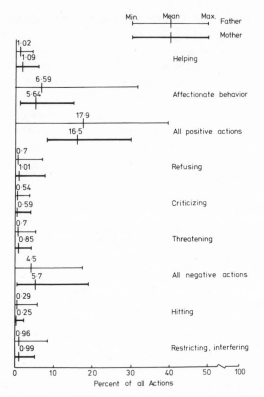

Figure 9.   Mother and father positively and negatively toned behavior.

No significant differences in line with mother's education emerged in these categories of behavior. The differences that were present did not all point in the same direction, either, although the frequency of both mother's and father's use of physical punishment ("Hitting") was slightly higher in the lower education group. However, one can conclude overall that warm affectionate behavior is not linked to any level of education (nor, by implication, to any class).

Responsiveness

A "quality of maternal responsiveness" has in the past been considered to be significant from a theoretical point of view and has been shown empirically to be important to the child's development. Stayton, Hogan, and Ainsworth (1971) measured "sensitivity of maternal responsiveness" by a rating, defining it thus:

> The sensitive mother is defined as one who is finely attuned to the baby's signals and communications and able to see things from his point of view. She is aware

of signals, interprets them accurately, and responds to them promptly and appropriately. (p. 1060)

They concluded that this quality was related to obedience and to manifestations of "internalized controls" in the child, even in the first year of life. Bell and Ainsworth (1972) suggested that maternal responsiveness was associated with a decline in the frequency of infant crying. Clarke-Stewart (1973) defined contingent responsiveness behaviorally as the proportion of child elicitors such as demands or distress, to which the mother provided a positive response; however, the appropriateness of the demand was not taken into consideration. It was found that maternal responsiveness was related to optimal secure attachment to mother and also to overall competence in these 9- to 18-month-old children.

Responsiveness is a quality that attaches to the contingent nature of an act; that is, a maternal or paternal act is responsive if it occurs as a reaction to a child's explicit demands or implicit needs. Hence, any count must take account of the contingencies the child furnishes; in other words, the sequence of acts has to be considered. Moreover, to obtain meaningful behavioral measures, note must be taken of whether the parental response is appropriate or inappropriate in the light of the circumstances and the reasonableness or otherwise of the child's demand. To classify such acts in appropriate ways is therefore a complex task, which requires judgments to be made, and which cannot be entrusted to a computer.

I decided to obtain measures of mothers' and fathers' responsiveness, but in view of the complications mentioned above, this had to be done by human scrutiny of the observation records. A representative subsample of 40 children was selected. This subsample consisted of 20 singletons and 20 twins, each of the latter being one randomly selected partner of a pair; each group was made up of 60% working-class and 40% middle-class children, and about the same proportions were lower and higher education groups. In view of the amount of labor involved, only one observation record for each child was examined, and the second observation was chosen because it was known that on the second visit, parents' customary reactions to the child were even more likely to gain the upper hand than during the first visit.

The child actions identified as elicitors were actions expressing the child's demands, needs, distress, bids for attention or help, and attempts at contact or play. Thus, touching or showing something to a parent, as well as crying and various forms of requests, was counted as an elicitor. For each elicitor, the parent's reaction within a maximum of 30 sec was classified as responsive or unresponsive, and the parent's action (or nonaction) was further qualified as "appropriate" or "inappropriate." The general criterion of "appropriateness" was what a "good" mother or father, sensitive to the child's welfare and developmental needs, would do in those circumstances.

Subjective judgment and cultural bias inevitably entered into these decisions, the bias being that of the author—a person trained in Western
psychological tradition. While a research assistant examined the records in
the first place, I checked all instances of unresponsiveness and of inappropriate responsiveness. The latter occurred very infrequently, an example
being a mother's giving a child an object with which he could hurt himself.
Examples of appropriate unresponsiveness were mother's not complying
with the child's request to carry the baby brother, or mother's not giving the
child coffee to drink, saying "You're too small," or father's not doing
something for the child that he could do for himself. Table 8 lists the definition of the variables derived from this analysis.

Figure 10 displays the frequency of all child elicitors. The fact that
many more elicitors were addressed to mother than to father is somewhat
deceptive since, if an elicitor was not addressed to a particular person, it
was counted toward the person who made the first response, and if there
was no response to an unaddressed elicitor, it was counted to mother. So the
higher frequency for mother may partly be due to her responding more to
unaddressed elicitors than father did. (We have some evidence for her
propensity to respond more to a child's compliance in general; see Chapter
6). Her longer time with the child of course, also accounts for part of the
excess.

The percentage of elicitors responded to, as well as the percentage of
appropriate responses and nonresponses ("Appropriateness"), is very high,
and there is practically no difference between mother and father for either
of these measures. However, father's variability is much greater than
mother's—a fact that echoes similar findings for affectionate behavior and
positive actions (Figure 9). That some fathers respond 100% of the time and

Table 8. Definitions of Variables from Responsiveness, Reactive Speech, and Repeated Command Analyses

Behavior label	Definition
Responsiveness %— mother or father	Proportion of child elicitors to which parent responded. Child elicitors: demands, expression of need, distress, bids for attention or help, attempts at contact or play.
Appropriateness %— mother or father	Proportion of child elicitors to which parent's response or nonresponse was judged appropriate. For criteria see section on "Responsiveness".
Total reactivity %— mother or father	"Responsiveness %," defined above, plus proportion of child speech addressed to parent to which parent reacted. For details see Chapter 8.
Repeated commands %— mother or father	Commands repeated twice or more for same issue, expressed as a percentage of total commands. For details see Chapter 6.

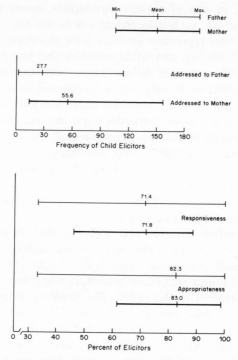

Figure 10. Mother and father responsiveness.

are 100% appropriate in their reactions may be traceable to the fact that they were "bothered" much less by the child than mother was, and hence their patience was tried less; and the 100% response may also be due to the counting rules described above.

Differences in responsiveness and appropriateness between college-attenders and non-college-attenders do not reach significance, but they are all in the same direction: higher means for the higher education group. The findings suggest that higher education bestows somewhat more appropriate sensitivity to children's needs on mothers (and their husbands), but the advantage is only slight. Since, however, Kamii and Radin (1967) and Tulkin and Kagan (1972) found significant differences for responsiveness between different education groups, in favor of the higher group, these differences are likely to be "real."

Multivariate Testing of Differences in Action Frequencies between Mothers' Education Groups

The differences between higher and lower mothers' education groups that have been discussed so far were evaluated for significance by univariate *t* tests. However, in view of obvious correlations among variables derived from the same person, such independent *t* tests are not, strictly speaking, appropriate. Multiple regression analyses were therefore performed to see whether the child, mother, and father variables that had proved significant by *t* test were still significant differentiators between mothers' education groups after the effect of the other variables (derived from the same person) had been taken into account. Mother's education level was the criterion, and child, mother, and father variables were, in turn, entered as the independent variables in three multiple-regression analyses.

The child variables that stayed significant discriminators between mothers' education groups in this multivariate testing were rate of speech, comply ratio, and total of active behavior (percentage of time). Expressions of pleasure and of displeasure, on the other hand, were now no longer associated with the mother's education.

The only mother variable that differentiated significantly between mothers' education groups under multivariate testing was the rate of mother–child speech. Reasoning, suggestions, prohibitions, and commands, however, were no longer significant predictors when they were entered into the regression equation in this order. The same variables were tested for father. His use of reasoning and of prohibitions was still significantly associated with mother's education level, but the other variables were not. These variables, then, which stood up to this more stringent testing, can be regarded as differing reliably and strongly between higher and lower mothers' education levels.

Education Level Differences in Vocabulary IQ and Ratings.

Vocabulary IQ was assessed by means of the Peabody Picture Vocabulary Test (PPVT) for group comparison rather than for individual prediction purposes. In view of the fluctuations in attention inevitably displayed by such young children, no reliance can be placed on the precise individual scores. The mean IQ overall was 86.4, *SD* 16.9, range 58 (estimated) to 135. Children of college-educated mothers had significantly higher IQs than children of non-college-attenders (91.6 versus 84.0, $p < .02$). The low overall average IQ was no doubt in part due to the preponderance in the sample of twins, who in this, as in other studies (e.g. Mittler, 1970), scored lower than singletons (see Chapter 4). But in addition, the low mean IQ may reflect the test's underestimation at these age levels. Deutsch (1969) and Radin (1974) also quote consistently lower IQs for the same children when tested on the PPVT than when tested on the Stanford–Binet. As has been suggested by some, the PPVT is probably best regarded as a test of vocabulary comprehension rather than as a test of intelligence.

Children, mothers, and some fathers were given overall ratings on the characteristics under study, as described in Chapter 2. Relatively few ratings showed differences according to mother's education level. For children, the ratings for compliance and speech maturity were significantly higher in the higher education group, reflecting similar differences in the behavior counts. Mothers in the higher education group received higher ratings for the use of reasoning, the use of psychological rewards, and verbal–psychological punishment. They also exerted significantly greater pressure on the child to comply with instruction in the experimental situation. Hess (1970) suggested that the degree of monitoring of the child's behavior may be a central variable in the influence of the home and that the less close monitoring in working-class homes may be at the root of many social-class differences. However, a rating for the degree of monitoring by mother, included because of this suggestion, showed practically no difference between social classes or mother education groups. Twenty-nine fathers who completed questionnaires were also given ratings. Fathers in the higher education group, like mothers, received higher ratings for the use of reasoning and verbal–psychological punishment and, in addition, for consistency of enforcement of rules and for encouragement of independence in their children. (Differences in mothers' ratings for the last two variables, though nonsignificant, were in the same direction.) The differences that were significant all indicate that both mothers and fathers in the higher education group lean toward a more cognitive and psychological approach to socialization, compared with parents in the lower education group.

Summary

1. Children of better-educated mothers (mothers who had at least some college education) were less physically active and engaged in more verbal communication and complied more with parents' requests than children of less-educated mothers.

2. There were no differences between education groups in children's seeking parents' proximity and nurturance (attachment behavior). This behavior constituted only 4.75% of all child actions.

3. Parents in the higher education groups, like their children, engaged in more verbal interaction than parents in the lower education groups. The triadic communication system was marked by reciprocity, but it was parents who chiefly determined the level of speech within a family.

4. In their control behavior, parents used commands and prohibitions together much more frequently than milder suggestions or explanations of orders. Although differences were not always significant, both behavior counts and ratings showed a consistent tendency for parents in the higher

education groups to lean more toward cognitive and psychological, rather than power-assertive, influence methods.

5. Parents' positive responses predominated over their negative responses. But there were no differences along educational lines in the incidence of positive or negative actions or the expression of affection.

6. Responsiveness to children's needs or wishes was very high, and there were no education group differences.

7. Differences between mother and father in mean levels of actions are summarized in Table 9. Mother was involved in more verbal interchanges with the child, and reasoned more with him, but she also intervened in negative ways more than father did. Father displayed more affection and positive actions in general to the child; he played far more with him and also complied more with his wishes than mother did.

8. High correlations between mother and father behavior indicate that over and above their differences, parents also created a common family system that marked off one family from another.

STRUCTURE OF CHILD AND PARENT INTERACTIVE BEHAVIOR

The foregoing section has described the incidence of, and certain group differences in, children's and parents' behavior toward each other. But we

Table 9. Mother—Father Action Differences ($N = 120$)

	Higher mean	p of difference[a]
Commands–prohibitions frequency[b]	M[c]	.517
Suggestions frequency	F[d]	.856
Reasoning frequency	M	.000
Comply ratio[e]	F	.000
Affection frequency	F	.028
Positive actions frequency	F	.044
Negative actions frequency	M	.000
Mother–(father–)child speech rate[f]	M	.000
Play with child frequency	F	.000
Physical punishment frequency	F	.353
Child comply ratio to M:F	F	.001
Child attachment rate to M:F	M	.001

[a] Correlated t test, two-tailed.
[b] Relative frequency out of each parent's total actions.
[c] M = Mother.
[d] F = Father.
[e] Comply/(comply + noncomply).
[f] Rate per minute of each parent's presence.

can gain greater understanding of such behavior by examining the way in which the different kinds of actions are associated with one another (correlational analysis). To achieve further simplification, it is useful to describe these behavioral characteristics in terms of a few underlying variables, in other words, to seek a simplified structure that describes the domain. The factor analysis to be reported in this section is intended to throw such light on the behavior that we are studying. The factors, in this view, are to be seen as dimensions arising from the data, in terms of which the behavior can be more parsimoniously described, and no motivational force need be ascribed to them.

The factor analysis is set out in detail in Appendix IV, and only a *summary* of the structure of child and parent behavior is presented here.

1. An eight-factor model best fitted child and mother behavior; a six-factor model fitted father behavior.

2. The outstanding dimensions that characterize child social behavior are factors denoting play with father and verbal and nonverbal attachment. Further factors point a contrast between speech and physical movement and between compliance and negative affect.

3. Both mother behavior and father behavior are characterized by the overriding importance of disciplinary approaches to the child: for both mother and father, there emerged factors of positive psychological control, of negative psychological control and of power assertion. Another dimension in both mothers' and fathers' domains is their affectionate behavior.

4. Intercorrelations between child and parent behavioral factors show that child speech, compliance, and attachment behavior are associated with positive qualities of mother and father. The child's physical activity and movement, and his dysphoric mood, on the other hand, are linked to parents' negative and coercive qualities.

5. Mother and father factors resemble each other, and such similar factors are significantly correlated, showing the existence of a common family approach.

INTERRELATIONS OF MOTHER AND FATHER CHARACTERISTICS

The domains of mother and father actions (based on behavior counts) have been delineated in the preceding sections. However, the overall ratings given to children, mothers, and some fathers can also provide insight into the dimensions and structure of children's and parents' interactive behavior. Ratings for child behaviors and their intercorrelations will be presented for each characteristic in the appropriate chapter. This section will consider the interrelations and structure discernible in mother and father characteristics, as seen in the ratings (for definitions see Table 6). To round off the picture, the discussion will also embrace the grouped behavior-count categories "positive action" and "negative action," variables from the responsiveness analysis described earlier, and the variable "repeated commands." The definitions of these variables were presented in Table 8.

The correlations shown in Table 10 present something of a conglomerate based on different subsamples, and hence, a factor analysis is not appropriate for them. The correlations of mother ratings, and the positive and negative action frequencies of both mother and father, are based on the subsample of 90, described above (singletons plus one of each twin pair); correlations involving father ratings are based on 29 fathers in Sample 90, who were given questionnaires; some ratings were omitted from the table because of a lack of correlations for them. "Responsiveness," "Appropriateness, "Total reactivity," and "Repeated commands %" were measures derived from behavior counts for the selected sample of 40, decribed above.

Carrying out individual significance tests for the hundreds of correlations arising from 31 variables is not a strictly valid procedure, because the correlations are not independent of one another. One should therefore regard the correlations shown in Table 10 as suggestive of a trend rather than as definitely significant (only those whose individual significance level is less than .05 are shown). One can, however, have greater confidence in rejecting the null hypothesis—or, in other words, in the "reality" of an association—if a correlation is replicated (at least, at the .05 level) in another sample. The correlations for mothers and fathers were therefore also computed for the 46 twin partners (Sample 46) excluded from Sample 90, although it must be recognized that this is not an independent sample. The 27 correlations (out of 48 "significant" ratings correlations) that were replicated in Sample 46 at the .05 level or beyond have been marked with a superscript b in Table 10. Most of the correlations among ratings have also been confirmed by similar correlations in the same direction among the pilot sample ($N = 30$).

The correlations that describe mothers' characteristics fall essentially into three coherent clusters, very similar to the main factors emerging from the factor analysis of action frequencies. The first cluster, in the top left-hand corner of the table, expresses mother's warmth and responsiveness, or "positive reinforcement." It groups together warmth, psychological rewards, play, support of dependency, positive actions, responsiveness, appropriateness, and total reactivity. The last three responsiveness measures form a subcluster indicative of a "quality of responsiveness" that runs counter to repeated commands, and these behavior count measures are mainly related to psychological rewards (praise, approval, etc.) rather than to the other ratings. The second cluster characterizes the cognitive aspects of discipline and socialization, corresponding to the factor "positive psychological control." It consists of reasoning, consistency of enforcement, and encouragement of independence. Note that reasoning overlaps these two clusters, forming a bridge between them. and that consistency of enforcement and encouragement of mature actions runs counter to the support of dependency. The last cluster, at the bottom of mothers' half of the table, is the antithesis of the first cluster and embodies the negative aspects of discipline, corresponding to the factor "negative psychological control." It consists of restrictions, verbal–psychological punishment, love withdrawal, physical punishment, negative actions, and repeated commands. It is the last three variables that make up the core of this cluster, which is typified more by its very consistent negative correlations with the first cluster than by positive interrelations among its own components. It has partly positive and partly negative associations wih Cluster 2.

Correlations among fathers' ratings are fewer and weaker than among mothers' ratings, no doubt because of the small numbers involved, and hence clusters are less clearly discernible. However, most of the correlations are of a similar nature, and the father variables also correlate in expected ways with the different clusters of mother characteristics.

While the structure apparent in these correlations, and particularly in the mother clusters, presents a picture of parent characteristics that is coherent and makes intuitive sense, it should not be forgotten that all the parent ratings were allotted by the same observer. It is therefore possible that part of the plausible coherence of these relationships is due to a halo effect arising from raters' stereotypical conceptions of a "good" or a "bad" mother. However, this reservation does not apply to positive and negative actions nor to the responsiveness variables, which are all derived measures based on detailed behavior counts. The observers who noted the behavior were not identical with the persons who rated mother and father characteristics, and it is also much less likely for a stereotype to influence a behavior count, since the observer had to decide only whether a given kind of behavior occurred or did not occur.

Summary

1. The correlations of ratings of mothers' characteristics fall into three clusters, paralleling some of the main factors arising from the factor analysis of behavior counts. They are (a) warmth or positive enforcement; (b) positive psychological control; and (c) negative psychological control.

2. Correlations among fathers' ratings are weaker and do not fall into easily identifiable clusters, probably because of the reduced number of cases.

Table 10. Pearson Product Moment Correlations of Mother and Father

Var. No.	Var. label	45	47	53	54	88	120	121	122	43	49
Mother variables											
45	Warmth rtg										
47	Psychol. rewards rtg	49[b]									
53	Play rtg	52[b]	40[b]								
54	Support of dependence rtg	47		33[b]							
88	Positive action %	27		21	27[b]						
120	Responsiveness %		46								
121	Appropriateness %		45				75				
122	Total reactivity %		53				60	77			
43	Reasoning rtg	42[b]	52[b]	33					40		
49	Consistency of enforcement rtg		25[b]		−36					29[b]	
55	Encourage mature action rtg				21					26[b]	37[b]
50	Restrictions rtg										32[b]
51	Verbal–psych. punish't rtg					−25					
52	Physical punish't rtg	−27[b]	−31[b]	−23[b]	−25	−24[b]				−36[b]	
84	Love withdrawal %						−36				
89	Negative action %		−31				−55	−34	−41		
123	Repeated commands %				−41	−48	−31	−36	−40		
Father variables											
65	Warmth rtg										
67	Psychol. rewards rtg		38		41			55	61		
73	Play rtg										
74	Support of dependency rtg										
90	Positive action %	23				44					
124	Responsiveness %								36		
125	Appropriateness %		36						36		43
126	Total reactivity %					32			48		
63	Use of reasoning rtg									45[b]	
69	Consistency of enforcement						56	57	53		
75	Encourage mature action rtg										
72	Physical punish't rtg										
91	Negative action %		−29				−54	−44	−37		
127	Repeated commands %		−34				−47	−41	−41		

[a] Only correlations with individual $p < .05$ shown. Decimal points omitted.
[b] This correlation also has $p < .05$ in subsample of 46 twins.

Characteristics (Ratings and Responsiveness Variables)[a]

55	50	51	52	84	89	123	65	67	73	74	90	124	125	126	63	69	75	72	91
24																			
	33																		
		27[b]																	
		31		28															
					41														
47[b]																			
		38																	
							50[b]												
							44												
						-41													
												77							
						-56						66	40						
								53[b]				55	52	59					
													52						
															42				
	42[b]				37					-39[b]						43[b]			
		25			65[b]									-39					
					41	45													

DISCUSSION

The summary descriptive statistics presented in this chapter provide only a skeleton framework outlining the rough dimensions overall that characterize the interaction between parents and children. The categories themselves (e.g., "Commands" or "Positive action"), too, are comparatively gross classifications, and many qualitative nuances are inevitably lost at this level of abstraction. Such qualitative aspects of the interaction are in principle recoverable by utilizing the adverbial indicators in the code or by studying the detailed records with their longhand comments. (A control sequence, quoted verbatim, is included in Chapter 6.) However, the data—rough as they are—provide normative information that has hitherto generally been lacking on the interactions between parents and 2-year-old boys in a natural setting.

The level of compliance of these 2-year-olds is relatively high: they comply with approximately two-thirds of their parents' requests and commands, a proportion similar to that found by Minton *et al.* (1971). So the "terrible twos" are by no means very rebellious.

The proportion of their behavior overall that these young boys devoted to seeking closeness with mother or father, (i.e., the incidence of what is generally called *attachment behavior*) is relatively modest: 4.75%. About twice as much is of the nonverbal as of the verbal kind, a reflection of the fact that most of these children are still acquiring fluency in speech.

Dyadic and triadic interactions may often be characterized as reciprocal or complementary. Reciprocity occurs when one partner responds to the action of another by the same kind of action to a roughly similar degree. It is exemplified by the saying "One kind act deserves another." Complementarity, on the other hand, occurs when the actions of the two partners are not the same but complement each other in a mutually fitting way (e.g., nurturant and dependent actions by parents and children, respectively).

The reciprocity inherent in the triadic system mother–father–child that I have described is in fact, striking. Greater amount of speech by college-educated mothers is echoed by greater amount of speech by their children. Greater compliance of the children of college-educated mothers has its counterpart in (slightly) greater compliance by their mothers and fathers. Indeed, the distribution of the compliance ratio is very similar for child, mother, and father, and a correlational analysis has shown that they vary together to a significant extent. This reciprocity between parent and child actions, however, breaks down when it comes to "positive" and "negative" actions: children engage in slightly more "negative" than "positive actions," but with both mother and father the reverse is very strikingly the case. This contrast may exist—partly, at least—because children (at 2½) are not in the habit of prohibiting any of their parents' behavior, and hence "negative" actions from this source will be virtually absent from the parents' count, whereas they make up a considerable proportion of the child's "negative" actions. But, in addition, parents do seem to try to exhibit positively toned rather than negatively toned behavior to their children (one might detect effects due to the presence of an observer here, of course), whereas 2½-year-old boys are much less given to controlling their momentary hostile or unpleasant feelings or asocial impulses. At any rate, "negative" actions are relatively prominent in the child's repertoire of actions. It should be noted that mothers' and fathers' total of "negative" actions would still remain well below that of the child and of their own total of "positive" actions, if one added prohibitions, hitting, and restricting to the narrower category of "negative actions," as from a broader point of view, one might well do. That parents engage in more positively toned actions than their children is confirmed by Patterson (1979), who noted that parents of both problem and nonproblem boys provided at least three times as much approval as did the children.

The complementarity of the relationships manifests itself in the high degree of responsiveness (and appropriateness of their reactions) that both mother and father show to the child's distress or bids for attention, help, etc. Another area where child and parent behavior is complementary rather than based on reciprocity is that of commands. The child issues, both absolutely and relatively, far fewer of these than do his parents—an unsurprising finding that confirms expected authority relationships. The incidence of parental commands and prohibitions far exceeds that of suggestions or of reasoning, but these proportions may well be characteristics of this age, and their relative standing may change at later ages.

Differences between mother education groups were evident in certain areas only—above all, in the greater amount of verbal interaction in the better-educated families and in the higher amount of motoric and physical behavior by children in the lower education groups. With greater verbal interaction also went greater reliance on cognitive and psychological influence methods by the better-educated parents, something that is now a well-replicated finding (see the beginning of this chapter). On the other hand, this study did not detect significantly greater sensitivity to children's needs by better-educated parents, although differences were in this direction. Since others have found significant discrepancies in this area, it may be that our differences simply did not register sufficiently strongly. Our data also showed that affectionate and emotionally positive behavior is not confined to a particular education level or class but occurs to virtually the same degree in all of them. Overall, differences between mother education groups were relatively few—and there were even fewer variables significantly related to social class, as determined by father's occupation. The absence of differences may partly be due to the fact that the focus of the study was on social interaction rather than on cognitive variables. But, in addition, the finding suggests that the gap in child-rearing practices—and in children's social characteristics—between different education and social groups may be narrowing in what is a fairly uniform urban society. (No non-European ethnic minorities were represented in the sample.)

The research provided some fascinating glimpses into the differing roles that mothers and fathers play in the socialization process. The detailed counts of unconstrained behavior in the home confirmed that mother is, overall, the main object of attachment for these 2½-year-old boys. This is true individually for 83 out of the 120 children whose fathers were present. This topic will be discussed in greater detail in Chapter 5.

Since romping with parents is by its nature a reciprocal activity father has to take an active part in it. Indeed, he, for his part, engages much more in such physical contact than mother does, both absolutely and relatively to his total actions; it represents about 3% of his actions, but only .9% of mother's actions. Mother, on the other hand, is involved in far more verbal interchanges of all kinds with the child and intervenes more in the child's doings, often in a negative way. As part of this she also employs a cognitive approach—reasoning—more as a method of inducting the young into society's ways than father does.

That father displays more affection and engages in more positive and fewer negative acts than mother may well be an artifact of the early evening hours when we observed, as probably is the amount of play. Nevertheless, it is clear that at this time, when he takes over from mother, he fulfils an important child-rearing role through play and positive interaction, although this emphasis is not meant to deny the inevitable role he plays in disciplinary encounters, too.

While we have seen that differences between mother and father behavior frequencies are often significant, these same mother and father measures invariably show significant positive correlations with each other, most of them being significant at the .001 level. This finding suggests that mother and father, over and above their differences, display considerable similarities, with both of them, say, showing relatively high use of reasoning or low use of physical punishment.

The data presented here do not allow us to trace the development of behavior over age. It would be of considerable interest to know what changes in the distribution and balance of behavior by both child and parents take place as a function of age. Some studies presenting behavior observation data for infants in the home have already been published (e.g., Clarke-Stewart, 1973), but there is a marked lack of them for later ages, no doubt because then they pose greater practical difficulties.

Let us now look at what the factor analysis has shown. The structure of behavior emerging from such an analysis is dependent on the aspects of living and acting that we set out to investigate and capture. Since our variables were all concerned with social behavior and socialization practices, the resulting factors are constrained within this domain and do not, for instance, include factors denoting parents' cognitive teaching approaches, except in so far as the cognitive variables of speech and reasoning entered into the parental factors of positive reinforcement and psychological control.

The factors do, indeed, delineate dimensions in socialization behavior that have been posited on theoretical grounds and have been found impirically in other investigations, which, however, were grounded in interviews and ratings rather than in direct observation. Our ratings and responsiveness measures also generated clusters of correlations for mothers and fathers paralleling the main factors that structure parents' socialization practices. The present dimensions, emerging from mothers' and fathers' actual complex behavior, do not, however, reduce to the simplicity of the three-factor solution that has been proposed for this domain by Schaefer (1965). Factors are ways of grouping individual actions, and we should note that the tendencies represented by the different dimensions can coexist within the same person.

A coherent and intelligible network of reciprocal influence runs through the correlations between child and parent behavioral factors (see summary). While the drawing of causal inferences from such correlations must be hazardous, it may seem reasonable to speculate that it is the *parents'* reasoning, suggestions, and approval that promote greater compliance in the child, whereas it is the *child's* physical activity and movement that call forth greater restraint and coerciveness by parents.

The factor intercorrelations demonstrate also that mother and father approaches to the child resemble and reinforce each other, so that a tendency in a certain direction exhibited by one spouse is echoed by a similar trend in the other. This finding is further evidence for the existence of a common family climate in which children are brought up, discussed earlier.

The factor structure of behavior, in sum, reflects the essential facets, including the asymmetry, of the authority–dependence relationship between parents and child.

CHAPTER 4

Being Two Makes a Difference

The Impact of Twinship on Parent–Child Interaction

One of the purposes of the project was to assess a possible genetic contribution to the child characteristics, and this was the chief reason for including twins in the sample. However, twins are also something of a "special" population. They share the same womb and the same maternal resources before birth, their birth is attended by special difficulties, and their physical state at birth is more precarious than that of singletons (these factors will be discussed below). Moreover, the presence of two children of the same age in the home is likely to alter quite dramatically the climate of the relations between children and parents—the environmental contingencies to which children are exposed. In terms of the immediate, harsh reality, it simply doubles the demands on mother's and father's time, effort, and patience.

Gosher-Gottstein (1979) of the Bar-Ilan University, Ramat Gan, Israel, recently investigated by prolonged home observations the infant-centered activities of twin and singleton mothers of infants, 1–19 months old. She found that twin mothers spent 35%–37% of their time on infant-related activities, versus 22%–29% for singleton mothers. Most of the time was devoted to the infants' physical needs the care of the newborn babies being the most time-consuming. But in all infant-related tasks, mothers of twins had less time to spend on each twin than singleton mothers had for their single child. Not only did mothers spend more time on home activities when they had twins, but fathers and siblings did so, too.

Hence, differences between twins and singletons merit examination in their own right. Comparisons between twins' and singletons' test performance have previously been reported. Day (1932), as well as Davis (1937), reported the language skills of twins to be considerably inferior to those of singletons, and Day (1932) also noted that twins' inferiority in language was much greater than in general intelligence-test performance. Mittler (1970b) found 4-year-old twins to be inferior in comparison with singletons on subtests of the Illinois Test of Psycholinguistic Abilities, as well as on the Peabody Picture Vocabulary Test. Several investigators (e.g., Koch, 1966; Mittler, 1970a; Zazzo, 1960) have reported twins' intelligence test scores to be below those of singletons. Record, McKeown, and Edwards (1970) elaborated on these results by identifying 148 twins whose partners had died before 1 month of age. The survivors, they found, had almost average verbal reasoning scores (98.8) at the age of 11, whereas the mean verbal reasoning score of 1,924 twins whose partners were alive was 95.6 (the population mean being 100). They concluded from this finding and from their negative findings regarding birth factors that lower intelligence scores in twins were due not to prenatal and perinatal handicapping conditions, but to postnatal experiences.

Kim, Dales, Connor, Walters, and Witherspoon's (1979) study appears to be unique in that the investigators directly observed and compared the social interactions of twins and singletons in nursery school. They found twins to be less affectionate, less aggressive, and at the same time, more solitary than singletons at age 3½, but none of these differences remained significant by age 5½.

None of these authors, however, examined directly the way in which twins differ from singletons in their day-to-day experiences in the home. Having both singletons and twins in our sample afforded a rare opportunity to study these effects by direct observation and to analyze the resulting differences in interaction between singleton and twin families. The differences in child speech that we found—not only between singletons and twins, but also between fraternal or dizygotic (DZ) and identical or monozygotic (MZ) twins—led us further to examine the prenatal and perinatal complications that accompany twin pregnancies and their relation to child speech.[1]

As noted in Chapter 2, almost the total male twin population born in Calgary in two successive years participated in this investigation. The most accurate method of determining zygosity (i.e., whether the twins are MZ or DZ) is by blood typing. This serological examination was carried out for between 16 and 22 different blood group systems at the hematology laboratory of the university hospital after all the psychological data had been collected. In five cases, when blood typing was impossible, zygosity was determined by finger ridge counts and a physical similarity profile.

Although blood typing has a very high degree of accuracy, in practice human error can intervene and—as with computers—it is wise to check

---

[1] Dr. Dorice Conway and Dr. Reginald Sauvé of the University of Calgary collaborated with me in this part of the investigation.

when there is a gross discrepancy between expectation, based on parents' and observers' well-based impressions, and the serological finding. In two cases, the hematology laboratory reversed their findings, when they did a second analysis on the twins. The likely causes of misclassification are technical; for example, some antisera react at low temperatures, and room temperatures can at times reverse any agglutination that may be present. Nevertheless, blood typing was considered the final arbiter for zygosity.

DIFFERENCES IN CHILD AND PARENT BEHAVIOR BETWEEN TWINS AND SINGLETONS

This chapter discusses twin–singleton differences in the incidence of child, mother, and father behavior, that is, the variables that describe children's social behavior and the socialization experiences that they encounter. How the dynamics of their interaction—that is, the effects that parents' practices exert on children's behavior and vice versa—differ between twins and singletons is examined in the discussions of specific social characteristics in the following chapters.

As was noted in Chapter 2, the twin and singleton groups do not differ significantly on the mother education variable, though the higher education groups are slightly more numerous among singleton families. Since mother's education is related to some of the variables under consideration, one must take care not to confound this source of variation with the effect of twinship as such. Table 11 shows variables for which twin–singleton differences are significant by independent t test. Definitions of the variable labels were shown in Tables 3 and 6. The probability levels for the t tests were based on an adjusted df of 88, or lesser number for father variables, as appropriate, as explained in Chapter 3. A separate multiple-regression analysis was carried out for each of these criterion variables, with mother's education and twinship, in this order, as the predictors. Superscript b indicates when twinship was no longer a significant predictor once the influence of mother's education had been removed; that is, in these cases, no significant twin–singleton difference remained over and above mother's education differences.

A separate analysis showed that in only one variable (mother's use-of-reasoning rating) would the elimination of the five single-parent twin families reduce the difference between twin and singleton means. We recalculated the twin–singleton difference for this variable, using two-parent twins only, but the difference still remained significant.

It should be noted that most measures are relative frequencies; that is, the individual action is expressed as a percentage of that agent's total actions. This approach was necessary in order to remove the effect of dif-

**Table 11. Twin–Singleton Differences with Associated Probabilities of .05 or Less
(t test, two-tailed)^a**

	Singletons higher than twins		
Child variables	p <	Mother variables	p <
Number of actions	.001	Command–prohibition—	
Vocabulary IQ (PPVT)	.05^b	% of actions	.001
Comply ratio	.05^b	Use of reasoning (ratg)	.01
Attachment rate	.05^{b,c}	Use of reasoning %	.001
Instrumental independence		Affection %	.001
Experimental measure	.02	Consistency of enforce-	
Instrumental independence		ment (ratg)	.01
(ratg)	.05^b	Suggestion %	.001
Internalized standards		Positive action %	.001
(ratg)	.001	Love withdrawal %	.05
Rate positive actions	.001^c	Rate mother–child speech	.001
Rate negative actions	.001^c	Helping %	.01
Percentage of time in toy play	.001^c	Threatening %	.01
Percentage of time in active		Refusing %	.02
behavior	.001^c		

		Father variables	p <
Total activity score	.001^c	Command–prohibition—	
Speech maturity (ratg)	.01	% of actions	.001
Rate child speech	.001^c	Use of reasoning %	.001
Speech—% of actions	.001	Affection %	.001
Seeking mother's permission—		Consistency of enforce-	
% of actions	.001	ment (ratg)	.01
Seeking father's permission—		Suggestion %	.001
%	.02	Positive action %	.01
		Rate father–child	
		speech	.001
		Refusing %	.01
		Use of material rewards	
		(ratg)	.05

	Twins higher than singletons		
Child variables	p <	Mother variables	p <
Attachment behavior—		Number of actions	.02
% of actions	.01		
Walking %	.01		
Expression of displeasure %	.001		
Approaching M %	.01		
Sitting on F's knee %	.05^b		

^{a} For reasons of space, only significant differences are shown. M = mother; F = father. "% of actions" and "%" denote percentage of the given agent's total actions. Analysis carried out on arcsin transformations. Probability levels are based on df: 88, or an appropriate lesser df for father variables.
^{b} When the contribution of the mother's education was allowed for as a prior predictor, twinship no longer added significantly to the prediction for this variable in a multiple-regression analysis, indicating no significant twin–singleton difference (p > .05).
^{c} The rate measures are affected by the generally higher rate of behavior of singletons; see also Table 12.

ferences in total actions. Such systematic overall differences are of interest in their own right; those between mothers and fathers were presented in Chapter 3, and those between twins and singletons will be discussed below. However, a comparison of, say, mother's commands between twins and singletons would be invalidated by the difference in the total number of actions, unless the commands were first equalized for total actions. The *t* tests and all subsequent analyses were carried out on arcsin transformations of these percentages (Winer, 1962).

The table shows a considerable number of significant differences between twin and singleton families, more than emerged when the mothers' education groups were contrasted. However, because carrying out independent *t* tests on 38 child, 31 mother, and 27 father variables is not a strictly valid procedure since it will produce some chance "significant" findings, multivariate analyses, reported below, were also performed. The results in Table 11 should, therefore, be regarded more as suggestive of a trend than as definite.[2]

We will first consider mother and father variables. The fact that none of the differences in *mother* and *father* behavior were rendered nonsignificant by first removing the influence of mother's education underlines the importance of the twin situation. It is these behavioral variables that carry its impact. The most important difference among these variables is that mothers and fathers of singletons simply spoke more to their children than twin parents did to theirs (rate of mother speech per minute: 2.00 for singletons, 1.24 for twins; rate of father speech: 1.38 for singletons, 0.89 for twins). This difference, moreover, is not an artifact of the coding system, since speech addressed to both twins simultaneously was counted for each of them, nor is the higher rate of parent-to-child speech for singletons a result of more behavior to singletons overall, since the number of mother's and father's total actions was greater for twins. (We cannot reconstitute the rate of speech addressed to both twins together by simply adding the rate of speech to the two twins together, since in doing so we would count twice any single utterance addressed to both.) As a corollary of greater amount of speech, mothers and fathers of singletons also engaged in more control behavior generally; that is, they used relatively more commands and prohibitions, more reasoning, and more sugggestions. In addition, mothers of singletons were rated as more consistent in enforcing the rules they had laid down. It is also of significance that while there was no difference at all in affectionate behavior between mothers' education groups, singleton parents

---

[2] In order to know which differences remain significant under a strict simultaneous confidence test, we can use the formula: overall $\alpha = 1 - (1 - \alpha_1)(1 - \alpha_2)\dots(1 - \alpha_n)$, which gives the overall probability of a chance finding's being accepted as significant when n tests are carried out (Bock & Haggard, 1968). If we set individual α levels at .002 for 38 variables, this will result in an overall probability of .07 (reasonable with this stringent criterion).

demonstrated more affection to their children than twin parents and displayed relatively more "positive actions."

Since the actions of the child, or of the parents, are intercorrelated, it is important to see whether they still distinguish between twins and singletons when account is taken of the intercorrelations of each agent's actions. For this purpose, multivariate regression analyses were carried out to analyze child, mother, and father criterion variables, with mothers' education and twinship, in this order, as the predictors. In order to conserve degrees of freedom, only seven child and mother variables and six father variables were included in this analysis. The details of the analysis are shown in Appendix V.

The mother and father variables included were rate of parent–child speech, use of reasoning frequency, command–prohibition frequency, affectionate behavior frequency, positive action frequency, and suggestion frequency. Consistency of enforcement rating was included only for mothers, as this rating was available for only a small number of fathers. In all these variables, twinship, as measured by twin–singleton family differences, accounted for a much larger percentage of variance than mother's education, with the latter in many cases explaining only a minute proportion of the variance.

All the twin–singleton differences in mother and father criteria remained significant in the multivariate analyses, and it is clear they cannot be entirely accounted for by differences in higher-placed variables, such as the rate of parent–child speech. Except for mother's consistency-of-enforcement rating and father's positive-action frequency, the criteria remained significant also when the seven variables were tested simultaneously (see above).

A separate analysis was conducted that broke down verbal interchanges into speech initiated by children or parents and speech reactive to these initiations (see Chapter 7 for details). Initiated speech—by each parent to each child separately—was expressed as rate per minute of each speaker's presence, and reactive speech was expressed as a proportion of the speech initiated by the other partner. Twin parents initiated less speech to each twin than did singleton parents to their child, and twins themselves initiated less speech to each parent than singletons did, but the difference was significant only for the children. However, parents initiated far more speech than the children in both twin and singleton families. Moreover, twin mothers and twin fathers reacted much less ($p < .001$ and $.05$, respectively) to the speech initiated by their children than did singleton parents. Their lesser verbal responsiveness is an outstanding factor, and it would seem that overall, it is the parents who are chiefly responsible for the lesser amount of verbal communication within each twin–parent dyad as compared with a singleton–parent dyad (though, of course, the amount of verbal interchange between the pair of twins combined and the parents is greater than that between a singleton and his parents).

As outlined in Chapter 3, mothers' and fathers' "responsiveness" and "appropriateness" were assessed in a subsample of 20 twins and 20 singletons. Again, twin parents were somewhat less responsive than singleton parents to the children's distress, bids for attention, etc., but not significantly so. However, twin mothers showed significantly less appropriateness in their reactions (Mann-Whitney U test, $p < .05$), and they were more unresponsive when unresponsiveness was inappropriate (difference was of borderline significance: $p = .0583$).

Now let us turn to the effect that the twin situation has on *child* behavior (Table 12). A crucial difference between twins and singletons here, too, is the fact that the amount of speech by twins was less, expressed both as a rate per minute and as a percentage of all their actions (singletons: 48.93%; twins: 38.61%). The initiated speech analysis demonstrated that twins initiated significantly less speech and also reacted significantly less to both mothers' and fathers' speech than singletons did. In addition, their speech was rated as less mature. Informal observation produced no evidence of "cryptophasia" or secret speech among twins. Reports in the past (Mittler, 1970a; Zazzo, 1960) of such secret speech were based on mothers' reports and may well have arisen from observation of immature speech, at

Table 12.   Significant Differences between Single-Parent Twins and Two-Parent Twins (Mann–Whitney U Test)

	Single-parent twins' mean higher or lower	p (two-tailed)
Child variables		
Attachment rating[a]	Higher	.001
Attachment rate[a,c]	Higher	.034
Internalized standards rating[a,c]	Higher	.049
Rate of negative actions[a,c]	Higher	.005
Rate of child speech[a,c]	Higher	.016
Mother variables		
Use-of-reasoning rating[a,c]	Lower	.002
Physical punishment rating[a]	Higher	.001
Rate of positive actions[a]	Higher	.017
Rate of negative actions[b]	Higher	.003
Rate of mother–child speech[a,c]	Higher	.005
Commands–Prohibition—% of actions[a,c]	Higher	.046
Love withdrawal—% of actions[a,c]	Higher	.003
Threats—% of actions[a,c]	Higher	.037

[a] Singletons > twins for this variable.
[b] Twins > singletons for this variable.
[c] Difference between twins and singletons for this variable also significant.
[d] No difference between twins and singletons for this variable.

times intelligible to no one but the twin partner. This, however, would be something different from a systematic "secret language."

The degree of internalization of standards of behavior that twins had achieved was also rated lower than that of singletons. All these differences persisted even after mother's education had been allowed for. On the other hand, the differences in vocabulary IQ (singletons' mean: 90.7; twins' mean: 84.4; see Chapter 3 for a discussion of the low average IQ obtained), in comply ratio, and in the rating for instrumental independence (at home) were not significant, once the effect of mother's education had been removed. In vocabulary IQ, but not in the speech measures, an interaction effect was noted: the vocabulary IQ of twins was *higher* than that of singletons when mothers had attended college. (Since the numbers were small and the difference was not significant, it is best regarded as an isolated chance finding.) The opposite effect held for non-college-attenders, where there was a large difference in favor of singletons, parallel to the generally found differential in IQ, and particularly in vocabulary IQ, between twins and singletons (e.g., Mittler, 1970b). We did not find that twinship had a more deleterious effect on any speech measure for children of college-attenders versus non-college-attenders, in contrast to Mittler (1970b), who found a more pronounced effect for middle-class than working-class children.

The total number of actions that singletons engaged in was much higher than that of twins; that is, they seemed to be more active. However, this finding may be an artifact of the observation situation, in that the observers, because they had to record two children's activities, picked up fewer actions by each twin than by singletons. The discrepancy in the number of actions overall affected the measures expressed as rate per time or as percentage of time, but the measures expressed as relative frequencies (percentage of actions) were not so affected, since they equalized for total number of actions. Thus, the "attachment rate" per minute was greater for singletons largely because they were recorded as engaging in more activity. On the other hand, on the measure "attachment behavior" (percentage of actions), standardized for total numbers of actions, twins were higher.

In the multivariate analysis of child variables (Appendix V), twin–singleton differences are shown to account for a very large proportion of the variance of total number of actions as well as rate of child speech. (The latter difference is still highly significant even after the greater number of actions of singletons has been allowed for. Other factors must therefore operate, too.) The difference in attachment-behavior frequency also remained significant in the multivariate analysis, but not so differences in vocabulary IQ, comply ratio, independence rating, and total activity score—the significance of the latter vanished once the effect of the number of actions was taken into account.

Summary

1.   The most important differences between twin and singleton parents for the sample as a whole, after allowing for differences in mother's education, are the following:

Mothers and fathers of singletons exhibit *higher* levels of verbal communication in general, of commands and prohibitions, of suggestions, of reasoning, and of affectionate behavior. Singleton mothers also engage in more positively toned actions.

2.   In a subsample, twin mothers showed less sensitivity in responding to their children's distress or demands than did singleton mothers.

3.   The most salient differences for the children (for the whole sample) are that singletons speak more and have internalized parents' standards and rules more. Twins, on the other hand, express both attachment and displeasure more frequently (relative to all their actions).

IDENTICAL AND FRATERNAL TWINS AND BIOLOGICAL FACTORS

Twin–singleton differences in the means of various intellectual characteristics had been expected, from knowledge of earlier literature. However, we also discovered that monozygotic (MZ) twins were significantly inferior to dizygotic (DZ) twins in vocabulary IQ, rate of child speech, and rate of speech by mother and father to child. These results (particularly the last one) were puzzling findings that called for further exploration.

Among the explanations we thought we could discard was the explanation by social class: there was no significant difference between MZ and DZ twins in father's occupation, nor in mother's education, as tested by chi square (cf. Table II), although higher education groups predominated slightly among DZ twins. Nor could we explain the MZ–DZ difference by the "twoness" of the twin situation, since the two types of twins were subject to the same constraints in this respect. The hypothesis was therefore formed that the speech differences among twins were due to the greater prenatal and perinatal difficulties to which MZ twins are reported to be subject (e.g., Allen, 1955; Benirschke & Kim, 1973; Record, McKeown, & Edwards, 1970). The lesser amount of speech by parents, on this hypothesis, would be a reaction to the twins' lower rate of speech. If the hypothesis were corroborated, it would obviously cast a completely different light on the twin–singleton differences in speech, too, because twins in general are subject to biological hazards in pregancy and birth that singletons are not exposed to. More than half of all twins weigh less than 2,500 g at birth, over a third are breech births, and one in six twin pregnancies ends in the death of one or both twins (Mittler, 1970b; Record, McKeown, & Edwards, 1970).

The "biological hypothesis"[3] was put to the test by examining the birth records of all our twins. The prenatal and perinatal factors commonly associated with a child's being "at risk" have been delineated (e.g., by Butler & Alberman, 1969). We examined the obstetric and pregnancy records of 43 sets of twins (15 MZ sets and 28 DZ sets)—records were not available for 3 sets of twins—and noted the following indicators: mother's age, parity and gravidy, toxemia or other pregnancy complication, length of gestation, presentation (breech or vertex), other birth complications (e.g., use of forceps), interbirth time, birth weight, Apgar score, and age at discharge. (The Apgar score rates an infant's condition one minute and five minutes after birth, based on heart rate, color, respiratory effort, etc.—Apgar, 1953.) The average birth weight was 2,490 g, the average length of gestation was 37.5 weeks, and nearly 40% were breech births. Although we did not examine the birth records of our singleton sample, all these indices point toward greater risk for these twins compared with singleton norms.

On analysis, it was found, however, that of all these biological factors, only the Apgar score correlated at the .05 level ($r = .20$) with twin type, the DZ twins having a slightly higher Apgar score (i.e., showing the better condition at birth). In other words, the MZ twins in our sample did not overall suffer from greater prenatal and perinatal complications that could help explain the differences in speech. Simple correlations between the criteria of vocabulary IQ, speech maturity rating, child speech rate, and the biological indicators again demonstrated the inability of the biological factors to account for speech performance: the only significant correlations were between vocabulary IQ and birth weight ($r = .24$, $p < .01$, but see below for interaction with education) and vocabulary IQ and toxemia during pregnancy ($r = .17$, $p < .05$). Since the latter finding may seem surprising, it should be noted that Mittler (1970b) also found a positive correlation for toxemia, and Broman, Nichols, and Kennedy (1975) showed the same relationship between edema (in blacks), hypertensive blood pressure (in whites), and IQ in the Collaborative Perinatal Project, based on 26,000 children.

Although the MZ and DZ twin groups did not differ significantly in their composition by mother's education, in view of the negative results noted above, it was decided to see if twin type added materially to the prediction of language, if it was entered as a predictor in a multiple regression *after* mother's education. The result was that mother's education accounted for a significant proportion of variance in vocabulary IQ, speech maturity

[3] Prenatal and perinatal factors are, of course, also part of the child's environment. They are biological only in the sense that they affect the fetus or newborn via organic, biological pathways.

rating, and child speech rate, but once this effect had been allowed for, twin type did not add significantly to the prediction. In other words, *the speech differences between MZ and DZ twins could be accounted for by mother's education alone.* Furthermore, when mother's education was held constant, birth weight no longer made a significant contribution to the prediction of vocabulary IQ. Our finding, therefore, is essentially in line with Mittler's (1970b) results, which indicated that there was no significant association between birth weight and language scores, though Broman *et al.* (1975) found an association between birth weight and IQ even within socioeconomic groups.

Mother's education, however, was found to be related to a number of the biological indicators. Since the mother with a higher education tended to be older (difference significant), we used mother's age (first) and mother's education (second) as predictors in another multiple-regression analysis with the biological indicators as the criteria. The following relationships persisted at a significant level, after allowing for the effect of mother's age: higher education was associated with longer gestation ($p <$ .01), with a shorter interval between the births of the first and second twin ($p <$ .01), and with lesser occurrence of respiratory distress ($p <$ .05). Six perinatal indicators (Apgar score $<$ 7, birth weight $<$ 2,500 g, bilirubin level $>$ 15 mg, interbirth time $>$ 30 min, length of gestation $<$ 37 weeks, and presence of respiratory distress syndrome) were also combined to form a Neonatal Stress Scale (cf. Denhoff, Hainsworth, & Hainsworth, 1972), and this was found to be negatively correlated with mother's education ($p <$ .05). These relationships are easily understood as the beneficial effects of a better social environment. It is less clear why higher education should also be associated with more breech births ($p <$ .05).

SINGLE-PARENT TWIN FAMILIES VERSUS TWO-PARENT TWIN FAMILIES

There were five families of twins in which mother was the only parent. Two mothers were separated, one was divorced, and two mothers were probably never married. One mother was working as a teacher and one at a food outlet, one was receiving full-time secretarial training, and two were not working—one had previously worked as a secretary and the other as a waitress. Two of the mothers had not completed high school, two were high school graduates, and one had attended college.

Table 12 displays the significant differences in child and mother variables between the single- and the two-parent families. Only for two mother variables are the single-parent twin families further removed from singleton families than are ordinary twin families; that is, they are more extreme than

two-parent twin families: single mothers employ reasoning even less than
married twin mothers, who, in turn, use it less than singleton mothers (the
singleton–twin difference here was also significant, as discussed above); the
rate at which single mothers of twins engage in negative actions (disapproval, criticism, etc.) toward their twins is higher than the rate for married
twin mothers, and the latters' rate is, in turn, higher than that of singleton
mothers. It is remarkable, however, that in the case of 10 variables, single-
parent twin families are more akin to singleton families (means closer) than
are other twin families.

What is striking here is that rates per minute are generally higher for
the single-parent families, largely because the simple total of both child and
mother actions is considerably higher for single-parent families (means:
1,040.4 for child and 1,131.2 for mother) than for all twin families (means
of 908.5 and 671.5, respectively). While the number of child actions lies
between that of twins and that of singletons, the number of actions by these
single mothers is, on average, nearly twice that of twin mothers overall and
more than twice that of singleton mothers. However, it should be noted that
there is great variation among the single-parent families, and three mothers,
in particular, were responsible for this abundance of actions. It seems then
that single mothers often do their best to make up for the absence of a
father, at least by quantity of interaction with their children.

The nature of the difference in interaction is revealing. In their
attempts to introduce their children to social norms, the single mothers
seem to come up against some difficulties: they issue more commands and
prohibitions than married mothers, but fewer of them are accompanied by
explanations (i.e., they tend to be more peremptory in tone). They also use
physical punishment, threats, and withdrawal of love more than married
mothers; in addition, they refuse the children's requests more (nearly significant) but are less consistent in enforcing their rules (nearly significant).
These signs of harsher disciplinary measures indicate that single mothers
are less secure and relaxed and more under stress and therefore feel driven
to resort to more negative sanctions by the weight of responsibility for discipline that rests on them alone. One mother put this into words in the
interview: "As a single parent I feel I can't allow them to get away with
things—if I don't no one else will." Another mother who was observed to be
rather irritable expressed concern that she might be hitting her children too
much. In a study designed to investigate the consequences of divorce,
Hetherington, Cox, and Cox (1978) show very similar effects in the area of
discipline. On the other hand, our single mothers, in contrast to Hetherington et al.'s divorced mothers, also speak more to their children than do
married twin mothers, and speech, as we have noted, is an important instrument of stimulation. The great variability among the single mothers noted
above also meant that some of them played a great deal with their children,

while one, for instance, was noted as simply watching them without playing with them at all. It seems that these single mothers tried to compensate for the absence of a father by greater stimulation, on the one hand, and, on the other, by sterner, more negative discipline that was also somewhat inconsistent.

The effects on the children of having a single parent only—or of having these particular single mothers, most of whom tried so hard—do not seem to have been entirely negative. These children speak more than other twins, which can be considered a sign of cognitive competence. Their mean vocabulary IQ is almost identical with that of other twins. While they internalize their mothers' standards more readily, they also overtly comply somewhat less with their mothers' immediate orders (difference nearly significant), and their rate of negative actions is higher (i.e., they make a greater display of overt disobedience, but at the same time show a tendency to follow mother's long-term rules or standards without having to be reminded of them). That the single-parent twins show greater attachment to their mothers than two-parent twins do (chiefly by verbal means) probably reflects greater insecurity in these children (cf. the discussion of attachment in Chapter 5), and it echoes a similar finding of increased dependency in children of divorced parents by Hetherington et al. (1978). On the other hand, all the rate measures will have been increased by these children's greater activity all round.

In concluding I should add that, unfortunately, we do not know what relationships with their fathers or substitute fathers the boys had. It would, of course, be unwise to base very confident generalizations on five families, but the findings agree very closely with those found in the specific study of the effects of divorce quoted above. The variability of the results demonstrates above all that the effects of a single-parent situation need not be all bad and that some mothers compensate quite effectively for the absence of a father, even under the extra stress that twins impose.

Summary

1. Single mothers of twins try to compensate for the absence of a father by sterner, more negative discipline, on the one hand, and by greater stimulation, on the other.

2. Children of these mothers exhibit more negatively toned actions and more attachment behavior, but they also show greater verbal competence than other twins.

3. Since these findings arise from only five families, no generalization should be based on them. They show that some single mothers *can* compensate effectively for the absence of a father, not that this typically happens.

OTHER ASPECTS OF TWINSHIP

Several other issues unique to being twins were investigated in the course of this study. It has been said that twin partners frequently establish a complementary relationship with each other, with one twin being the leader and the other the follower, the so-called dominance–submission relationship (Koch, 1966). We investigated this question by asking mothers whether one twin was more dominant than the other. Of the 46 mothers, 35 indeed identified one twin as being more dominant, but often they qualified this by saying, "A is now, but B used to be," or "B asks A, A is like a big boss in the house, but B is dominant in a fight," or "Most of the time B follows A, but this does switch once in a while." Other mothers, however, did not qualify their statements. It is apparent that in many cases there is no clear-cut, well-established status relationship between the twins but that it depends on the situational context.

We then looked at differences in a variety of child and parent behaviors between the "dominant" (i.e., the twin whom mother had declared to be mainly dominant) and the nondominant twin. Examples of these variables were birth weight, vocabulary IQ, speech rate, degree of compliance or attachment, mother's warmth and use of reasoning or psychological rewards. None of these differences were, in fact, significant at the .05 level: birth weight, for instance, was almost exactly the same for the two groups. The only difference that was significant at the .10 level was child rate of speech. While this one difference could easily have been due to chance, it is significant that several mothers mentioned that the "dominant" twin talked more. These comments strengthen the finding from the behavior count, and together they suggest that the amount of speech is related to competence in dealing with the environment and hence to being perceived as a leader; this relationship again reflects the importance of speech. The reason for the general absence of distinguishing characteristics between the two groups may well be that at the age of $2\frac{1}{2}$, status relationships between the twins are still in a very fluid state, though some of these may become crystallized at a later age.

There is evidence that the greater genetic resemblance of MZ twins leads to greater similarity between them in interests, activities, and also time spent together (Loehlin & Nichols, 1976), but this evidence relates to twins aged 6 or older. It seems possible that MZ twins aged $2\frac{1}{2}$ might also spend more time in common activities, such as playing together, playing with father, and watching TV, than DZ twins do. We investigated this hypothesis by noting, from the behavior record, how much time twins spent in such common activities. This time measure was then expressed as a proportion of the time the twins spent in active behavior altogether, and the average of MZ twins' social interaction, thus computed, was compared with that of DZ twins by Mann–Whitney U test. The difference was found to be nonsignificant. Hence, it seems that greater genetic resemblance did not, at this age, result in more time spent in common activities or in closer social contact; in other words, MZ twins did not create a more common environment for themselves. Both MZ and DZ twins may, however, evoke similar actions in each other when they are together (see Chapter 9).

In the experimental playroom sessions (each twin was seen separately), a child had the choice of a number of toys to play with. To test for possibly greater commonality of interests in MZ twins we tabulated the difference in toy choices between twin partners separately for MZ and DZ twins. Again, there was no evidence of greater similarity of interests for MZ twins, since the average difference in toy choices was slightly greater for them than for DZ twins.

Whether parents made greater differences between DZ twins than between MZ twins because they were influenced by a stereotype that fraternals should be treated differently will be discussed in Chapter 9.

One effect of twinship that our observers noted, although we did not quantify it, was the impact that the twins' existence had on a singleton sibling who was one to three years older than they. While a toddler usually feels displaced in his parents' attention and affection by the arrival of a baby, this effect was exacerbated when twins arrived on the scene, as we noted in several families. Not only did the twins, because of their more urgent needs, demand and get far more of the parents' attention than the older child, but by the time they were 2½, they also tended to form a pair together who played and acted together, excluding the older child in the process. In these cases, the older child, perceiving himself isolated or downgraded by the twins, would develop intense feelings of rivalry. He would become the classical "difficult child," interfering with the interlopers and their play, or throwing temper tantrums. While we showed earlier that twins were the recipients of less speech and fewer demonstrations of affection by parents than singletons—and, no doubt, received less than the older sibling himself received when he was the only child—when three young children compete for parents' attention and time, it is the older singleton who has the hardest time of it.

DISCUSSION: THE EFFECTS OF TWINSHIP—BIOLOGICAL, ENVIRONMENTAL, OR BOTH?

The influence of the twin situation has been shown to be very pervasive in this male sample. It is particularly noticeable in *parent* behavior (see Table 11), where it is not swamped by social-class effects. It was explained above why, with our data, we could not simply add parents' speech to both twins together. If one could do this, it would no doubt be found that mothers and fathers speak more to both twins than parents speak to a singleton. However, what affects the child is how much speech each twin receives, and a twin experiences fewer verbal interchanges of all kinds with his parents than a singleton. Mothers, and particularly fathers, also play more with singletons, but the difference does not reach significance. Differences between twins and singletons for father's compliance with the children's requests, mother's and father's use of psychological rewards, and their use of verbal–psychological punishment do not reach significance, but they are in the expected direction, singletons having higher means, and they indicate a general trend of more "psychologicalness" by singleton parents.

The impact of the twin situation on *children's* behavior is more diluted by social-class effects and by intercorrelations among the types of behavior themselves. It expresses itself above all in decreased quantity and lowered quality of speech, and in greater need for attachment to parents. Differences in compliance and independence, however, seem to disappear once mother's education and children's language skills have been taken into account. While there are significant differences for *rates* of positive and negative actions, no such differences appear when these actions are expressed as percentages of the child's total actions (i.e., when they are freed of the influence of the higher rate of activity of singletons).

Do the effects on the twins—particularly those on speech—arise directly from biological factors or from being a pair together, or, on the other hand, are they mediated by parents' behavior? Our analysis of MZ–DZ differences provides some evidence on this question as far as language performance is concerned. The MZ–DZ comparison tested the hypothesis that biological factors in the MZ twins' pre- and perinatal environment are responsible for their inferior language skills. The results clearly demolished this hypothesis and, instead, unexpectedly reconfirmed the importance of social class or education influences.

As noted previously, biological factors for our twins and singletons could not be compared directly, but the birth data for our twins presented above suggest that the difference between them and singletons must be considerably bigger than between the MZ and DZ groups. Conway, Lytton, and Pysh (1980) showed also that among language measures, amount of speech by children and mothers distinguished most clearly between 24 twins and 24 singletons. An examination of the birth data of these children demonstrated that both the biological factors of the perinatal environment and parental practices in the postnatal environment significantly affected children's language performance, but postnatal environment was much more important. It shoud also be noted that in the present investigation, the social-class influences did not swamp the twin-singleton differences, as they did the MZ–DZ differences. Taking all the evidence together, it seems justifiable to conclude that the perinatal environment, potentially affecting children's neurological constitution, is a less important influence on the development of speech and language skills than is the postnatal environment provided by the parents. Broman *et al.* (1975), with their sample of 26,000 children, also very convincingly demonstrate that social-class variables have a much greater effect on IQ at age 4 than do prenatal or perinatal complications.

How does the postnatal environment operate in practice? It is clear that parents are under much greater time pressure when they have twins and, what is perhaps more important, that they are also under greater stress. For one thing, there are often inevitable conflicts between the twins—one twin biting the other as a method of attack or defense was reported by a number of parents at this age, and they naturally found this difficult to deal with—and then there are the competing demands of the twins themselves and of other siblings. Moreover, transcending the conflicts, the twins also acquire relative cohesion as a pair who often act and play together, in parallel or in complementary or reciprocal fashion. Such intimacy may often mean that language becomes less important as a means of communication, and speech evolves into inarticulate grunts or monosyllables, unintelligible to others (often misinterpreted as twins' "secret language"). In general, their self-sufficiency will lead twins to seek less contact with others and hence to relative social isolation from adults.[4] However, our data show that their cohesion as a unit did not, at their age, results in a flow of chatter among themselves. In fact, the mean number of utterances by one twin to the other over about four or five hours of observation was only 22.

All members of twin families initiated fewer conversations with each other than did members of singleton families, and while differences between twin and singleton parents were nonsignificant, it was the parents who predominantly initiated verbal interchanges in all kinds of families. Moreover, twin parents responded significantly less to the conversations that each twin initiated—no doubt because of other pressing demands on them. Whether it is greater pressure or stress, or whether parents simply react to the cohesion of the pair and are content to leave twins to entertain each other, it does seem to be the parents who are chiefly responsible for the lesser verbal communication in twin families. While reduced interaction and intervention may indeed have some positive effects, it also means an impoverishment of the children's environment and less stimulation to their speech. Moreover, twin mothers' responses and unresponsiveness seem less sensitively modu-

---

[4] Zazzo (1960) has called this the "couple effect" and has suggested that twins' behavior can best be understood in terms of the psychology of the couple.

lated to serve their children's needs—or, very probably, they cannot afford to show the same appropriate sensitivity to their children's demands that singleton mothers show.

The data do not provide evidence about the direction of causality for the greater need for attachment shown by twins. There was no difference between twin and singleton parents' rated support of dependence or encouragement of independent behavior. The fact that twins show greater attachment to their parents may be traced to the lesser display of affection by the latter, since the twins may feel the need to reassure themselves of their parents' love. However, it may also be a consequence of twins' greater general immaturity compared with singletons.

We must conclude that twinship, as an enduring ecological factor, has a considerable impact—probably a greater one than social class—on children's socialization experiences and development. We should put this fact into the perspective of the effects of spacing of siblings in general. In an analysis of the effects of different family configurations (birth order, number of siblings) on the national Merit Scholarship Examination scores of almost 800,000 17-year-olds in the United States, Breland (1974) demonstrated that the close spacing of siblings means more adverse effects on the intellectual development of the younger one than spacing further apart. Twinship is the extreme instance of close spacing and shows the same result—only more so. In Breland's analysis, twins (N = 6,382) held the 72nd rank among 82 different family configurations for males. Zazzo (1960), too, found that whereas singletons in general had an advantage of seven IQ points over twins (on a nonverbal test), when siblings close to each other in age were compared with twins the advantage dropped to 2.25 points.

It should be noted that twins' deficit applies more to the verbal sphere than to general intelligence (Day, 1932; Koch, 1966; Mittler, 1970b). Breland (1974) also found that word usage, the most purely verbal part of the Nation Merit Scholarship test, showed birth-order differences most clearly, and hence he concluded that the primary source of the score differences (for twins, too) was verbal in nature.

Do twins catch up? Wilson (1975) concluded from a longitudinal study of 142 sets of twins—using the Wechsler Preschool and Primary Scale of Intelligence (an individual test with verbal and nonverbal parts) at ages 4, 5, and 6—that twins' initial deficit largely disappears by age 6. However, a doubt must remain, since twins have scored lower (mainly on verbal tests) than comparison singletons at age 11 (Record et al., 1970), on induction to the army (Husen, 1959) and at age 17 (Breland, 1974). In the latter case, they were compared with other entrants to the National Merit Scholarship tests, a group that itself represents a selected top part of the populations, so that it is clear that twins can rise to considerable achievement. Men like the

Picard brothers, the underwater explorers, or the author Thornton Wilder also bear witness to this fact.

Breland (1974) concluded from his general findings as regards twins, larger families, and closely spaced sibships that "children isolated from other children during early developmental stages may have an advantage as far as verbal achievement is concerned" p. 1015). Conversely, children thrown too much into the company of other children—and this applies particularly to twins—suffer a disadvantage. Zajonc and Marcus (1975) deduced from their "confluence model" of intellectual development that detrimental effects would accompany the close spacing of siblings. They explained the effect by essentially the same reasoning as the above; that is, the intellectual climate of the family will be diluted as a function of (1) the number of children and (2) the time gap between them, as the intellectual contribution of young children is bound to be small relative to that of parents or older siblings. Our data add credibility to the same hypothesis, and so do Zazzo's (1960) results and Record et al.'s (1970) findings concerning twins whose partners had died. Our evidence suggests further that it is parents' socialization practices and way of communicating with their children that are—at least, partly—responsible for these effects on twins.

FAMILY PORTRAITS

The following comments on outstanding characteristics of families were written by observers after their visits and give a sense of the "feel" of the differing family climates.

Singleton family (mother's education: some college): Frank has a 1-year-old sister. This is a highly verbal family. Much time is spent talking with Frank, and consequently, his speech is well developed. He talks in sentences and at some length. Mother and father both reason with this child, and he is often offered choices and required to make decisions.

Frank's mother is very conscious of current child-rearing practices and deliberately puts much of what she reads into practice. She reports having spent a great deal of time with Frank, as an infant, providing him with sensory training (e.g., colors, shapes, open crib). This sensory training seems to be continuing, except at a reduced rate; for example, much time is spent singing, reading, and doing puzzles.

Frank appears very sensitive to his parents' reactions. On two occasions, although his parents' disapproval was not overt, he stopped misbehaving, first, to ask "what they should do with him" and, second, to go to his room. Also, he asks permission before acting on occasion.

Twin family R (mother's education: nurses' training): The R's are a middle-aged couple with three children: a daughter 5 years old and the twin boys. Mr. R is out of town for a month at a time and then home for 10 days. Mrs. R is a nurse at a home for the aged, and the twins are left with a baby-sitter. Mrs. R and all three children had colds this week, but nothing serious. All four are irritable—children whine continuously—twins' speech almost unintelligible—two-word sentences or whined requests. Mother most inconsistent—makes threats, promises, and doesn't follow through—bribes. Observed to feed boys. Older sister a real problem—is cruel to twins—hitting, fighting etc. Mother seems almost to bait the children into this whiny behavior. Said she is unable to discipline children and that if she didn't go to work she would lose her temper with them. Says father is a strict disciplinarian. Exhausting!

Father present for second observation and sister out to play part of the time. This does make a difference in children's behavior. Father spends a lot of time playing and talking with them. Plays "let's be boys," excluding mother and sister. Encourages play fighting—sets one twin against the other or both against sister. Overrides mother's commands. Compares children unfavorably to each other. Much more conversation this observation, less whining—father follows through on most commands—enforces manners. Children fed selves this time except for last few spoonfuls. Mother sinks into the background when Daddy's home. Pete seems more sure of father's affection than Dan.

Twin family S (mother's education: left school after grade eleven): The S family live in a comfortable, well-kept home. The family consists of the parents; Len, 9 years; Laura, 6 years; Susan, nearly 4 years; and the twins, Chris and Charles. In addition, there are two paternal uncles who until recently lived with the family and are still frequent visitors.

Mr. S works long hours as a working manager but seemed quite friendly and helpful with the twins in the short time they were together. He is outshone by Mrs. S, who plays with the twins almost constantly and has an incredible amount of energy and patience. Chris and Charles are allowed to "help" their mother in many household activities, and she happily accepts a lot of interruptions from them.

Len and Laura have little to do with the twins, and Len is not able to tell them apart. Susan is almost their contemporary and did spend some time playing with the twins and occasionally coming into conflict with them.

Charles seems the more active, noisy twin, and he went to father more often than Chris, who was inclined to seek help and comfort from mother.

CHAPTER 5

Attachment

We now come to a detailed consideration of the first of the behavior systems—or child characteristics—studied in this investigation. *Attachment* has to do with the bond that a child forms with those who nurture him and thus is at the heart of socialization.

Attachment behavior has of recent years been the subject of considerable attention and study under the banner of a new perspective, first propagated by Bowlby (e.g., 1969) and inspired by and derived from animal ethology. This new perspective has meant viewing attachment in its evolutionary context and seeing it as a biological function that confers survival advantage in an "environment of evolutionary adaptedness" (Bowlby, 1969). Its biological function, according to Bowlby, is the protection of the young against predators, a protection that increased the survival chances of cave-dwelling hunters, as it must increase those of present-day bushmen. Viewing attachment behavior thus from the perspective of its biological function implies the assumption that it has some innate, genetic basis, an assumption that is usually left unspoken. Ethologists and comparative psychologists have studied attachment behavior among birds, mammals, and subhuman primates, as well as humans. It may be thought that attachment is instrumental in forming bonds within small groups and that it became intensified with man as groups of humans started to live in caves or other confined dwellings. In addition to its original biological function, the infant's attachment to one or more adults who rear him also represents a behavior system that enables the child to become integrated into his social environment and its ways.

Attachment has been defined in terms of its function and consequences, for example, by Maccoby and Masters (1970), as "behavior that maintains contact of varying degrees of closeness between a child and one or more other individuals and elicits reciprocal attentive and nurturant behavior from these individuals" (p. 75). Ainsworth (1973) has additionally stressed that affect is involved, for example, "An attachment is an affectional tie that one person forms to another specific person. . . . One may be attached to more than one person, but one cannot be attached to many people" (p. 1).

The investigation of *dependency* historically preceded that of *attachment*, and the two terms overlap to some degree, both in definition (Maccoby and Masters' definition above is intended to apply to both terms) and in the indices by which they are measured. However, the usual distinction made is that *attachment* is applied to a bond to one or a few specific people, whereas *dependence* is applied to a behavior system directed at a class of persons (Gewirtz, 1972). *Dependence* traditionally carried with it a negative connotation of immaturity, and the absence of this connotation was considered by Bowlby one of the advantages of the term *attachment*. Indeed, the importance of the attachment system for Bowlby lies in the fact that secure attachment to a mother figure carries with it a positive implication for future healthy personality development, whereas the same would not be true of "dependence on mother." What Bowlby and Ainsworth emphasize as crucial is attachment as the enduring feeling or bond with a person (see above definition). This can be distinguished conceptually from its manifestation, *attachment behavior;* for example, institution-reared children tend to show a great deal of clinging and following behavior but are less likely to form lasting selective bonds (Rutter, 1979). In fact, attachment behavior, at least in its strong form, cannot escape some negative implications of insecurity, since, as Ainsworth (1972) notes, the strongest attachment behavior occurs when the infant is intensely alarmed and apprehensive. Indeed, if its biological function is to elicit protection, this will ensure that it is emitted relatively more by immature organisms in a situation of insecurity.

The term *attachment*, with its positive connotation has often been used for this kind of interactive behavior in research with infants less than 2 years of age, whereas the same behavior in older children has been labeled *dependence*, denoting negative properties. Such a distinction can, however, not be a rigid one, since the frequency and adaptiveness of the behavior wane only slowly.

Excellent reviews of the literature on attachment and dependency are available in Ainsworth (1973), Gewirtz (1972), and Maccoby and Masters (1970). Rutter (1979), in a review of later findings, considers attachment from the perspective of the role it plays in maternal deprivation. Only a selective review of the literature will be presented here.

Attachment (and dependency, measured by the same behavioral indices) has been studied by means of ratings and reported intensity (e.g, Emmerich, 1966; Schaffer & Emerson, 1964; Sears, Maccoby, & Levin, 1957), as well as by observation of attachment behavior in the home (e.g.,

Ainsworth, Bell, & Stayton, 1972; Schaffer & Emerson, 1964), in nursery school (e.g., Emmerich, 1964; Heathers, 1955), and in experimental situations (e.g., Sears, Rau, & Alpert, 1965). The experimental situation that has been most thoroughly exploited in recent years is Ainsworth's mother–stranger–child situation (e.g., Ainsworth & Wittig, 1969; Maccoby & Feldman, 1972). The incidence and intensity of attachment behavior has been related to mother's responsiveness (in the home) and to the situational context in which it occurred (in both the home and the laboratory; e.g., mother leaving or returning, presence of stranger). Attachment behavior toward father has recently also received attention (e.g., Cohen & Campos, 1974; Lamb, 1976). Further, researchers have attempted to identify the structure of attachment behavior via correlations among its various indicators (e.g., Emmerich, 1966; Heathers, 1955). Masters and Wellman (1974) put forward a well-reasoned argument contending that the most fruitful approach to deciding whether a class of behaviors called *attachment* can be identified is to take as criterion whether a large proportion of children shift from one type (class) of common behavior to another as the situation changes (e.g., starting to cry on mother's leaving the room). They consider correlational analyses less appropriate for this purpose, as they tend to generate contradictory relationships of dubious validity. Sroufe and Waters (1977) have criticized the assumptions that underlie much of attachment research; they are critical, on the one hand, of research that views attachment as an individual difference dimension, or trait, measured monotonically by its strength or frequency and, on the other, of studying such behavior simply as part of a contingency system between child and caregivers. They advocate instead placing greater emphasis on the organization of this behavior in varying contexts, which can generate a qualitative typology of children such as Ainsworth has espoused. (The typology is arrived at by typing children as secure, avoidant, or ambivalent in their attachment, based on complex behavioral criteria; cf. Ainsworth, Blehar, Waters, & Wall, 1978.) In this way, Sroufe and Waters claim, attachment behavior can be seen as stable across its various transformations, and it can be maintained as a useful developmental construct, in spite of its critics.

Attachment behavior and its role in socialization is presented here from two perspectives: it is viewed, first, as a process that takes its place in a living stream of behavior and, second, as an individual difference dimension, or child characteristic. To index attachment behavior, I have used six individual actions, and the analysis of behavior sequences will show how their individual frequencies change under different conditions. For the individual difference analysis, individual actions have been summed to form two indices (see below for details of definition and justification).

The sequence analysis is predicated on the assumption that attachment behavior is a behavioral system that can be aroused by certain stimuli—in particular, immediately preceding parent actions—and suppressed by others. It is also assumed that this behavior can influence subsequent parent actions. The analysis therefore sought to identify the kinds of mother and father behavior that, in the immediate present, significantly facilitate or inhibit—or, in other words, control—child attachment behavior. A further analysis also determined which categories of mother and father actions (viewed as consequents) are facilitated or inhibited by the child's attachment behavior. This last analysis illustrates how the usual parent–child direction of effects can, in fact, be reversed. Since parent practices, not only may act on child behavior (or vice versa) in the immediate present but may, by accumulation, have an effect over a time span, too, I also made an attempt to look for such consequences in the medium term and to examine their causal direction. This analysis is discussed in a later section.

Obviously, for a complete theory of attachment, data about other relationships are needed, too. For instance, the child's own prior actions and state may be influential, and if one included information about them in the analysis, one would be able to assess the effects of previous state on present state (possible perseveration), in addition to effects arising from the actions of an interactant. (However, a recent study by Maccoby, Martin, Baran, and Jacklin [1979] showed that while such perseveration effects have some influence, they do not materially alter the nature of the parent–child, or the child–parent, contingencies.) Further, the situational context, or the quality of the parents' interaction with the child, is an important factor. Some research on these questions has been carried out, chiefly by experimental means (e.g., Ainsworth & Wittig, 1969; Maccoby & Feldman, 1972; Sears, Rau, & Alpert, 1965).

This study enters into these questions only to some extent (e.g., in the "responsiveness" analysis). However, a microanalysis of the discrete actions that define *attachment behavior* (see below) and of the contingencies surrounding them is of value, as a first approximation: it defines the major part of the situational context; it provides insight into specific conditions that elicit attachment behavior and the consequences that it engenders; it describes normative patterns; and it thereby throws light on the nature and functions of this behavior system. A qualitative typology, such as the one evolved by Ainsworth and advocated by Sroufe and Waters (1977), has considerable value, but it supplements an analysis of behavioral frequencies and cannot supplant it. Indeed, a sound typology must be based on a careful assessment of such frequencies.

ATTACHMENT BEHAVIOR AND PARENT ACTIONS: SEQUENCE ANALYSIS

Attachment behavior here is conceived of as actions designed to maintain more-or-less close contact with one or more individuals. In keeping with this definition and in line with many previous researchers' practice (cf. Maccoby & Masters, 1970), the kinds of behavior selected were those indicating proximity seeking, attention seeking, and approval seeking. Since mother, by arrangement, did not leave the house during the observation, the only indicators of the child's attachment that were used in this investigation were positive ones. Initially, four actions were identified: approaching, touching, and seeking the attention and seeking the help of mother and father. In the factor analysis of child behavior counts (see Chapter 3), two separate clusters, corresponding to proximity seeking and attention seeking, emerged as two factors, particularly when the behavior was addressed to father. One factor added sitting on father's lap to approaching and touching. Another factor bracketed seeking permission with seeking attention and help. Based on these empirical results, the two clusters of three actions each were therefore ultimately selected as attachment indicators. Some doubt must attach to the use of approach behavior as an attachment measure (cf. Tracy, Lamb, & Ainsworth, 1976). Similarly, help seeking is somewhat questionable, since it can be argued that only in situations where help is not realistically needed is it a proper indication of attachment. However, a high incidence of help seeking suggests many occurrences of this type, and it can be interpreted as an attention-getting device. The bracketing together of these actions on two factors and their general nature justify treating them as two kinds of indicators of attachment, the first set (approaching, touching, sitting on lap) representing proximal or nonverbal, and the second (seeking attention, help, and permission) distal or verbal attachment behavior. We have further evidence on this matter from the correlations within each set of behaviors and from the differential controlling effects that each set exerts. We will return to the question of attachment behavior as a "response class," or as two response classes, when we have reviewed this evidence.

All parent actions addressed to the child were recorded as single actions, (e.g., approaching, talking, leaving the child), and these labels are self-explanatory. A second analysis was carried out on the same actions, classified into the superordinate "grouped behavior categories" listed in Table 3.

Analysis

Specially written computer programs examined the sequential contingencies that obtain between child and parent behavior, and in this chapter, we are concerned with the analyses of attachment behavior, carried out separately for mother and father. The program searched the record and stored and tabulated each parent action or utterance as an antecedent (A_i); it allowed one to specify any action as successor (R_j)—in this case, the child attachment indicators—and these were searched for within two 10-sec intervals and tabulated.

A further analysis reversed the direction of search; that is, it placed the child's attachment behavior in the position of antecedent and then searched for parents' grouped categories of behavior as successors. No analysis was undertaken to trace in one single process the sequence from parent antecedent to child attachment behavior to parent subsequent response (second-order dependencies), as this would have produced a very large number of cells (294 when seven grouped categories are used for parent behavior and six categories for child behavior), many of them with zero frequency. Details of the calculations (including detailed tables for attachment behavior) involved in the sequence analysis are provided in Appendix VI.

Sequence analyses were carried out, and statistics computed, for each child separately. Table 13 and Figure 11, however, present the analyses of frequencies summed over all 136 children. Such summed counts analyses were carried out for all child characteristics because the larger numbers of the summed frequencies yield a more stable and interpretable data base. (When frequencies are low, the formula for the significance of differences provides only an approximate estimate.) As can be seen in Table 14 and 15, the number of individual children for whom significant relationships between antecedent and successor were found was in fact relatively small. This fact illustrates the strength of the summed analysis and represents one of the reasons for pooling occurrences across children. While the trends that emerge from the summed analysis do not necessarily apply to any particular child, they do represent the functional relationships between the given antecedents and the successors overall, based on sums that are weighted according to the different individual data bases, with individuals, as it were, submerged. It should be noted that data were not collapsed across agents.

Effects of Parents' Single Actions on Attachment Behavior

The mean rate per minute of the four chief attachment indicators initially selected (approaching, touching, seeking attention, and seeking help) addressed to mother (for mother's time present) was .11, and for father (for father's time present), the mean rate was .08. The difference between them is significant by two-tailed t test: t (119) = 5.12, $p < .001$. All six attachment indicators combined, addressed to mother, made up an average of 3.16% of all child actions; those addressed to father made up 1.59% of child actions. Nonverbal attachment behavior was twice as frequent as verbal behavior (see Figure 6).

Table 13 and all subsequent tables show only those antecedent actions that were significant facilitators–inhibitors for at least one attachment indicator, and they omit nonsignificant effects. The antecedents in Table 13 are arranged in order of generality of effect: from the most broadly facilitating to the most broadly inhibitory. The comments on the results are based on the "facilitating power" (*FP*), that is, the relative strength of the facilitation exerted by a given antecedent (see Appendix VI for the formula).[1] The effects of attachment behavior on parents' single actions were not analyzed because of the mass of data and the complexity involved.

The total of mother–child dyads in this analysis was 204,974, that of father–child dyads 172,627. Most of these dyads, in fact, represent the occurrence of a child successor action that is not attachment behavior and that is not preceded by a mother or father antecedent within the specified time limit. This procedure—necessary to arrive at a total count of dyads involving the child—inflated father–child dyads particularly; in reality, father actions were far fewer than mother actions, as can be seen in Appendix VI, Table VIIIA.

Talking to the child (counted as a "neutral action" among the superordinate grouped categories) strongly activiates attachment behavior, and so do a number of positively toned actions (e.g., approval). This would suggest a direct effect of a positive stimulus controlling a positive response. However, ignoring child (a "negative action") was the strongest facilitator of attachment behavior for mother; for example, it multiplied the occurrence of attention seeking 15-fold. Mother's ignoring, it should be noted, has more widespread effects than father's. Leaving the child similarly exerts a strong activating effect on approach, in particular. That an adult who ignores a child, busying himself instead with paperwork, spurs a child on to greater attention-seeking efforts than does an adult fully attentive to the child was found in an experimental setting by Gewirtz (1954). Our results also parallel in a natural setting certain experimental findings on social deprivation that suggest that social deprivation enhances the effectiveness of later social reinforcement (e.g., Gewirtz & Baer, 1958).

'Sitting on lap' is facilitated in general by friendly parent actions, and in particular, mother's or father's holding the child in their arms is seen as a regular prelude to his sitting on their lap. The fact that threat also effectively boosts the occurrence of a child's sitting on mother's lap suggests that attachment behavior can serve a propitiating, appeasing function, when the child has fallen out of parents' favor. This relationship, as well as the findings noted above suggest that deprivation of social contact and social threat increase attachment motivation.

Some of the relationships between stimuli and consequents demonstrate that the analysis was sensitive to the temporal ordering of actions: thus, if the child action "approaching mother" is "inhibited" by mother's physical contact, affection, and care, this simply indicates that approach has

---

[1] For a table showing base rates, conditional probabilities, and significance level of differences, see Appendix VI, Table VIIIA.

Table 13. Patterns of Facilitation and Inhibition of Child Attachment Behavior (Parents' Single Actions)[a]

	Child attachment behavior (consequents)					
	Approaching	Touching	Sitting on lap	Seeking attention	Seeking help	Seeking permission
	Mother (N = 136)					
Mother antecedents	*FP*	*FP*	*FP*	*FP*	*FP*	*FP*
Ignoring child	1.38[b]	7.90[b]		15.31	10.02	3.80[b]
Talking to child		1.33	1.20	1.09	.51[b]	2.43
Suggesting	1.38		1.07[b]	.92	3.84	1.35
Command	2.79		.87		1.44	1.16
Approval				2.57	3.55	2.71
Reasoning	.59					3.56
Prohibition						2.24
Leaving child	7.78					
Threatening			3.31[b]			
Expressing pleasure			2.33[b]			
Giving object to child					3.33[b]	
Physical affection	−.44[b]		5.35			
Holding child	−.65		20.20			
Dressing child	−.55[b]		3.79[b]			
Feeding child	−1.0 [b]					
Helping	−.49[b]					
Providing food	−.71		−.70[b]			
Showing, reading to child	−.58		−.78			

Father ($N = 120$)

Father antecedents	FP	FP	FP	FP	FP	FP
Talking to child	.75	3.25	2.79	1.82	3.48	3.40
Command	6.50		2.00		6.63	4.09
Suggesting	2.80		1.66^b	3.43	9.24	
Expressing pleasure	2.01^b		3.22^b	6.02^b		
Prohibition	1.80		2.57			
Physical affection		6.34^b	10.95			
Reasoning	1.75^b					10.17^b
Holding child			24.85			
Ignoring child				35.22		
Leaving child	22.81					
Showing, reading to child	−.73					

[a] Nonsignificant effects are omitted. FP = facilitating power. Minus sign for FP indicates antecedent acts as inhibitor.
[b] The difference between conditional probability and base rate for these variables is not significant when all consequents combined are taken into account, with $\alpha = .10$ (i.e., individual $p > .017$).

normally already preceded such care. On the other hand, holding the child "facilitates" sitting on lap, since the former often is a prelude to the latter.

Seeking attention, help, and permission are the verbal attachment indicators. All three share a distinctive pattern of facilitation by mother, demonstrating a certain cohesion among them. The use of reasoning by both mother and father strongly boosts the occurrence of seeking permission, which suggests that the latter is not only an index of attachment but also a sign of rudimentary socialization, and the relationship indicates the way the child is being taught social means of attaining his ends.

Table 14 shows the number of children for whom individually significant facilitating effects exist. The pattern is fairly similar to that of the pooled data, but the number of significant facilitating or inhibiting effects is relatively small. "Ignoring child" is conspicuous by its absence, probably because of the low incidence of ignoring for individual families. This again illustrates the strength of the summary analysis.

Table 14. Number of Children for Whom Certain Parent Single Actions Are Significant Facilitators (Inhibitors) of Attachment Behavior[a]

Parent antecedents		Child attachment behavior (consequents)									
		Approaching		Sitting on lap		Seeking attention		Seeking help		Seeking permission	
		M	F	M	F	M	F	M	F	M	F
Leaving child	Fac	2									
	In										
Talking to child	Fac	1	1			2	2			2	
	In	1									
Dressing child	Fac										
	In	1									
Giving object to child	Fac										1
	In										
Holding child	Fac			3	2						
	In										
Refusing	Fac										1
	In					1					
Suggesting	Fac	2	1					1	1		
	In										
Command	Fac	14	6								
	In										
Prohibition	Fac	1									
	In										

[a] M = mother ($N = 136$); F = father ($N = 120$); Fac = facilitator; In = inhibitor.

Bidirectional Effects of Parents' Grouped Actions on Attachment Behavior and Vice Versa

Figure 11 displays the bidirectional effects of the superordinate categories of parents' behavior (see Table 3 for definitions) on the child's attachment behavior and vice versa, presented for the pooled data of 136 children. Each kind of mother and father behavior is viewed as an antecedent (arrow pointing toward the attachment behavior) and as a consequent (arrow in reverse direction). Arrows for nonsignificant effects have been omitted.[2]

When parent actions act as antecedents (arrows pointing inwards), all their significant effects are facilitative; that is, they tend to increase, not to decrease, the likelihood of some attachment behavior's occurring. It is worth noting that parents' negative actions in general boost *verbal* attachment behavior (lower part of Figure 13) more strongly than do positive actions, and in particular for attention seeking and permission seeking, negative actions are the strongest elicitors of all. This agains suggests a conciliatory, appeasing function for these forms of attachment behavior, too. Help seeking, on the other hand, does not appear to fit this function so clearly, since it is elicited most of all by mother's and father's use of a suggestion. (The finding that "reasoning control" does not significantly facilitate permission seeking, whereas "reasoning," as noted earlier, does, can be explained by the fact that "reasoning control" consists of commands, etc., accompanied by justification, whereas "reasoning" counts all instances of explanations.)

In contrast, no *nonverbal* forms of attachment behavior (upper part of figure) are facilitated by negative actions, and the only one that is increased significantly by positive actions is sitting on lap—though, as was noted earlier, this can also serve an appeasing function.

Individual relationships for parents' grouped actions are shown in Table 15. With parent actions as antecedents (top part of table), a paucity of significant relationships is apparent. The relationships that do exist parallel very closely those for the pooled data.

What effects does the child generate by his attachment behavior? The salient fact here is that this behavior appears to exert greater controlling power over parents' actions than parents' actions exert over attachment behavior. In the pooled data (Figure 11), there are more significant effects from child to parents (arrows pointing outward) than the other way around. We can also notice, for instance, that the child's verbal attachment behavior has larger effects on mother's positive and negative actions than these

[2] For a table showing base rates, conditional probabilities, and significance level of differences see Appendix VI, Table IXA.

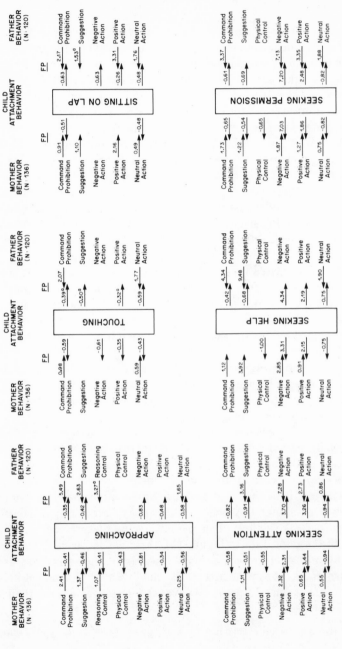

Figure 11. Patterns of facilitation and inhibition of child attachment behavior (grouped parent actions). (Nonsignificant effects are omitted.) FP = facilitating power. Minus sign for FP indicates antecedent acts as inhibitor. Arrows point from antecedent to consequent. [a]The difference between conditional probability and base rate for these variables is not significant when all consequents are taken into account, with $\alpha = (p > .017)$.

mother actions have on the child (the effects are facilitative in both directions).

The most significant effects are in the direction of reducing the incidence of parents' subsequent behavior below base rate, except that verbal attachment indicators, showing a common pattern different from that of nonverbal ones, increase both positive and negative actions; that is, they impel parents to adopt actions that are polarized as either positively or negatively toned.

The greater control exercised by child behavior is also evident from the figures for individual children (Table 15), in that the significant effects of attachment indicators on parent actions are more numerous than effects from parents to child. This echoes the findings from the pooled data. It should be noted that whenever there is a preponderance of facilitative effects for individual children, the *FP* for the pooled data in Figure 11 is positive, and conversely, a preponderance of individual inhibitory effects is accompanied by a negative *FP* in Figure 11. The individual analyses therefore bear out the overall picture arising from the pooled data.

Nonverbal attachment behavior mainly *inhibits* parents' positive actions, as distinct from *verbal* attachment behavior, which chiefly *facilitates* positive actions. This contrast illustrates the difference in function of the two classes of attachment behavior. From the manner in which nonverbal attachment behavior interacts with different parental behavior categories, we may infer that its function is to maintain and prolong existing close relationships and, specifically, to secure proximity with parents. Once the child is in physical contact with his mother, or sits on her lap, he has achieved this purpose, and any further positive action on her part becomes superflous. On the other hand, we can infer that verbal attachment behavior seeks to reinstate good relationships when the child has fallen out of favor; hence, its purpose is accomplished if it elicits positive actions as signs of restored favor.

The results of the pooled data and those for individual children as regards the relative facilitation of negative and positive actions by verbal attachment behavior show a seeming inconsistency. Verbal attachment behavior increased positive actions for a greater number of individual parents, but the pooled data generally show a larger percentage of increase (stronger facilitation) for negative actions. The two sets of results are, however, not incompatible and can perhaps best be understood through an analogy from economics. Suppose certain price changes were introduced for radio and TV sets. This might have the effect of increasing the sale of TV sets more than the sale of radio sets (in terms of numbers sold), while at the same time, the percentage of increase in the overall value of radio sets sold could exceed the percentage of increase in the overall value of TV sets sold.

Table 15.   Number of Children for Whom Significant Relationships Exist between Attachment Behavior and Parent Grouped Actions[a]

| | | Child attachment behavior (consequents) | | | |
| | | Nonverbal attachment behavior | | Verbal attachment behavior | |
Parent antecedents		Mother	Father	Mother	Father
Command–prohibition	Fac	15 (7,8)	6 (4,2)		
	In				
Suggestion	Fac	2 (2,0)	1 (0,1)	1 (0,1)	1 (0,1)
	In				
Negative action	Fac			3 (2,1)	
	In				
Positive action	Fac	1 (1,0)	2 (0,2)	1 (0,1)	
	In				
Neutral action	Fac	1 (0,1)	9 (6,3)	5 (1,4)	
	In	1 (0,1)		1 (1,0)	
Command–prohibition	Fac		2 (1,1)	1 (1,0)	
	In	15 (5,10)	7 (2,5)	4 (1,3)	
Suggestion	Fac				
	In	1 (1,0)		1 (0,1)	
Negative action	Fac			39 (21,18)	8 (7,1)
	In	2 (1,1)			
Positive action	Fac	2 (1,1)	1 (1,0)	82 (42,40)	28 (13,15)
	In	22 (12,10)	10 (3,7)		1 (1,0)
Neutral action	Fac				
	In	111 (85,26)	59 (39,20)	56 (41,15)	17 (13,4)

[a] Fac = facilitator; In = inhibitor. Figures in brackets are numbers of twins (first) and of singletons (second). N of twins = 92 (76 for father); N of singletons = 44.

Both sets of findings are "real." But in considering the higher *FP* for negative actions, we should remember that *FP* expresses the relative increase of the successor in multiples of its base rate, and therefore, the higher *FP* for negative actions can be explained in part as a function of the latter's lower base rate, which can be raised to a multiple of its original size more easily than the higher base rate of positive actions. (Not all differences in *FP* can be explained in this way, nor does the explanation negate the reality of the facilitating effects.)

In view of these considerations, the individual effects *in this case* carry with them the more important psychological implications. We will therefore look to them for an answer to the question whether the child's verbal attachment behavior—viewed partly as an attempt to reestablish harmonious relationships—"pays off." Verbal attachment behavior produces many significant negative, as well as positive, reactions from individual parents. However, judging by the far larger number of significant effects on parents' positive actions, for the individual child the odds are that verbal attachment behavior will pay off more often than not, though by no means invariably so.

In the reciprocal interaction chain existing between parents and child, if the child's attachment behavior could, in fact, terminate a preceding parental negative action, this would, indeed, reinforce the attachment behavior. Whether this happens was investigated for the three children for whom individually mother's negative actions were a significant antecedent (cf. Table 15) by noting the significance and strength of the facilitation–inhibition of subsequent parental actions for each child separately. No actual behavior chains were followed through, as is explained in the "Analysis" section. The following sequences emerged. Child 1: Mother's negative action increased attention seeking ($FP = 6.53$), which in turn increased negative action ($FP = 5.98$) (it also increased positive action, $FP = 1.90$, and decreased neutral action, $FP = -.94$). Child 2: Mother's negative action increased help seeking ($FP = 18.17$), which in turn increased negative action ($FP = 7.96$) (and decreased neutral action, $FP = -1.00$). Child 3: Mother's negative action increased permission seeking ($FP = 10.18$), which in turn increased negative action ($FP = 5.78$) (and decreased neutral action, $FP = -.57$, and command–prohibition, $FP = -.59$).

It is clear that for these children, an aversive cycle was operating and that their verbal attachment behavior, triggered by parents' negative action, served to increase subsequent negative action further still. However, it may be that the persistence of mother's negative actions represents a perseverative echoing, across the child's attachment behavior, of her prior state of mind, a hypothesis that this analysis could not test. For these three children, negative action was particularly important, since only for them was it a significant facilitator of attachment behavior. The situation will be different for others: as noted above, the odds are that verbal attachment behavior will pay off.

"Attachment Behavior" as a Class of Response

Let us now return to the question whether the "attachment" indicators can legitimately be considered a "class of response." One way of determining this is to examine whether the several indicators tend to be facilitated–inhibited by the same parent antecedents and whether they, in turn, elicit similar parent behavior. Judged by the parent grouped actions that control them (Figure 11), the six attachment verbs show only weak evidence of forming one coherent class, though at least no significant stimuli have a sign opposite the prevailing direction. If we consider the effects exerted by the attachment indicators on parents' grouped actions, the evidence against the one-class model, and in favor of two distinct subgroups, becomes quite marked. Seeking attention, help, and permission—the verbal, or distal, attachment indicators—show the strongest signs of being a cohesive unit, particularly those actions addressed to father. The other three—nonverbal, or proximity-seeking, attachment indicators—are somewhat less closely bound together.

Similarity indices were calculated by computing the number of significant facilitators–inhibitors that all pairs of attachment indicators have in common and expressing this as a percentage of all possible shared facilitators, taking into account the number of significant facilitators available. These similarity indices were worked out separately for verbal and nonverbal attachment indices and for combinations that crossed these two groups, with parents' grouped actions as antecedents and as consequents. The values of the indices ranged from 100% to 58.8%, and the trend in general was the same for mother and father and for whether attachment was considered a consequent or an antecedent of parent behavior. The similarity indices averaged over the four analyses were 92.55% for the verbal indicators, 93.38% for the nonverbal ones, and 70.23% for the cross-group combinations, demonstrating again the cohesion of the two classes of response.

Taking the pattern of facilitation by single parent actions as a criterion (Table 13), the same story emerges as for the grouped action analyses: verbal attachment behavior is more recognizable as a class than nonverbal, and only father talking to child facilitates all six indices.

The relative frequencies of the six attachment indicators were also intercorrelated, separately for mother and father. Five out of six intercorrelations within the two classes of attachment behavior for mother, and all six for father, were significant beyond the .05 level. Only 1 out of 18 cross-group correlations, however, was significant. It is this network of correlations, of course, that forms the foundation for the separate relevant factors that emerged in the factor analysis.

All the findings, therefore, converge to suggest that the attachment indicators naturally fall into two cohesive classes of response: the nonverbal and the verbal. Some evidence also points to a weaker association between the two primary classes forming a loose overall "attachment" group.

Differences in Facilitation (Inhibition) Effects between Twins and Singletons

The same sequence analyses that were carried out on the summed counts of all children were also performed on the summed counts of twins and singletons, separately.

Similarities between twins and singletons in these analyses far outweigh the differences. However, some significant facilitating (inhibiting) effects were unique to one or other of these subgroups (cf. Appendix VII). Thus, singletons were particularly apt at inhibiting their parents' restrictive control or negative actions by several attachment behaviors. The analysis of individual children (Table 15) demonstrates that significant effects occurred relatively more frequently between singletons and their parents in both directions; in other words, both partners in the dyad were more prone to influence the behavior of the other to a marked degree than was the case in twin families. The execption to this generalization is the area of negative actions, which twins aroused as much in their parents as singletons did. Looking at the effect of parents' negative actions we notice, too (Appendix VII), that some of them (threatening and restricting) stimulated twins more to seek father's proximity—very likely to propitiate him. It seems that parents' negatively toned actions are a particularly sensitive area for twins. Attention seeking, in particular, seemed to elicit parents' negative actions strongly, and, in turn, mothers, by their prohibitions, inhibited attention seeking very effectively. This kind of attachment behavior was, no doubt, especially irksome to them in view of the greater pressures on parents' time and attention in twin families.

Summary

1. The evidence indicates that attachment behavior falls into two cohesive classes of response, verbal and nonverbal, with nonverbal being more typical of the younger child.

2. The sequence analysis probes the immediate impact of parental actions on the child's attachment behavior, as well as reverse effects. It shows that parents' leaving or ignoring the child prompts the child to seek more contact with them by approaching them or seeking their attention. This constitutes a kind of homeostatic feedback mechanism.

3.   Parents' negative actions in general significantly stimulate verbal but not nonverbal attachment behavior.

4.   Attachment behavior exerts greater control over subsequent parent actions than parent actions do over attachment behavior.

5.   The most notable effect of attachment behavior is to reduce the incidence of parents' subsequent actions in general, as shown by the pooled data and by the results for individual children.

6.   The exception is the increase in both positive and negative parental actions, brought about by verbal attachment behavior, with positive actions being increased more frequently. Nonverbal attachment behavior, however, reduces positive actions, as it does other actions.

7.   The function of nonverbal attachment behavior appears to be to maintain existing close relationships with the parents; verbal attachment behavior seems to serve the purpose of reestablishing harmonious relationships that have been disturbed. On the whole, it is successful in achieving this goal.

ATTACHMENT TO MOTHER AND ATTACHMENT TO FATHER

As was noted earlier in the chapter, the four attachment indicators initially selected (approaching, touching, seeking attention, and seeking help) were used to calculate an attachment rate to mother, per minute of her presence, and an attachment rate to father, per minute of his presence. In this section, we will explore in greater detail the ramifications of differential attachment to mother and father and the role these two attachment figures play in the child's early experiences.

The attachment rate to mother (.11) was significantly higher than that to father (.08), allowing for his lesser time with the child. However, the correlation between these two measures was .406 ($p < .001$), showing that beyond this difference, a general attachment tendency pervaded the child's behavior, expressing itself to both mother and father, high attachment to one going with high attachment to the other, and similarly for low attachment. It should be made clear that this "attachment tendency" is defined operationally by the number of instances of attachment behavior that the child displayed toward mother and toward father.

Since the overall trend was toward greater attachment to mother, it is of interest to see how many individual children bucked the trend and what were the variables that characterized them and their parents. I therefore divided the 120 children whose fathers were present for at least some of the observations into two groups: one whose attachment rate to mother was greater than that to father, called the *mother-attached group*, and the other, whose attachment rate to father was the greater, called the *father-attached group*. There were 83 children in the first group and 37 children in the second. Among the first group, there were 49 twins and 34 singletons, and among the second group, 27 twins and 10 singletons. The ratio of twins to singletons in the mother-attached group therefore is 1.44, whereas in the father-attached group, it is 2.7. This suggests that there is a much greater likelihood for twins to take father as their preferred attachment object than for singletons to do so. In fact, less than a quarter of the singletons did so. The reason that more twins tend to display greater attachment behavior to father (though only a minority even of twins did so) lies probably in the greater competition for mother's time, attention, and comfort that exists in twin families. In many cases, when mother is, for one reason or another, unavailable, a twin naturally directs his bids for attention or comfort to the other parent. In fact, some competition effects were observed; for example, 13 of the 27 twins in the father-attached group had twin partners who where mother-attached. In these families, each twin gravitated toward his own favorite parent. In one case where one twin was in the father-attached group, his mother-attached partner never emitted any attachment behavior to father at all!

What distinguishes the father-attached group from the mother-attached group? To find out, I correlated membership in the father-attached group versus mother-attached group with all major child and parent variables. Since membership in the father-attached group was coded 1 and membership in the mother-attached group 0, a positive correlation (between a variable and membership in one or the other group) means that the father-attached children are higher on this variable than the mother-attached children, and a negative correlation means that the father-attached children are lower. The correlations significant at the .05 level or better are shown in Table 16, but since multiple correlations were involved, the correlations

Table 16. Correlations for Membership of Father-Attached Group (Coded: 1) versus Mother-Attached Group (Coded: 0) with Parent and Child Variables[a]

Child variables	r	Mother variables	r
Vocabulary IQ	−.24[b]	Encourage mature action rating	−.27[b]
Compliance rating	−.24[b]	Positive action rate	−.30[c]
Attachment rating	.22[b]	Rate mother–child speech	−.30[c]
Instrumental independence rating	−.28[c]	Physical punishment frequency	.26[b]
Speech maturity rating	−.39[d]		
Rate of speech	−.26[b]		
Rate child–mother speech	−.35[c]		
Expression of displeasure	.23		

[a] Sig. beyond .05 level. Reduced sample $N = 82$.
[b] $p < .05$.
[c] $p < .01$.
[d] $p < .001$.

shown to be "significant" by independent tests should be interpreted only as trends rather than a definite associations. It will be seen that only child and mother variables, but no father variable, produced significant correlations; that is, no father variable discriminated between the groups.

It can be seen that children attached more to father than to mother tend to show the more "mature" characteristics—vocabulary IQ, etc.—to a lesser degree, and they are rated as showing more attachment behavior in general. However, these need not be the direct characteristics of father-attached children as such, since the generally low correlations could easily by explained by the slight preponderance of twins in this group. (Twins differed from singletons in the same direction, even where this difference was not significant; cf. Chapter 4.) The same can be said for the mother variables that show a significant association with membership in the' attachment groups, except for physical punishment frequency, which is *lower* for twin mothers (but higher for the father-attached group).

To see how well a combination of mother and father variables would discriminate between the mother-attached and the father-attached groups, a discriminant function analysis was performed, with all mother and father counts and mother ratings as the discriminating variables. Nineteen of the variables together provided a significant separation of the two groups ($p <$ .05) with the following *mother* variables, in the order listed, proving to be the best discriminators (the criterion being change in Rao's V): mother–child speech; physical punishment relative frequency; encourage mature action rating; reasoning relative frequency; and positive actions relative frequency. For all these variables, the mother-attached group was higher, except for mother's physical punishment, which was more frequent in the father-attached group. It is interesting to note that a high degree of physical punishment by mother is one of the incentives for the child to form a greater attachment to father.

The fact that more attachment behavior is directed to mother than to father is all the more significant since, as we noted in Chapter 3, observations were carried out during what was father's "playtime" and we found considerably more rough-and-tumble play with father than with mother. For these 2-year-old boys, father was the appropriate person for romping,[3] and mother, the appropriate person for comfort and attention, overall. Our finding that mother is the main object of attachment for about 70% of the children and father for 30% agrees very closely with Schaffer and Emerson's (1964) figures: they found that by 18 months, nearly one-third of the children directed the most intense attachment to an individual other than

---

[3] "Affiliative" behavior (e.g., vocalizing, showing, offering), which, like romping, involves less emotional intensity than attachment behavior, has repeatedly been observed to be addressed more frequently to father than to mother (Belsky, 1979; Lamb, 1976, 1977).

the mother. Other investigators have also found greater attachment behavior to mother than to father during the first year (Ban & Lewis, 1974; Lamb, 1976), as well as during the second year of life (Cohen & Campos, 1974; Kotelchuck, cited in Lewis & Weinraub, 1976). All these investigations, except Schaffer and Emerson's (1964), however, were conducted in laboratory situations. Lewis, Weinraub, and Ban (1973), however, found equality in attachment behavior directed toward mother and father for 1 to 2-year-olds in the laboratory, and Lamb's (1977) findings on 7- to 13-month-old children, observed in the home, are similar. It may be, as Lamb (1977) suggests, that it is children who are under stress who tend to seek out mother more, but our data provide no evidence on this, as these situations were not singled out in the analysis.

The majority of studies do show mother to be the child's main attachment object, but this, of course, does not mean that she is the only one. Almost all fathers were the target of the child's attachment behavior to some extent. Moreover, other types of interaction also have a significant influence on children's development, and the different kinds of experiences that children derive from their interactions with father (e.g., play) are important.

Schaffer and Emerson (1964) found that for young infants, a person's amount of interaction with the child, or availability, by itself was not associated with the child's attaching himself to that person. What was important was willingness to interact intensely with the child, even though for a shorter period. However, mother, as the primary caregiver, has more opportunity to be responsive to the child and to become a salient object in his world, and hence, on theoretical grounds, one would expect her to become the prime object of attachment, too. It is worth noting that what distinguished the father-attached group in our sample was not father's outstanding qualities but mother's less positive interactions and more punitive approach to the child. It is not so much father's aggreeable qualities but what the child sees as mother's disagreeable one that induce him to search for another attachment object.

Summary

1. Mother is the major attachment object of children of this age. This was true for the overall average and for 70% of children individually.

2. Among the father-attached group, there was a disproportionate number of twins, a fact explained by the competition for parents' time and attention in twin families.

3. Compared with mother-attached children, the father-attached children were less mature, and their mothers displayed fewer positive qualities.

CORRELATES AND DETERMINANTS OF
ATTACHMENT BEHAVIOR

The sequence analyses of behavior chains that we discussed in the earlier sections of this chapter examined the immediate effects of parent actions on child attachment behavior and vice versa, the contingencies that children and parents institute for each other. Since these actions were analyzed in their proper order in time, there was some justification for interpreting the direction of effects as being indicated by the order, namely, antecedent influencing successor. However, it might well be objected that looking for the effect of parents' actions only within the next 20 seconds is taking a very myopic view, since parents' actions are bound to affect their children's behavior (and vice versa) beyond the immediate moment. The sequence analysis does not tell one what the remote or generalized effects of parental behavioral tendencies, accumulated over time, are on the child's behavioral tendencies. Such remote effects are due to the accumulation of many recurrent actions and their reinforcing properties, combined with the operation of memory, which will permit behavioral tendencies to take root. The generalized effects of parents' on child's behavioral tendencies (or vice versa) may quite conceivably differ from the immediate effects. First, the long-term cumulative effect of one person's behavioral tendency on another's response tendency may differ from the effect that same behavior has on the other's response on the spot; for example, a parent's command may typically secure the child's compliance on the spot, yet a parent's tendency to issue many imperious commands may tend to make the child more disobedient in the long run, since obedience in the long run includes following a parent's implied wishes and standing rules, when there is no overt command. Second, the effects may differ because the parent's long-term behavioral tendency will take into account the perceptions and expectations that the parent holds of the child and the child's history, and the parent may in this way, in fact, compensate for actions she felt compelled by circumstances to take unwillingly, even in a number of situations.

The general approach to identifying remote or generalized effects is by way of a correlational analysis. This was employed in two distinct and separate ways in this research. The "remote effects analysis" was designed to discover whether parent behavior at one point in time had an effect on child behavior at a later point in time (or vice versa). In order to uncover such effects, if they existed, the analysis examined the relationship of the densities (or rates per unit of time) of child and parent action at Time 1 with their densities at Time 2, the two points in time being the two observations sessions that we had with each family and that usually were one week apart. This analysis was confined to frequencies of certain observed behavior categories. The "trait analysis," on the other hand, took as its data base the rates of certain parent and child behaviors or their relative frequencies, determined over all sampled occasions. Using these behavior–frequency-based variables as well as ratings as summary measures of child or parent characteristics, the analysis sought associations between them.

Remote Effects of Parent Actions and Child Attachment Behavior on Each Other

The remote effects analysis was carried out by what is technically known as a *cross-lagged panel analysis*, which bases itself on a well-defined network of intercorrelations between one child and one parent variable at a time, as diagrammed in Figure 12(a).

What we are essentially interested in is the correlation of the rate of a parent behavior category—say, commands–prohibitions—during Observation 1 with the rate of child's attachment behavior during Observation 2, and vice versa, the correlation of child's attachment behavior during

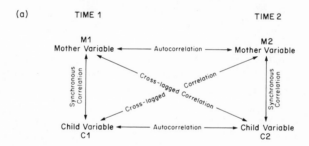

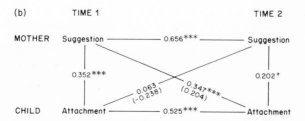

Figure 12. Diagrams for cross-lagged panel layout and for analysis of mother's suggestion rate versus child's attachment rate. (Figures in parentheses are partial correlations, holding constant the applicable Time 1 variable.) *** $p < .001$.

Observation 1 with parents' commands–prohibitions during Observation 2 (i.e., the cross lagged correlations). In such a cross-lagged panel analysis, the differential between these two correlations, called the *cross-lagged differential*, is of focal interest, since it may give us a clue to the direction of causality in these relationships. The data base for the correlations was the rates per minute of mother's and father's grouped categories of behavior (see Table 3) and the rate per minute of child's attachment behavior addressed to mother (or to father, in the analysis of father's actions).[4]

The analysis was performed for all 136 children and their mothers and for those fathers who were present for the two observations (99 fathers). The significance levels for the correlations, displayed in Table 17, however, for reasons mentioned in Chapter 3, were calculated as if only one partner out of each twin pair had been included, that is, on a reduced N of 90 for the mother and of 69 for the father analysis. It will be noted that all synchronous correlations between attachment rate and mother and father behaviours are positive and that most are significant, though the correlations for physical control and negative actions for mothers are weak. It is clear, therefore, that an association exists between the child's attachment rate and the rates of many parent grouped categories of behavior as they occur during one observation. A number of cross-lagged correlations are significant, too, demonstrating an association over time between the relevant child and parent behaviors.

However, which is the cause and which the effect? To answer this question, we have to turn to the cross-lagged differentials, only one of which, that for suggestion and attachment, was significant ($p < .02$) for mother.[5] To make the argument clear, the correlations for these variables have been diagrammed in Figure 12(b). Since the correlation between mother's suggestion rate at Time 1 (T1) and the child's attachment rate at Time 2 (T2) is significantly greater than the correlation between the attachment rate at Time 1 and the suggestion rate at Time 2, the hypothesis that suggestion increases attachment is supported.

For reasons set out in detail in Appendix VIII, there is also evidence that attachment decreases suggestion over a medium time-span. The positive correlations between suggestion and attachment then reflect the strong positive influence of suggestion on attachment, which is, however, partly counterbalanced by the opposite, negative pull of attachment on suggestion,

---

[4] The original, narrow definition of attachment behavior—consisting of approaching, touching, seeking attention, and seeking help—was employed, since this analysis was carried out before verbal and nonverbal attachment behavior were specifically defined on the basis of other analyses.

[5] The rationale for this analysis is set out in Kenny (1975), who also provides the formula for evaluating the significance of the cross-lagged differential, attributed to Pearson and Filon.

resulting particularly in a reduced correlation between attachment T1 and suggestion T2 (.063).

Other hypotheses as regards the direction of effects are possible, and they are discussed in Appendix VIII.

Thus, the cross-lagged analysis allowed us to make an inference as to the direction of effects for mother's suggestion and the child's attachment behavior. When a mother tends to engage in this less imperious form of control, regularly saying to the child, for instance, "Would you like to ..." or "What about doing so and so?" this *increases* the child's tendency—at least, over a medium time-span—to seek her proximity and nurturance, perhaps because it increases her attractiveness. The child's attachment behavior will, in turn, however, *decrease* her propensity to use suggestions (or reduce the need for it), thus setting up a feedback loop mechanism.

The only cross-lagged differential for father's actions that approaches significance is father's neutral actions and attachment behavior ($p < .10$), which suggests a causal and positive effect of attachment behavior on neutral actions. In view of the marginal significance of the effect, however, I will not dwell on this any further. The absence of any other very clear-cut finding from this analysis confirms Kenny's (1975) statement that it seems difficult to obtain significant cross-lag differentials with even moderate sample sizes (as this one was).

Attachment Viewed as a Behavior Tendency

Correlational or "trait" analysis has been the traditional method in socialization research in attempting to answer questions such as, "How does parents' warmth or restrictiveness affect the child's attachment or dependence?" As Yarrow, Waxler, and Scott (1971) have shown, the correlational analysis and the analysis of behavior sequences can complement each other fruitfully, as the two methods of analysis taken together may lead the researcher to interpret the nature of things rather differently than he would have done had he employed only one approach. The difficulty in using correlations is that they do not, of course, by themselves indicate the direction of effects, although some general considerations may give us hints as to the nature of the relationships.

The measures that represent the generalized behavior tendencies in the analyses to be discussed below are partly the summed behavior counts (relative frequencies or rates) and partly the overall impressionistic ratings of the characteristics under study, allotted to children and parents by separate raters. (For details see Table 6). Vocabulary IQ and the demographic variables of age, mother's education level, and the fact of twinship (versus being a singleton) were also included in the analyses.

Table 17. Cross-Lagged, Synchronous and Autocorrelations for Parents' Grouped Actions and Child Attachment Behavior for Observation 1 and Observation 2 (Rates per Minute)[a]

		Mother–child (df 88)				
		Child attachment behavior: autocorrelation T1 × T2: .525[b]				
	Autocorrelations	Synchronous correlations		Cross-lagged correlations		Difference: $p < .02$
Maternal variable	T1:T2[b]	CT1:MT1	CT2:MT2	CT1:MT2	MT1:CT2	
Commands–prohibitions	.652	.234[c]	.318[d]	.294[d]	.277[d]	
Suggestions	.656	.352[b]	.202[e]	.063	.347[b]	
Physical control	.495	.220[c]	.108	.075	.202[e]	
Negative actions	.589	.180[e]	.228[c]	.143	.112	
Positive actions	.673	.404[b]	.528[b]	.324[d]	.370[b]	
Neutral actions	.740	.327[d]	.350[b]	.239[c]	.345[b]	

Father–child (*df* 67)

Paternal variable	T1:T2	CT1:FT1	CT2:FT2	CT1:FT2	FT1:CT2
		Child attachment behavior: autocorrelation T1 × T2: .453[b]			
Commands–prohibitions	.689	.277[c]	.438[b]	.290[c]	.170
Suggestions	.470	.176	.266[c]	.173	.040
Physical control	.657	.324[a]	.467[b]	.285[c]	.408[b]
Negative actions	.625	.389[b]	.542[b]	.387[a]	.243[c]
Positive actions	.556	.386[a]	.455[b]	.341[a]	.165
Neutral actions	.694	.335[a]	.328[a]	.384[a]	.163
					Difference: $p < .10$

[a] C = child; M = mother; F = father; T = time. Child behavior: attachment behavior to mother and father, respectively, as rate per minute.
[b] $p < .001$.
[c] $p < .05$.
[d] $p < .01$.
[e] $p < .10$.

Table 18. Pearson Product Moment Correlations between Attachment Measures and other Child Variables (Sig. beyond .05 Level)—Reduced Sample: Singletons and Even-Numbered Twins (Maximum $N = 90$)[a]

	Attachment rating	Attachment relative frequency	Nonverbal attachment rate	Verbal attachment rate
Criteria intercorrelations				
Attachment relative frequency		—		
Nonverbal attachment rate		.53[c,d]	—	
Verbal attachment rate	.24[b,c]	.44[c,d]		—
Child and demographic variables				
Twinship[e]		−.25[b]		.28[f]
PPVT IQ			−.23[b]	
Age		−.27[f]	−.35[c,d]	
Compliance	EM		−.24[b]	
Compliance rating	−.44[c,d]			

Comply ratio	c	−.32^f		.22^b
Instrumental independence measure	EM		−.23^b	−.25^b
Instrumental independence rating		−.32^f		
Activity shift	c	−.23^b		.57^{c,a}
% time active behavior	c	−.33^d		.34^{c,f}
Speech maturity rating		−.33^{c,f}		
Frequency child command	c			−.26^b
Rate child speech	c			.51^a
Rate child–M speech	c			.55^a
Rate child–F speech	c			.54^a
Neg. action frequency	c	.32^f		
Twins' social interaction	c	−.32^{b,c}		.31^b

^{a} M = mother; F = father; EM = experimental measure; c = count. Two-tailed tests.
^{b} $p < .05$.
^{c} Correlation significant ($p < .05$) in same direction in sample of 46 twins.
^{d} $p < .001$.
^{e} Twins coded 1, singltons 3.
^{f} $p < .01$.

Table 18 presents the intercorrelations among the four attachment criteria and between them and other child and demographic variables. The "attachment rating" represents the average of ratings of four component behaviors, as explained in Table 6. The "attachment relative frequency" is attachment behavior (narrowly defined) expressed as a percentage of the child's total actions. Only correlations significant beyond the .05 level are shown; thus, if a variable—such as, for instance, mother's education—does not appear, it means that it showed no significant association with any of the criterion variables. Relationships between the criteria and parent variables were explored via a series of multiple-regression analyses to be discussed below.

The intercorrelations between the two attachment rate measures and attachment frequency are moderately good, but this is to be expected, since they are based on partly identical behavior counts. However, the attachment rating correlates significantly only with the verbal attachment rate, and the correlation is relatively low. The raters, it appears, were more influenced in their ratings by distal attention bids than by proximal ones. But in addition, they took other factors into account, such as the intensity of the attachment behavior displayed as well as reaction to separation from mother (one of the component scores). These aspects were not included in the six verbs that made up the behavior count of attachment, since they were difficult to pin down by any single action. What is of interest is also that in spite of the common method, the two rate measures correlated only −.004 (i.e., practically zero). This fact demonstrates again the independence of the domains tapped by these two complementary measures.

Relationships with Demographic and Child Variables

Let us now consider the relationships with deomographic and other child variables that place attachment behavior in the framework of the child's social behavior in general. That age correlates negatively with nonverbal attachment rate indicates—as did Sears *et al.*'s (1965) and Ragozin's (1978) findings—that the tendency to seek parents' proximity decreases with age. This developmental trend almost defines nonverbal attachment behavior as immature behavior. Verbal attachment behavior, on the other hand, had a near-zero correlation with age. It was noted in Chapter 4 that twins were more inclined to show attachment behavior than singletons, and this can be seen here in the negative correlation of twinship with the relative frequency of attachment behavior (twins being coded 1, and singletons 3). This is very likely a consequence of the fact that twins generally tended to be somewhat more immature. On the other hand, twins tended to show a lower verbal attachment *rate*, which, however, can be understood in terms of their lower activity level all round, compared with singletons, as explained in Chapter 4.

The significant negative correlation of nonverbal attachment behavior with vocabulary IQ once again underlines the immature nature of this kind of behavior (other attachment criteria also had negative, though nonsignificant, correlations with IQ). Emmerich (1966) also found that brighter children were less dependent, and Crandall, Preston, and Rabson (1960) found the same for high-achieving children.

The correlations of the experimental measure and the rating of independence with two attachment criteria are negative, as expected. The negative correlations between the attachment and independence ratings could be explained as the result of an inverted halo effect (a rater who perceived a child as greatly attached would also see him as less independent), but the negative correlations of the nonverbal attachment rate and the attachment frequency cannot be so explained.

The relationships between the attachment and compliance measures are somewhat equivocal. The nonverbal attachment rate has a positive correlation with the comply ratio (comply / [comply + noncomply]), indicating that the child who shows more nonverbal attachment also is more compliant. The verbal attachment rate and the attachment frequency also show positive, though nonsignificant, correlations with the comply ratio. On the other hand, the attachment rating has negative correlations with both the comply ratio and the compliance rating. The correlations based on behavior counts provide some evidence that attachment (or dependence) may indeed supply the motivation for compliance, as Sears et al. (1957, 1965) and Stayton et al. (1971) suggest on theoretical grounds. The negative correlations of attachment rating with two compliance measures can be understood as the result of raters' seeing attachment in a negative light, as bothersome behavior that naturally goes with noncompliance. (Note, though, that one of these negative correlations holds with a count variable, the "comply ratio.") The pilot study of this project also replicated the negative relationship between attachment and compliance ratings on an independent sample of 30 two-year-old boys. While the rating tapped a somewhat different concept of attachment than did the nonverbal attachment rate, as has already been stated, both aspects exist and are readily intelligible. In previous studies, correlations between dependence (globally assessed) and "conscience" have typically been near zero, as Yarrow et al. (1968) have shown. Sears et al. (1965), interestingly enough, found negative correlations between conscience and attention seeking and reassurance seeking for boys, similar to our negative correlations for the rating measure.

The positive correlations between nonverbal attachment rate and the activity measures, and between the verbal attachment rate and the speech rate measures, are no doubt due to the influence of the child's general level of activity on all these measures. Nonverbal attachment is significantly associated with general play activity, whereas verbal attachment goes with speech, as one would expect. On the other hand, the correlations between the attachment rating and the activity measures as well as the speech maturity rating are all negative, again pointing to attachment as a sign of lack of maturity.

Lastly, the positive association between the attachment rating and the negative action frequency is readily intelligible, since instances of whining and crying featured largely in the raters' assessment of attachment, and these actions also formed part of the "negative actions" count category.

We consider the role attachment behavior plays in the child's total development and experience in the "discussion" section below.

Prediction from Parent Characteristics

Which parent characteristics are significant predictors of the child's attachment behavior? To answer this question, stepwise multiple regression analyses that take into account the intercorrelations among the parent variables were performed for the main attachment variables. Criteria for including parent variables as predictors in the analyses were that (1) the variable had a significant ($p < .05$) simple correlation with one of the attachment critera; or (2) the variable was theoretically important for this domain. Only the rating *or* the behavior count measure for a given characteristic—and among count measures *either* the rate *or* the relative frequency measure—was included. Both mother and father behavior counts were considered for inclusion, but father ratings could not be used because they were available for only a few fathers. In addition, the demographic variables of mother's education, twinship, and vocabulary IQ were included *after* all the other variables had been entered. This was a deliberate decision made because the parental characteristics were the chief focus of the investigation, and I wished to assess their full contribution to the prediction, including the indirect effects of the demographic variables that they carried with them. The order of entry into the stepwise multiple regression within these two blocks was determined by the amount of variance in the criterion that the variable was able to account for over and above previously entered variables, the decision being made by the computer program (SPSS) employed.

Tables 19, 20, and 21 display the results of the three analyses for the sample of 90, which contains only one of each twin pair. The column "R^2 change" shows the increment in R^2 due to the given variable, that is, the additional amount of variance that the variable explains, over and above the higher-placed variables. This index has been called the variable's *utility* and can be taken as an indication of the variable's importance in the prediction, when other predictors and their intercorrelations are taken into account. In addition, however, the simple correlations also provide useful information.

There is little overlap between the significant predictors of the three attachment criteria, which indicates that they tap relatively distinct aspects of

Table 19. **Multiple Regression Prediction of Attachment Rating (Singletons and Even-Numbered Twins)** $(N = 90)^a$

Predictors			Multiple R^2 $(p < .001)$	R^2 change	Simple r
Reasoning rating	M		.168	$.168^b$	$-.409^c$
Rate mother–child speech		c	.253	$.086^d$	.177
Consistency of enforcement rating	M		.315	$.062^d$	$-.342$
Paternal negative action freq.		c	.370	$.054^d$	.271
Maternal verbal psychological punishment rating			.398	$.029^e$	$.237^c$
Paternal positive action freq.		c	.423	$.025^f$	.108
Paternal play frequency		c	.445	$.022^f$	$-.153$
Encourage mature action rating	M		.466	$.021^f$	$-.199$
Maternal negative action freq.		c	.477	.011	.269
Support of dependence rating	M		.489	.012	.140
Maternal love withdrawal freq.		c	.499	.010	.066
Material rewards rating	M		.507	.008	$-.083$
Maternal physical punishment frequency		c	.516	.010	.161
Maternal positive action freq.		c	.523	.006	.004
Maternal command prohibition frequency		c	.530	.007	$-.085$
Monitoring rating	M		.535	.005	$-.160$
Maternal affection frequency		c	.538	.003	.039
Paternal reasoning frequency		c	.541	.002	.059
Rate father–child speech		c	.544	.003	$-.015$
Paternal physical punishment frequency		c	.545	.002	$-.032$
Maternal play frequency		c	.546	.001	$-.120$
Paternal affection frequency		c	.546	.000	.009
Psychological rewards rating	M		.546	.000	$-.163$
Twinship^g			.571	$.024^f$	$-.042$
Vocabulary IQ			.572	.001	$-.094$
Mother's education			.572	.000	.007

^{a} Twinship, Vocabulary IQ, and mother's education entered separately after all other variables. No father ratings included because of number of missing cases.
^{b} $p < .001$.
^{c} Correlations significant $(p < .05)$ in same direction in sample of 46 twins. c = count; M = mother.
^{d} $p < .01$.
^{e} $p < .05$.
^{f} $p < .10$.
^{g} Twins coded 1, singletons 3.

the attachment construct, a fact confirmed also by the existence of only one significant (but low) correlation between the rating and the verbal attachment rate. In considering the findings for the rating, it should be pointed out that possible contamination between child and parent ratings was guarded against by having separate investigators rate child and parents.

Multiple-regression analyses can produce very variable results, even with only very slight changes in a variable (cf. Wainer, 1978), and in finding the best linear composite to predict the criterion in a given sample, the analysis "capitalizes on error variance." It is therefore useful to have findings from a replication on another sample available. In this case, we replicated all the analyses on the 46 twins eliminated from the main sample to arrive at the sample of 90. Although this is, of course, not a completely independent sample, any confirmatory results will strengthen confidence in the "reality" and robustness of the findings shown here. As can be seen from Table 19, there are eight predictors (apart from twinship) that made significant contributions to the prediction of the attachment rating, as judged by a significant increment in R^2. In the replication sample, however, three of these corelated with the criterion in the reverse direction. The variables that contributed significantly to the prediction in the same direction in both samples were[6]: mother's reasoning rating (reasoning leading to *decreased* attachment), mother's verbal–psychological punishment rating, and father's positive action frequency, both of the latter having a positive relation with the criterion. These, then, appear to be the stable predictors. In examining the simple correlations, however, we notice that the correlation for father's negative actions is higher (and significant) than that of his positive actions, which is nonsignificant. The same holds for mother's parallel variables. A reasonable interpretation of the overall picture is that attachment, as perceived by the raters, is discouraged by a cognitive approach to discipline (reasoning and consistency of enforcement of rules) but is encouraged by father's and mother's positive as well as negative actions—the latter including such behavior as criticizing or threatening, actions that would also be counted toward the rating for verbal–psychological punishment.[7] The raters, we notice again, were especially alive to negative aspects of attachment behavior (e.g., whining, crying, and attention

---

[6] A significant contribution to prediction (i.e., significant increment in R^2), it should be noted, is different from a significant simple correlation—only replications of the latter are marked in the table.

[7] Mother's negative action frequency, it will be noted, does not make a significant contribution to prediction. It is quite possible for one variable that happens to gain entry to the regression first to crowd out another predictor, correlated with the first one, so that the second variable seems less important, although it has an equal, or sometimes even higher, correlation with the criterion than the first variable. It seems likely that mother's verbal–psychological punishment rating acted in this way to relegate her negative action frequency to a lower, nonsignificant place.

seeking), which are often elicited by parents' negative actions. This relationship parallels the repeated finding that parental rejection gives rise to increased dependency in the child (e.g., Sears *et al.*, 1957; Smith, 1958). However, the direction of effects need by no means necessarily be from parent to child: it may well be that a child whose attachment behavior exeeds his parents' tolerance and expresses itself in a particularly burdensome fashion (e.g., by whining or constantly seeking his parents' attention) will also arouse a negative reaction from his parents. Such mutual interdependencies between attachment behavior and parents' negative actions do not by themselves contradict the fact that father's positive actions also seem to influence—or to be influenced by—the child's attachment. Differing circumstances may well give rise to seemingly similar child behavior that will assume a different tone and meaning according to these circumstances (see "Discussion" section).

Results for the nonverbal attachment rate for the sample of 90 are shown in Table 20. The variable that made a significant contribution to the prediction of the nonverbal attachment rate in the same direction both in the sample of 90 and in the sample of 46 was father's play frequency. It should be stressed that this variable is not a rate per unit of time but a frequency expressed as a percentage of the agent's total actions, and hence the general level of activity will not introduce an element of spuriousness into the correlations. Mother's play frequency and maternal affection frequency also had significant correlations with the criterion in both samples. Although in the analysis shown, the latter was relegated to a lower position by the stepwise regression procedure, it was a significant predictor in the sample of 46. It is apparent that in the long run, nonverbal attachment is fostered by parents' affection and willingness to play with the child.

These results are in line with a few other findings—though they are somewhat patchy—pointing to parents' affection or "warmth" as the basis for the child's dependence (Hatfield *et al.*, 1967; Yarrow *et al.*, 1968). Positive actions overall, however (which include other actions beside affection), have only a weak and diluted relationship with nonverbal attachment. The sequence analysis (Figure 11) also demonstrated rather weak effects between parents' positive actions in general and nonverbal attachment behavior, with positive actions facilitating only the child's sitting on his parents' lap.

The results of the multiple-regression analysis for the verbal attachment rate are shown in Table 21. Of the five variables (apart from twinship) shown as significant predictors here, mother's consistency of enforcement rating and her positive action frequency were also significant in the sample of 46. These, then, seem to be the most replicable predictors. Verbal, as distinct from nonverbal, attachment is fostered most by an approach that emphasizes cognitive structure. Justification for this interpretation lies not

Table 20.   Multiple Regression Prediction of Nonverbal Attachment Rate
(Singletons and Even-Numbered Twins) ($N = 90$)[a]

Predictors		Multiple R^2 ($p < .001$)	R^2 change	Simple r
Maternal play frequency	c	.230	.230[b]	.480[c]
Paternal play frequency	c	.294	.064[d]	.441
Maternal love withdrawal freq.	c	.346	.051[e]	−.141
Paternal negative action freq.	c	.360	.014	.070
Verbal psychological punishment rating	M	.371	.011	−.157
Material rewards rating	M	.380	.009	.141
Consistency of enforcement rating	M	.386	.007	−.054
Support of dependence rating	M	.397	.010	−.016
Psychological rewards rating	M	.405	.008	.068
Maternal affection frequency	c	.411	.005	.261[c]
Maternal positive action freq.	c	.426	.015	.090
Paternal suggestion frequency	c	.433	.008	−.065
Rate father–child speech	c	.445	.011	−.053
Maternal reasoning frequency	c	.449	.005	.027
Encourage mature action freq.	M	.452	.003	−.119
Maternal suggestion frequency	c	.455	.003	−.018
Rate mother–child speech	c	.458	.003	.070
Maternal negative action freq.	c	.460	.001	−.040
Paternal reasoning frequency	c	.460	.001	−.014
Twinship[f]		.513	.053[d]	.148
Paternal affection frequency	c	.520	.007	.017
Restrictions rating	M	.522	.002	−.092
Paternal positive action freq.	c	.523	.001	.005
Mother's education		.537	.014	.036
Vocabulary IQ		.551	.014	−.234

[a] Twinship, vocabulary IQ, and mother's education entered separately after all other variables. No father ratings included because of number of missing cases.
[b] $p < .001$.
[c] Correlation significant ($p < .05$) in same direction in sample of 46 twins. c = count; M = mother.
[d] $p < .01$.
[e] $p < .05$.
[f] Twins coded 1, singletons 3.

only in the predictors listed above but also in the significant simple correlations of several other predictors with this criterion, namely, mother's and father's suggestion frequency and mother's reasoning frequency, all of which indicate a cognitive emphasis. But parents' affective relations also play a part: both categories of positively and negatively toned actions are important correlates of verbal attachment behavior, one of the negative actions being mother's withdrawal of love, which had a significant simple correlation with verbal attachment and was a significant predictor in the sample of 46. The temporary withdrawal of love (e.g., mother's not wishing to talk to the child or sending the child to his room) deprives the child temporarily of interaction with mother and acts as a form of rejection. It seems to increase his long-term tendency to seek psychological, verbal contact with her, although this was not evident as an immediate consequence in the sequence analysis of single parent actions, probably because of the low frequency of this particular code.

In which direction do effects flow? We have evidence from the cross-lagged panel analysis that it is mother's suggestions that increase the child's

Table 21. Multiple Regression Prediction of Verbal Attachment Rate (Singletons and Even-Numbered Twins) ($N = 90$)[a]

Predictors		Multiple R^2 ($p < .001$)	R^2 change	Simple r
Rate mother–child speech	c	.224	.224[b]	.473
Rather father–child speech	c	.274	.050[c]	.368
Maternal positive action freq.	c	.321	.047[c]	.265[d]
Maternal negative action freq.	c	.371	.050[c]	.219
Support of dependence rating	M	.384	.013	.163
Consistency of enforcement rtg.	M	.407	.023[e]	.182
Paternal positive action freq.	c	.419	.013	.250
Restrictions rating	M	.428	.009	.185
Paternal affection frequency	c	.435	.007	.136
Paternal play frequency	c	.441	.006	.030
Maternal suggestion frequency	c	.445	.004	.412
Maternal reasoning frequency	c	.448	.003	.298
Maternal love withdrawal freq.	c	.451	.003	.351
Psychological rewards rating	M	.455	.004	.203
Paternal suggestion frequency	c	.457	.003	.332
Paternal negative action freq.	c	.459	.001	.187
Maternal affection frequency	c	.459	.001	.200
Material rewards rating	M	.460	.001	.027
Paternal reasoning frequency	c	.460	.001	.192
Maternal play frequency	c	.461	.000	.084
Verbal psychological punishment rating	M	.461	.000	.113
Encouragement mature action rating	M	.461	.000	.139
Twinship[f]		.499	.038[c]	.276
Vocabulary IQ		.502	.003	.148
Mother's education		.502	.000	.152

[a] Twinship, vocabulary IQ, and mother's education entered separately after all other variables. No father ratings included because of number of missing cases.
[b] $p < .001$.
[c] $p < .05$.
[d] Correlation significant ($p < .05$) in same direction in sample of 46 twins.
[e] $p < .10$.
[f] Twins coded 1, singletons 3.

attachment behavior over time, at least, in the medium term. We have no real evidence on this question for mother's withdrawal of love, although it seems most plausible that this mother action influences her child's attachment behavior, by some mechanism such as the one described above, rather than the other way round. As far as the positive and negative action categories are concerned, however, we may conclude that the influence runs both ways. From Figure 11 we see that both are significant antecedents as well as consequents. If we may extrapolate from the sequence analysis of immediate consequences to long-term relationships (cf. also Table 15), we can conclude that negative actions are the more powerful instigators of verbal attachment behavior, whereas postive actions are its more frequent consequences.

The significant association between mother's support of dependence and her restrictiveness, on the one hand, and child's attachment behavior, on the other, repeatedly reported in the literature (cf. Maccoby & Masters, 1970), found very little support in this study. This was in spite of the fact that because of the previous findings, ratings for these mother characteristics were included in the design.

Parental Responsiveness and Attachment Behavior

An important piece of evidence for the biological adaptiveness of attachment behavior—and for the mutual adaptedness of mother and child—is the finding that mother's sensitive responsiveness is associated with "secure attachment" in the infant (Ainsworth, Bell, & Stayton, 1972; Clarke-Stewart, 1973). The present research program was not designed to test this hypothesis, since attachment behavior here was assessed by its frequency and strength. Because of the reported association, however, I set out to explore the relationship between mother's and father's responsiveness and the strength of attachment behavior, as defined by the rate measures, as well as by the attachment relative frequency and the attachment rating. The responsiveness measures included in this analysis were the variables listed in Table 8, which had been calculated for the "responsiveness sample" of 40 children.

None of these measures showed a significant bivariate correlation, either positive or negative, with the nonverbal or verbal attachment rates. Further, when the "responsiveness" and "appropriateness" percentages were added to the significant predictors from the sample of 90 to predict nonverbal and verbal attachment rates in multiple-regression analyses, they did not add anything significant to the prediction. Thus, there was an essentially zero relationship between these responsiveness and appropriateness measures and the attachment rates.

However, when the total reactivity percentages (i.e., total responses to bids for attention, etc., and to speech) were used to predict the verbal attachment rate in a multiple-regression analysis, father's reactivity percentage made a marginally significant additional contribution to the prediction of the verbal attachment rate, with which it correlated negatively. Similar negative bivariate correlations that just failed to reach significance were found between mother's and father's total reactivity and the attachment relative frequency, and a significant ($p < .05$) negative correlation between father's total reactivity and the attachment rating. Conversely, mother's "inappropriate unresponsiveness" (i.e., where a sensitive, not exasperated mother would have responded) correlated positively ($p < .01$) with the attachment relative frequency, and father's "appropriate unresponsiveness" (i.e., justified by the circumstances) correlated positively ($p < .01$) with the attachment rating. (No multiple-regression analyses including the responsiveness measures were carried out for these two criteria.) Here we have a consistent picture: parents' responsiveness, as a whole, reduced the need for the child to seek closeness with them, whereas their unresponsiveness, whether justified or not, increased the child's motivation to reassure himself of their love. In an observational study, Smith (1958) also found that the more the mother complied with the child's requests, the less help and attention he requested.

Attachment Behavior in the Experimental Stiuation

Attachment to mother was measured in the experimental playroom situation, as described in Chapter 2. Little need be said about this experimental measure, as it did not correlate significantly with any parent measure or with any other child measure, except (negatively) with the amount of interaction between twin partners. This fact illustrates the unfruitfulness of the experimental approach in this investigation, possible reasons for which were set out in Chapter 2.

Summary

1. Correlations between the nonverbal attachment rate, the verbal attachment rate, and the attachment rating are low to near zero: these indices seem to represent somewhat separate domains of attachment behavior.

2. Correlations with other child variables, replicated in a subsample, show that the attachment rating is related to ratings of noncompliance and immaturity of speech, indicating that the rating captures the less positive aspect of attachment (e.g., whining and crying).

3. In the medium term, mother's use of milder suggestions increases both kinds of attachment behavior, counted together, which, in turn, decreases (perhaps renders less necessary?) mother's use of suggestions.

4. The trait analysis shows the long-term impact of parental practices on the child's attachment behavior (and vice versa). The results of this analysis are complex and vary in detail, depending on the type of attach-

ment behavior examined. The findings that have been replicated can be summarized as follows:

    a. A warm climate of play and affection by mother and father are closely associated with nonverbal attachment behavior.

    b. Taking the evidence from the sequence analysis and from the trait analysis together, we may conclude that mother's negative attitudes arouse the child's verbal attachment behavior, whereas her positive actions are more its consequence, though both kinds of maternal behavior "predict" attachment behavior.

    5. The analysis of a subsample shows that parents' unresponsiveness to the child's bids for attention, demands, or speech stimulates the child's attachment behavior, as measured by various indices.

DISCUSSION

The attachment process is at the core of parents' and children's interactions with each other—indeed, it is an important part of people's interactions with each other throughout life. What is its function? How does it develop? What elicits it, and what kind of reactions does it arouse? These are questions that we are now ready to discuss. We will examine them by bringing together the evidence from both types of analysis presented in this chapter: the analysis of the dynamics of attachment behavior, viewed as a process (sequence analysis), and the analysis of the individual differences in attachment behavior, seen as a child characteristic or "trait" (correlational analysis).

The research has identified two clases of attachment behavior: nonverbal (consisting of approaching, touching, and sitting on lap) and verbal (consisting of seeking attention, help, and permission). The three actions making up each group cohere together quite strongly, and each is characterized by specific patterns of parent actions that activate it and that are, in turn, aroused by it. The evidence for combining the two subclasses to form one overarching class of responses is much weaker, and the chief justification for calling all these behaviors by the common name *attachment behavior* is that they all serve to maintain closeness and to elicit nurturant behavior from the person(s) to whom they are addressed, the *attachment object*.

For the purpose of the trait analysis, we measured attachment by its frequency and summed instances of this behavior to form two main indices of attachment as summary traits. Ainsworth (1972) suggests that to do this is unsatisfactory

> ... unless one is willing to equate it (strength of attachment) with the degree of insecurity and frequency of fear, for there is no doubt that the strongest attachment behavior occurs when the infant is intensely alarmed, intensely apprehensive that his mother may leave him, or intensely distressed because he has in fact been separated from her. (p. 119)

I am willing to adopt this view, however, since this is what the data presented here show. Particularly, nonverbal attachment is a sign not only of insecurity but also of immaturity: a greater degree of nonverbal attachment went with lower age (even within our limited age range) and with lower vocabulary IQ. As Maccoby and Masters (1970) put it:

> Dependency [operationalized by the same behavioral measures as attachment] is an immature response system, in the sense that the frequency of this behavior declines with age, as the child acquires a more adaptive repertoire of alternative techniques for getting what he wants. Among children of a given age, then, the more dependent children are the ones who have proceeded slowly in the process of acquiring these alternative repertoires. (p. 141)

("Getting what he wants," I suspect, has to be interpreted as getting the contact, attention, and reassurance of love that he wants.)

Taking this view of attachment behavior, however, does not deny the fact that it is a normal, ubiquitous, and crucial process or behavior system, and that in particular a certain degree of attachment to his caregivers is essential for the child during the stage of immaturity. It would seem quite tenable to argue that it has biological utility in that it tends to ensure protection—from predators in the far-off days of savannah living, and from other dangers now. Moreover, it lays the foundation for a network of relationships that characterizes living in small groups, as humans do. In fact, as noted in the introduction to this chapter, attachment behavior is likely to be emitted relatively more by immature organisms in a situation of insecurity, if its biological function is to elicit protection. That mother turns out to be the preferred attachment object in most studies, including this one, is a reflection of the fact that she, in most cases, is the primary person who protects the child against harm and injury.

It is consonant with such an interpretation of attachment that the various attachment *rate* and *frequency* measures are positively associated with compliance, since attachment, in this view, forms the framework within which compliance with the essential directions of the more mature protector will develop. As Stayton *et al.* (1971) write, "the ethological literature suggests that the attachment bond disposes an infant to obey his mother's signals" (p. 1067).

On the other hand, attachment behavior also has a negative, demanding side to it when, in excess, it is burdensome to parents. This aspect was reflected mainly in the attachment *rating* and showed up in the latter's positive associations with *non*compliance and with mother's psychological punishment.

The analysis of sequences of behavior presented here, I suggest, implies two kinds of parent stimuli for attachment behavior. Positive and neutral parent actions act as discriminative cues: they may either simply set the stage for nonverbal or verbal attachment behavior to be manifested (for example, talking to the child), or they may render it superfluous (for example, reading to the child). An analogy might be with mother's setting the supper table, which provides the setting for the child to eat.

The other type of stimuli are parent's negative actions. The findings suggest that negative actions in general—and ignoring, in particular—disturb a relationship that the child feels motivated to reinstate by his verbal attachment behavior, even if this behavior is not reinforced. These actions can be seen as stimuli that arouse (verbal) attachment behavior. Similarly, in the correlational analyses, unresponsiveness or the absence of reactions by parents was a negative stimulus that was seen to increase attachment behavior as measured by several indices, including verbal attachment rate.

The different parent stimuli are connected differentially to the two classes of attachment behavior, and the latter can be interpreted as having differing psychological functions related to the specific parental behaviors with which they interact. Nonverbal attachment behavior uses proximal receptors to ensure physical proximity, and it tends to be more characteristic of the younger child. (The younger child, in fact, engages in more attachment behavior all round, which is weighted more heavily with the nonverbal kind.) The sequence analysis showed that nonverbal attachment behavior is not particularly elicited by parents' negative actions, and positive actions set the stage mainly for sitting on lap. Nonverbal attachment behavior therefore seems to have the function mainly of maintaining and prolonging existing affectionate and harmonious relationships. Its consequent effect on parents is to reduce the incidence of all types of behavior; that is, the very act seems to be its own end—and peace thereafter.

The correlational trait analysis confirmed this picture for the long-term relationships: nonverbal attachment behavior seems to be fostered by a warm climate of parental affection and play with the child.

Verbal attachment behavior, on the other hand, uses distal receptors to achieve psychological proximity, and it characterizes younger and older children within our age range equally. The sequence analysis demonstrated that it is aroused particularly by parents' negative actions, and this finding suggests that is has the function of reinstating the harmonious relationship that was thus disturbed. Negative actions put the child into a state of deprivation (potential lack of protection?), which he seeks to remedy by verbal attachment behavior. The latter's effect on parents, however, is to activate behavior that is polarized not only as positively toned but also as negatively toned. While verbal attachment behavior is therefore not uniformly effective in achieving its presumed purpose, on balance it tends to do so, since it increases positive actions more frequently than negative ones.

The trait analysis via mulitple regression also demonstrated a dual relationship between verbal attachment and positive and negative actions, both of which seemed to be effective predictors of attachment. From the evidence of the sequence analysis, however, we can conclude that though positive and negative actions are both associated with verbal attachment, they are not both its causes. The most reasonable inference is that a negative and critical parental attitude is a major cause of verbal attachment, whereas positive actions are more its consequence. This holds for immediate as well as long-term effects. We have to reconcile this finding with the fact that mother's less attractive qualities seem to cause the child to attach himself more closely to father. This seeming contradiction may be resolved, however, if we assume that positive, appealing characteristics (and interactions) determine the *choice* of attachment object, but that negative actions increase the *strength* of attachment behavior. We should note that in addition, verbal attachment is also fostered by a cognitive approach in parents' dealings with their child.

It is quite possible that genetic factors also contribute to individual differences in attachment behavior. This possibility was ignored but not forgotten in this presentation, because attachment here was seen as an interactive process in which parents' actions would have a considerable part to play, both as causes and consequences, over and above any genetic predisposition. The contribution of genetic factors to attachment behavior, however, seemed minimal in the present investigation (see Chapter 9).

Since verbal attachment is aroused by negative actions, it appears that this behavior subserves a motivational drive system, and in this sense, the results support the theory that attachment possesses biological utility, particularly for young children (Ainsworth, 1972; Bowlby, 1969).

CHAPTER 6

Compliance and the Rudiments of Conscience

The process whereby the child acquires control over his own behavior so that it conforms to the requirements of his society, irrespective of the presence of an external agent of authority, is sometimes considered synonymous with socialization, though this may be taking an unduly narrow view of this process. Be this as it may, the development of internalized controls, together with the development of attachment and of independence, form a trinity of processes central to early child–parent relations. Hence, there exists a considerable body of literature dealing with the development of internalized controls, or "conscience," in the child. This literature has its theoretical origins in the psychoanalytic school, and we owe the empirical studies in this area mainly to workers who have derived testable propositions from psychoanalytic postulates and cast them in an experimental mold. These historical roots partly account for the emphasis on the internalization of controls, that is, the development of self-inhibition in the absence of external restraint. The latter topic is, however, important also for anyone who considers the establishment of an autonomous, self-regulating conscience a desirable goal of development. Investigators holding the view that this process must, in part, be a product of environmental forces have related it to specific parental child-rearing practices as well as to parents' attitudes, or the "climate," of the home.

Most of the studies in this area have used ratings, based on interviews or questionnaires, as their data source for investigating individual differences in "conscience" by way of correlations, although some (e.g., Sears *et al.*, 1965) have derived behavioral measures from observation in an experimental laboratory setting. Apart from Baumrind (1971), who dealt with compliance, among other child characteristics, only two investigations, both of recent vintage (Stayton *et al.*, 1971; Minton *et al.*, 1971), appear to have based themselves on naturalistic observation in the home. Both dealt with very young children (12 and 27 months, respectively) and appear to be the only ones that have studied overt compliance with mother's commands and requests, as opposed to internalized controls.

Yet, overt compliance has its own importance, and it is chiefly workers in the tradition of social learning theory who have devoted themselves to specifying the conditions that facilitate or impede it, though not in the context of parent–child relations (e.g., Bandura & Walters, 1963; Carl-smith, Lepper, & Landauer, 1974; Walters & Parke, 1964). Theoretically, one would expect the achievement of overt compliance with parental wishes and standards in response to external control and in the expectation of immediate sanctions to be the precursor of the internalization of these stan-dards within the child, operating in the absence of any external agent of control (cf. Sears *et al.*, 1957, pp. 363–366). "Achieving a certain level of conformity may become a 'milestone' representing the formation of conscience in various theories" (Kohlberg, 1969, p. 371). Yet, it is not clear how internalized control takes over, first from external constraint and then from the anticipation of it, nor do we know much about the factors that facilitate this shift of control. Empirically, Stayton *et al.* (1971) did not, in fact, find a significant relation between the infant's compliance with com-mands and a rating of degree of internalized control, but this finding was based on a reduced sample of five.

Research in this area does not commit the researcher to the proposition that compliance is an absolute good or that the more of it we have the bet-ter. What degree of compliance is desirable is, of course, a value question, but some factual base for answering it can eventually be obtained from empirical research into the concomitants and consequences of compliance, for example, into how far autonomy, creativity, or moral integrity are associated with it. We are all aware, from instances in recent history as well as from Milgram's (1974) vivid demonstrations, of the dangers of automatic obedience to "higher orders," or to the commands of those regarded as being in positions of trust. Many people, therefore, are uneasy about research on "compliance," because of the specter of parroting automata, of tools of an unscrupulous state, that the word conjures up. Yet, parents can-not escape the need to induct their children into the norms of society, and they inevitably impose certain rules of conduct and restrictions on them.

Many writers on moral development agree that in the early years, the concepts of overt compliance and internalized, autonomous conscience overlap and are difficult to distinguish, though at a later stage they diverge. Thus, Kohlberg (1969), in the paragraph quoted above, continues:

> Further development, however, may lead to a relaxation of conformity with
> assurance that impulse control has been achieved, or it may lead to an apparent

non-conformity as autonomous and individual principles of values are developed.
(p. 371).

No one has put it better than Harding (1953):

> The growth of a person, simultaneously as an individual and a social being, does
> for a time show itself in a gradually increasing conformity to the adult standards
> of a social group. But it would be disastrous to assume that these standards must
> continue to be the measure of development. Group conformity and social
> development may in the early years of life be closely connected and perhaps dif-
> ficult to distinguish. But a dissociation of the two ideas . . . is of the utmost
> importance in understanding the social development of the more mature
> members of a group. (pp. 47–48)

Thus, the goal that Western values stress is the development of an
inner-directed conscience, where the direction of behavior derives from an
internal standard that is not simply the repository of group norms. With
2-year-olds, however, we studied chiefly compliance as the forerunner and
outward manifestation of internalized controls, as well as in its own right.
In examining the contingencies governing compliance or noncompliance in
unconstrained parent–child interactions, we combined an ethological framework (see Chapter 1) with concepts derived from social learning theory.
Hoffman (1970) wrote:

> Social learning theory seems best suited to account for the early forerunners of
> morality which consist of the expression and inhibition of specific acts defined by
> socialization agents as good or bad and rewarded or punished accordingly, and
> other acts having stimulus elements in common. (p. 345)

It is difficult to obtain trustworthy measures of the internalized control
of behavior at this age, partly because very young children have only just
begun to monitor their own behavior, and partly because it is not easy to
observe the operation of conscience within the span of relatively limited
visits. If a child does *not* climb on tables, we do not know whether he
refrains because he has made his parents' rules on this matter his own or
because he has never done this kind of thing or because he does not feel in
the mood for it just now. When the study was already in progress, a direct
rating measure of internalized control was included, since it was thought
that it was better to have some measure of it, however approximate and
imperfect, than to have none at all. This variable is discussed below. It must
not, however, be thought that the internalization of parents' standards is
here equated with the expression of an autonomous conscience—at this age,
it is more probably the internal representation and anticipation of the feared
consequences of external constraint. Nevertheless, it signals that control has
shifted to the child's own monitoring system, and it thus can be regarded as
a rudimentary form of conscience.

Although the analyses that examined the child's compliance differed
somewhat in design from those for attachment behavior, the perspectives

from which we viewed the area of compliance were the same: the process of compliance was investigated as it revealed itself in parent–child behavior sequences; and compliance and internalized control as child characteristics were studied by correlational "trait" analyses. Various subsidiary aspects (e.g., the "second-order effects" of father's presence on mother's control behavior) were also examined and are considered in subsequent sections of this chapter.

COMPLIANCE AND PARENT ACTIONS: SEQUENCE ANALYSIS

Analysis

The aim of this set of analyses was to determine which parent actions are facilitating and which inhibitory antecedents of child compliance; both immediate and more remote (second order) antecedents were taken into account by separate analyses. A somewhat technical explanation of the analysis is necessary to enable readers to follow the discussion of the findings below.

Two separate programs, somewhat different from those used for the analysis of attachment behavior, analyzed the compliance sequences. I will now describe the count algorithm that was basic to both programs. Separate analyses were run for mother and father. The program searched the record and stored and tabulated each parent action or utterance, other than a mode of verbal control, which was then arbitrarily defined as an A_h action (prior antecedent). It then searched for a parent mode of verbal control over the next two 10-sec intervals and tabulated it as a B_i action. If none was found, "no control" was recorded. It searched further for a child comply or non-comply for two 10-sec intervals, tabulating it as an R_j action (successor). If none was found, "neither" was recorded.

Thus we have the following scheme, arranged in time sequence:

$$T-2 \longrightarrow T-1 \longrightarrow T$$

parent antecedent, A_h,	parent verbal control,	child comply/
e.g., negative action	B_i, e.g., command–prohibition	noncomply/neither, R_j

The count, it will be seen, took note of one more event, prior in time, than did the attachment program. All programs used *event*-based counts with time serving only as a limiting boundary.

The four parental grouped behavior categories that were not modes of verbal control, defined in Table 3 (namely, physical control, negative actions, positive actions, and neutral actions) constituted the parent antecedents (A_h) at time $T-2$. Using these superordinate categories simplified the understanding of the relationships, but individual verbs could in principle also be searched for.

Instances of mother (or father) verbal control (B_i) at time $T-1$ were classified into three categories: command–prohibition (collapsing these two categories from Table 3), suggestion, and control with reasoning. Child actions R_j (at time T) were classified as comply, noncomply, or neither comply nor noncomply. The last category deserves special mention. It was assigned after the various modes of control if the child did not comply or definitely disobey (i.e., in instances when mother or father showed by their behavior that they did not really mean their request to be followed and dropped the matter), and it would also be scored if it was not clear whether the child did or did not comply. In such instances, it would be misleading to count either comply or noncomply.

"No verbal control" by the parent and "neither comply nor noncomply" following it have a special status: every parent action was counted as one of the prior antecedents A_h at time $T-2$; if no mode of verbal control B_i occurred, but then a comply or noncomply ensued, the triad parent antecedent (A_h)—no mode of control (B_i)—comply or noncomply (R_j) was scored. This could happen in a double sequence when one command was followed first by a noncomply and then by a comply, or when a child refused his mother's offer—the latter was not counted as a form of control. If no mode of verbal control and then no comply or noncomply followed a parent prior antecedent, "no verbal control" and "neither comply nor noncomply" were scored, but only *once*, however many child actions (not comply or noncomply) occurred. As an example, "Mother shows child a picture in a book, child talks to mother, child climbs on mother's knee, child looks at book (end of second time interval)" would produce one triad: "Mother shows something (A_h)—No mode of control (B_i)—Neither comply nor noncomply (R_j)." Hence the frequencies of "no verbal control" and of "neither" following on "no verbal control" are artifactual figures. It can be seen that in the matrix of joint events all possible parent antecedents, A_h, were counted, but not all possible child actions. However, the unconditional probability (base rate) of a child successor, R_j, occurring in the record was computed by dividing the frequency of the successor by the total number of child actions counted in the record.

It would be theoretically possible to extend the analysis to the subsequent parent response to the child's comply, treating the latter as a third antecedent. However, such a third-order dependency analysis was thought too complex to carry out in the present state of experience with sequence analyses, and it would also be liable to result in a great many cells with zero frequency. Instead, parents' responses to child's comply were analyzed by hand for a subsample of children (see below).

Program I was designed to identify two kinds of first-order dependencies in the data, and hence, two separate conditional probabilities were calculated: (1) The conditional probability of a child response R_j occurring, given that a particular parent mode of control B_i had occurred in the two preceding time intervals, summing over all prior parent actions, $A_h : p(R_j \mid B_i)$. This is displayed in Table 22. (2) The conditional probability of a child response R_j occurring, given that a particular prior parent action A_h had occurred, summing over all intervening modes of parent control B_i − $p(R_j \mid A_h)$. This is shown in Table 24. The probability of the difference between the conditional probability and the base rate was evaluated by the method explained in Chapter 5, and the "facilitating power" was also computed.

Program II arranged the same basic counts in a somewhat different manner by regarding the verbal control (B_i) as the first antecedent of the child's comply or noncomply response (R_j) and parents' prior action (A_h) as the second antecedent. The program was designed to answer the question whether the occurrence of a given prior parent action, in addition to verbal control, significantly increases the facilitation or inhibition exerted by verbal control alone. In more formal terms, the analysis determined whether, in a given case, the first-order dependency was adequate to describe the process or whether second-order dependencies were operating. The program computed the second-order conditional probability of a child response (R_j) occurring, given that *both* a particular mode of control *and* a particular parent prior action had occurred: $p(R_j \mid B_i, A_h)$. (Parent prior actions within two 10-sec intervals preceding the verbal control were counted.) It compared this probability with the first-order probability, $p(R_j \mid B_i)$ in the same way that Program I compared the first-order probability with the base rate. The crucial question is whether the difference between the first- and the second-order probabilities is significant, and the probability of this difference was therefore evaluated by the method previously described.

Effects of Parents' Actions on Compliance and Noncompliance

The patterns of facilitation and inhibition are first presented for the data summed over all children (see Table 22). (Reasons for pooling the data were presented in Chapter 5.) Let us first consider the degree of compliance that the children displayed overall. If we omit "no verbal control," the average percentage of comply to all mother's verbal control statements together is 54.3%, the average for noncomply is 33.0%, and that for "neither" is 12.7%. The corresponding percentages for father are 61.1% comply, 28.6% noncomply, and 10.3% "neither." Thus, "neither" plays a comparatively minor role in the ecology of obedience once the parent has expressed a request, as one would expect. Differences between mother and father for comply and noncomply are significant (see Table 27).

Table 22. Patterns of Facilitation and Inhibition of Child Comply and Noncomply by Parents' Verbal Control[a]

		Child successors					
		Comply		Noncomply		Neither	
		Mother control (N = 136)					
Antecedents	N:	10015		5879		60490	
Mother mode of control	Base rate:	.053		.031		.321	
		CP	FP	CP	FP	CP	FP
Command-prohibition		.52[b]	8.76	.32[b]	9.34	.16[b]	−.50
Suggestion		.58[b]	9.88	.31[b]	8.88	.12[b]	−.64
Reasoning		.46[b]	7.59	.31	8.98	.23[b]	−.27
No Verbal Control		.02[b]	−.59	.01[b]	−.64	—	—
		Father control (N = 120)					
	N:	4562		2031		25319	
Father mode of control	Base rate:	.027		.012		.151	
		CP	FP	CP	FP	CP	FP
Command–prohibition		.60[b]	20.94	.28[b]	22.26	.12[b]	−.21
Suggestion		.66[b]	23.01	.25[b]	19.73	.09[b]	−.38
Reasoning		.57[b]	19.85	.23[b]	17.92	.20[c]	.33
No verbal control		.02[b]	−.22	.01[c]	−.11	—	—

[a] CP = conditional probability; FP = facilitating power = (conditional probability − base rate)/base rate. Minus sign for facilitating power indicates antecedent acts as inhibitor. The p values indicate significance of difference between conditional probability and base rate (significance test adapted from Goodman, 1965).
[b] $p < .001$.
[c] $p < .05$.

The "comply ratio" to both mother and father together (CR = Comply/[Comply + Noncomply]) was .65, averaged over all children. This ratio is somewhat higher than the proportions listed above because the commands, etc., followed by neither comply nor noncomply were not counted in the denominator of the ratio for this calculation. (Minton et al., 1971, also found about 60% compliance with commands in a home situation.)

Father's seeming ability to secure greater compliance with his wishes is not necessarily due to his greater forcefulness or commanding air. Mother issued far more control statements than father: 87.5 commands and prohibitions on average per mother, as against 37.4 per father. This difference is partly due to mother's spending more time with the child than father did, but even per minute present, her command–prohibition rate was .38 and his .25, so the reason may also be that she generally feels more responsible for the child's behavior and has a tendency to intervene more. It may well be for this reason that the child turns a selectively deaf ear to her. Though mother's rate of control statements is significantly higher than father's, the correlation between the numbers of commands and prohibitions issued by mother and father is .51 ($p < .001$), indicating considerable similarity in parents' disciplinary approaches.[1]

First-Order Antecedents

Let us now look at the effect that various modes of control (the first-order antecedents) have as controlling stimuli for comply, etc., ignoring the second-order antecedents A_h at time T-2 (Table 22). For mother, the probability of comply is highest following suggestion and then decreases progressively for command–prohibition and reasoning. The probability of noncomply is highest following command and decreases slightly for reasoning and suggestion. The probability of "neither" is depressed by the occurrence of any mode of verbal control. After no verbal control, the probability of comply or noncomply is very slight, as might be expected. The relationships for father are very similar, except that the probability of noncomply decreases progressively from command–prohibition to suggestion to reasoning. It appears that suggestion is the parent's, and particularly the mother's, most effective instrument of control. The significance of differences between categories of verbal control in eliciting comply, etc., was tested by chi square. All six tests for command–prohibition versus suggestion, command–prohibition versus reasoning, and reasoning versus suggestion, for father and mother separately, proved significant at the .001 level.

If we examine the question which of the two, comply or noncomply, is facilitated more readily by the various modes of control by comparing the respective "facilitating powers" (*FP*) (see Chapter 5), we see that suggestion facilitates comply more than it does noncomply, relative to their base rates, whereas both command–prohibition and reasoning are relatively more effective facilitators of noncomply. These relationships apply for both mother and father, except that reasoning in the case of father boosts comply more than noncomply. However, what is most striking is that all father's modes of control boost both comply and noncomply much more powerfully than do mother's modes of control. This is a reflection of the greatly reduced natural occurrence of both comply and noncomply to father in the record (i.e., of their lower base rates), which in turn is due to the lower number of control statements he issued. As was pointed out in the last chapter, a lower

---

[1] In the following tables and figures, the probability of the difference between conditional probability and base rate (shown by letter superscripts) was evaluated independently for each successor. For simultaneous confidence testing, lower significance levels have to be assigned, following the method described in Chapter 5. For Table 22, with three successors to be evaluated simultaneously, in order to reach an overall significance level of .10, which is reasonable with this stringent criterion, we assigned the following significance levels, with more lenient probabilities being assigned to the more important variables: comply, .05; noncomply, .05; "neither," .0001.

base rate can more easily be boosted to many times its original size than a higher one.

The numbers of individual children for whom the various modes of verbal control showed significant facilitating or inhibiting effects on compliance or noncompliance were tabulated and are shown in Table 23. The pattern of relationships was similar to that for the pooled data, with the exception that command–prohibition, and not suggestion, was the most frequent facilitator of comply for both mother and father (it also facilitated noncomply for a larger number of children than any other form of control). This seemingly greater effectiveness of commands–prohibitions is due to the fact that they occurred more frequently than suggestions as antecedents with all families, and, in general, a larger number of antecedents tends to produce significance more readily. However, the finding arising from the pooled data—namely, that suggestion is the most powerful facilitator of

Table 23. Number of Children for Whom Parents' Modes of Verbal Control Are Significant Antecedents ($p < .05$) of Comply, Noncomply, or Neither[a]

	Child successors					
	Comply		Noncomply		Neither	
	Facil	Inhib	Facil	Inhib	Facil	Inhib
Mother Antecedents	Mother ($N = 136$)					
Commands–prohibitions	136	0	130	0	4	101
	(92,44)		(90,40)		(0,4)	(77,24)
Suggestion	125	0	106	1	0	82
	(82,43)		(71,35)	(1,0)		(62,20)
Reasoning control	83	0	54	0	3	23
	(51,32)		(32,22)		(1,2)	(18,5)
No verbal control	1	94	0	96	N.A.	N.A.
	(0,1)	(76,18)		(73,23)		
Father antecedents	Father ($N = 120$)					
Commands–prohibitions	115	0	95	0	6	42
	(74,41)		(61,34)		(1,5)	(33,9)
Suggestions	89	0	53	1	9	33
	(53,36)		(27,26)	(1,0)	(3,6)	(26,7)
Reasoning control	30	0	7	0	7	2
	(17,13)		(3,4)		(3,4)	(2,0)
No verbal control	3	37	0	23	N.A.	N.A.
	(0,3)	(29,8)		(16,7)		

[a] Facil. = facilitator; Inhib. = inhibitor. Figures in brackets are numbers of twins (first) and of singletons (second). N of twins = 92 (76 for father); N of singletons = 44.

comply—is true both absolutely (for the conditional probability) and relatively to the base rate (for the facilitating power). It is also less influenced by statistical artifact and seems more meaningful psychologically.

Table 24 displays the effects of parents' prior actions, summed over all modes of control. These are here also treated as first-order antecedents. The results are very similar for mother and father. We first note that all conditional probabilities are considerably lower than those for verbal control (Table 22). This is a platitudinous and unsurprising finding in that any form of verbal control is much more likely to be followed by compliance or noncompliance than any other action is. However, at least it strengthens intuitive confidence in the trustworthiness of the counts.

As seen in the FP index, all four categories of antecedents are significant facilitators of both comply and noncomply, but they differ in degree of facilitating power—for both comply and noncomply their strength is in the order: physical control, negative action, positive action, neutral action. Physical control and negative action are more facilitative of noncomply than of comply, relative to their respective base rates, and the reverse holds for positive and neutral action. However, it is notable that for both comply and noncomply, physical control and negative action are more powerful activators and galvanizers than are positive and neutral action. As the comparison is within each successor (columns) and for the same base rate, this finding cannot be explained as an effect of initially lower base rates for one side of the comparison.

Effects for individual children (shown in Table 25) can be seen to be far fewer than when verbal control was considered the antecedent.

Table 24. Patterns of Facilitation and Inhibition of Comply and Noncomply by Parents' Prior Actions over All Modes of Control[a]

		Child successors						
		Mother (N = 136)				Father (N = 120)		
		Comply		Noncomply		Comply		Noncomply	
Antecedents	N:	10015		5879		4562		2031	
Parental prior actions	Base rate:	.053		.031		.027		.012	
		CP	FP	CP	FP	CP	FP	CP	FP
Physical control		.16[b]	2.05	.15[b]	3.75	.14[b]	4.00	.11[b]	8.20
Negative actions		.13[b]	1.39	.09[b]	1.98	.13[b]	3.76	.07[b]	4.87
Positive actions		.12[b]	1.26	.05[b]	.68	.11[b]	3.00	.04[b]	2.28
Neutral actions		.07[b]	.40	.04[b]	.33	.08[b]	1.91	.03[b]	1.77

[a] CP = conditional probability; FP = facilitating power = (conditional probability − base rate)/base rate.
[b] $p < .001$ for difference between conditional probability and base rate (significance test adapted from Goodman, 1965).

Table 25. Number of Children for Whom Parents' Prior Actions Are Significant Antecedents ($p < .05$) of Comply or Noncomply[a]

| | Child Successors | | | |
| | Comply | | Noncomply | |
	Facilitator	Inhibitor	Facilitator	Inhibitor
Mother antecedents	Mother ($N = 136$)			
Physical control	4	0	10	0
	(1,3)		(6,4)	
Negative actions	23	0	18	0
	(9,14)		(5,13)	
Positive actions	57	0	11	2
	(19,38)		(5,6)	(2,0)
Neutral actions	49	5	24	7
	(12,37)	(5,0)	(5,19)	(6,1)
Father antecedents	Father ($N = 120$)			
Physical control	3	0	4	0
	(1,2)		(2,2)	
Negative actions	14	0	3	0
	(5,9)		(0,3)	
Positive actions	42	0	7	2
	(17,25)		(3,4)	(2,0)
Neutral actions	55	0	15	0
	(21,34)		(9,6)	

[a] Figures in brackets are numbers of twins (first) and of singletons (second). N of twins = 92 (76 for father); N of singletons = 44.

Second-Order Antecedents

We now turn to the results of Program II, which sought to determine whether taking account of a second antecedent, too, would materially change the facilitating (inhibiting) effect that the first antecedent—verbal control—alone had on compliance or noncompliance.[2]

The actual frequencies of comply, noncomply, and neither shown in Figures 13 and 14 (in parentheses) differ from those shown in Table 22. This is because this analysis omitted instances of comply, etc., that were not pre-

[2] The differences between nine first-order conditional probabilities (successors) and the pertinent second-order conditional probabilities were assessed for significance. Individual significance levels were assigned so as to result in an overall significance level of .10 for the simultaneous confidence test, with more lenient probabilities assigned to the more important variables, as explained above. Differences that do not remain significant under simultaneous confidence testing are marked accordingly in the figures.

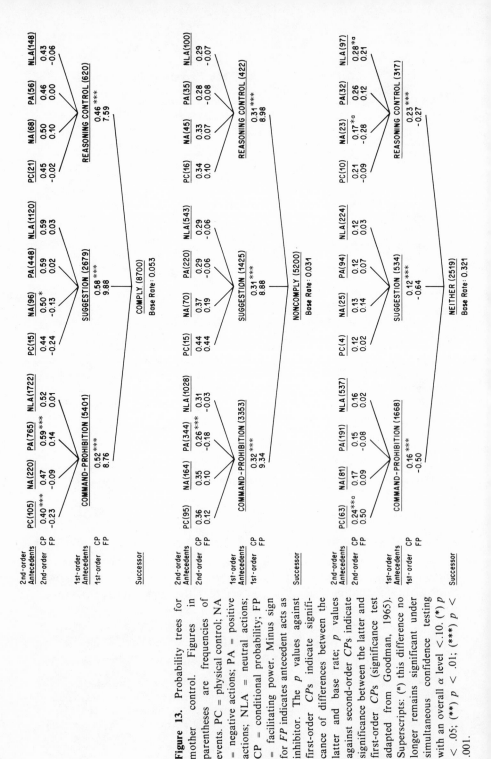

Figure 13. Probability trees for mother control. Figures in parentheses are frequencies of events. PC = physical control; NA = negative actions; PA = positive actions; NLA = neutral actions; CP = conditional probability; FP = facilitating power. Minus sign for FP indicates antecedent acts as inhibitor. The p values against first-order CPs indicate significance of differences between the latter and base rate; p values against second-order CPs indicate significance between the latter and first-order CPs (significance test adapted from Goodman, 1965). Superscripts: (ª) this difference no longer remains significant under simultaneous confidence testing with an overall α level <.10. (*) p < .05; (**) p < .01; (***) p < .001.

ceded by a form of verbal control. The base rates of the successors and the conditional probabilities and *FP*s of the first-order antecedents, shown in these figures, are the same as those that appear in Table 22.

In the present analysis, when parents' prior actions are considered as second-order antecedents, it can be seen from the second-order conditional probabilities that relatively few of the possible combinations make a significant difference to the control already exercised by the first-order antecedents. It will be noted that even where the second antecedent is significant, the *FP*s[3] are much lower than those for the first-order antecedents shown here, or those in Table 24. In other words, the extra facilitating effect afforded by a prior antecedent, over and above that exerted by verbal control alone, is much less than when the same antecedent—say, positive actions—is considered a first-order antecedent on its own. Those effects that remain significant are, however, of interest. Let us consider the results for mother (Figure 13). When physical control is added to command–prohibition, far from enhancing the latter's effectiveness, it actually detracts significantly from its facilitating effect on compliance. The addition of positive action, on the other hand, strengthens the facilitating effect of command–prohibition on compliance and makes noncompliance a less likely consequence. Again, the effectiveness of suggestion in eliciting compliance is weakened by the addition of negative action as a second-order antecedent; that is, the mother is less likely to achieve the child's compliance by a simple suggestion, if this was preceded by some aversive action on her part. "Neither comply nor noncomply" is somewhat more likely when physical control is added to commands, and it is a little less likely when negative actions are added to reasoning. These effects, however, do not stand up when they are evaluated by the stricter simultaneous confidence test.

Looking at the parallel results for father (Figure 14), we see that the effects of the different modes of verbal control are very similar to those for mother. Physical control and positive action, when added to command–prohibition as second-order antecedents, produce effects that parallel those for mother, except that they are somewhat weaker. Physical control by father, as a second-order antecedent, however, significantly increases the facilitating effect of suggestion on *noncompliance* and lessens that on compliance.

The number of children for whom second-order antecedents were significant additional facilitators (inhibitors) was ascertained. There were relatively few children for whom, individually, the addition of a second-order antecedent made a significant difference to the facilitation afforded by verbal control alone. Where there were more than one or two children for whom a given combination was significant, the trend of the pooled data

[3] *FP*s here express the facilitating power of second-order antecedents relative to first-order antecedents: $FP = [p(R_j|B_i, A_h) - p(R_j|B_i)]/p(R_j|B_i)$.

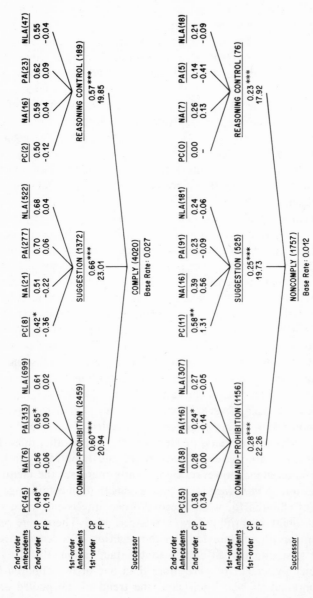

Figure 14. Probability trees for father control. "Neither" not shown as no second-order antecedent was significant. Figures in parentheses are frequencies of events. PC = physical control; NA = negative actions; PA = positive actions; NLA = neutral actions; CP = conditional probability; FP = facilitating power. Minus sign for *FP* indicates antecedent acts as inhibitor. The *p* values indicate significance of differences as for Figure 13.

a This difference no longer remains significant under simultaneous confidence testing with an overal α level < .10. *p < .05; **p < .01; *** < .001.

results was confirmed. This applies in particular to the effects of positive actions preceding commands: they supplied an added boost for the facilitation of comply and weakened the facilitation of noncomply.

Differences in Facilitation Effects between Twins and Singletons

The analyses that were carried out for the pooled data of the whole sample were repeated for the pooled data of twins and singletons separately. It was noted that the base rate of compliance (i.e., the proportion of comply out of all their actions) was *lower* for twins than for singletons, and conversely, the base rate of noncompliance for twins was *higher*. Similar differences were observed for the conditional probabilities of compliance and noncompliance following the various modes of verbal control. It has already been shown, too, that singleton parents engaged in more control behavior all round—commands–prohibitions, suggestions, and reasoning—than twin parents did (cf. Chapter 4).

A discriminant function analysis carried out on the 11 *FP*s that index the relative strength of facilitation exerted by the various modes of verbal control on compliance behavior showed that these measures overall discriminated significantly between twins and singleton groups (see Appendix IX). On the other hand, a parallel discriminant function analysis carried out for college-attenders versus non-college-attenders did *not* discriminate significantly between these groups, showing that control–compliance effects did not differ essentially between the levels of mothers' education.

To summarize the differences between twins and singletons in control–compliance relationships: parents' actions, whether they be verbal control or other prior actions, seem to have greater energizing influence on individual singletons than on twins, in that significant facilitating effects occur in general relatively more frequently for individual singletons, and significant inhibitory effects occur more frequently for twins (Table 23 and 25 display the figures). However we noted for compliance, as we did for attachment behavior, that twins seem to be especially sensitive to their parents' aversive actions, including physical control, which here appear to drive twins to more noncompliant behavior. Singletons, however, seem to depend, in their expression of obedience or disobedience, less on some overt mode of parental verbal control than do twins. Singletons may be actuated more readily by other subtler parental actions, e.g., praise or nonverbal gestures.

Parent Responses to Child Compliance and Noncompliance

As was noted earlier, to extend the formal sequence analysis to a parent's subsequent response to the child's comply or noncomply would amount to a third-order dependency analysis, and it was thought that this

would result in too complex and fragmented results. It was therefore
decided simply to identify parents' responses to comply and noncomply, and
for this purpose, a hand analysis of the data was carried out for 53
randomly selected children (36 twins and 17 singletons). Absent fathers
reduced the number of fathers for whom data are available to 49. The
analysis was done by hand in order to obtain a more fine-grained picture
that would take into account certain complexities that could not easily be
accommodated in a computer program, such as separating parents' reactions to compliance–noncompliance from their reactions to positive or negative actions in general; identifying which parent responds, or whether both
parents respond to compliance with a given parent's request; noting two successive parent responses to one child action; eliminating parental actions
that are not genuine responses to the preceding child action; and noting the
ultimate outcome of noncompliance sequences.

In this analysis, parents' responses were classified into categories
similar to the grouped actions (defined in Table 3). "Verbal control,"
however, here includes suggestions, as well as commands and prohibitions
(see Table 26). Both mother and father responses to a child's compliance or
noncompliance within two 10-sec intervals were counted, and several
responses to a child's actions were recorded, where these occurred.
However, care was taken to exclude parent actions that were not genuine
reactions to the child's compliance–noncompliance, as judged by the
context. "No response" was recorded if the parent who issued the request

Table 26.   Mean Percentage of Parents' Responses to Child Compliance and
Noncompliance[a]

	Comply				Noncomply			
	Mother		Father		Mother		Father	
	Mean	Rank	Mean	Rank	Mean	Rank	Mean	Rank
Parent responses	%	Order	%	Order	%	Order	%	Order
Positive response	15.35	4	12.80	4	10.75	4	11.94	4
Negative response	1.76	5	1.54	6	6.00	5	4.11	5
Neutral response	24.25	2	22.02	2	16.26	3	17.90	3
Verbal control	20.78	3	18.50	3	26.48	2	25.63	2
Reasoning control	1.75	6	0.98[b]	7	3.89	6	2.53	7
Physical control	0.88	7	2.11	5	3.45	7	3.55	6
No response	35.18	1	42.07[b]	1	33.19	1	34.34	1

[a] N: mother = 53; N: father = 49; N: comply = 5286; N: noncomply = 3357.
[b] $p < .05$ for difference between mother and father (two-tailed t test).

subsequently did not respond to the child's comply or noncomply. The percentages of different categories of response displayed in Table 26 are for all responses, whether first or later responses, within the two time intervals.

Among the reactions by parents to the child's compliance, by far the most common one, for both mother and father, was to make no response at all, followed in frequency by a neutral response (see rank order in Table 26); that is, in over 50% of cases the child was given no particular reward or reinforcement for his compliance. Father was distinctly more likely than the mother to make no response at all (difference significant). The next most common response was for mother or father to continue the chain of request–comply/noncomply by issuing another request or suggestion. Positive resonses are only the fourth most likely reaction to occur for both mother and father. This would include such actions as smiling at the child, praising him, playing with him, or cuddling him. The above four categories of response, in fact, make up 95% of both mother's and father's responses to the child's compliance.

The remaining categories are obviously rarer, and for them, the rank order differs somewhat for mother and father. The next most common response by father was some form of physical control: slapping or restraining. For mother it was a nonphysical negative action, such as showing displeasure or criticizing or threatening the child. Although both physical control and negative action immediately followed the child's compliance and were judged to be related to it, they are more intelligible in the context of the whole situation of which the compliant act formed a part; for example, parents may be reacting to another ongoing obnoxious action by the child. Justification of orders or rules was the next category of mother's responses—and the last one for father. In these cases, mother or father evidently felt that some kind of explanation for the matter at issue was appropriate, even after compliance. The greater use of reasoning by mother, compared with father, after compliance (the difference is significant) reflects her general tendency to resort to this form of control in interacting with the child more than father did.

The responses to the child's noncompliance were somewhat, but not dramatically, different from those to his compliance. "No response" was still the most frequent form of reaction, but verbal control, as one might expect, was the second most frequent response for noncompliance. Negative action and physical control, although low in the rank order, showed a greater frequency than after compliance: together they made up 9.45% of mother's responses and 7.66% of father's.

The kind of response that parents make to the child's compliance seems more a function of the overall probability of occurrence (base rate) of the different action categories than it is determined contingently by the nature of the child's act. The responses, on the whole, are not particularly reinforcing for compliance. Mother's rank order for response to comply, shown in Table 26, follows exactly the rank order of the overall probabilities of occurrence of these categories, this rank order being (leaving aside "No action") neutral actions, then verbal control, positive actions, negative actions, reasoning, and physical control. The more flexible approach of the hand analysis precluded a formal testing of the difference between conditional probability and base rate. Nevertheless, by comparing the proportions of different categories following noncomply (these proportions equal conditional probabilities) with their base rates, some changes in magnitude can be detected, which also imply changes in rank order from base rate: following noncomply the proportions of neutral actions and positive actions go down, whereas those of reasoning and physical control, and especially of verbal control, rise. The choice of verbal control is realistic and appropriate, if eventual compliance is the goal, since compliance is likely to follow verbal control 54% of the time for mother and 62% of the time for father. However, the probability of parents' choosing any category other than verbal control bears no relation to the probability of compliance following it. This can be seen if we compare the rank order of the remaining categories, as employed by mother after noncompliance, with the probability of child compliance's occurring after the respective category (probability in parenthesis): neutral action (.07), positive action (.12), negative action (.13), reasoning control (.46), and physical control (.16).

The outstanding fact is that both compliance and noncompliance are most often (roughly one-third of the time) followed by no response by parents within the following 20 sec. This suggests that either another act of compliance (noncompliance) intervened before parents responded, or that they are willing to drop the matter or pretend that nothing had happened.

Hetherington et al. (1978) studied parents' responses to child's compliance and noncompliance in a laboratory playroom situation, and Minton et al. (1971) investigated mothers' reactions to child violations in the home. Their findings reveal some similarities, and also some striking differences compared with the foregoing results. Hetherington et al. (1978) (comparisons are based on their figures for boys in intact families) found, as I did, that mother engaged in physical control rather less and in explanations more than father. Minton et al. (1971) also noted that mother's most common actual response to a violation was verbal prohibition or direction. On the other hand, in both the other studies, parental response of some kind to compliance or noncompliance occurred more frequently, and "no response" occurred less frequently than in the present study. One can only speculate as to the reasons for these differences: they may arise from differing definitions of what constitutes a violation and a parental response or, in the case of the Hetherington study, from the fact that the data were based on nursery-school-age children who were observed in a laboratory and not their own homes.

"Second-Order Effects" of Father's Presence on Mother's Control Behavior

Previous writers have shown that mothers' and fathers' interactions with their children are affected by the presence of the other spouse. Thus, Clarke-Stewart (1978) and Lamb (1976) found that both parents interact less with their infants when both of them are present than when each parent is alone with the child. Parke and O'Leary (1975) concluded, to the contrary, that fathers are stimulated to greater interaction with their neonate children by mother's presence. This last finding, however, may be due to the special circumstances (hospital surroundings) and the novelty of interacting with newly born infants.

We have already noted that fathers tend to issue fewer commands, both absolutely and in proportion to time present, but are obeyed more than mothers. It was therefore of special interest to discover how father's presence would affect the nature of the disciplinary interactions between mother and child—from mother's first command or suggestion to her later response to the child's compliance or noncompliance. Because fathers were alone with their children for relatively short periods only, the number of control instances did not warrant carrying out the converse comparison, that is, analyzing how mother's presence or absence affects father's disciplinary interactions with the child. However, comparisons between mother and father, when both were present, were possible.

The first part of this analysis—the examination of mothers' and fathers' control behavior and children's reactions to it—was carried out for the total sample by a specially written computer program. This separated out the time when mother was alone with the child from the time when both parents were present. Within each of these time periods, the program counted all control statements—commands, prohibitions, suggestions, and reasoning control—that each parent issued and expressed these as rates per minute. The percentage of these control verbs that was followed by comply or noncomply was also calculated, but if the number of control verbs by mother or father was less than five, this percentage was excluded from the analysis, as it would carry little meaning. The comparisons are shown in Table 27.

The effect of father's presence on the kind of interaction that mother has with the child when she sets out to change his behavior is clear-cut (top part of the table): mother uses fewer control verbs (i.e., intervenes less in the child's doings) and is obeyed relatively more. In more general terms, the amount of interaction between mother and child is reduced by father's presence—this general statement will be confirmed by findings on speech to

Table 27.   Second-Order Effects Due to Father's Presence and Comparisons between Mother and Father: Control and Comply $(N = 120)^a$

	Rates of control verbs per min	Percentage of comply by child	Percentage of noncomply by child
Mother alone	.674 ⎱$_b$	53.15 ⎱$_c$	32.90
Mother—both present	.436 ⎰	56.00 ⎰ ⎱$_b$	32.59 ⎱$_b$
Father—both present	.370	60.86	28.53 ⎰
Mother—total time	.536 ⎱$_b$	54.31 ⎱$_b$	33.00 ⎱$_b$
Father—total time	.376 ⎰	61.06	28.55 ⎰

^{a} Percentages are calculated out of number of control statements issued during given period. (Wilcoxon matched pairs signed rank test, two-tailed, for difference between bracketed means.)
^{b} $p < .001$.
^{c} $p < .10$.

be discussed in Chapter 7, and it is consonant with Clarke-Stewart's (1978) and Lamb's (1977) findings on younger infants. It is indeed understandable that when father is present, he takes over some of the responsibility for the child and mother feels less need to intervene.

The relations between mother's and father's control behavior and the child's compliance to each, when both parents are present and overall, are presented in the lower sections of Table 27. Even when father is present, too, and mother therefore feels relieved of some of the responsibility for the child's doings and safety, she still engages in more attempts to change the child's behavior than father does, although the difference does not reach significance. On the other hand, he achieves more compliance with his commands, etc., when both parents are present, as he does overall. The possible reasons were discussed earlier in this chapter. It is noteworthy that his presence also increases the likelihood of the child's complying with mother's directions, so that it seems his mere presence adds authority to her requests. In many cases, of course, father also backed mother's wishes in some nonverbal way or by an earlier request, although the comply was counted for the parent who issued the immediately preceding request. (We examined the effects of father's reinforcement of mother's commands by hand in a subsample; this analysis is presented in the next section).

The figures shown here were broken down into the subgroups of twins and singletons. The results for the periods when mother was alone with the child and when both parents were present were very similar to the general trend of the findings reported above. The rate of control verbs per minute and the percentage of comply were higher for singletons in all periods; the percentage of noncomply was higher for twins. Differences, however, tended to be more significant for mother than for father.

As described earlier, the response by parents to the child's compliance or noncompliance were analyzed by hand on a subsample of 53 children.

This analysis was carried out separately for "mother alone" and "both present" periods (the latter for 49 children, whose fathers were present). For the period when both parents were in the home, a three-stage analysis was performed from the original control statement to the subsequent parental response to compliance or noncompliance, in order to establish whether there was a tendency for the originator of the request also to react to the child's response. A count was therefore made of who issued a given command, etc., in the first place, and who replied to the ensuing compliance or noncompliance by the child. Responses by mother and father were counted if they occurred within two 10-sec intervals of the child's response, and if both replied, both responses were counted. The results can be seen in Table 28. There was, indeed, a strong tendency for the originator to react to the child's responses to his/her request. However, we also see that mother reacted more to the child's compliance with her own commands than father did to compliance with his commands; moreover, she reacted more to the child's compliance with father's commands than father did in the reverse situation (second and third lines in Table 28.). The resulting chi square is significant ($p < .005$). However, when we look at the reactions to noncompliance, we notice there is no significant difference in mother's and father's respective reply rates.

In what way did father's presence exert an influence on the *manner* in which mother responded to the child, and how did mother's and father's reactions differ from each other when they were both present? Table 29 tells this tale and shows where significant differences occurred. Father's presence stimulated mother to respond more positively and less neutrally to the child's compliance than she did when she was on her own. Father's presence

Table 28. Mother versus Father Responses to Child Compliance and Noncompliance ($N = 49$)[a]

	Comply				Noncomply			
	Command etc. given by				Command etc. given by			
	Mother		Father		Mother		Father	
Response by	N	%	N	%	N	%	N	%
Same parent	627	74.6	533	67.1	338	69.0	259	67.3
Other parent	140	16.6	177	22.3	98	20.0	84	21.8
Both	74	8.8	84	10.6	54	11.0	42	10.9
	841		794		490		385	

$\chi^2 = 11.23; p < .005$ $\chi^2 = 0.437$; nonsignificant
(two-tailed test)

[a] "Same parent" means same parent who issued command.

Table 29. Mean Percentage of Parents' Responses to Child Compliance and Noncompliance: "Mother Alone" versus "Both Present" Periods $(N = 49)^a$

		Mean percentage			
		Positive response	Reasoning control	Neutral response	No response
Responses to comply	M alone	13.11 $\}_b$		28.39 $\}_c$	31.49
	M—Both present	17.35		22.20	34.95 $\}_b$
	F—Both present	13.30 $\}^b$		19.59	42.52
Responses to noncomply	M alone		5.18 $\}_a$	18.82 $\}_c$	30.99 $\}_e$
	M—Both present		2.27	14.90	39.21
	F—Both present		1.62	18.29	34.05

^{a} Superscripts refer to significance of differences between bracketed figures. Only variables for which significant differences exist are shown. M = mother; F = father.
^{b} $p < .02$.
^{c} $p < .10$.
^{d} $p < .001$ (two-tailed t test).
^{e} $p < .05$.

also caused her to react differently to the child's noncomply: she used fewer neutral responses and far fewer explanations and more frequently made no response at all. It is interesting to note that when both were present, father ignored the child's *comply* far more frequently than mother, and he ignored the child's *noncomply* less frequently than she did (though the difference was not significant).

Summary

1. Mothers issued commands or prohibitions on average every 2½ minutes, but fathers only every 4 minutes during the time that either of them was with the child. The children complied with father's directions more than with mother's, and overall they complied about 60% of the time.

2. The probability of compliance by the child is highest after a mild suggestion by his parents, though this result may be an artifact of the coding (see "Discussion" section). A direct command or prohibition is the next most effective mode of verbal control, indicating that an authoritative stance best secures compliance on the spot.

3. Among parental actions other than verbal control, physical control and other negative actions (e.g., criticism) facilitate noncompliance more than compliance; the reverse holds for positive and neutral parental actions.

4. If we look at the additional effect that joining other parental actions to verbal control has on the child's compliance, we find that physical control and negative actions, when added to commands, lessen the effective-

ness of the latter in securing compliance, whereas joining positive action (e.g., smiling, praise) to commands increases this effectiveness.

5. The effects of compliance–noncompliance on parents' subsequent actions are relatively small: about one-third of the time, parents make no response, thus neither rewarding compliance nor punishing noncompliance. The only deviation from generally expected probabilities is that after non-compliance, there is an increased likelihood that parents will use some form of verbal control.

6. Father tends to leave it to mother to respond to the child's compliance, but he responds equally with her to noncompliance.

7. Father's presence has an indirect effect on mother–child relations: mother then intervenes less and is obeyed more than when she is alone with the child.

OTHER ASPECTS OF PARENTS' CONTROL BEHAVIOR

Incidence and Effects of "Repeated Directions"

There are many occasions when parents do not secure immediate compliance with their requests. They may then make their wishes known repeatedly, either by directly repeating their original direction or by varying the form, for example, making a general critical remark, promising the child something if he carries out their wish, uttering a threat, or intervening physically. We regarded all these variations in parents' attempts to influence the child, if they were addressed to the same issue, as "repeated directions". Such repeated directions are of special interest in an account of parent–child disciplinary encounters. Are they characteristic of some special quality in the relationship between parent and child? How often do they happen? Are some parents more prone to them than others, and what kind of parents are those who use them frequently? How effective are they? What kind of situation tends to elicit them? Moreover, to understand the triadic interaction between mother, father, and child, it is also important to know when father reinforces mother's request by repeating it himself (and vice versa) and how effective such reinforcement is.

A special analysis of control sequences was therefore carried out by hand for the sample of 40 children for whom parents' responsiveness was also examined (cf. Chapter 3). To count as "repeated direction," the sequence had to start with one of the modes of verbal control (prohibition, suggestion, or reasoning control), and it had to pursue the same issue without interruption. However, the repetition of the wish did not have to be a direct mode of control; it could take some other form, as indicated above. When two directions followed each other in quick succession so that the child did not have a chance to show compliance or noncompliance, they were, however, not coded separately. We also noted whether the outcome of the whole sequence was compliance, noncompliance, or "neither." Intermediate noncomplies or doubtful responses were not counted in the final outcome.

The most important comparisons appear in Table 30. It will be noted that the percentage of complies to all directions appears to be higher here than that reported earlier in this chapter. The reason is that the percentage

Table 30. Repeated and Reinforced Directions ($N = 40$)[a]

	Mother means	Father means	p of difference between M and F
% of repeated directions series out of all directions	17.53	13.28	.004
% comply to single directions	73.03 ⎱ p: .003	74.15 ⎱ p: .427	.154
% comply to repeated directions series	65.62 ⎰	69.75 ⎰	.258
% of M directions reinforced by F (col. 1) and F directions reinforced by M (col. 2)	2.47	8.16	.000
% comply to M directions reinforced by F (col. 1) and F directions reinforced by M (col. 2)	77.46 ⎱ p: .237	68.82 ⎱ p: .486	.380
% comply to all directions (single and series)	71.76 ⎰	74.45[b] ⎰	.023

[a] Significance levels refer to difference between bracketed figures. (Wilcoxon Matched Pairs Signed Rank Test: two-tailed.) M = mother; F = father.
[b] The reader may be puzzled why this figure is higher even than the mean of % comply to single directions (74.15%). This occurred because the % comply to all directions, for each child, was weighted by the frequency of comply to single directions plus the frequency of comply to repeated directions series and these frequencies will differ. A fictitious example would be:

Child	% comply to single directions	% comply to repeated directions	Weighted % comply to all directions
A	17/17 = 100%	2/5 = 40%	19/22 = 86.4%
B	6/13 = 46%	5/5 = 100%	11/18 = 61.1%
Average of A & B:	73%	70%	73.75%

Correlations

	Repeated direction %—F	Child comply ratio	Compliance rating	Internalized standards rating	Relative frequency child requests
Repeated direction %—M	.45[b]	−.32[a]	−.41[b]	−.64[c]	.40[b]
Repeated direction %—F	—	−.32[a]	−.06	−.06	.34[a]

[a] $p < .05$.
[b] $p < .01$.
[c] $p < .001$.

shown here refers to the final outcome of the repeated-directions series, leaving out of account the intermediate noncomplies or "neithers."

Mother evidently had a greater tendency to repeat her directions than father did. However, repeating the request did not increase the likelihood of the child's complying with it; on the contrary, that likelihood was smaller for repeated directions for both mother and father. It appears, then, that once the child has shown some resistance to the parent's wish, as evidenced by the fact that the request has to be repeated, the resistance will continue, although the parent is still likely to get his way in the end. Indeed, the percentage of comply as the final outcome of repeated directions is still considerably higher than the percentage of comply to all control statements counted singly (54.3% for mother and 61.1% for father; see p. 148).

The percentage of repeated directions out of all directions was used as an index of a parent's propensity to repeat requests. By correlating this measure with various indices of child's compliance, we could determine whether "repeaters" tended to have more or less compliant children than those who repeated dirctions less frequently. (The tendency to repeat ranged from 3% to 32% for mothers and from 0% to 41% for fathers.) From the correlations at the bottom of the table, it can be seen that mother repeaters had children who were less compliant and had internalized parental standards less, as indexed by all measures, than nonrepeaters. Repetition by fathers, on the other hand, was significantly associated with noncompliance only for the measure "comply ratio." Since this, however, is derived from an actual count of instances of compliance and noncompliance, it is the most direct and most immediately valid indicator of the child's compliance, and hence the most important one. We must remember, of course, that correlations by themselves do not tell us the direction of the effect: it may be that hearing his parents repeat directions regularly makes a child less obedient to any single one of them, but, on the other hand, a less compliant child may also generate in his parents a tendency, or may force his parents necessarily, to be repetitive in their directives. It is noteworthy that the strongest association obtains between mother's repeating requests and the child's *not* having made parental standards his own. Again, the direction of influence may flow either way, and indeed, we seem to have evidence here of the existence of a reciprocal "coercive cycle."

It is interesting to note that the parents' tendency to repeat directions is echoed by the child's inclination to utter many requests and that mother's propensity to repeat is reflected by a similar disposition in father. The tendency to escalate directions, rather than to leave it at a single one, is evidently symptomatic of a family and expresses a systematic family "climate." That mother's tendency to repeat directions has a negative connotation for her whole attitude toward the child can be seen from the significant negative correlations that this measure has with the positive actions, responsiveness, and appropriateness and the positive association it shows with her negative actions (cf. Table 10). Father's tendency to repeat has similar significant negative relations with *mother's* benevolent characteristics and positive relations with her adverse ones, but not with his own traits. It appears that this is a practice in which he takes his cue from mother and that it is not part of a cohesive personality configuration for him in the way that it is for her.

The repeated direction analysis was carried out for singletons and twins separately. Repeated directions seemed to play the same role for each of these subgroups as they played for the sample as a whole; that is, the same kind of relationships between mother and father and between compliance to single and repeated directions were apparent in both subgroups, except that some of the differences were no longer significant. However, mothers issued relatively more repeated directions to twins than to singletons, though the difference did not reach significance. This finding no doubt reflects singletons' greater readiness to comply, which makes repeated directions unnecessary.

Instances in which father repeated mother's direction (in other words, reinforced it) and reverse cases of mother's reinforcing father's direction were identified, and the results of the analysis are also shown in Table 30. Mother tends to reinforce father's directions more than three times as often as father reinforces mother's; that is, she feels impelled to intervene more often. However, an interesting reversal of relationship can be observed: when father reinforces mother's directions, this increases the likelihood of compliance with her wishes, but when mother reinforces father's directions, this decreases the chance of the child's complying. This reversal of effects is noteworthy, even though the differences barely reach significance. It seems to indicate once again (as does the greater percentage of comply to father's commands overall in this subsample) the greater effectiveness of father's control for these boys, a thread that has been running through this whole chapter.

Example of Control Sequence

An example of a control sequence gives the flavor of such mother–child interactions that mere figures cannot, of course, capture. This sequence is taken from the coded record and amplified by explanations in longhand that are written underneath the code at the time of transcription. It comes from a twin family (border-line middle class) with no father in the house. All but one of mother's commands are addressed to one child, and the whole interaction occupied 90 sec during dinner (M = mother; C = child):

> C: My nose is dirty. M: What do you say? C: My dirty nose. M: What do you say? C: Clean it off. M: What do you say? (*C demands again.*) M: Is that how you ask nice? (*C demands again, then whines, then demands again with a*

yell.) M: Where's "please"? (*C demands again.*) M: Where's "please"? (*C demands again.*) M: Say "Please." (*C still does not comply. M feeds both twins.*) M (*to both*): Don't spill this milk. C: My nose is dirty. M: What do you say? C: Please. (*M shows her approval and cleans his nose.*) M: You can say sorry. C: Sorry. M: Just bad boys say bad words. Don't say bad words. (*C says something in compliance with M's wishes and M shows her approval. End of sequence.*)

(Where actual words are not quoted, the record does not specify what they were but only indicates, say, a demand or approval.)

How Different Issues Affect the Mode of Control and the Use of Repeated Directions

How does mother modulate her mode of control and which issues make her repeat her directions? These questions were examined in the subsample of 40 children. The proportions of commands–prohibitions, suggestions, and reasoning control evoked by different issues were ascertained, and so were the proportions of repeated directions (out of all directions) that the different issues called forth. These percentages can be seen in Tables 31 and 32.

"Stopping nuisance" and "care of objects" are among the top three issues to evoke mother's commands–prohibitions, and they are also among the top three to elicit repeated directions. The "nuisance" that parents would want to stop would include behavior such as yelling, demanding attention, whining, or crying. "Care of objects" involved issues such as

Table 31. **Proportions of Different Modes of Control for Different Issues: Mother Control ($N = 40$)**

	Mean percentage		
Issues	Command–prohibition	Suggestion	Reasoning control
Stopping "nuisance"	86.1	5.8	8.3
Eating and drinking	78.2	13.5	8.3
Care of objects	76.6	8.9	14.5
Interfering with siblings	72.3	17.5	10.2
Personal care and dressing	72.0	24.8	3.3
Giving things	71.5	22.4	6.1
Body movement	70.1	22.8	7.0
Ordinary dealing with objects	66.3	29.1	4.6
Clearing up	65.6	20.9	13.5
Asking for attention and affection	53.2	44.6	2.4
Verbal self-expression	41.9	56.5	1.6
Play	30.0	64.0	6.0
Overall mean	61.0	31.6	7.4

Table 32.   Proportions of Repeated Directions Out of All Directions for Different Issues (Maximum N = 40)

	Mother		Father	
	Rank order	Mean percentage	Rank order	Mean percentage
Clearing up	1	33.8	2	28.4
Care of objects	2	33.3	6	21.8
Stopping "nuisance"	3	30.2	5	22.0
Giving things	4	28.7	8	17.8
Interfering with siblings	5	27.1	3	23.9
Eating and drinking	6	22.7	4	22.4
Ordinary dealing with objects	7	20.7	1	30.0
Personal care and dressing	8	19.6	9	15.6
Body movement	9	19.0	7	18.3
Play	10	17.0	10	14.8
Verbal self-expression	11	11.8	12	11.6
Asking for attention and affection	12	9.6	11	12.1
Overall mean		17.5		13.3

standing on sofas and other furniture, throwing cookies on the floor, playing with matches, and so forth.

Looking at the proportions of different modes of control (Table 31), we can see that "stopping nuisance" is most likely to arouse a direct imperative and least likely to evoke suggestion or reasoning control. At the other end of the scale, there are issues that are more likely to elicit a milder suggestion than an imperative (e.g., play and asking the child to say something, like, "Say 'please,'" or "Count"), although overall, the predominant mode of control by far is command–prohibition. The reason that suggestion is such a frequent mode of control for play lies partly in the coding convention that repeated requests in a play situation would be coded as suggestions, whatever form they actually took. It will be noted also that parents ask for attention or affection mainly by making suggestions to this effect. Mothers use justification of their orders relatively more when the careful treatment of objects (toys, furniture, etc.) is at stake, when clearing up is to be done, and when the child in some way interferes with his brothers and sisters. It is, indeed, somewhat surprising—but also reassuring—that mother deals with interference with siblings by reasoning and suggestions to the extent that she does, in view of the potential physical danger to the sibling that may sometimes be involved.

The distribution of father's modes of control is very similar to mother's and is therefore not shown separately. Generally speaking, he uses reasoning control less than mother does and commands–prohibitions more, and this tendency is particularly pronounced when clearing up is at issue. The situation in which father explains and justifies his orders most (and does so as much as mother) is when the child interferes with siblings. It appears that both mother and father make a point of laying down general principles of behavior when the child is actually, or is in danger of, getting physically involved with his siblings.

The child is brought up most sharply, it seems, when he makes a nuisance of himself to his parents, and when proper and effective eating manners and the care of objects are involved. In such situations, pertaining to household convenience and damage to property, however, the children frequently do not obey immediately, and hence these issues also most often elicit repeated directions from mother. Father uses relatively fewer repeated commands when it is a question of the care of objects or of the child's being a nuisance, perhaps because one command by him suffices, or because he is less concerned about these matters. However, ordinary handling of objects (e.g., getting a toy or putting a chair in a certain place) rouses him to relatively many repeated commands, as does interference with siblings.

These, then, are the occasions when parents are most insistent, when the children take some persuading before they obey, and which as a result become sources of irritation. They strike one mainly by their ordinariness and the fact that they represent frequently occurring incidents in any family with young children. Since only a few of them involve any danger to persons, it looks as if in this latter area commands are swiftly obeyed. In general, however, there is a correlation (correlation of .61 between rank orders of use of commands–prohibitions and repeated directions for mother) between the imperiousness of the command and the likelihood that repeated and escalated directives will occur.

The following incident shows the child interfering with a sibling. It demonstrates how mother, by giving an explanation, makes her order understandable to the child and at the same time provides a cognitive structure and base from which the child can generalize to similar situations. The example also shows how parents often intermingle physical control with the use of reasoning. This was a singleton family, and the mother had some college education.

> (*Child plays roughly with 6-month-old baby brother, sitting on him.*) Mother: Get off him. (*Mother slaps child; child cries a little and talks to mother.*) Mother: Don't sit on him. You weigh too much. (*Child gets off brother.*)

In the following example, also a mix of physical control and reasoning, the mother is actuated by her concern for the protection of the furniture. This, too, was a singleton family, and mother had not completed high school.

> Mother: Hurry, get down. (*From table.*) Want me to get mad? Baby will copy you. (*Child romps around on table, not taking any notice.*) Mother: Don't, Frank. (*Mother removes him physically from table and places him near window from where he can look out.*)

Summary

1. Mother has a greater tendency to repeat directives (for the same issue) than father. The probability of gaining the child's compliance, however, is less (for both parents) after a series of repeated directives than after a single one; nevertheless, the percentage of complies even after series of repeated directions is 66%–70% (not counting intervening instances of noncompliance).

2. "Repeaters" tend of have children who are less compliant and who have internalized parental rules less well, and this relationship suggests the existence of a "coercive cycle," with parents and children instigating higher-intensity behavior in each other.

3. Mother, father, and child resemble, and perhaps imitate, each other in the propensity to repeat directives. This tendency has negative connotations for other maternal qualities.

4. Mother reinforces father's commands by one of her own more frequently than he reinforces hers. Her reinforcement reduces the chance of the child's complying, whereas his increases this probability.

5. Among the different modes of control, commands–prohibitions are used most prominently to stop the child from making a "nuisance" of himself (e.g., whining and crying); explanations are used most when it is a matter of ensuring careful treatment of objects, or when the child interferes with a sibling.

CORRELATES AND DETERMINANTS OF COMPLIANCE

As for attachment behavior, the more long-term and generalized effects of parents' actions on the child's compliance and vice versa were examined by a "remote effects" analysis and by multiple regression, or "trait" analyses.

Remote Effects of Parent Control Behavior and Child Compliance on Each Other

The purpose of the remote effects analysis was to discover whether parent behavior at one point in time had an effect on child behavior at a later point in time (or vice versa). In the case of compliance, we looked for such effects not only from one observation session to another—usually one week apart—but also from one situation to another, similar, situation within the same observation session.

We will first look at the effects from one observation to another, which were examined by cross-lagged panel analyses, a method described in the last chapter. The analyses were based on rates per minute of instances of parental control (i.e., the density of control) and on the percentage of comply out of the total of control verbs. The correlations are shown in Table 33. As in the analyses of attachment behavior, the significance levels were based on reduced degrees of freedom, first, because only one of each twin pair was counted, and furthermore, because some fathers were absent from one of the two observations.

The stability of the various modes of control across observations, it will be seen, was quite good, that of the comply percentage rather less so, particularly for comply to mother. The synchronous correlations between child comply percentage and mother's mode of control were almost all negative, though weak. It does appear that the density of mother's control statements and child comply are antithetical to each other. To tell us in which direction the influence flows, we look to the cross-lagged correlations and their differentials, as explained in the last chapter. Only one of these differences was significant: that for compliance and reasoning (diagrammed in Figure 15). The immediate effects of density of reasoning control and compliance on each other are negative, as indicated by the synchronous correlations. When we look at the remote effects, however, we notice that reasoning control at Time 1 (T1) is positively correlated with compliance at Time 2 (T2), and that compliance T1 is negatively correlated with reasoning control T2. These relationships suggest as the most plausible interpretation (1) that compliance decreases the density of reasoning control from Observation 1 to Observation 2, as we see here, *and* (2) that rate of reasoning in the medium term increases compliance. Psychologically one can interpret this as indicating that the child's tendency to comply reduces the need for mother to use reasoning in order to influence the child, both in the immediate present and over a medium time span. A high rate of reasoning control, on the other hand, in the long run creates a climate of compliance, although in the immediate present, the reverse tendency—of compliance's reducing the need for reasoning control—is more powerful.[4]

While the direction of influence cannot be clearly interpreted for the other modes of control used by mother, because of the lack of significant cross-lagged differentials, it should be noted that the signs of the correlations in the other cases are the same as for reasoning control: the correla-

---

[4] The rival hypothesis would be that density of reasoning control is the causative factor in the negative correlations, so that at T1, it reduces compliance in the immediate situation, while showing stability to T2, thus producing a negative correlation between compliance T1 and reasoning control T2. This hypothesis, however, becomes implausible in view of the positive cross-lagged correlation between reasoning T1 and compliance T2, but particularly in view of the nature of the partial correlations (shown in parentheses), which indicate the residual associations, with the influence of the possibly "causative" variable at T1 removed in each case.

Table 33. Cross-Lagged, Synchronous, and Autocorrelations for Child Compliance and Parent Control Behavior Observation 1 versus Observation 2[a]

Maternal mode of control	Autocorrelations T1:T2	Child compliance: autocorrelation T1 × T2: .176[b]				Difference: $p < .05$
		Synchronous correlations		Cross-lagged correlations		
		CT1:MT1	CT2:MT2	CT1:MT2	MT1:CT2	
Commands–prohibitions	.575[c]	-.251[d]	-.226[d]	-.079	.115	
Suggestions	.623[c]	-.059	.042	-.042	.031	
Reasoning control	.479[c]	-.196[b]	-.083	-.142	.174[b]	
Total control verbs	.652[c]	-.220[d]	-.137	-.091	.115	

Paternal mode of control	Autocorrelations T1:T2	Child compliance: autocorrelation T1 × T2: .332[e]				
		CT1:FT1	CT2:FT2	CT1:FT2	FT1:CT2	
Commands–prohibitions	.674[c]	.000	-.132	.014	-.098	
Suggestions	.426[c]	.129	.040	.095	.011	
Reasoning control	.512[c]	.042	-.081	-.010	-.077	
Total control verbs	.570[c]	.066	-.085	.051	-.060	

[a] C = child; M = mother; F = father; T = time. Child compliance: Percentage comply out of total control verbs by mother and father, respectively. Parental modes of control are rates per minute.
[b] $p < .10$.
[c] $p < .001$.
[d] $p < .05$.
[e] $p < .01$.

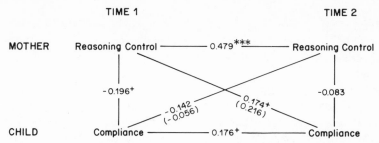

Figure 15. Cross-lagged panel for mother's rate of reasoning control and child's percentage of comply. (Figures in parentheses are partial correlations, holding constant the appropriate Time 1 variable.)

tions between compliance T1 and mother's mode of control T2 are negative; the converse correlations are positive. Similar relationships as for reasoning control may therefore hold for the other variables, too.

For father control, the synchronous correlations and the cross-lagged correlations are all very near zero, and the signs are less consistent, so that interpretations seem inappropriate. However, we should note that the stability of compliance to father across observations is greater than that to mother.

We also wanted to see whether the density of parent control behavior during one situation had an effect on child compliance during another, similar situation within the same observation session; that is, we wanted to detect effects, if any, that were intermediate between the immediate effects of the sequence analysis and the more distant effects, extending over a week from one observation session to another. For this purpose, we identified and extracted free play situations, which often recurred within the same observation. The ideal would be for these situations to be taken from the beginning and the end of the observations, but this was not always possible; however, a minimum of 15 min separated the comparable situations, and each situation was 30–45 min in duration. Such comparable free play situations, as well as contrasted dinner and bedtime preparation situations, were identified for 56 children by hand. The criterion for the selection of the children used in this analysis was that in their records such situations should be clearly identifiable and should occur with the requisite minimum interval between them. A specially written program then calculated the densities of the different modes of control for each situation, that is, their rates per minute, for mother and father separately, and identified instances of child comply that were expressed as a proportion of the total control verbs of mother and father.

Cross-lagged panel analyses for mother–child dyads were carried out in the same way as those for entire observations, described above. The results were very meager. Only the stability coefficients across situations for some of the modes of control were positive and significant, and the total of control verbs had a significant synchronous negative correlation with compliance at T2. Almost all other correlations were negative, and all were nonsignificant at the .05 level, nor were there any significant cross-lagged differentials.

It seems, therefore, that the effects of densities of control behavior on the proportion of comply over short time intervals are very weak. The larger data base accumulated over an entire observation generates somewhat more stable relationships and more noticeable effects, though even these have not proved to be very strong. Note that the effects we detected in the sequence analysis are of a somewhat different nature: those effects indicated that the occurrence of certain modes of control raised the probability of compliance above its base rate; they did not show how far the densities of control and compliance varied together.

The levels (mean rates) of mother's modes of control and of the child's compliance during two free play periods and during dinner and preparation for bedtime were also compared with each other. The only significant difference found was that the mean rate of mother's commands–prohibitions was higher during the dinner period than during the free play period (t (54) $= 2.97$ $p < .004$, two-tailed test). A dinner situation, as might be expected does indeed give rise to more commands and prohibitions by mother than does a free play period.

Compliance and the Rudiments of Conscience: Relationships with Demographic and Child Variables

We now turn to compliance regarded as a child characteristic, measured by summary indices. We obtained a rating of overt compliance (cf. Table 6), based on observation, interview, and the 24-hour diary. The behavior count that served as another summary index of this child trait was the comply ratio, that is, the ratio of all instances of compliance (C) to all instances of compliance and noncompliance (N): $CR = C/(C+N)$. It should be noted that this index leaves out of consideration instances when neither comply nor noncomply followed a given direction. Hence, the overall mean of this index to mother and father (.65) was higher than the average percentage of comply to all control verbs together.

As mentioned at the beginning of this chapter, a rating of degree of internalized control was introduced when the study was in progress. This rating is available for 66 children of the reduced sample of 90, and it was based, in part, on observation of rudimentary manifestations of self-restraint. Such an instance occurred, for example, when a child started to climb on furniture with his shoes on but then spontaneously took them off first. Another example was observed when a child started to cry at the table, got up from his seat, and headed toward his bedroom. He stopped for a moment as if to consider his choice, stopped crying, and came back to his place at the table. The parents had not said anything to him about going to his room at this point. Later, during the interview, the mother reported that L is sent to his room when he cries and is given permission to come out when he stops crying. At times, we caught a glimpse of how a rule actually becomes internalized by the child's repeating it to himself. Thus, one child repeated the rule: "You mustn't drink your milk all at once; you must drink it a bit at a time" twice to his mother during the course of a meal. Children also sometimes revealed that internalization had taken place by taking over the parents' role themselves and stopping a younger sibling from doing something, (e.g., touching a wall electric outlet) that they themselves had been forbidden to do.

Observers were also instructed to note when behavior that mother had proscribed at the time of the first observation did not occur on the second occasion. In addition, during the interview, the investigator listed many possible misdemeanors, and the mother was asked whether she had, in the past, proscribed such activities and whether the child now obeyed the rule, if it had been made, without having to be reminded. While such behavior was the highest degree of moral development that could be assessed in this situation, the self-restraint practiced by the child may well, of course, be due to fear of punishment by the external agents of control who were normally present. Control is "internalized" only in the sense that the child has adopted the rule without an immediately preceding prohibition, and such restraint cannot be equated with an internalized "autonomous conscience."

The internalized standards rating was allotted by the interviewer, who was present for one observation and also rated the parents, whereas the compliance rating was assigned by the main observer. These two observers viewed the same acts of overt compliance by the child, but the internalized standards rating was based on evidence that rules had already been internalized. Relatively few instances could be observed, and the rating was perforce chiefly based on the relevant questions from the interview. The distinction between acts indicating internalization of rules and overt compliance to commands was clearly defined, and contamination between the ratings by the two separate raters will, therefore, have been minimized.

Table 34 displays the correlations among the three compliance measures and between them and other child variables (for the sample of 90) that were significant at the .05 level or beyond.

The experimental measure of compliance had only nonsignificant associations with the compliance measures based on home observation and interview, and it correlated significantly almost only with other child experimental measures. Since compliance in the experimental situation therefore appears to represent a dimension somewhat different from compliance in

Table 34. Correlations between Compliance Measures and Other Child Variables (Sig. at .05 Level or Beyond). Reduced Sample—Singletons and Even-Numbered Twins (Maximum $N = 90$)[a]

		Compliance rating	Comply ratio	Internalized standards
Criteria intercorrelations				
Compliance ratio		$.66^{b,c}$		
Internalized standards		$.46^{b,c}$	$.41^{b,c}$	
Child and demographic variables				
Mother's education		$.21^d$	$.30^e$	
Twinship[f]				$.31^e$
Vocabulary IQ		$.22^d$		
Attachment rating		$-.44^{b,c}$	$-.32^e$	
Nonverbal attachment rate	c		$.22^d$	
Instrumental independence	EM			$.35^{c,e}$
Instrumental independence rating		$.42^b$	$.32^e$	$.50^{b,c}$
No. of form-board pieces placed	EM			$.28^d$
Speech maturity rating		$.40^{b,c}$	$.27^e$	$.47^{b,c}$
Rate of child speech	c	$.20^d$	$.26^d$	$.32^e$
Rate of child–mother speech	c		$.22^d$	

[a] c = count; EM = experimental measure.
[b] $p < .001$.
[c] Correlation significant ($p < .05$) in same direction in sample of 46 twins.
[d] $p < .05$. (two-tailed test).
[e] $p < .01$.

the home situation, and the main focus of this investigation has been on the development of compliance in the home, we will confine ourselves to the latter.

Let us first examine the question whether *compliance* can be regarded as a unitary concept about which meaningful statements can be made. The three compliance criteria based on home observation (but not the experimental playroom measure) correlate fairly well with one another. A certain amount of commonality seems to exist between the different indices, and one can therefore speak with some degree of confidence of a coherent construct of *compliance*, measured via different methods. In particular, the correlations between the rating devised to measure the child's degree of internalized control and the measures of overt compliance (.46 and .41, $p <$ .001) justify the working hypothesis that overt compliance is the outward manifestation of the internalized control, at least at this age.

Social class, as measured by the father's occupation, does not show a significant correlation with any compliance measure; the mother's education, on the other hand, which can be viewed as a kind of socioeconomic-status indicator, does correlate significantly with some criteria.

If we look at the correlations with other child variables, we see that there is a consistent positive relationship with independence rating and experimental measure. The correlations between indices of compliance and attachment rating and rate, however, are inconsistent in direction. The inconsistency here suggests that the attachment rating measures a somewhat different quality than simply frequency of attachment behavior, as discussed in Chapter 5. The pilot study of 30 children provided a replication of this analysis and confirmed the positive association of compliance with instrumental independence and the negative one with attachment (ratings).

Prediction from Parent Characteristics

In asking which parent variables significantly predict child compliance, we are placing compliance in the position of criterion and parent variables in the position of predictors, a choice that is to some extent arbitrary (cf. Bell, 1977). At least for some variables, the roles could quite plausibly be reversed, as is discussed below.

To identify parent predictors, multiple-regression analyses for the compliance criteria were carried out for the sample of 90, as for the attachment variables. The principles for the selection and entry into the regression equation of parent variables were the same as those that applied in the case of the attachment analysis (cf. Chapter 5).

In reviewing the relationships between parent predictors and child compliance, it should be borne in mind that mother and child ratings were assigned by different raters, in order to avoid contamination, except that the rating for internalized standards was alloted by the rater for mother. While the possibility of contamination exists in this latter case, it is rendered unlikely even here because the average correlation of 11 mother ratings with the internalized standards rating (same rater for mother and child) is lower than the average correlation for the same mother ratings with the child compliance rating (different raters for mother and child; average correlations .134 and .191, respectively, taking absolute values).

The results of the individual multiple-regression analyses are displayed in Tables 35–37. We note that individual simple correlations are generally low to moderate, but the overall prediction afforded by all predictors together is fairly good, the multiple correlation for comply ratio reaching .686. The correlations of a few predictors fluctuate in direction across the criteria. However, in every one of these cases, the one correlation that is out

Table 35.   Multiple-Regression Prediction of Compliance Rating $(N = 90)^a$

Predictors			Multiple R^2	R^2 change	Simple r
Consistency of enforcement rating	M		$.146^b$	$.146^b$	$.382^c$
Psychological rewards rtg.	M		$.211^b$	$.065^d$	$.341^c$
Encourage mature action rtg.	M		$.253^b$	$.042^e$	.330
Maternal physical punishment frequency		c	$.286^b$	$.033^e$	$-.249$
Maternal suggestion frequency		c	$.309^b$	$.023^f$	$-.019$
Verbal–psychological punishment rating	M		$.328^b$	.019	$-.117$
Maternal love withdrawal frequency		c	$.336^b$	.008	$-.131$
Reasoning rating	M		$.345^b$	.009	.316
Paternal affection frequency		c	$.350^b$	.006	.085
Maternal play frequency		c	$.355^b$	.004	.135
Paternal physical punishment frequency		c	$.358^b$	.003	$-.158$
Maternal comply ratio		c	$.360^b$	.002	.160
Paternal suggestion frequency		c	$.363^b$	.002	.079
Monitoring rating	M		$.365^b$	.002	$-.063$
Restrictions rating	M		$.367^b$	.001	.152
Material rewards rating	M		$.368^d$	.001	.060
Maternal affection frequency		c	$.368^d$	.001	.044
Mother's education			$.289^d$	.021	.208
Vocabulary IQ			$.398^d$	.010	.216
Twinship^g			$.400^d$	.002	.074

^{a} M = mother; c = count. Twinship, IQ and mother's education entered separately after all other variables. No father ratings included because of number of missing cases.
^{b} p: $< .001$.
^{c} Correlation significant ($p < .05$) in same direction in sample of 46 twins.
^{d} $p < .01$.
^{e} $p < .05$.
^{f} $p < .10$.
^{g} Twins coded 1, singletons 3.

of line with the others is completely nonsignificant (in most cases, in the religion of .01 to .07), so that it can be considered a chance occurrence, and no importance need be attached to the inconsistent direction. Thus, maternal physical punishment frequency has generally negative correlations with the criteria, though it also displays a nonsignificant positive one. (The associations of paternal physical punishment frequency with the criteria, however, are consistently negative). The same chance flunctuations can be noted for monitoring rating, material rewards rating, and love withdrawal frequency (main direction is negative) and for paternal play frequency, maternal affection frequency, and maternal suggestion frequency (main direction positive). The interpretations of the overall relationships can therefore reasonably be based on the predominant direction.

For a convenient overview, Table 38 presents a summary of these parent characteristics, viewed as predictors, which had a simple correlation with any of the criteria or yielded an increment in R^2, significant at the .10 level or better. The increment in R^2, can be seen as a measure of the predictor's "usefulness" (cf. Darlington, 1968) and is the chief basis for the interpretation of the relationships.

Table 36.   Multiple-Regression Prediction of Comply Ratio ($N = 90$)[a]

Predictors			Multiple R^2 ($p < .001$)	R^2 change	Simple r
Consistency of enforcement rating	M		.141	.141[b]	.375[c]
Maternal play frequency		c	.202	.061[d]	.270
Maternal comply ratio		c	.255	.053[e]	.188
Restrictions rating	M		.286	.031[f]	.288
Psychological rewards rtg.	M		.317	.314[f]	.307
Maternal love withdrawal frequency		c	.336	.019	−.121
Reasoning rating	M		.353	.017	.282
Paternal physical punishment frequency		c	.367	.014	−.177
Monitoring rating	M		.381	.015	−.017
Paternal play frequency		c	.392	.011	.175
Maternal affection frequency		c	.403	.011	−.018
Encourage mature action rtg.	M		.409	.005	.269
Material rewards rating	M		.417	..008	−.050
Paternal affection frequency		c	.423	.006	.069
Paternal suggestion frequency		c	.424	.002	.079
Maternal suggestion frequency		c	.425	.000	.090
Maternal physical punishment frequency		c	.425	.000	−.209
Verbal–psychological punishment rating	M		.425	.000	−.012
Mother's education			.468	.042[e]	.301
Twinship[g]			.470	.003	.149
Vocabulary IQ			.471	.000	.086

[a] M = mother; c = count. Twinship, IQ, and mother's education entered separately after all other variables. No father ratings included because of number of missing cases.

[b] $p < .001$.

[c] Correlation significant ($p < .05$) in same direction in sample of 46 twins.

[d] $p < .01$.

[e] $p < .05$.

[f] $p < .10$.

[g] Twins coded 1, singletons 3.

Table 37.   Multiple-Regression Prediction of Internalized Standards Rating
$(N = 66)^a$

Predictors		Multiple R^2	R^2 change	Simple r
Encourage mature action rtg.	M	.123[b]	.123[b]	.351
Material rewards rating	M	.184[b]	.060[c]	−.220
Paternal suggestion frequency	c	.235[d]	.051[c]	.246
Verbal–psychological punishment rating	M	.278[d]	.043[e]	−.143
Maternal play frequency	c	.319[d]	.041[e]	.222
Maternal physical punishment frequency	c	.343[d]	.024	.118
Monitoring rating	M	.359[d]	.015	.001
Consistency of enforcement rating	M	.374[d]	.016	.302
Reasoning rating	M	.378[d]	.004	.191
Psychological rewards rtg.	M	.383[b]	.005	.025
Maternal comply ratio	c	.386[b]	.003	.077
Paternal affection frequency	c	.388[b]	.002	.008
Maternal affection frequency	c	.392[b]	.004	.157
Paternal physical punishment frequency	c	.395[c]	.003	−.105
Maternal love withdrawal frequency	c	.396[c]	.002	.072
Maternal suggestion frequency	c	.397[c]	.000	.227
Paternal play frequency	c	.397[c]	.000	−.018
Twinship[f]		.420[c]	.024	.311
Vocabulary IQ		.440[c]	.020	.237
Mother's Education		.441[e]	.001	−.005

[a] M = mother; c = count. Twinship, IQ, and mother's education entered separately after all other variables. No father ratings included because of number of missing cases.
[b] $p < .01$.
[c] $p < .05$.
[d] $p < .001$.
[e] $p < .10$.
[f] Twins coded 1, singletons 3.

The table lists the predictors in the order of the generality of their influence on the multiple correlations across the criteria, with positive contributions being placed before negative ones, and demographic variables coming last. The most important positive predictors of compliance are mother's consistency of enforcement of rules, her encouragement of mature action, her use of psychological rewards (praise and approval), and her play with the child. The most important negative one is the amount of physical punishment by mother. How do these findings compare with those of other published studies?

If one collates—at the level of individual studies and individual measures of conscience—the results linking child-rearing practices to the child's development of internalized controls, one is at first overwhelmed by a sense of confusion. Many apparent contradictions in the findings, however, arise from the use of different measures of conscience as criteria (e.g., in Sears *et al.*, 1965). In surveying the research by Sears *et al.* (1957), Sears *et al.* (1965), Burton, Maccoby, and Allinsmith (1961), Yarrow, Campbell, and Burton (1968), Grinder (1962), Hoffman and Saltzstein (1967), and Minton *et al.* (1971), a considerable degree of consensus emerges, as Hoffman (1970) rightly points out. Warmth, the use of praise, high standards of obedience and moral training, and, to a lesser extent, the use of reasoning (induction) are positively related to the development of

Table 38. Summary Table: Significance Levels of Increments in R^2 and of Simple Correlations ($p < .10$ or Better)[a]

Predictors		Criteria					
		Compliance rating		Comply ratio		Internalized standards	
		Increment in R^2 $p<$	Simple r $p<$	Increment in R^2 $p<$	Simple r $p<$	Increment in R^2 $p<$	Simple r $p<$
Consistency of enforcement rating	M	.001	.001	.001	.001		.05
Encourage mature action rtg.	M	.05	.01		.05	.01	.01
Psychological rewards rtg.	M	.01	.01	.10	.01		
Maternal play frequency				.01	.01	.10	.10
Reasoning rating	M		.01		.01		
Maternal comply ratio				.05	.10		
Paternal suggestion frequency						.05	.05
Maternal suggestion frequency		.10	(−)				.10
Restrictions rating	M			.10	.01		
Maternal physical punishment frequency		.05	.05 (−)		.05 (−)		
Material rewards rating	M					.05	.10 (−)
Verbal-psychological punishment rating	M					.10	(−)
Mother's Education			.05	.05	.01		
Vocabulary IQ			.05				.10
Twinship. Twin: 0; Singleton: 1							.05

[a] Simple r's are positive, except where (−) is indicated.

conscience (in almost all studies), whereas the use of physical punishment and the severity of punishment are negatively related to it in all studies except Burton *et al.* (1961), an investigation that is discrepant in several ways.

Thus, our results, derived from direct home observation, are in broad agreement with evidence from other researchers employing different methods. Warmth, however, although measured by both rating and behavior counts, in this study did not seem to have any significant influence on compliance, in contrast to findings by, for example, Sears *et al.* (1965) and Yarrow *et al.* (1968). However, it may be regarded as having found its place as part of maternal play (where it is joined to cognitive stimulation), which had a relationship with two of the criteria.

Among the less important predictors, I should single out for comment the use of verbal–psychological punishment (which shows a slight negative influence on compliance). This measure is the rater's estimate of mother's tendency to criticize and to withdraw emotionally from the child. "Love withdrawal" (coded according to the indices listed by Hoffman, 1970, p. 348) was also included in the behavior counts. The correlations of the psychological punishment rating and of love withdrawal (count) with the criteria were almost all negative, though none was significant, in contrast to the reasoning rating, which showed several significant positive relationships, thus confirming the distinction between induction and love withdrawal delineated by Hoffman (1970).

Mother's comply ratio was positively correlated with child's comply ratio and made a significant contribution to its prediction. (Father's comply ratio showed an even stronger association but was omitted from the multiple regression because of an additional number of "missing cases," that is, cases that showed too few instances of compliance). These associations are evidence of reciprocal mother–father–child relationships: each person's compliance is reflected by that of the others.

Even after all child-rearing variables had been taken into account, mother's education still added significantly to the prediction of the comply ratio. It was also significantly and positively correlated with the compliance rating, though not with internalized standards. Social-class differences, therefore, while they were consistent in direction, were not as strongly associated with compliance—or with parental control practices—in this study as they were in Minton *et al.* (1971).

The contribution that twinship made to the prediction, though small, suggests that singletons tend to internalize rules more readily than twins, perhaps because parents can, and do, give singletons closer attention.

Two replications of these analyses are available. The first one is the pilot study of 30 singleton and twin boys that preceded the main study. Multiple-regression analyses were run for compliance rating and ratio, and the following variables contributed significantly to the prediction in both samples, thus indicating some stability in the findings: mother's consistency of enforcement, amount of play, and use of reasoning (all positive); and her use of material rewards (negative). The second replication is not completely independent, in that it consists of a multiple-regression analysis of a compliance composite measure for the 46 twins who were randomly eliminated for the analysis of the sample of 90. Nevertheless, it can serve as a certain check on the findings presented so far. It confirms the importance of consistency of enforcement, encouragement of mature action, and the maternal comply ratio.

Are parental responsiveness to the child's demands and needs, and the appropriateness of such responses related to the child's compliance and internalized control? This question was examined in the selected sample of 40 children, for whom parents' "responsiveness" and "appropriateness" were assessed. (These variables were defined in Table 8, and the analysis was outlined in Chapter 5.) It should be noted that the definition of *responsiveness* excluded parents' responses to the child's compliance or noncompliance and focused on responses to his wishes or distress so that circularity of reasoning was avoided. Such responses often, of course, entailed parents' complying with the child's wish, so that mother's responsiveness score, for instance, correlated .70 with her comply ratio. A multiple-regression analysis was carried out for one of the compliance criteria (the comply ratio), and the findings are shown in Table 39. For this analysis, the respon-

Table 39. Multiple-Regression Prediction of Comply Ratio Including Responsiveness Predictors $(N = 39)^a$

Predictors		Multiple R^2	R^2 change	Simple r
Restriction rtg.	M	$.213^b$	$.213^b$	.461
Responsiveness %	F	$.311^c$	$.098^d$	.283
Responsiveness %	M	$.381^c$	$.070^e$	.362
Consistency of enforcement rtg.	M	$.443^c$	$.063^e$	.441
Appropriateness %	M	$.489^c$	$.045^e$	.222
Maternal play frequency		$.511^c$	.022	.287
Maternal comply ratio		$.532^c$	.021	.298
Appropriateness %	F	$.538^c$	.006	.216
Psychological rewards rtg.	M	$.541^b$	.002	.228
Mother's education		$.629^c$	$.089^d$	.281

^{a} M = mother, F = father.
^{b} $p < .01$.
^{c} $p < .001$.
^{d} $p < .05$.
^{e} $p < .10$.

siveness and appropriateness variables for mother and father were added to the predictors that had made a significant contribution to the prediction in the larger sample. It can be seen that all the responsiveness and appropriateness variables were positively correlated with the comply ratio, and that three of the four variables were important contributors to the prediction, pushing some of the other variables into the background. This strong relation between responsiveness and compliance echoes a similar finding by Stayton *et al.* (1971).

No regression analysis was carried out for internalized control. However, father's responsiveness and total reactivity (i.e., his reactions to the child's speech, as well as his needs) correlated fairly highly with the child's internalized control (at the .05 and .001 level, respectively), though mother's corresponding variables did not. It is clear, however, that both mother's and father's responsiveness foster overt compliance in the child. Father's responsiveness, moreover, promotes the growth of internalized control. That father's attentiveness to the child's needs prompts the child to make parents' standards his own suggests that father plays a particularly important role in the development of moral standards. The significant positive association between responsiveness and compliance stands in stark contrast with the association (significant or near-significant) between parents' *un*responsiveness and attachment behavior.

It is, of course, a truism to say that correlation does not imply causation. Hoffman (1975), however, adduces theoretical and empirical arguments for the likelihood of the proposition that parent practices are the antecedenets rather than the consequents of the child's moral behavior, even if the child's behavior also initially influences the parents. I would qualify this conclusion according to the nature and logic of the relationships. Thus, verbal–psychological or physical punishment need not necessarily give rise to lesser compliance in the child: it may well be that mother felt impelled by the child's disposition to criticize or send him to his room frequently or felt driven to use physical force. On the other hand, for certain variables, a parent–child direction of causation seems to be strongly suggested by the logic of the relationships: it is difficult to conceive that children, through regular compliance, would generate in their mothers a greater tendency to be consistent in enforcing rules, or to use reasoning as a form of control, or to encourage mature, self-reliant action (unless these are all reactions to the child's general maturity). For these variables, the probability is high that the direction of influence runs from mother to child; in other words, consistency in enforcing rules, the use of reasoning, and the encouragement of maturity and independence by mother tend to foster greater compliance by the child. Reciprocal influences, however, may be at work in the case of responsiveness and compliance, each enhancing the other.

Summary

1. Compliance emerges as a fairly coherent construct when assessed by the different measures: compliance rating, comply ratio (a count variable), and internalized standards rating. It therefore seems justifiable to regard overt compliance as the outward manifestation of internalized control.

2. In the medium term, reciprocal influences operate between mother's use of reasoning and compliance: reasoning strengthens compliance, which, in turn, lessens the need for reasoning.

3. Compliance, seen as a child characteristic, is positively correlated with independence and speech maturity, a relationship that has been replicated. Compliance, therefore, can be seen as a sign of maturity and competence.

4. Triadic reciprocity is evident between mother, father, and child in their mutual compliance with each other's requests.

5. Predictions from parent characteristics that have been replicated are that mother's consistency of enforcement, her amount of play with the child, her encouragement of independence, and her use of psychological rewards are positively related to compliance, but that use of material rewards is negatively related to it. Analysis of a subsample also indicates a positive relation between mother's and father's responsiveness and compliance.

6. The logic of the relationships suggests that in the case of (a) consistency of enforcement and (b) encouragement of independence, the direction of influence runs from mother to child. The direction of influences is more ambiguous for the other parent characteristics.

DISCUSSION

While compliance may be a requisite for survival for social organisms and particularly their young, the ultimate goal of most parents is the development of an internalized, autonomous conscience, rather than of compliance itself, as discussed in the introduction to this chapter. It is therefore of importance to note that overt compliance here was found to be related to a measure of internalized standards—though the latter, as pointed out earlier, would at this age represent only the rudiments of conscience and not a fully flowering, inner-directed morality. As Maccoby (1968) noted, even later, when standards of conduct seem to be self-directed, they may still depend on some far-removed reference person or group whose sanctions are feared or whose opinions are valued. As this group becomes more dif-

fuse, it will cease to be a readily identifiable entity, and the locus of control
will appear to have shifted from it to a "small inner voice."

Compliance as a process and the facilitative and inhibiting effects that
different parent antecedent actions (the "controlling stimuli") exert on it
were studied in the sequence analysis. We noted that suggestions resulted in
comply more frequently than did commands–prohibitions (Table 22).
However, an exception to the usual definition of suggestion should be noted:
repeated commands or requests during play were scored as suggestions so as
not to load the parents' command total (which was viewed as an index of
restrictiveness) with commands such as "Put the elephant over there."
(Indeed, the highest frequency of use of suggestions occurred in a play
context.) The effectiveness of suggestion is therefore very likely due to the
less conflict-laden situations—both play and others—in which it tended to
be used, when the child would have fewer motives for disobeying (cf. Table
31). Reasoning, on the other hand, elicited fewer complies than command–prohibition did, but these were compensated for not by more noncomplies but by more "neithers," so that it appears that parents, having justified their demands or prohibitions, were more willing to let matters be
forgotten.

Commands–prohibitions, suggestions, and reasoning control were analyzed as the immediate antecedents of comply and noncomply. These
"modes of verbal control" do not, however, exhaust the range of behavior
that influences the child. Physical control obviously comes under this category, and other, more general actions that are less focused on a specific
child behavior are also potentially means of control. They could be positive,
e.g., praise or demonstration of affection) or negative (e.g., criticism or
expression of coldness), and they were analyzed as "prior antecedents" that
may or may not have been followed by verbal control.

These parent actions did indeed have an energizing effect on the child's
rule-following behavior, as is shown by the fact that both comply and noncomply were facilitated by all categories of prior antecedents (cf. Table 24).
The fact that physical control and negative actions were even stronger facilitators of comply than were positive actions and neutral actions suggests that
the occurrence of the first two action categories indicates a definite conflict
about some behavioral rule that may then be followed by comply. Since,
however, physical control and negative actions were even more facilitative
of noncomply (as seen in the FPs), it does appear that parents' aversive acts
tended on the whole to have negative consequences, but a positive, or at
least neutral, approach (which was more facilitative of comply than noncomply) tended to produce positive results.

Physical control, negative action, and direct command are examples of
"power assertion" (Hoffman, 1970). The relative potency of physical control and negative action compared with positive action in facilitating

comply, as well as the lower probability of comply following on reasoning than following on command, seems at first sight to argue against a humanistic–rational view of socialization, since such a view holds that the establishment of internalized moral standards is fostered by parents' use of induction (reasoning) rather than coercive commands (cf. Hoffman, 1970). Nor can we escape an antihumanist conclusion from our findings by arguing that overt compliance is unrelated to an internal agency of morality, in view of the moderate but significant correlation between overt compliance and a rating of internalized control (r = .44). However, the limitations of the sequence analysis must here be borne in mind: it is situation-bound, and it shows how immediate compliance can be secured most effectively, that is, by command or, in more conflict-free situations, by the less imperious suggestion. The long-term impact of power assertion on socialization is a different matter, which will be discussed in connection with the "trait" analysis below.

There are also some modifying comments to be made on these somewhat astringent conclusions. First, we found that the likelihood of compliance was less after parents repeated their directions—be they commands or suggestions—than after a single direction (Table 30). Evidently, there is a limit to the effectiveness of commands, though one might also surmise that it is the less-obedient boys who force their parents to issue repetitive directives—and indeed, these two effects may reinforce each other.

Second, the mode of control that parents employed was to some extent adapted to the circumstances. The one they adopted most frequently was a simple imperative, and this tendency was especially pronounced when they wanted to stop something that seemed a nuisance to them (e.g., whining or yelling). They coupled an explanation with a command relatively often when they were concerned that the child should treat objects in the house carefully, as well as when the child was getting physically involved with his sibling or interfering with the latter's toys. It seems, then, that matters of real importance called forth explanations that would serve to establish more general rules and help the child to build cognitive structures.

A third modification to the conclusions arises from the analysis of second-order antecedents (Figures 13 and 14). This sought to determine whether taking account of parents' prior actions as second-order antecedents significantly altered the facilitating (inhibiting) effects that the first-order antecedents (verbal control) alone exerted on compliance or noncompliance. It did so in relatively few cases, and when it did, the extra facilitation was weak. However, here the (from the parents' point of view) undesirable effects of physical control and the desirable effects of positive actions could be seen more clearly. Physical control had an effect opposite to that presumably intended by parents since, when it was added to command–prohibition, it lessened the facilitating influence of the latter on compliance; it seems brute force is not the most effective method, after all. Positive action, on the other hand (such as smiling, hugging, and praise), when added to command–prohibition, increased the likelihood of compliance and therefore would seem to be a preferable strategy for parents.

When we consider parents' responses to the child's compliance or noncompliance (Table 26), it appears that the family system of complementary interchanges is built on an expectation of compliance by the child. (The probability of parents' complying with the child's request is similar to that of child compliance.) If compliance happens, it is accepted, but not, in general, particularly rewarded. If noncompliance occurs, this does not, apart from the 25% likelihood of another command, trigger a rationally calculated response. Mother and father, in other words, do not carry a probabilistic calculus in their heads, adjusting their response to the probability of obtaining eventual compliance. One-third of the time, they make no response, and the likelihood that any particular action category will follow comply is of the same order as the probability of occurrence of the category in the observation as a whole, though after noncomply, this order changes somewhat. So, it seems that parents' reactions are only to some extent influenced by the child's behavior in these interchanges. One may speculate that if parents often conduct such disciplinary encounters not in a manner adapted to their ultimate purpose, this may be because they are so emotionally involved that they neglect rational procedures in favor of actions that meet their own needs of the moment. Parents may, of course, also often be guided quite rationally by particular circumstances, not noted here, and their experiences with their individual children. As we saw above, the *mode* of control they employ is usually appropriately adaptive to the situation.

The conclusion that the influence that the child's compliance or noncompliance has on mother's behavior is relatively small was also reached by Minton *et al.* (1971). Their findings indicated, they suggest, that differences among mothers in the disposition to explain or punish are more a function of a psychological dimension in the mother. Our finding on compliance, however, contrasts with what we found regarding attachment behavior, the effects of which on parents' action was seen to be greater than the influence the other way round. Close observation of parents' interactions with their children, then, leads to the conclusion that when it is a question of ensuring the child's compliance with their own rules, parents' behavior is conditioned by their own goals and emotions more than by the child's doings, but in the matter of establishing close bonds between child and parents, it is the child's actions that shape parents' behavior more than the other way round.

In spite of our parents' seemingly casual approach to these interchanges, the final outcome of noncompliance sequences is likely to be positive: in about 66% of cases, the child eventually complies with a series of directions (cf. Table 30).

How does father's presence affect mother's behavior compared with when she is on her own with the child? As may be expected, in his presence she makes fewer attempts to change the child's behavior—but she is obeyed more. When father repeats and reinforces mother's directions, this also has a beneficial effect on the degree of compliance shown by the child, whereas mother's reinforcement of father's directions has the opposite effect. It seems that father's commands—perhaps because of their greater rarity—still carry more weight.

When both parents are present, it appears that mother feels impelled to take notice of the child's positive response to her or to father's directions (though less so than when she is alone with the child), whereas father is more inclined to take such a response for granted—or leave the positive reinforcement of the child to his wife. When it comes to displays of disobedience, however, father feels as much involved and constrained to react to the child as does mother. The findings of a greater degree of compliance to father than to mother, and of father's ignoring compliance more readily than noncompliance, confirm similar results in Hetherington *et al.'s* (1978) study of intact and divorced families.

It also seems that father's presence spurs mother on to be "on her best behavior" and to reinforce the child for his compliance by more positive acts (e.g., smiling and hugging). It looks as if she knew what was expected but does not always carry it out to the same extent when she is alone with the child. However, mother is willing, and no doubt glad, to let father, when he is about, deal with a child's noncompliance on many occasions—hence, the generally fewer responses and more instances of "no response" by her than when she is on her own.

Father's presence does, indeed, change the quantity and the character of mother's responses to the child in such disciplinary encounters in a beneficial way. Overall, however, as noted already in Chapter 3, mother not only is the primary caregiver but also assumes the major responsibility for the child's induction into the ways of his family and of the world beyond.

In Chapter 3, I documented some differences in control and compliance behavior in line with mother's educational level: the better-educated parents showed greater reliance on cognitive and psychological influence methods, and their children complied more. However, the fine-grained analysis of interaction sequence exhibited no noticeable differences between educational groups in the effects that, say, command produced on compliance, whereas such differences were observed between twins and singletons. This would seem to be another indication that class and educational differences in child rearing are becoming less marked.

The correlational analysis examined compliance as a child characteristic or "trait." The comply ratio (a behavior count) and the ratings of overt compliance and of internalized standards displayed sufficient commonality to allow one to speak with some confidence of a coherent construct of compliance, measured by different methods. The correlations of these compliance indices with other child variables suggest overall that the child who shows compliance is seen as independent in carrying out tasks and in initiating his own actions and as possessing fewer of the more burdensome characteristics of attachment. The positive associations with speech maturity and rate of speech provide further evidence that compliance at this age is a sign of maturity and general competence in living. Nevertheless, attachment to parents when shown in a nonverbal way—a behavior that we saw serves to cement harmonious relationships—may also indicate greater readiness to comply with their wishes.

The parent variables most strongly predictive of the development of compliance are practices that lead to cognitive structure, generalization, and generally age-appropriate development (encouragement of mature and independent action, consistency in enforcing rules, and the cognitive aspects of play). The strong effect that consistency of enforcement (which, contrary to simple pressure for compliance, has a cognitive *and* an authority aspect) had on compliance in this study confirms Baumrind's (1971) conclusion as regards the influence of authoritative parental control on the child's social responsibility. (See also Chapter 10).

The development of compliance also appears to be influenced by social reinforcement (i.e., praise and approval, play in its affective aspects, and, to a lesser extent, reciprocal compliance by parents) that satisfies some of the child's motivational needs. Under this heading, too, would come being sensitively and appropriately responsive to the child's needs, which is also positively associated with compliance. (In contrast, attachment behavior is associated with unresponsiveness: it seems, unresponsiveness creates the need to reassure oneself, but responsiveness breeds responsibility.) Warmth and affection, as directly measured, are conspicuously absent from the list of affective variables fostering compliance, though they may form part of play. On the other hand, emphasis on material incentives and the arousal of anxiety (and pain) by means of physical and psychological punishment are related to noncompliance.

This investigation suggests that the use of reasoning—often considered the cornerstone of moral generalization—plays a lesser role in the prediction of moral behavior, once other variables have been taken into account, and in particular that it plays no significant part in the prediction of internalized standards, relatively the most advanced aspect of moral behavior tested here. This may well be an effect of the age of the sample, since rules and abstractions are likely to be more effective—and to be used more by parents—as cognitive competence increases with age.

Placing child compliance in the position of criterion and parent variables in the position of predictors implies the working hypothesis that the direction of effects runs from parents to child. This is not meant to deny the existence of endogenous forces within the child that may mold moral behavior and that will influence the mutuality of the encounters between parents and child. For most parent practices, the direction of effects will, in fact, very likely run more strongly from parent to child, simply because the balance of power is heavily in parents' favor, though in some instances (e.g., in the case of physical punishment), the child's disposition may be an instigating factor. However, the best interpretation for some of the effects we have observed will lie in the mutuality of influences constantly at work between parents and child. Thus, we have noted a reciprocity between parents' and child's compliance, one enhancing the other, suggesting that yielding to another person's wishes is a two-way affair. The relation between parents' responsiveness and the child's compliance may indicate similar reciprocal effects. The association between the use of repeated directions and noncompliance suggests reciprocal influences in the opposite sense, indicating the operation of a coercive cycle. Lastly, the cross-lagged panel analysis has shown both positive and negative influences to be operating between reasoning and compliance, with reasoning strengthening compliance, and compliance in turn lessening the need for reasoning.

In sum, if we can for the moment assume a direction of influence that runs from parent to child, the findings demonstrate the positive effects of cognitive factors (as well as of positive social reinforcement) and the negative effects of aversive emotional and physical stimuli on the development of moral behavior as an ongoing disposition in the young. In contrast, the analysis of the stimuli controlling compliance in the immediate situation (sequence analysis) led to a different result: it demonstrated the effectiveness of power assertion. The findings on compliance as a trait provide a necessary counterweight to the picture drawn by the short-term sequential contingencies and redress the balance in favor of a model of humans as rational creatures.

Moral behavior may have a biological basis and be of evolutionary and adaptive significance, as Stayton et al. (1971), among others, suggest: "As an infant moves about to investigate his world, his mother must be able to control his actions across an enlarged and often hazardous environment" (p. 1066). And again: "a disposition to comply develops in a social environment which does not deviate unduly from the environment of evolutionary adaptedness and . . . such a disposition does not require specific training" (p. 1060). It is reasonable to suppose that obedience by the young to the signals of adults is of survival value to the individual, particularly when natural dangers threaten.

Such theorizing would lead one to think further that obedience may be mediated by the development of attachment to adult caregivers. This latter hypothesis has not been subjected to rigorous proof, though this investigation provided some limited support for it, but only as far as nonverbal attachment behavior is concerned (see above). It should be noted that theorists such as Ainsworth posit a relationship between obedience and "secure attachment" (Stayton *et al.*, 1971), a quality that we did not measure. There is evidence, however, that the tendency to obey adults is widespread among primates and mammals. Altmann (1963, quoted in Stayton *et al.*, 1971), for instance, described how young moose and elk comply immediately with mother's vocal signals and intention movements when there is any sign of danger. McCann (1956, quoted in Stayton *et al.*, 1971) reported similar behavior in wild mountain sheep.

In the human case, matters are more complex. However, biologists suppose that living in groups and the emergence of large societies necessitated certain biological adaptations that enabled individuals to act effectively as members of large communities, whether as rulers or as followers (Young, 1971). Waddington (1967, quoted in Hogan, 1973) believes that the dynamics of human culture necessarily presuppose the role of "authority-acceptor." Wilson (1975) even posits the existence of "conformer genes," for which, however, there is very little evidence. This investigation, in fact, uncovered no significant genetic determination for compliance (cf. Chapter 9). As Young (1971) suggests, it is not clear how important genetically determined individual differences in compliance would be nowadays, when cultural and verbal transmission has assumed a much more important role.

Stayton *et al.* (1971) suggest that obedience is a natural disposition that does not require training. These authors, however, also used indices like maternal "sensitivity" and "cooperation," which they found to be conducive to the development of compliance. Since these constructs are themselves attempts to capture recurring patterns of behavior or practice in a fairly objective way, it can be seen that some practices are more effective than others in this area. We also noted that certain parent practices (e.g., responsiveness) fostered compliance, while others did not, and whether one calls such actions "practices," "climate of the home," or "training" is in the end only a semantic question. As Stayton *et al.* also recognized, in any case, learning is involved. Whether or not children are inherently disposed to compliance, parents very consciously inculcate certain rules and standards in their offspring, and they do so partly because the nature of the rules of social living is not always clear to young children, and partly because at times, parents' and children's goals are bound to diverge. Similar arguments apply to training for independence; attachment, on the other hand, is in a different category and in most families is simply allowed to grow, perhaps because this is behavior that really "comes naturally" to the child and that does not require the teaching of any specific content. This difference between compliance and attachment also emerges from our finding that for compliance the strongest influence runs from parents to child, whereas with attachment behavior, influence runs more strongly the other way.

As we have seen, compliance at this age may justifiably be regarded as the forerunner and outward manifestation of internalized control. However, there is a danger that compliance, especially if inflexibly and unreasonably insisted upon, may lead to a "Milgram-type" slavish conformity. This is not necessarily the case, though, if compliance is adaptively and rationally enforced. Our findings suggest that, in fact, compliance at this age is consonant with independence and maturity, and a compliant 2-year-old may well develop into a socially responsible adult who is governed by an inner-directed, rather than a conformity-driven, conscience (cf. Baumrind, 1973).

CHAPTER 7

Child–Parent
Communication

By the time a child is 2 years old he has two years of speech development, or, more strictly, development of communication, behind him. Bruner (1978), without any exaggeration, could claim:

> . . . the child communicates before he has language. He does so in order to carry out certain functions that are vital to the species. These primitive communicative acts are effected by gesture, vocalization, and the exploitation of context. (p. 65)

As regards speech itself, a 2-year-old has normally mastered two-word utterances (although this need not always be the case even with nonhandicapped children) and therefore is about to pass beyond Stage I in Brown's system (1973), the upper limit of which is marked by a mean length of utterance (MLU, i.e., mean number of morphemes) of 2.0. In short, between 2 and 3 years old, children start to speak in sentences.

Brown (1973) has found that the mean length of a child's utterance is a more useful benchmark of his speech development than is his age, since certain syntactical developments in the child's speech are closely bound to MLU, whereas age is a much less certain indicator. Brown has segmented the early stages of lanugage into five stages, Stage I extending from MLU 1.0 to 2.0, Stage II from 2.0 to 2.5, etc., with increments of .5 in MLU for each succeeding stage. The rate of progress through these stages, of course, varies for different children; thus, among the three children studied by Brown (1973), Eve covered Stages III to V between the ages of 22 and 26 months, but Adam and Sarah traversed these stages between 36 and 42 months. Nelson's (1973) study has provided norms based on a somewhat larger number of children (18), and for these, the mean MLU at 2 years was 1.91 (beginning of Stage II), with a range from 1.03 to 3.37, while at 30 months the mean MLU was 3.23 (Stage IV), with a range from 1.80 to

4.46. Clearly, thus, Brown's Stages II–V are the salient markers and the most apposite descriptors of the child's linguistic development between 2 and 3 years of age, though for some children, the later stages do not appear until after age 3.

While these stages are defined by mean length of utterance, their main task in the evolution of syntax is the development of noun and verb inflections (e.g., present progressive) and the use of articles, prepositions, auxiliaries, etc. These are the "grammatical morphemes" that modulate the child's language, making it more adaptive and unequivocally intelligible. The order in which they make their appearance over two or three years is surprisingly invariant among different children, as evidenced not only by Brown's children but also by the 21 children studied by de Villiers (1973). However, a morpheme is not acquired suddenly and with complete dependability from one day to the next. For a considerable period, the use of the morpheme fluctuates, with the probability of its presence in an obligatory context increasing steadily over time (Brown, 1973).

After the emergence of syntax in two- to three-word utterances, studies of language development have focused on the acquisition of particular subsystems of adult grammar (e.g., negation and past tense). An illustration of the development of negation comes from the "Harvard children" (Klima & Bellugi, 1973):

> Stage I: *No the sun shining. No singing song.*
> Stage II: *I can't catch you. That no Mommy.*
> Stage III: *I don't want cover on it. This not ice cream. It's not cold.*

In Stages II and III, as Brown (1973) noted, children are working mainly on simple sentences; that is, the most complex constructions they use are simple sentences, and they hardly ever produce conjoined or embedded sentences. But this changes by the time later stages are reached. The following examples of the enormous advance in linguistic sophistication that occurs between 24 and 30 months are taken from a girl's speech, recorded in Bloom, Lightbown, and Hood (1975) and in Bloom (1975a).

At 24 months, Kathryn, who, with an MLU of 2.83, was relatively advanced, expressed action by *that one a ride*, intention by *I want try again*, negation by *no bring lambs* (visitors had not brought any lambs), and occasionally produced a well-formed sentence, such as *I find my balloons*.

At 30 months, the following sophisticated conversation was recorded (Bloom, 1975a):

> (During the last session, six weeks previously, mommy had been ironing in the kitchen while Lois and Kathryn played in the living room)

Lois:	*Kathryn:*
	you came here last night, when my mother was ironing/

I came here last night?	yes/ my mother, my mother ironed/
Oh, your mother ironed last night? What did she iron?	yes/ oh, she ironed some clothes/
Hm. And what did Kathryn do? Hm. Did you play with me tomorrow? Yes? Will you play with me yesterday?	Oh, I played with you/ yes/ yes/ last yesterday/ last night/

(Mommy had not been ironing the previous night)

Note that Kathryn's verbal facility coexists with somewhat primitive ideas about time relationships, in other words syntactic capacity outruns understanding. The same age can be marked by the opposite tendency; in the following example, a 32-month-old twin girl gropes for the expression of meaning that is somewhat beyond her verbal power (Conway, 1974): "(Norma had already indicated that her imaginary school was 'way back far away' and that she had a boy friend there.) *Norma and Linda went to Norma's school and they was away school and Norma's school boy way.*"

These then are the characteristics and developments that mark child speech in the third year. This is not the place to engage in a detailed discussion of the processes underlying this development. Such discussions can be found elsewhere (e.g., Bloom, 1975a,b; Brown, 1973; Campbell & Wales, 1975; Ervin-Tripp, 1973; McNeill, 1975; Miller & Ervin-Tripp, 1973). Ervin-Tripp's (1973) line of reasoning is indeed convincing: it is difficult to make one theory encompass and fit all the facts. If we follow her account, three processes—at least—are involved in the development of language: comprehension of adult speech and its continual expansion, imitation and repetition, and the induction of classes and rules by analogy. In addition, an often neglected factor in the acquisition of adult syntax and semantics is the simple act of playing and experimenting with language and its sounds in an unconstrained way, particularly in the twilight between consciousness and sleep at night (Weir, 1962) or in the early morning (Keenan, 1974).

Speech is, no doubt, a very important *vehicle* of parent–child social interaction, but in our investigation, it was the meanings conveyed by parents' speech to the child and the child's speech to parents that were the focal point of attention, rather than the syntactic, structural characteristics of that speech. Hence, speech was broken down into certain semantic categories, it was recorded whenever it occurred, and the *amount* of speech by the child and parents was calculated, but the syntactic structure of neither child's nor parents' speech was examined in detail. Such an analysis would have been a study in its own right and was beyond the resources of this project. In any event, speech—even grossly defined and measured, as it was here—was found to be an important indicator of the child's cognitive competence and highly predictable from certain demographic variables and features of the environment.

The behavior code in this investigation contained a number of separate categories indiciating verbal–social transactions in different keys between parents and children, for example, orders, suggestions, seeking attention (verbally), expressing affection or criticism (verbally), as well as a general "communicates" category, used for informational speech and questions. (See Appendix I for a complete list.) A special symbol also enabled us to record when verbaization accompanied some other action. All such utterances were counted as "speech acts" and converted into rates of speech (per minute) by a specified speaker to a specified addressee (or to no addressee). Thus, we have rates of child-to-mother speech and vice versa, child-to-father speech (per minute of his presence) and vice versa, and an overall rate of child speech.

WHO INITIATES CHILD–PARENT DIALOGUES AND WHO RESPONDS?

Speech by one person is naturally intertwined with speech by another, one remark eliciting a reply, which, in turn, evokes a response, and so forth. In order to gain some insight into the dynamics of child–parent communication and to discover who–parent or child–is mainly responsible for the level of verbalization in a family, it seemed important to disentangle speech that initiated a dialogue from speech that was elicited by a partner's verbal overtures. Child–mother and child–father dialogues could be examined in this way, but not mother–father dialogues, since the latter were not generally recorded, as they did not impinge directly on the child(ren).

Initiated speech was defined as a speaker's utterance that was not preceded by a speech act by him or by his interlocutor (addressed to him) within the previous 10 sec. *Reactive speech*, by the same reasoning, had to follow the initiator's utterance within 10 sec. While these definitions may seem somewhat mechanical and arbitrary, and may, indeed, count in instances that were not true initiations, it has to be remembered that the definitions had to be suitable for a computer program that was specifically written for this analysis.

Total amount of speech and initiated speech acts were divided by the number of minutes when both interlocutors were present together ("rate per minute"), thus making allowance for fathers' shorter presence. Since opportunities for responding to speech exist only when the partner has spoken first, we equalized for differences in these opportunities by expressing reactive speech as a percentage of the partner's initiations, rather than as a rate. When there were fewer than five instances of initiations by the partner, reactive speech was not counted for that person.

The means of the various categories of speech, displayed in Table 40, show considerable differences, depending on who is speaking and who is being addressed. Mother and father both address significantly more speech to the child than he does to them. Not only do the parents speak more to the child overall than vice versa, but each of them also initiates more of the dialogues. Differences between parent and child verbal responsiveness are particularly large: when given the opportunity, both mother and father make a verbal response to the child's verbal overtures on the average more than twice as often as the child does in the reverse situation. That mother and father initiate more dialogues and respond more to the child than he does to them is true of the vast majority of children individually. Indeed, *every* mother without exception responds more to her child's speech than he does to hers.

It is clear also that mother and child initiate more dialogues with each other and communicate more with each other in general than do father and child, in relation to time present. This preponderance of mother–child interchanges also applies individually to two-thirds of the families. Mother also responds more to the child than father does, relative to the child's initiations. However, the child responds equally to mother and father (the only comparison in the table that is not significant). These relationships suggest that responsiveness to speech is governed more by the child's internal

Table 40. Mean Initiated, Reactive, and Total Amount of Speech by Child, Mother, and Father over Total Observations (Maximum $N = 136$)[a]

	Means		
	Overall speech rate (per min)	Initiated speech (rate per min)	% of partner's speech reacted to by speaker
Mother to child	1.58	.44	75.4
Father to child	1.15	.38	71.8
Child to mother	1.07	.29	34.4
Child to father	.79	.23	33.9
M–C interchange	2.57[e]		
F–C interchange	1.94		

[a] Reactive speech not counted when N of partner's initiated speech < 5.
[b] $p < .001$ (for bracketed figures) (Wilcoxon Matched Pairs Signed Rank Test, two-tailed).
[c] $p < .01$.
[d] $p < .05$.
[e] This figure differs from the sum of C–M and M–C speech because it is based on 120 children, but the former are based on 136 children.

predisposition and propensities than by the characteristics of the interlocutor's speech, since mother and father differ in these characteristics, but the child responds relatively equally to both.

The conclusion that a child's reactive speech is relatively independent of the parent's initiated speech is confirmed by an examination of the product–moment correlations between the various speech measures, shown in Table 41, which show that the correlations between a parent's initiated speech and the child's reactive speech to that parent are near zero. On the other hand, the degree to which the child responds verbally to mother and to father is very consistent, in spite of their differing initiations—another indication that the sources of this responsiveness are more internal. The correlation between the child's initiated speech to mother and to father is at least moderate.

In spite of differences in *level* of speech between mother and father, *correlations* between mother's and father's total speech rates, between their initiated speech rates, and between their percentages of reactive speech are all moderate. In other words, there exists a system of communication, characteristic of a family.

Father's and child's initiations to each other show a moderate association, as one might expect. On the other hand, mother's and child's initiations to each other are poorly correlated. This is somewhat surprising in view of the fact that the total speech rates of child to mother and mother to child (as well as of child to father and father to child) are very highly interrelated. One would expect the latter close association, since speech by the

Table 41.   Intercorrelations of Initiated, Reactive, and Total Amount of Speech by Child, Mother, and Father over All Observations[a]

	SCM	SMC	SCF	SFC	ICM	IMC	ICF	IFC	RCM	RMC	RCF
SCM	—										
SMC	89	—									
SCF	50	44	—								
SFC	39	43	89	—							
ICM	74	51	24	10	—						
IMC	29	59	03	18	13						
ICF	24	13	76	55	25	−08	—				
IFC	02	11	48	76	−10	28	34	—			
RCM	73	55	46	34	46	01	28	−01	—		
RMC	41	48	21	25	26	43	07	22	27	—	
RCF	47	37	53	32	36	03	47	03	61	20	—
RFC	26	20	27	33	28	16	14	25	25	36	24

[a] Decimals omitted. SCM = speech rate child to mother; SMC = speech rate mother to child, etc.; ICF = initiated speech rate child to father; ICF = initiated speech rate father to child, etc.; RCM = reactive speech of child as a percentage of mother's initated speech, etc. For N = 90 (mother variables) $p_{(.05)}$: r = .21; $p_{(.01)}$: r = .27; $p_{(.001)}$: r = .34. For N = 82 (father variables) $p_{(.05)}$: r = .22; $p_{(.01)}$: r = .28; $p_{(.001)}$: r = .36.

child is almost always intermeshed with speech by the parent. Initiations by the child, however, it seems, do not always mirror initiations by mother, or vice versa, but represent an aspect of the parent–child communication system that varies independently for mother and child.[1]

"Second-Order Effects" Arising from the Presence of Both Parents

The observation sessions were broken down into periods when either mother or father were alone with the child (the "one parent" condition) or when both were present. On average parents were present for 141 minutes of observation, mother was alone with child for 97 minutes, and father was alone for 12 minutes. Mothers, therefore, were in the child's company for 238 minutes, but fathers for only 153 minutes, on average.[2] These time differences have to be borne in mind in interpreting the various mean speech measures.

Table 42 presents the speech measures broken down into the two conditions, "one parent" and "both present." The main point of interest is how the pattern of communication with the child changes for each parent when the other one is present, too. We notice that, in general, both mother's and father's speech decreases in the other's presence, except that father's initiated speech rate remains constant. In absolute terms, father emitted only 4.7 initiating utterances, on average, when he was the only parent present, so the rate for the "father alone" condition is based on a very short time period and few utterances. The differences between mother and father are all in the same direction, with mother having more verbal interchanges with the child, but while these differences are significant for the total duration of the observations (see Table 40), they lose their significance for the periods when both parents are present. It appears that mother reduces her communication with the child in this situation more than father does in similar circumstances.

The differences in child-to-parent speech by and large mirror those in parent-to-child speech, except that when father is alone with the child, the child shows greater responsiveness to father's utterances than he does to

[1] Since the correlations presented in Table 41 are not independent of one another, independent significance levels have to be interpreted with considerable caution. For a strict interpretation of significance, it would be better to apply the formula, presented in Chapter 4, that takes account of the fact that 66 correlations are being tested simultaneously (cf. Bock & Haggard, 1968). So that the experiment-wise significance level remains at .10 (a reasonable level, in view of the strict formula applied), significance levels for individual correlations have to be set at .0016. Therefore, following this criterion, only correlations of .34 or higher (if they involve mother and child variables) and those of .36 or higher (if they involve any father variables) should be accepted as "significant."

[2] Cases where fathers were absent from both observations were disregarded for these calculations; hence, the figures differ a little from those shown in Chapter 3.

Table 42.   Mean Initiated, Reactive, and Total Amount of Speech in the "One Parent" and "Both Present" Conditions ("Second-Order Effects")
(Maximum $N = 136)^a$

	Means					
	Overall speech rate (per min)		Initiated speech (rate per min)		% of partner's initiated speech reacted to by speaker	
	One parent	Both present	One parent	Both present	One parent	Both present
Mother to child	1.88	1.31^b	.48	.40^c	77.7	73.6^d
		e		e		f
Father to child	1.39^b	1.12^b	.38^c	.38^c	75.4^d	71.8^d
Child to mother	1.25	.90	.32	.26	35.9	34.5
Child to father	1.01	.77	.24	.22	39.8	33.6

^{a} Reactive speech not counted when N of partner's initiated speech < 5. Statistics for child-to-mother and child-to-father speech were not tested for significance.
^{b,c,d} Figures with the *same* superscripts do not differ significantly from each other.
^{e} $p < .001$ for bracketed figures (Wilcoxon Matched Pairs Signed Rank Test, 2-tailed).
^{f} $p < .05$.

mother's in the parallel situation. This relatively greater readiness to respond is very likely due to the small absolute number of father's initiations that the child had an opportunity to react to (see above). Differences between various child-to-parent speech measures were not tested for significance, as they were not the focal point of attention.

The overall effect of having both parents present appears to be (1) to increase the amount of communciation that occurs between parents and child *in toto* (this can be seen by adding mother and father speech together), and (2) to share out whatever parents wish to say among them, so that each of them speaks somewhat less and the child speaks less to each of them.

Twin–Singleton and Mother Education Level Differences

The impact of twinship on the overall speech rates of child, mother, and father was discussed in Chapter 4 (see Table 11), and the influence of mother's education was discussed in Chapter 3 (see Figures 3 and 7). The findings can be summarized very shortly: There is a very much greater degree of verbal interaction between a singleton and his parents than between a twin and his parents, as measured by both the child's speech and the parent-to-child speech. However, if one added together the parents' speech to both twins (the reason that we could not, in fact, do this was explained in Chapter 4), this would no doubt on average exceed the amount of verbal communication from parents to a singleton. There is also a greater degree of verbal communication in the families of college-attenders than in those of lesser education, but the differences here are less dramatic than in the twin–singleton comparisons. These differences are shown in the two left-hand columns of Table 43.

The other columns of Table 43 display the comparisons between twins and singletons and between higher and lower mother's education level for initiated speech and reactive speech. Again, all singleton means are higher than twin means, though the differences in mother's and father's initiated speech do not reach significance. The means of college-attenders are also generally higher, but the differences between them and those of non-college-attenders are less marked than the singleton–twin differences. In the case of father's reactive speech, the direction of the difference is even reversed; that is, the lower-education-level fathers respond more to their children. It should be mentioned that when observations are broken down into the "one parent" and the "both present" conditions, the direction of the differences remains the same as for the total observations.

Who is responsible for the lower level—and, presumably, sophistication—of verbal communication in the twin and in the lower education families—parent or child? The differences in speech initiations (between twins and singletons, etc.) are wider and more strongly significant for the child than for the parents. Nevertheless, both singletons *and* their parents initiate more dialogues than do twins and their parents, and the same goes for college-attenders and their children; moreover, parents in general initiate considerably more verbal interchanges than their children do and respond twice as much. The conclusion therefore imposes itself that the prime responsibility for the level of communication in a family is the parents'.

The observers rated each child on "speech maturity," basing their ratings on the articulateness and comprehensibility of the child's speech and on the completeness of his utterances. In this, too, singletons and children in the higher education group showed superior accomplishments ($p < .01$ and .05, respectively).

That higher education in parents leads to greater verbalization in parent–child relations has been documented in a number of studies (see introduction to Chapter 3) and is being confirmed here. One of the main benefits of more advanced education is that it confers greater verbal ease on its recipients; in using this facility, parents also transmit it to their children. The reasons that may underlie the more restricted level of verbal communication in twin families were discussed in detail in Chapter 4.

The extremes of verbal communication between parents and children, or the lack of it, are illustrated in the following two comments by the observers. The first one concerns a singleton: "His speech is as advanced as

Table 43. Twin–Singleton and Mother Education Level Differences in Speech Measures over Total Observations (Maximum $N = 136$)[a]

	Overall speech rate (per min)		Initiated speech (rate per min)		Reactive speech (percentage)	
	Singletons higher p	College-attenders higher p	Singletons higher p	College-attenders higher p	Singletons higher p	College-attenders higher p
Child to mother	.0001	.0011	.0002	.0192	.0000	.0005
Child to father	.0001	.0587	.0178	.0172	.0000	.4537
Mother to child	.0001	.0072	.4289	.2611	.0000	.1423
Father to child	.0001	.2015	.5040	.9350	.0398	[b]

[a] Wilcoxon Matched Pairs Signed Ranks Test, two-tailed.
[b] Lower education level has higher mean – $p = .2906$.

that of a 3- or 4-year old, and his parents talk with him continuously." The next one is about twins, but I should stress that such extreme behavior is not a necessary, or usual, accompaniment of having twins in the family:

> The twins sit at a separate table from the parents during the meal; they can hardly be heard uttering a sound, only father says a word now and again to mother—no conversation between twins and parents during mealtime. Parents seem to have little time for the boys.

It would be rash to conclude that such discouragement of speech was the sole cause of these twins' low verbal competence, since genetic factors may also be involved (see Chapter 9), but it will certainly have contributed to it: their speech maturity ratings were 2.0 and 2.5 on a five-point scale, and their rate of speech was also below average (one of them below the twin average). By contrast, the speech maturity rating of the singleton mentioned above was 5.0, and his rate of speech was above the singleton average.

In Chapter 4, we noted that speech among the twin pair in our experience did not seem to compensate, or account for, the lesser amount of parent–child communication, since the average number of utterances by one twin to the other was only 22 over the whole duration of the observation. It should be understood, however, that we recorded as twin–twin speech only statements, requests, question, etc., that one twin directly addressed to the other. The category "twin–twin speech," therefore, does not comprise monologues or "collective monologues" that twins may engage in each other's presence and to which the other twin may react by parallel speech or sound play rather than by way of referential, meaningful interchange. It is this kind of parallel speech, rather than actual dialogues, that has been reported (Keenan, 1974) as occurring abundantly between young twins as they talk in bed in the early morning.

Summary

1. In all speech categories—initiated, reactive, and overall—parents speak more than the child, and mother more than father. In particular, parents respond to the child's speech twice as often (about 75%) as the child does to the parents.

2. Transcending these differences in level, mother, father, and child overall speech rates are highly interrelated, a fact that demonstrates the existence of a triadic family system of communication.

3. The effect of both parents' being present in the home is (a) to increase the amount of communication between parents and child *in toto*, and (b) to share out what parents wish to say to each other, thereby decreasing the amount of speech for individuals. This finding is in accord with that of other research (e.g., Clarke-Stewart, 1978; Lamb, 1976).

4. In initiated, reactive, and overall speech rates, singleton families surpass twin families, and higher education groups surpass lower ones. In view of the relationships noted in number 1 above, we must conclude that these differences in the level of verbal interchange are primarliy determined by the parents.

EXAMPLES OF PARENT–CHILD INTERCHANGES

I have reconstructed some examples of parent–child interchanges from the code plus the longhand notes and quotations written on the record by the observers. They vary in length, but they are all segments of longer conversations that, because of lack of longhand comments, could not be fully reconstructed. The examples are not concerned with the child's attempts to understand and explore the world he lives in, nor with parents' cognitive explanations or efforts to expand or model speech for the child; that is, they are not the type of examples usually provided in accounts of language development (e.g., C: Horsey there. M: He's black, etc.). Instead, they have to do with play, with the child's social behavior (including nurturance seeking), with the parents' attempts to direct and guide it, and with the ordinary, more-or-less emotion-laden business that makes up the daily round of family life. This kind of interaction occurs with greater frequency than cognitive–informational interchange at this age, and it also was the focal point of our investigation. Since longhand notes were not taken in full, the child's speech cannot be reported verbatim.

The first example, initiated by the child (a twin), shows him seeking nurturance—and help as a manifest sign of nurturance. The conversation occurred during a free play situation. Mother had asked the child to retrieve a ball from under a chair (C = child; M = mother; F = father):

C: Get my ball. M: I'm busy. You get it. C: You hold my hand. M: Silly boy. C: Not silly. Hold hand. (*M then holds C's hand and they get the ball together.*)

The next example illustrates the persistently recurring preoccupation with training the child in "politeness," mingled with some understandable inconsistency:

M: Do you want some more? (*C eats some more.*) M: You like that, don't you? C: More meat. M: What do you say? C: Please. (*C gets some meat.*) C: I want tomato. M: But you don't like tomato.

The next example shows both parents trying to humor the child (a twin). During play, the child had been whining (reason not known) and mother laughed:

C: Don't laugh. I don't like mommy being funny. (*M laughs again.*) C: Not funny. M: When you whine and cry you are very funny; that's why mommy laughs. Have you a smile for mommy? C: No, I have a *mad* for mommy. M: I love you. C: I'm very angry. F: I'll do my magic for you, if you have a smile for mommy. M: Have a smile. C: No, a *mad* smile. M: Make a mad smile. (*C frowns and grimaces. M laughs.*)

The following is a typical dinner conversation, with the child wanting more independence than his mother thinks he can handle and also wanting more of the "goodies " than she is willing to concede. Mother— quite appropriately—is not responsive to all the child's wishes:

(*C has some grapes.*) C: I'll get seeds out. M: No, I'll do it. It's too hard for you with this knife. C: I want to. M: No, this knife is too sharp. (*Some further conversation ensues.*) C: Give me grapes. (*M gives them to him.*) C: Want my knife. M (*not giving him the knife*): Is this enough grapes? C: More. M: Better get started if you're going to eat all those grapes. (*M gives him more grapes.*) C: More. M: Eat that many, that you've got. We'll save some for tomorrow. We'll save these for lunch. (*More conversation follows.*) C: More. M: No more.

The following conversation during "playtime" between a single mother and her twins illustrates the mutual interaction and turn-taking that occurs among twins and shows how carefully the mother has to balance out attention and help between them. It demonstrates again how 2-year-olds constantly need and seek help, even during play. Communication is, of course, filled out and completed by nonverbal action. This mother deserves A+ for effort! (C = one twin; T = the other twin):

(*T yells loudly and excitedly.*) M: You're sure in rare form. C: Give me dough (playdough). M: It's very hard. (*M shows C how to shape the playdough and also gives some to T. Conversation between M and T.*) M (*smiling at T*): You're goofy. M to C: Make a Kitty. C: You make something for me. (*M helps C with the dough.*) M to T: Make a diamond. (*T tries.*) M: Push harder! (*T tries.*) M to T: Good. Your're doing fine! M to C: Give me a piece for a tail (*for the Kitty*). (*C pulls off a big piece.*) M to C: Just a little piece. (*C gives it to her.*) (*M, smiling at C, hands him the kitty.*) C: Make a turtle. M: Not just yet. (*T shouts something loudly.*) M to T: Do you have to go potty? T: No. C: Make a turtle. M: Just a minute. I have to make one for T first. M to T: What do you want? T: A bulldog. M: No, that's too hard. T: Then a turtle (*M helps T to produce it.*) T: Look! M to T: Yes, that's nice. Make some more—make some diamonds. T: No, I want a puppy. M to T: No, that's too hard. C: Make me one (*turtle*). (*C hands M the damaged kitty.*) M to C: Put Kitty's head back on. (*C tries clumsily. Conversation between twins and M and among the twins.*) M: Would you like some pencils? C and T: Yeah? (*M gives them a pencil each.*) M to both twins: Then you can put eyes and a nose on the turtles. (*Conversation between M and C.*) M to T: You're doing that nicely. C: Make me a turtle. M to C: I'm doing it, just a second. M (*handing C the finished turtle*): Put eyes and a nose on it. (*C does so.*)

The last short interchange to be quoted illustrates nicely how a parent may—probably quite unconsciously—apply the maxim "Do as I tell you, don't do as I do!":

F (*entering the room*): Who let that damn cat in? C: Damn Cat. F: Don't swear. (*C says no more, and F leaves the room.*)

CORRELATES AND DETERMINANTS OF THE CHILD'S
LINGUISTIC COMPETENCE

Relationships with Demographic and Child Variables

If we view linguistic competence as a "trait," measured by the summed speech acts (overall speech rate) and by the speech maturity rating, which other child and parent characteristics are associated with it? Similarly, which other child and parent characteristics are correlated with the child's propensity to initiate dialogues or to respond verbally to his parents? These are the questions that the "trait" or correlational analysis attempts to answer. Table 44 shows the significant correlations between the speech measures and other child and demographic variables for the "sample of 90."

The sheer amount of speech (speech rate) and the quality of speech (maturity rating) are moderately related, and it appears therefore that the speech rate is not just an index of garrulousness but has implications for speech quality and competence. We also see that the reactive speech measures (i.e., the proportion of mother's or father's initiations to which the child responds) have a denser network of relations with other criteria and other child variables than have the rates of initiated speech. Responsiveness to parents' speech, therefore, is a more pervasive characteristic of the child indicative of other areas of his functioning than is the more idiosyncratic initiated speech.

Among the demographic variables, twinship has the greatest impact on level of speech competence, as noted in Chapter 4, followed by mother's education, with father's occupational status ("social class") having very little association with speech behavior.

The correlations of the speech maturity rating and the speech rate with other child variables have, for the most part, already been encountered in previous chapters, but they are here drawn together to provide an overview of the interrelations of speech with other child social behavior. There is a perceptible trend in the correlations for speech measures to be associated with indices of maturity and competence—with age and vocabulary IQ (the speech rate has a near-significant correlation with the latter in the sample of 90 and highly significant ones in the sample of 46 twins and the pilot sample), with achievement of internalized standards, with independence, and, negatively, with the attachment rating (the very consistent positive correlations of all speech rate measures with verbal attachment rate are due to the fact that the verbal expression of attachment is a subset of speech in general). That verbal responsiveness to parents is a sign of maturity is also indicated by the fact that it goes with lesser amounts of negatively toned behavior (e.g., whining or crying). It is interesting to note, too, that the more time twins spend in social interaction with each other ("twins' social interaction ratio"), the greater is the amount of speech that they produce all round, which suggests that a high level of interaction among twins is itself a sign of maturity (it is, in fact, also significantly correlated with vocabulary IQ).

It must again be stressed that the correlations that should be regarded as most dependable are those that are consistent across several measures and those that have been replicated in other samples. Few of the correlations for the speech rate are replicated at the .05 probability level in the sample of 46 twins, but the correlations of this variable with mother's education and the independence rating are significant at the .10 level in this smaller sample. The speech rate also shows significant correlations in the pilot sample of 30 children with vocabulary IQ and compliance rating. There is thus some evidence for the dependability of many of the associations that speech rate shows. The considerable number of replications that the speech maturity rating has achieved in the sample of 46 twins must be somewhat suspect, however, as they may be due to a halo effect operating (same observer allotting the ratings in the two samples).

Prediction from Parent Characteristics

As was done with the other child characteristics, multiple-regression analyses were performed for the two measures of speech competence viewed as criteria, to see which parent characteristics would best predict speech fluency and maturity. The parent predictors were selected on the same principles that applied for the other characteristics (see Chapter 5 for details). Twinship, vocabulary IQ, and mother's education were entered on a separate step after all other variables. It should be pointed out again that ratings for child and parents were assigned by different raters so as to avoid contamination.

Tables 45 and 46 display the results of these analyses. The most remarkable aspect of these findings is the very high degree of predictability of the child's rate of speech—in fact, it is the most predictable of all the child characteristics studied (multiple R^2: .828). The implication is that speech is a very pervasive function, with ramifications in many of the child's experiences, and that it is influenced by—and, conceivably, also influences—a large number of parents' modes of action and behavior. Some of this high predictability, it is true, will derive from the high correlations with the rates of mother–child and father–child speech, which are reciprocally interrelated with child speech, stimulating it, as well as being stimulated by it. Note, however, that child speech incorporates all of the child's utterances, not only those addressed to mother and father, and also that the "initiated

Table 44. Correlations between Child Speech Measures and Other Child Variables (Sig. at .05 Level or Beyond) Reduced Sample: Singletons and Even-Numbered Twins (Maximum $N = 90$)[a]

		Speech maturity rating	Overall child speech rate	Initiated speech rate child–mother	Initiated speech rate child–father	Reactive speech percentage child–mother	Reactive speech percentage child–father
Criteria intercorrelations							
Speech maturity rating			.47[b,c]			.40[b,c]	.31[c,d]
Child speech rate	c	.47[b,c]		.50[b,c]	.44[b,c]	.66[b,c]	.50[b,c]
Child and demographic variables							
Social class						.21[e]	
Mother's education		.25[e]	.29[d]	.24[e]		.28[d]	
Twinship[f]		.23[e]	.69[b]	.26[e]		.48[b]	.35[b]
Age		.23[e]				.28[c,d]	.23[e]
Vocabulary IQ		.49[b,c]				.27[c,d]	.26[c,e]
Compliance rating		.40[b,c]		.21[e]			
Compliance ratio	c	.27[d]	.26[e]	.25[e]			.25[c,e]

Measure	Code						
Internalized standards rating		.47[b,c]	.32[a]				
Attachment rating	c	-.33[c,d]		.21[e]			
Verbal attachment rate	EM	.24[c,e]	.51[b]	.48[b]	.51[b]	.32[a]	.36[b]
Instrumental independence measure		.42[b,c]	.30[a]				.23[e]
Instrumental independence rating	c	.25[c,e]		.24[e]			
Child command frequency	c		.22[e]	.24[e]			
Percent time active behavior			.22[e,g]			.34[b]	
Total activity score	c		.60[b,c]				
Negative action frequency	c				.32[e]	-.25[c,e]	-.30[c,a]
Twins' social interaction ratio	c					.41[c,d]	.33[e]

[a] c = count; EM = experimental measure.
[b] $p < .001$ (two-tailed test).
[c] Correlation significant ($p < .05$) in same direction in sample of 46 twins.
[d] $p < .01$.
[e] $p < .05$.
[f] Twins coded 1, singletons 3.

Table 45. Multiple Regression Prediction of Child Speech Rate $(N = 90)^a$

Predictors		Multiple R^2 $(p < .001)$	R^2 change	Simple r
Rate mother–child speech	c	.502	$.502^b$	$.708^c$
Rate father–child speech	c	.628	$.126^b$	$.569^c$
Maternal positive action rate	c	.674	$.045^b$	$.320^c$
Maternal affection frequency	c	.693	$.020^d$	.159
Paternal command–prohibition frequency	c	.706	$.012^e$	.046
Maternal command–prohibition frequency	c	.723	$.017^d$	.253
Paternal positive action rate	c	.731	.008	$.353^c$
Play rating	M	.737	.005	.211
Paternal negative action rate	c	.740	.003	.188
Maternal negative action rate	c	.743	.004	.223
Paternal reasoning frequency	c	.746	.002	.339
Consistency of enforcement rating	M	.748	.002	.264
Paternal suggestion frequency	c	.750	.002	.430
Maternal reasoning frequency	c	.751	.001	.441
Psychological rewards rating	M	.752	.001	.217
Encourage mature action rating	M	.752	.001	.264
Maternal love withdrawal frequency	c	.752	.000	$.341^c$
Maternal suggestion frequency	c	.752	.000	$.460^c$
Twinship^f		.828	$.076^b$	.690
Mother's education		.828	.001	.293

^{a} Twinship, IQ and Mother's Education entered separately after all other variables. No father ratings included because of number of missing cases. c = count; M = mother.
^{b} $p < .001$.
^{c} Correlation significant ($p < .05$) in same direction in sample of 46 twins.
^{d} $p < .05$.
^{e} $p < .10$.
^{f} Twins coded 1, singletons 3.

speech" analysis indicated that the degree of verbal interchange in a family depends chiefly on the parents' initiative.

Speech maturity, or quality, is not as easily predictable as is quantity of speech, but there is a considerable degree of overlap in the predictors of these two measures, and the signs of the predictors are generally positive for both criteria. In the case of maternal affection and paternal commands–prohibitions, which have positive correlations with speech rate, but negative ones with speech maturity, the negative correlations are almost zero and can be attributed to chance.

Let us first consider the variables that are important predictors for both criteria. In identifying these, we must take account not only of those predictors that produce a significant increment in R^2, but also of those with high simple correlations with the criterion, which were relegated to a lower place in the equation by dint of their interrelations with other predictors. Father's speech to the child is particularly important in explaining the variance of both speech rate and speech maturity, and this fact underlines the importance of father's interaction with the child for the latter's growing competence. Both mother's and father's suggestions (i.e., milder, cognitively modulated forms of control) are also important predictors for both speech criteria. Similarly important for explaining both criteria are positively toned actions (mother's for the speech rate and father's for speech maturity), mother's and father's use of reasoning, and mother's encouragement of independence in general.

Mother's speech to the child, which is the outstanding predictor of child's speech rate, does not appear as a predictor of speech maturity at all, because it did not pass the normal criterion for entry to the regression on account of its interrelations with other predictors (though it has a significant

Table 46. Multiple-Regression Prediction of Speech Maturity Rating (N = 90)[a]

Predictors			Multiple R^2 ($p < .001$)	R^2 change	Simple r
Encourage mature action rating	M		.160	.169[b]	.401[c]
Rate father–child speech		c	.228	.067[d]	.327[c]
Maternal suggestion frequency		c	.258	.030[e]	.252
Paternal positive action rate		c	.291	.034[f]	.138
Maternal love withdrawal frequency		c	.303	.011	.186
Psychological rewards rating	M		.319	.017	.195
Maternal negative action rate		c	.330	.010	.009
Maternal affection frequency		c	.341	.011	−.028
Paternal reasoning frequency		c	.346	.006	.247
Paternal command–prohibition frequency		c	.352	.005	−.037
Maternal positive action rate		c	.354	.002	.108
Play rating	M		.357	.003	.025
Maternal reasoning frequency		c	.358	.001	.196
Maternal command–prohibition frequency		c	.358	.000	.066
Paternal suggestion frequency		c	.358	.000	.267[c]
Vocabulary IQ			.467	.109[b]	.490[c]
Mother's education			.470	.003	.110
Twinship[g]			.473	.003	.249

[a] Twinship, IQ, and mother's education entered separately after all other variables. No father ratings included because of number of missing cases. c = count; M = mother.
[b] $p < .001$.
[c] Correlation significant ($p < .05$) in same direction in sample of 46 twins.
[d] $p < .01$.
[e] $p < .10$.
[f] $p < .05$.
[g] Twins coded 1, singletons 3.

simple correlation with speech maturity). Additional parent characteristics that take an important place in the prediction of the speech rate alone are mother's affection, as well as her use of love withdrawal, and mother's and father's degree of command giving (i.e., their directiveness).

The most dependable predictors are those that have been replicated in the sample of 46 twins. Again, replicated predictors exist for the speech rate: parents' speech to the child, their positive actions, and mother's use of suggestions and love withdrawal. For the maturity rating, *father's* speech rate and his use of suggestions are replicated predictors. While speech flourishes, it appears, mainly in a positive and warm climate of parent–child relations, some sterner words (e.g., commands–prohibitions) also stimulate it, probably because they, too, express a cognitive approach by the parents.

The speech rate was submitted to another multiple-regression analysis, confined to the "responsiveness sample" of 40 children. The variables that added significantly to the prediction in the multiple-regression analysis for the sample of 90 were entered as predictors, plus the responsiveness and appropriateness percentages of mother and father. (For definition of these see Table 8.)

It can be seen from Table 47 that the responsiveness and appropriateness variables did not add significantly to the prediction. Mother's and father's rates of speech and degree of command giving made the more important contributions in this analysis, as in the previous one. However,

Table 47. Multiple-Regression Prediction of Rate of Child Speech Including Responsiveness Predictors ($N = 39$)

Predictors		Multiple R^2 ($p < .001$)	R^2 change	Simple r
Rate mother–child speech	c	.557	.557[a]	.747
Rate father–child speech	c	.675	.118[a]	.591
Maternal command–prohibition frequency	c	.706	.031[b]	.340
Paternal command–prohibition frequency	c	.737	.031[b]	.035
Maternal responsiveness %	c	.752	.015	.216
Maternal rate of positive actions	c	.760	.008	.272
Maternal affection frequency	c	.764	.005	−.017
Paternal responsiveness %	c	.770	.006	−.084
Paternal appropriateness %	c	.773	.003	.097
Maternal appropriateness %	c	.774	.001	.409
Twinship[c]		.799	.025[b]	.687

[a] $p < .001$.
[b] $p < .10$.
[c] Twins coded 1, singletons 3.

mother's appropriateness was fairly strongly related, and her responsiveness was somewhat related to the child's rate of speech (though the former was crowded out by other variables and placed in a lower position in the prediction). Both tendencies exerted a greater influence on the child's speech than did father's parallel characteristics, which had near-zero correlations with the criterion. We can conclude that a mother's being appropriately responsive to her child does enhance the latter's speech capability, probably because appropriateness indicates a rational attitude in the mother that communicates itself to the child and prompts him to more verbal (i.e., cognitive) behavior.

Summary

1. The child's rate of speech and the speech maturity rating (quantity and quality of speech, respectively) are the two well-interrelated aspects of speech competence measured here.

2. Speech competence is affected adversely by the fact of twinship. Child characteristics to which both speech criteria are positively related, are compliance, internalized control, and independence; there is also a replicated relationship between speech maturity and vocabulary IQ. Language competence is thus a sign of cognitive maturity.

3. Quantity of speech is the most highly predictable of all the child characteristics and is more predictable from parent measures than is speech maturity. Replicated relationships between parent variables and speech (either measure) show that a positive emotional climate and cognitive stimulation are both conducive to good development of language. Mother's sensitivity in responding to the child is also predictive of speech competence. Mother seems to exert greater influence on the quantity of speech, father more on its quality (see discussion in Chapter 10).

DISCUSSION

The verbal communication system between parents and child spans and pervades all aspects of parent–child relations. The socialization process works on language, as well as through language, and indeed, speech is a form of socialization. The language that the child hears and the language that he uses, as Bernstein (1975) suggests, shapes the child's view of reality. His parents' speech acts as a cognitive stimulus that assists the development of the child's cognitive structures; but it also puts a stamp on the family's social interaction and climate.

Some of these influences very probably work through the mode and structure of speech that parents employ, and this has often been thought to be defined by social class (cf. Bee *et al.*, 1969; Bernstein, 1975; Tulkin & Kagan, 1972). We were not able to record the details of the syntactic structure of speech by either parents or child, but even the coarse measures of speech that we used (rate of speech per unit of time, and a rating of the maturity of the child's speech) provided some insights into the role that speech plays in the socialization process. It should also be remembered that Conway *et al.* (1980) showed that *amount* of maternal speech, not a measure of speech complexity, best explained the singletons' superiority—as compared with twins—in amount, as well as maturity of speech (use of sentences). Amount of speech therefore seems a powerful and important factor in itself, and the rate of child speech in this investigation, in fact, showed a significicant correlation with the rating of the child's speech quality.

Characteristics of the family communication system have been summarized above, but a few points deserve further comment.

The rate of child-to-mother initiation was found to be unrelated to that of mother-to-child, whereas initiation to father was moderately related to the father's initiation to the child. (See Chapter 10 for a discussion.) Further, the child's initiations had fewer associations with other child traits than did his reactive speech. Initiations in general appear to be a more isolated, idiosyncratic child characteristic, more subject to situational influences, having little relationship with other areas of the child's functioning.

The child's reactive speech is somewhat related to the parents' degree of responsiveness, but it is not influenced by their readiness to initiate dialogues. But the child's tendency to respond is related to a number of other child traits and hence seems to be a pervasive characteristic, deriving from internal predispositions and forming part of the fabric of the child's personality.

Our parents responded to approximately 75% of their children's speech, and this high degree of responsiveness in the home should be contrasted with a response rate of 39% by mothers to their 2½- to 5-year-old children, when observed in free play in a laboratory playroom by Baldwin and Baldwin (1973). The response rate of 34% that our children displayed, however, corresponds very closely to that shown by the children in the Baldwins' laboratory situation (35%). It seems, then, that mothers respond relatively more in a naturalistic home situation than they do in a laboratory, although it should be borne in mind that the rate of utterance by children and mothers was much higher during the 30 min laboratory observation than it was during our longer home observations. Watts (1978) and Yuzwak (1979) found that mothers generally conversed more with their young children in the home than in the laboratory, though not all speech categories showed significant differences. The higher responsiveness in the home is somewhat surprising, as one might intuitively expect mothers to be more responsive in the laboratory, where they can give their children their undivided attention and where they may feel more put on their mettle. However, the inhibition that some parents may feel in the unaccustomed laboratory situation is an influence that works in the opposite direction. Moreover, it may be that in the home, the child feels freer to express his needs, and more situations arise in the ordinary routine of family life where parents feel the necessity to respond to the child's needs or to resolve mild conflicts between siblings or to guide the child's social behavior.

Higher education, as has been found in many previous studies (see Chapter 3), brings with it greater emphasis on a verbal–cognitive approach in child rearing that is echoed by the children—hence, higher speech rates in higher education groups. Possible genetic influences should, however, not be overlooked (cf. Chapter 9).

Differences in speech rates between twins and singletons (with singletons and their parents speaking more) were much more marked than those between differing education groups, and here it would be implausible to invoke genetic explanations. As was noted earlier for the general case, in the case of twin families, too, the level of verbal interaction must be primarily a function of lesser speech by parents, since they do more of the initiating and responding than the children. Such reduced speech is understandable in view of the greater demands on parents' time and attention that a pair of twins makes, and it may also be explained as parents' reaction to the cohesion of the pair (even though this cohesion did not express itself verbally).

The correlational or "trait" analysis showed speech to be a sign of competence and maturity, with the rating of speech quality being rather more indicative of these traits than speech rate.

The speech rate, however, turned out to be the most highly predictable of all the child characteristics we studied, which means that it is very closely bound up with many parent characteristics. (This high predictability was also corroborated in the sample of 46 twins.) Speech quality was somewhat less easily predictable.

Our findings suggest that a warm and positive attitude, particularly on the part of the mother, facilitates speech development. Some other research (e.g., Clarke-Stewart, 1973; Radin, 1971) has similarly shown a connection between maternal affection and the child's cognitive advancement, but such a finding is by no means universal (cf. McCall, Appelbaum, & Hogarty, 1973). It is very likely that maternal affection, as Clarke-Stewart and Apfel (1978) suggest, works through other aspects of mother's interaction with the child, for example, stimulation or responsiveness.

Love, it seems, is not enough; and indeed, maternal stimulation has, more often than maternal affection, been shown to be an important facilitator of a child's cognitive development (e.g., Clarke-Stewart, 1973; Hanson, 1975) and of language development in particular (e.g. Elardo, Bradley, & Caldwell, 1977). It is not surprising that we found similar relationships for our measures of cognitive stimulation, namely mother's and father's level of speech and their use of suggestions.

Our finding that responsiveness (not merely of a verbal kind), and particularly sensitive responsiveness, encourages linguistic competence is similarly in line with other research results, linking maternal responsiveness to infant competence (e.g., Clarke-Stewart, 1973; Elardo et al., 1977). One may hazard the inference that appropriate responsiveness sets an example of rationality that encourages the child to verbalize his thoughts and feelings, something that indicates a tendency toward at least cognitive, even if not rational, processes.

The evidence regarding the effects of directiveness is somewhat contradictory. Some authors have shown that directing and controlling the 2- to 3-year-old child's activities tends to retard intellectual advancement or language development (e.g., Clarke-Stewart et al., 1979; Nelson, 1973), and some have even claimed that " . . . the mother's use of inhibitory and input-control techniques . . . promotes the development of a nonrational, non-verbal stance towards the environment" (Olim, 1975, p. 321). On the other hand, McCall et al. (1973) showed that children whose IQ increased from 3 years on had parents who used medium or fairly severe penalties. Our finding that parents' directiveness facilitates language development would suggest that a certain firmness, provided it is rational and embedded in generally affectionate relationships, can also be cognitively stinulating, and this is in line both with the last-mentioned author's findings and with Baumrind's (1971) demonstration that authoritative parental attitudes and practices lead to competence in the child.

By setting forth the evidence that shows that, and how, parental behavior influences language development, I do not wish to enter the argument about the thesis of a universal, innate predisposition for language, propounded by Chomsky (1965) and others. This research has no evidence to produce for or against this proposition. Nor do I mean to deny the importance of genetic factors in determining individual differences in verbal competence. Indeed, while parental behavior may seem to act as an environmental influence, it may also operate via genetic transmission. Nevertheless, the characteristics of his environment and the kind of transactions the child has with his parents will, in any event, play an important role in language and intellectual development.

Language is the hallmark of the human state. It represents a reflectiveness beyond physical action, and it is a tool of concept formation, for often we think by and through language. Introducing the child to the verbal conventions of his society is probably the most fundamental *cognitive* aspect of socialization, since his linguistic competence will influence his relations with others, the complexity of his cognitive structures, and his status in the world at large.

CHAPTER 8

Other Domains of Interaction

POSITIVELY AND NEGATIVELY TONED ACTIONS

The individual action verbs coded for child and parents can be broken down in many different ways. Thus, verbs indicating proximity seeking and attention seeking were grouped together to form the attachment system. Any action that also had the attribute of demonstrating compliance or noncompliance with the parents' wishes was counted as a component of the compliance system. But in addition to these groupings, and partly overlapping with them, an exhaustive superordinate classification system incorporating all actions was also established. This classified child, mother, or father actions on an *a priori* basis into seven categories (see Table 3). The two categories that this section explores are the child's positively and negatively toned actions.

These categories are important in that they summarize through their component actions (see Table 3 for a list) the contribution that the child makes to the family's emotional climate. On the one hand, his positively toned actions, added together, summarize the contribution he makes toward the family's harmonious living, and on the other, his negatively toned actions express his contribution toward building up family conflict and tension.

On what basis do we arrive at an acceptable definition of these categories? What is aversive, or unpleasant, ranges from a mild irritant to extreme pain, and a list of such actions will vary from person to person to some extent. Patterson and his colleagues (e.g., Patterson & Cobb, 1971), who also set out to identify a class of "noxious responses" and "aversive stimuli" for the purposes of their investigation, therefore decided that it was not feasible to draw up a universal taxonomy of aversive stimuli. Instead, they proceeded on an *a priori* basis to establish a list of such actions; this list was then validated by having mothers rate the behaviors for aversiveness and by showing that the responses served as suppressors for ongoing prosocial behavior, that is, that they reduced talk below its normal rate of occurrence. (Other actions suppressed talk, too, and therefore suppression of talk was not a sufficient criterion, and an *a priori* definition was the essential basis for categorizing aversive stimuli and separating them from the positive reinforcers that also suppressed talk.)

In this investigation, too, the child's negative and positive actions were defined on an *a priori* basis. Negatively toned actions, however, were only partly defined in this way, namely, as those actions that parents generally find aversive. The list thus arrived at (e.g., yelling, whining, hitting, non-compliance) largely overlaps with Patterson and Cobb's (1971) list. But in addition, other actions were empirically classified as negative acts, namely, all actions that were immediately followed by parental prohibition, even if on other occasions, they were classified under different categories. Thus, laughing was generally classified as a positive, since it is a way of showing pleasure, but when it was followed by parental prohibition, it was categorized as a negative, something that we came to recognize as "naughty laughter." Positively toned actions were defined *a priori* as those that parents could generally be expected to welcome (e.g., showing affection, showing pleasure, helping, compliance). This list also largely coincides with Patterson and Cobb's (1971) list of "positive reinforcers." It will be seen from Table 3 that parents' positively and negatively toned actions were defined in a similar way, though some modifications were made in recognition of the different connotations that parental actions also have. Thus, while hitting by parents is undoubtedly an aversive stimulus, it was considered more useful to establish a separate category (physical control) for it.

Parents' Responses to Child's Positively and Negatively Toned Actions

First, we will turn to the hand analyses of parents' responses to their child's positive and negative that were carried out on the randomly selected subsample of 53 children (36 twins and 17 singletons) on whom similar analyses were conducted for compliance and noncompliance. The reasons for doing such an analysis by hand rather than by computer were set out in Chapter 6, and the main benefits to be gained from a hand analysis of positive–negative actions were that it enabled us to note two successive parent responses to one child action and to eliminate parental actions that are not genuine responses to the preceding child action.

The classification of parents' responses and the rules for counting in this analysis are the same as those given in Chapter 6. It should be noted that the percentage of responses for the various categories displayed in

Table 48 refers to the sums of first and later responses that either mother or father may have made to a given child action.

Acts of compliance made up 70% of positive actions and acts of noncompliance represented 39% of negative actions. It is therefore not surprising that the rank orders of mother's response frequencies after child positive and negative are the same as those after compliance and noncompliance, respectively (cf. Table 26). The rank orders of father's response frequencies here are identical to mother's, but father's rank orders differ somewhat from the corresponding rank orders after compliance and noncompliance in that in the latter case, physical control assumed greater importance.

The comments made for compliance–noncompliance apply here, too, and only the most salient points will therefore be touched upon. Mother engages in more verbal control, and particularly reasoning, than father, and this reflects her general inclination toward greater verbal intervention. The levels of verbal control and reasoning by both parents are understandably higher after negative than after positive actions. The rank order of mother's response categories after positive actions is exactly the same as the rank order of the overall probabilities of these categories (father's rank order differs somewhat from the overall probabilities). The likelihood of a particular response by mother occurring is therefore more a function of the overall probability of that response than it is a function of the child's preceding act, except that child's negative expectably evokes more parental verbal control than neutral actions do.

Table 48. Mean Percentage of Parents' Responses to Child Positive and Negative Actions[a]

	Child positive actions				Child negative actions			
	Mother		Father		Mother		Father	
Parent responses	Mean %	Rank order	Mean %	Rank order	Mean %	Rank order	Mean %	Rank order
Positive response	16.02	4	14.61	4	8.16	4	7.55	4
Negative response	1.55	5	1.74	5	4.79	5	4.04	5
Neutral response	22.39	2	19.42	2	14.20	3	11.93	3
Verbal control	18.09	3	14.52[b]	3	26.90	2	22.90[e]	2
Reasoning control	1.37	6	0.98	6	3.99	6	2.68[b]	6
Physical control	0.67	7	0.92	7	2.50	7	2.09	7
No response	39.90	1	47.80[b]	1	39.49	1	48.85[d]	1

[a] N for mother: 53; N for father: 49; N positive actions: 7549; N negative actions: 8592.
[b] $p < .02$.
[c] $p < .05$.
[d] $p < .01$ for difference between mother and father (two-tailed t test).

Both positively and negatively toned actions, like compliance and non-compliance, are most likely—40%–50% of the time, in fact—to be ignored by parents, and father is distinctly less likely than mother to make a response. In the hurly-burly of family life, it seems, the child's praiseworthy, as well as his changeworthy, acts often receive no overt attention and are neither reinforced nor discouraged.

The child's positively and negatively toned actions that were clearly addressed to both parents were analyzed to see whether mother or father or both would response to them. Table 49 shows that the response comes most often from mother alone and least often from both together. However, it is also apparent that when the child acts in a disagreeable way, both parents feel more often obliged to respond and to become involved than when he engages in an agreeable action. The hard data indeed bear out the popular impression that disagreeable actions attract parents' notice more than agreeable ones do.

What Do Parents See as "Objectionable" Behavior?

It is of interest to note which actions parents perceive as objectionable since this is the behavior that will arouse conflict and elicit restrictions. In order to shed light on this question, a count was made of all the actions that the 53 mothers and 49 fathers of this subsample forbade. The seven most frequently forbidden actions are listed in Table 50 in rank order.

Each of these actions was, on average, forbidden at least once by mother. However, even the action at the top of the list (playing with an object—it could have been a toy or the TV set) was never forbidden by 10 of the 53 mothers and by 21 of the 49 fathers. It is noteworthy that the two top-ranking actions—on the face of it, quite innocuous—were evidently rendered objectionable by the circumstances in which they occurred on specific occasions. Behaviors generally considered noxious, like hitting and whining, appear lower on the list, no doubt because they happened infrequently.

Table 49. Parents' Responses to Child's Positive and Negative Actions Addressed to Both[a]

Respondent	Positive actions % responding	Negative actions % responding
Mother	51.4	48.5
Father	43.6	41.4
Both	5.1	10.1

[a] "No response" was not included in the total.

Table 50. Most Frequently Forbidden Actions[a]

	Mother (N = 53)				Father (N = 49)			
Actions forbidden	Total frequency	Highest individual frequency	Mode	No. of mothers forbidding	Actions forbidden	Total frequency	Highest individual frequency	Mode	No. of fathers forbidding
Playing with object	237	19	2.5	43	Playing with object	75	14	1	28
Talking	107	11	1	37	Talking	63	6	1	27
Disorganizing	87	9	1.5	29	Disorganizing	41	5	1	23
Romping	70	4	1	26	Hitting	29	4	1.5	15
Undetermined action (e.g., squirming)	57	8	1	26	Eating	25	8	1	14
Hitting	55	7	1	25	Undetermined action (e.g., squirming)	25	5	1	13
Crying, whining	54	10	1	21	Romping	22	2	1	16

[a] Actions that were never forbidden: permitting, approving, expressing affection verbally, helping.

Fathers forbade fewer actions and fewer fathers forbade them—they were, of course, less involved with the children; but the list of activities that they objected to is very similar to that for mothers.

The actions that were never forbidden by mother or father are few in number—a sobering thought; moreover, 2½-year-olds engage very infrequently in some of the actions that were never forbidden, like approving and expressing affection verbally. It should be added that only one mother forbade hugging—but she did so seven times!

Correlates and Determinants of Positively and Negatively Toned Actions

As with the other areas of social interaction presented in previous chapters, correlations of the summed counts of positive and negative actions were used in two ways. We attempted to gain some insight into the direction of the causal effect—whether it runs from parent action to child positive–negative or vice versa—by means of a cross-lagged panel analysis that related the density (or rate per minute) of parent behavior during the first observation to the density of child behavior during the second observation a week later, and vice versa. The counts of positive–negative actions were also transformed into relative frequencies (proportions out of all child actions), and these frequencies were submitted to correlational and multiple-regression analyses to determine to what extent parent behavior can predict the child actions.

Remote Effects of Parents' and Children's Positive and Negative Actions, or: Who Influences Whom?

The general rationale and methods of cross-lagged panel analysis have been described in previous chapters. The densities (rates per minute) of the child and parent grouped action categories formed the data base for the intercorrelations that were calculated for 136 children and mothers, and for the 99 fathers who were present for both observation sessions.[1]

It will be seen that the rates at which children and parents engaged in the various actions in the two observations, usually one week apart, are quite stable, as shown by the autocorrelations. The synchronous correlations between the child actions and most parent actions are moderately high, too, the chief exception being correlations with parents' neutral actions. This indicates that in most cases, there is a significant association between the rates at which child positive and negative actions and certain parent actions occur during one observation. Furthermore, a number of cross-lagged cor-

---

[1] The significance levels for the correlations, shown in Table 51, were, however, for reasons set out in Chapter 3, calculated as if only one partner out of each twin pair had been included, that is, on a reduced N of 90 for the mother analysis and of 69 for the father analysis.

relations are significant, too, showing that the association between these child and parent actions persists over time. In the main, the passage of time attenuates the relationships, but in a few cases, the effects actually become stronger.

In those instances where the differential between the cross-lagged correlations are significant, a basis exists for arriving at a "most plausible" inference about the direction of causal effects. Such significant cross-lagged differentials occurred only for mother–child interaction.

For every one of these significant differences, the cross-lagged correlation linking mother behavior at Time 1 (T1) to child action at Time 2 (T2) is the larger one. (See Figure IA, Appendix X.) Therefore, the hypothesis that it is mother's behavior that influences child action seems tentatively supported. Rival hypotheses and detailed arguments underlying the interpretations are discussed in Appendix X.

The relationships between mother's negative actions and child's positive actions display some special characteristic. The most plausible interpretation suggested by these relationships is (1) that mother's negative action (i.e., her disapproval, criticism, etc.) *increase* the rate of the child's more acceptable behavior in the medium term *and* (2) that the child's positive actions (i.e., compliance, affectionate behavior, etc.), *decrease* mother's negative actions over time. The facilitative influence of mother's negative on the child's positive over time is, indeed, somewhat weakened by the counterpull of the decreasing effect of the child's positive on mother's negative. The near-zero synchronous correlations might, at first blush, tempt us to conclude that mother's negative and the child's positive exert no immediate influence on each other at all. However, this apparent absence of influence, in view of the evidence of the cross-lagged correlations, is more likely due to a balancing of forces, the inhibiting effect in one direction balancing out the facilitating influence in the other, with the resultant force being (almost) zero.

For some of the interrelations displayed in Table 51, the synchronous correlations between parent and child actions are quite strong and positive at both points in time; the two cross-lagged correlations are also fairly strong and of roughly equal magnitude. With such a configuration of correlations, the most plausible inference we can draw is that influence is mutual and that effects flow in both directions; that is, parent behavior increases child action, and vice versa, child action increases parent behavior. Thus, for example, mother's suggestions and positive increase the child's positive, as well as vice versa; her commands–prohibitions and physical control increase the child's negative, and parallel effects flow in the reverse direction, too. Similar reciprocal influences are also operating, for example, between father's and the child's positive, and between father's and the child's negative. However, these positive intercorrelations, without a definite

Table 51. Cross-Lagged, Synchronous, and Autocorrelations for Parents' Grouped Actions and Child Positive and Negative Actions for Observation 1 and Observation 2: Rates per minute[a]

Mother–child interactions (df 88)
Child positive action: Autocorrelation T1 × T2: .634[b]

Maternal Variables	Auto correlations	Synchronous correlations		Cross-lagged correlations		Significant differences
	T1:T2	CT1:MT1	CT2:MT2	CT1:MT2	MT1:CT2	
Commands–prohibitions	.594[b]	.450[b]	.397[b]	.327[c]	.524[b]	$p < .05$
Suggestions	.625[b]	.450[b]	.444[b]	.253[d]	.380[b]	
Physical control	.526[b]	.235[d]	.219[d]	.108	.370[b]	$p < .05$
Negative action	.550[b]	−.045	.080	−.023	.229[d]	$p < .05$
Positive action	.682[b]	.353[b]	.391[b]	.283[c]	.363[b]	
Neutral action	.754[b]	.137	.122	.066	.208[d]	

Child negative action: Autocorrelation T1 × T2: .650[b]

	T1:T2	CT1:MT1	CT2:MT2	CT1:MT2	MT1:CT2	
Commands–prohibitions	.594[b]	.663[b]	.619[b]	.389[b]	.453[b]	
Suggestions	.625[b]	.424[b]	.392[b]	.343[b]	.344[b]	
Physical control	.526[b]	.590[b]	.575[b]	.306[c]	.453[b]	
Negative action	.550[b]	.497[b]	.419[b]	.216[d]	.433[b]	
Positive action	.682[b]	.300[c]	.237[d]	.248[d]	.175[e]	
Neutral action	.754[b]	.113	.040	−.035	.113	$p < .05$

Father–child interactions (*df* 67)

Child positive action: Autocorrelation T1 × T2: .683[b]

Paternal variables	Auto correlations	Synchronous correlations		Cross-lagged correlations	
	T1:T2	CT1:FT1	CT2:FT2	CT1:FT2	FT1:CT2
Commands–prohibitions	.676[b]	.497[b]	.322[c]	.262[a]	.351[c]
Suggestions	.427[b]	.500[b]	.258[d]	.237[d]	.208[e]
Physical control	.755[b]	.168	.285[d]	.130	.239[d]
Negative action	.696[b]	.203[e]	.206[e]	.019	.223[e]
Positive action	.630[b]	.403[b]	.361[b]	.266[d]	.293[d]
Neutral action	.746[b]	.149	.014	.054	.051

Child negative action: Autocorrelation T1 × T2: .692[b]

	T1:T2	CT1:FT1	CT2:FT2	CT1:FT2	FT1:CT2
Commands–Prohibitions	.676[b]	.421[b]	.277[d]	.245[d]	.264[d]
Suggestions	.427[b]	.222[e]	.137	.162	.126
Physical control	.755[b]	.381[c]	.226[e]	.230[e]	.334[c]
Negative action	.696[b]	.409[b]	.218[e]	.241[d]	.328[c]
Positive action	.630[b]	.128	-.008	.102	-.009
Neutral action	.746[b]	-.087	-.141	-.120	-.100

[a] C = child; M = mother; F = father; T = time. Child and parent variables are rates per minute.
[b] p < .001.
[c] p < .01.
[d] p < .05.
[e] p < .10.

direction being indicated, may also be due to high *rates* of parent and child behavior being associated with one another.

The main findings of the analysis are summarized in Figure 16. Summing up these relationship between parents' action categories and the child's positively and negatively toned actions, we can conclude that mother's influence on the child far outweights the child's effect on mother. Whenever a significant cross-lagged differential allows us to draw an inference as to the most plausible direction of effects, there is a mother-to-child effect, although sometimes a supplementary child-to-mother effect also exists.

Mother's tendency to engage in negative actions (e.g., disapproval and criticism) increases the child's negative (e.g., noncompliance, whining, and crying) in the medium term, and this is a one-way influence. However, her commands–prohibitions and physical control and the child's negative actions seem to feed and enhance each other in a mutually reinforcing "coercive cycle." But these same forms of control also tend to increase the child's more acceptable behavior in the medium term, without a similar influence's running in the opposite direction. On the other hand, a homeostatic feedback loop mechanism is operating between mother's negative and the child's positive: not only does mother's negative increase the child's positive at a later point in time, but the latter also plays a complementary role; that is, it, in turn, tends to decrease mother's negative. In other words, mother and child modulate their own behavior, reacting to the partner's behavior in a kind of feedback loop. In the case of father's interactions with the child, no definite direction of effects could be established, and the most plausible inference suggests that mutual influences are operating.

Relationships with Other Child Variables and Prediction from Parent Characteristics

The correlational analyses that will be discussed in this section were carried out on the child's positively and negatively toned actions, expressed as relative frequencies, that is, as percentages of the child's total actions. I

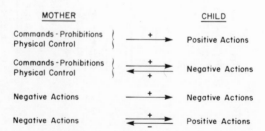

Figure 16.   Summary of remote effects showing most plausible direction of effects.

Table 52. Correlations of Child Positive and Negative Action Frequency with Other Child Variables (Significant at .05 Level or Beyond): Reduced Sample—Singletons and Even-Numbered Twins (Maximum $N - 90$)[a]

		Positive action relative frequency	Negative action relative frequency
Vocabulary IQ		$.21^b$	
Compliance rating		$.24^b$	$-.57^{c,d}$
Comply ratio	c	$.44^c$	$-.62^{c,d}$
Internalized standards rating		$.28^{b,d}$	$-.28^{b,d}$
Attachment rating			$.32^{d,e}$
Instrumental independence rating		$.31^{d,e}$	

[a] c = count.
[b] $p < .05$.
[c] $p < .001$ (two-tailed test).
[d] Correlation significant ($p < .05$) in same direction in Sample of 46 twins.
[e] $p < .01$.

decided to base the analyses on relative frequencies rather than on the rate measures, since the rates of child positive and negative were significantly and *positively* intercorrelated, a relationship that will largely be due to the influences of the child's general activity level. This underlying variable would then generate some artifactual parallel correlations with the rates of positive *and* negative actions, correlations that would be both misleading and difficult to interpret. The positive and negative action frequencies, on the other hand, had only a low positive correlation with each other. The rate measures, therefore, are less appropriate for the analysis of positive–negative actions than they are in, say, the area of attachment, where the rate of attachment behavior has important psychological implications of its own. The correlations of the relative frequencies with other child variables that proved significant are shown in Table 52.

The positive correlations of compliance rating and comply ratio with positive actions and the negative correlations of these variables with negative actions are "in-built" in the data, since positive actions comprise compliance and negative actions comprise noncompliance as subsets. The similar correlations with the internalized standards rating can be understood as extensions of the same relationship. These correlations, therefore, are not invested with any psychological significance. However, it is of interest to note that positive actions are associated with vocabulary IQ and with instrumental independence (i.e., with attributes that are generally perceived as positive), while negative actions are related to attachment, as rated by the observers. This latter relationship again demonstrates that the rating captured the negative, bothersome aspects of attachment behavior. Most of these relationships were also replicated in the sample of 46 twins, though this is not a fully independent sample.

The power of parent characteristics to predict the child's positively and negatively toned actions was examined in multiple-regression analyses, the results of which are displayed in Tables 53 and 54. The overall prediction of positive actions is fairly good, though once the R^2 has been adjusted for shrinkage, it is reduced to .331. The main contributions to the prediction of positive actions (i.e., the variables that produce a significant increase in R^2) are provided not only by positive and kindly parent traits, such as mother's warmth, but also by sterner characteristics, like mother's encouragement of mature actions and consistency in enforcing rules. In exploring these relationships, it is also useful to consider the more important simple correlations, since some of the parent variables may be significant correlates of the child's positive, although the regression procedure has displaced them to a lower position in the equation because of the intercorrelations among the predictors. Thus, the use of psychological rewards also has a significant

Table 53. Multiple-Regression Prediction of Child Positive Action Relative Frequency ($N = 90$)[a]

Predictors			Multiple R^2	R^2 change	Simple r
Encourage mature action rtg.	M		.098[b]	.098[b]	.314[c]
Warmth rating	M		.184[d]	.085[b]	.303
Consistency of enforcement rating	M		.225[d]	.042[e]	.275[c]
Maternal negative action frequency		c	.260[d]	.034[e]	−.221
Maternal play frequency		c	.293[d]	.033[e]	.289
Paternal command–prohibition frequency		c	.309[d]	.016	.086
Paternal positive action frequency		c	.320[d]	.011	.160
Comply ratio	F	c	.327[d]	.007	.163
Paternal negative action frequency		c	.343[d]	.016	−.069
Comply ratio	M	c	.352[d]	.009	.074
Paternal play frequency		c	.353[d]	.001	.173
Twinship[f]			.410[d]	.057[b]	−.059
Maternal command–prohibition frequency		c	.416[d]	.006	.060
Maternal positive action frequency		c	.429[d]	.014	.088
Psychological rewards rating	M		.432[d]	.002	.225[c]
Mother's education			.451[d]	.019	.118
Vocabulary IQ			.459[d]	.008	.212

[a] Twinship, IQ, and mother's education entered separately after all other variables. No father ratings included because of number of missing cases. c = count; M = mother; F = father.
[b] $p < .01$.
[c] Correlation significant ($p < .05$) in same direction in Sample of 46 twins.
[d] $p < .001$.
[e] $p < .05$.
[f] Twins coded 1, singletons 3.

Table 54. Multiple-Regression Prediction of Child Negative Action Relative Frequency ($N = 90$)[a]

Predictors			Multiple R^2 ($p < .001$)	R^2 change	Simple r
Paternal negative action frequency		c	.159	.159[b]	.399[c]
Paternal command–prohibition frequency		c	.215	.056[d]	.310
Play rating	M		.266	.051[d]	−.240
Maternal reasoning frequency		c	.312	.046[d]	.327[c]
Verbal–psychological punishment rating	M		.337	.025[e]	.259
Maternal love withdrawal frequency		c	.348	.011	.247
Support of dependency rating	M		.361	.013	−.262
Maternal physical punishment frequency		c	.370	.009	.210[c]
Maternal command–prohibition frequency		c	.378	.009	.225[c]
Paternal physical punishment frequency		c	.383	.005	.115[c]
Paternal reasoning frequency		c	.389	.006	.129
Maternal negative action frequency		c	.390	.001	.361[c]
Comply ratio	M	c	.394	.004	−.350[c]
Maternal positive action frequency		c	.396	.002	−.106
Psychological rewards rating	M		.397	.000	−.213
Paternal positive action frequency		c	.397	.000	−.032
Twinship[f]			.525	.128[b]	−.072
Comply ratio	F	c	.528	.003	−.276
Vocabulary IQ			.529	.001	−.013
Mother's education			.529	.000	−.138

[a] Twinship, IQ, and mother's education entered separately after all other variables. No father ratings included because of number of missing cases. c = count; M = mother; F = father.
[b] $p < .001$.
[c] Correlation significant ($p < .05$) in same direction in Sample of 46 twins.
[d] $p < .05$.
[e] $p < .10$.
[f] Twins coded 1, singletons 3.

positive association with the child's positive, but it was displaced to a lower position because of its correlation with the warmth rating.

The maternal behaviors that can be said to predict the child's positive most reliably are those that have also been shown to be significantly predictive in the replication of this analysis in the, not fully independent, "sample of 46." These characteristics are mother's use of psychological rewards (praise and approval), her encouragement of independence in the child, and her consistency in enforcing her rules. In view of the fact that acts of compliance form a subset of positive actions, it is not surprising that these three variables are also some of the most important predictors of compliance (cf. Chapter 6). However, not all these influences are necessarily one-way. It will be remembered from the cross-lagged panel analysis of remote effects that the negative association between the child's positive and mother's negative shown here may be accounted for by the fact that the child's positive inhibits mother's negative, whereas mother's negative tends to facilitate the child's positive.

Another multiple regression of the child's positive actions was performed for the "responsiveness sample" of 40 children (both twins and singletons), with the responsiveness and appropriateness variables added to those predictors that had added significantly to the prediction in the "sample of 90." In this analysis, only father's responsiveness percentage explained a significant additional proportion of the variance ($p = .10$). In addition, however, father's appropriate unresponsiveness had a significant simple negative correlation with the child's positive actions. Thus it is mainly father's responsiveness and his unresponsiveness that both have predictable effects on the child's agreeable actions.

The overall prediction of the child's negative is slightly better than that of the child's positive, and the R^2 adjusted for shrinkage is .392. It is chiefly father's, and secondly mother's, aversive behaviors that contribute significantly to the prediction of negative actions. (The absence of play with the child [negative correlation] can also be interpreted as aversive behavior.) Maternal reasoning frequency is somewhat incongruous among these "predictors," and it may well be that the direction of effects here is, in fact, reversed, that is, that it is the child's aversive actions that elicit many justifications and explanations from mother. Some variables with significant simple correlations with child negative have been displaced to lower positions in the prediction (e.g., mother's negative and mother's command–prohibition frequencies, because of their correlations with the parallel father variables).

To identify the characteristics that are most reliably associated with child negative actions, we look again at the variables for which significant correlations have been replicated in the sample of 46. They are essentially aversive actions by parents: father's and mother's negative, maternal physical punishment and command–prohibition frequencies, the degree to which mother does not comply with the child's wishes, and the use of reasoning frequency. However, it will be recalled that the cross-lagged panel analysis suggested that in some of these cases, reciprocal effects may be operating; for example, mother's commands–prohibitions will increase child's negative actions, but similar effects flow in the reverse direction. Still, the main effects seem to flow from parent to child, though among the variables included in the remote effects analysis, only mother's negative actions exhibit a clear unidirectional mother-to-child effect.

In the multiple-regression analysis of the "responsiveness sample," mother's unresponsiveness and inappropriateness added significantly to the prediction of the child's negative actions, and both mother's and father's tendency to issue repeated commands also had high simple correlations with this child variable. Here again, the logic of the relationships leads one to suspect that the direction of effects may well run from child to parent; that is, it is the child's disagreeable actions that produce unresponsiveness or repeated commands in the parents, but there is no evidence available on which a definite conclusion could be based.

Summary

1. Parents' responses to the child's positive and negative actions follow the same pattern as their responses after compliance–noncompliance (the former comprise the latter as a subset).

2. Parents' most frequent prohibitions are elicited by very ordinary actions, such as playing with an object or talking. More noxious behavior, such as hitting other family members, evokes prohibition, too, but occurs relatively rarely.

3. The remote effects analysis indicates that in the medium term, the mother's influence far outweighs the influence of the child's positive and negative actions, though some mutual effects operate, too.

4. Replicated correlations with other child variables show an interesting set of relationships among child qualities: positive actions are significantly associated with independence (rating) and negative actions with attachment (rating).

5. Predictions from parent characteristics that have been replicated are the following: The child's positive actions are predicted by mother's use of psychological rewards, her consistency in enforcing rules, and her encouragement of independence. The child's negative actions are predicted mainly by his parents' aversive actions, for example, mother's and father's negative actions, maternal physical punishment, unresponsiveness, and repeated directions. For some of these relationships, however, the cause–effect direction may well run from child to parent.

INSTRUMENTAL INDEPENDENCE

As a child grows older, his reliance on his parents for ministering to his physical needs, for helping him to cope with his world, and even for frequent physical contact and nurturance inevitably lessens. This growth of independence and autonomy plays an important role in the social interchanges between the child and his parents, since they will—to varying degrees—deliberately encourage and foster it as one of the goals of socialization. Nevertheless, the literature on this topic is surprisingly meager; most of the empirical work in the area dates from the 50s and 60s, and of late, the subject seems to have fallen into almost complete neglect, except for research on "achievement motivation," which has been viewed as a closely related variable (see below).

The term *an independent child* usually implies that the child possesses certain positive characteristics, like initiative, self-assertion, and striving to do things unaided, as well as that he seeks nurturance relatively infrequently (Parke, 1969; Zigler & Child, 1973). Independence is therefore taken to mean more than a simple lack of dependence, and the two traits are not necessarily to be considered as opposite poles of one bipolar continuum. However, the literature is not always consistent on this point. Beller (1955), for instance, postulates a negative, but not completely inverse, relationship between dependence and independence, and his results confirm this position. Heathers (1955), however, differentiates between "instrumental independence" and "emotional independence," and he bases this distinction on the differing needs that these behavior systems serve, *instrumental independence* being defined as coping with problems unaided. In this sense, it then becomes the obverse of instrumental dependence. Kagan and Moss (1962) and Emmerich (1966) similarly distinguish between instrumental and emotional dependency.

Beller (1957) operationalizes independence by questions tapping "autonomous achievement striving" (e.g., "How often does the child derive satisfaction from his work?") and thus *a priori* assumes that these two characteristics are equivalent. Crandall, Preston, and Rabson (1960) further establish an empirical relationship between independence and achievement striving by their finding that preschool children who were rated high on achievement effort were less emotionally dependent on adults than were children who displayed fewer achievement efforts. Indeed, others, too, often consider independence to be closely related to achievement (Hartup, 1963; McClelland *et al.*, 1953; Zigler & Child, 1973). In view of the theoretical and demonstrated relationship between these two facets of the child's social behavior, studies of the parental antecedents of achievement orientation will be considered below, together with those of independence, pure and simple.

Instrumental independence, then, was included in this investigation as an important social characteristic and aspect of the child's ongoing interactions in his family. It was defined as the degree to which the child engages in activities independently, and the overall rating was allotted by averaging subratings on the following components: child feeding himself, dressing himself, going to the bathroom by himself, dealing with difficulties by himself, and initiating his own activities. These areas were rated on the basis of observation and mother's answers to relevant questions. Instrumental independence was therefore clearly not conceived of as the opposite pole to our attachment construct, since the latter was defined by behaviors that have in the past been considered indicative of *emotional* dependence. A negative correlation between independence and attachment was, however, expected, and a slight, though significant, one (−.32) was indeed found.

Independence—manifested by the child's initiating his own activities, going to the bathroom without mother, etc.—is an attribute of the child's behavior that could not easily be incorporated in a code of simple actions, and therefore no behavior counts for independent actions are available.

Scores for independent behavior were also assigned in the experimental situation. While the experimental measure of independence was more productive in generating relationships with other variables than were the experimental measures of compliance and attachment, the correlations largely replicated those for the independence rating based on observation and interview, and the experimental measure will therefore not be discussed further.

Correlates and Determinants of Instrumental Independence

The correlates of instrumental independence among other child variables are shown in Table 55. Instrumental independence, as rated by the observers, increases with age, as one might expect. What is notable about the relationships is, above all, that independence is correlated with a great many positive characteristics that indicate both maturity and amicable

Table 55. Correlations of Instrumental Independence Rating with Other Child Variables (Significant at .05 Level or Beyond): Reduced Sample—Singletons and Even-Numbered Twins (Maximum N = 90)[a]

		Instrumental independence rating
Age		$.27^{b,c}$
Vocabulary IQ		$.30^{d}$
Attachment rating		$-.32^{d}$
Compliance rating		$.42^{c,e}$
Comply ratio	c	$.32^{d}$
Internalized standards rating		$.50^{c,e}$
No. of form-board pieces placed	EM	$.29^{b,c}$
Activity shift score	c	$-.21^{b,c}$
Speech maturity rating		$.42^{c,e}$
Rate of child speech	c	$.30^{d}$
Frequency of child request	c	$.28^{c,d}$
Positive action frequency	c	$.31^{c,d}$

[a] c = count; EM = experimental measure.
[b] $p < .05$.
[c] Correlation significant ($p < .05$) in same direction in Sample of 46 twins.
[d] $p < .01$ (two-tailed test).
[e] $p < .001$.

interactions with parents. The more independent boys, for example, tend to have higher vocabulary IQs, and the association between these two characteristics has been confimed by other studies (e.g., Emmerich, 1966). These boys also tend to comply more with parents' requests. On the other hand, independence is negatively correlated with negative traits: restlessness (activity shift score is an index of this) and the demanding aspects of attachment that the rating captured (though independence is not the direct inverse of attachment—we did, indeed, see some children who were both highly attached and highly instrumentally independent).

We should, however, express a reservation about this seemingly clear picture: since almost all the ratings were assigned by the same observer a halo effect may well have produced some of these plausible relationships. The exception is the internalized standards rating, which was allotted by a different person, and the fact that it has the highest correlation of all with instrumental independence lends credence particularly to the association between independence and compliance. Almost all the significant relationships shown here have also been found to be significant in one of the two replication samples, the sample of 46 twins (which is not a fully independent sample) or the pilot sample. The exceptions are the vocabulary IQ and the rate of child speech, whose correlations in the other two samples are also positive but do not reach significance.

To determine the set of parent characteristics that would best predict instrumental independence, a multiple-regression analysis was carried out on the sample of 90, and the parent variables to be entered as predictors were selected by the same rules that applied for other multiple-regression analyses. The results are shown in Table 56.

The overall prediction afforded by this set of variables is fairly good, although the R^2, when adjusted for shrinkage, is reduced to .388. Individual simple correlations are only moderate to low, except for the correlation with mother's encouragement of mature action. Encouragement of independence and mature action (in relation to the child's ability) was operationalized as mother's tendency to insist on his helping with dressing himself, going to the bathroom by himself, eating with appropriate utensils by himself, and solving his problems for himself as far as possible (e.g., getting a toy from a shelf by climbing on a chair, rather than asking his mother to get it down for him). It is not surprising that this maternal characteristic turned out to be the best single predictor of the child's independence. Mother's command–prohibition frequency made an additional significant contribution to the prediction. Looking at the variables that have important simple correlations with independence, but that were displaced to a lower position in the prediction because of intercorrelations among the predictors, we note that these are mother's reasoning frequency, her restrictiveness, and her consistency in enforcing rules. If we assume that the direction of effects runs

Table 56.   Multiple-Regression Prediction of Instrumental Independence Rating
$(N = 90)^a$

Predictors			Multiple R^2 $(p < .001)$	R^2 change	Simple r
Encourage mature action rating	M		.363	$.363^b$	$.603^c$
Maternal command–prohibition frequency		c	.407	$.044^d$	.291
Paternal affection frequency		c	.422	.015	−.043
Maternal reasoning frequency		c	.438	.016	.261
Verbal psychological punishment rating	M		.451	.013	.048
Restrictions rating	M		.459	.008	.308
Material rewards rating	M		.467	.008	$.118^c$
Paternal play frequency		c	.475	.008	−.112
Rate father–child speech		c	.480	.005	.104
Maternal love withdrawal frequency		c	.485	.004	.136
Maternal play frequency		c	.487	.002	.016
Paternal reasoning frequency		c	.488	.001	.103
Support of dependence rating	M		.490	.002	$-.178^c$
Rate mother–child speech		c	.491	.001	.171
Psychological rewards rating	M		.492	.001	.022
Consistency of enforcement rating	M		.494	.002	.307
Maternal affection frequency		c	.495	.001	−.135
Paternal physical punishment frequency		c	.495	.000	−.030
Maternal physical punishment frequency		c	.495	.000	−.033
Vocabulary IQ			.517	$.022^e$	.305
Mother's education			.536	$.019^e$	.132
Twinship^f			.539	.003	.152

^{a} Twinship, IQ, and mother's education entered separately after all other variables. No father ratings
   included because of number of missing cases. c = count; M = mother.
^{b} $p < .001$.
^{c} Correlation significant ($p < .05$ in same direction in Sample of 46 twins.
^{d} $p < .05$.
^{e} $p < .10$.
^{f} Twins coded 1, singletons 3.

from parents to child, the overall picture appears to be that a demanding and
authoritative approach that does not neglect offering a rationale for the
demands and rules that parents make is conducive to independent behavior in
the child.

The most dependable predictors are those that are replicated in parallel
analyses. The two replications of this analysis that are available both confirm the significant association between mother's deliberate fostering of independence and the child's mature behavior. In the sample of 46, mother's
consistency of enforcement and support of dependence (the latter in a negative sense) also made significant contributions to the prediction.

The relationships between the child's independence and parents'
responsiveness were explored by simple correlations in the responsiveness

sample of 40 children. The general trend was quite clear in that all responsiveness and appropriateness variables had positive associations, and unresponsiveness and the frequency of repeated commands had negative associations with independence; however, none of the correlations reached significance even at the .10 level. A separate regression analysis was run for this subsample, and mother's and father's responsiveness and appropriateness variables were added to the variables that contributed significantly to the prediction of independence for the sample of 90. In this analysis mother's encouragement of mature actions was still the most prominent predictor, but her appropriateness made the second most important, and significant, contribution to the prediction, and thus appropriate responsiveness to the child appears to be another salient determinant of the growth of independence.

How do these findings on parent antecedents of independence compare with the relationships reported in the literature? That encouragement of independent behavior by parents actually results in greater independence is supported by several sets of findings (Baumrind & Black, 1967; Nakamura & Rogers, 1969; Witkin et al., 1962; Yarrow, Campbell, & Burton, 1968) and contradicted by none. Independence training has also been shown to be positively related to achievement motivation in boys (Winterbottom, 1958), and this is particularly so for "optimally timed" independence training (Schmalt, 1975). The independence-training–high-achievement hypothesis is challenged only by Chance (1961, cited in Zigler & Child, 1973), who found that independence training was negatively associated with actual achievement measures in the elementary school, but this appears to be an isolated finding.

Several studies have indicated that there is a negative association between restrictiveness and independence and spontaneity (e.g., Antonovsky, 1959; Baumrind & Black, 1967; Hatfield et al., 1967). However, the evidence is conflicting as regards achievement measures: some studies have shown that they are negatively affected by authoritarian control or restrictions on independent activity (Shaw & Dutton, 1962; Winterbottom, 1958). On the other hand, a whole series of studies suggest the precise opposite, namely, that parental restrictiveness leads to higher achievement or achievement motivation in the children (e.g., Drews & Teahan, 1957; Hoffman, Rosen, & Lippitt, 1960; Maccoby, 1961; McClelland et al., 1953, Watson, 1934). Such seeming inconsistency in the findings can, however, be understood better if one considers in greater detail the definition of *restrictiveness*. If it entails restrictions on exploration or independent activity and initiative, as in Baumrind and Black (1967) and Winterbottom (1958), it will result in lowered independence and achievement. However, often expectations of mature behavior and demands for independent actions are labeled restrictiveness, too; for instance, Yarrow et al. (1968) labeled such expectations of maturity as clearing up toys "restrictiveness for neatness" (I relabeled it "encouragement of independence" in the discussion above). It is this kind of "restrictiveness" that involves demands for mature behavior—say, in the area of neatness, table manners, or self-caring—that seems conducive to independence. It should be noted, however, that our measures of restrictiveness went beyond maturity demands and encompassed the amount of general restrictions imposed, though these did not usually apply to exploration or initiative.

Baumrind and Black (1967) also found consistency and use of reasoning to be related to independence. Baumrind's 1971 study suggested that a "nonconforming" pattern in parents (i.e., one that stresses individuality and self-expression) went with independence in boys, whereas an "authoritative–nonconforming" pattern (which characterizes parents who use firm control but do not restrict the child's experimenting or decision making, and who are nonconforming, too) went with independence in girls.

The trends that emerge from these reports in the literature suggest that granting the child freedom to make decisions and to take initiatives—thus permissively fostering independence, while at the same time demanding a mature standard of behavior in an authoritative way, and even a certain parental sternness—is associated with greater independence in the child. Our findings as regards parental practices favoring the growth of independence are in general agreement with these trends, but they emphasize, on the one hand, the importance of a demanding and authoritative attitude and, on the other, the need to be appropriately responsive to the child.

The growth of independence, it should be noted, is, however, not solely dependent on parental practices, since a genetic factor made a significant contribution to the variation of instrumental independence (see Chapter 9).

A few thumbnail sketches of independent and nonindependent children, as recorded in the observers' informal notes, follow:

> Family M: Parents have set high standards of behavior for this child and make their approval and praise conditional on his meeting these standards. He seems a very warm and affectionate child—mature for his age in that he performs chores for mother and father, long attention span, is made responsible for own behavior, etc. At the same time I felt he was wanting more "babying."
> Family P: He is the most independent 2-year-old I have observed to date—dresses himself, washes self, serves self at table, etc. Both parents give freely of their time and attention to R.—verbal praise frequent. He seems a happy child—not overly subdued, yet respecting parental limits.
> Family B: This child at present knows all the letters of the alphabet and most of the numbers from 1 to 10, but, in direct contrast, he makes no effort to dress himself.

Summary

1. Replicated relationships with other child characteristics show instrumental independence to be associated with age, and with many posi-

tive qualities of the child: maturity of speech, with compliance and internalized standards, and with an absence of restlessness.

2. The most dependable (replicated) parental predictors of instrumental independence are mother's encouragement of independence and nonsupport of dependence. These are expectable findings; in addition, however, sensitivity in responding to the child and a certain demandingness also play an important part in fostering independence.

PHYSICAL ACTIVITY LEVEL

Neither raising nor lowering the child's activity level is of central importance in parents' socialization aims—except in extreme cases of hyperactivity—but it is a child characteristic that has often been thought to be to a large extent under genetic control, and for this and other reasons, it might be expected to enter into illuminating relations with other child dispositions. Activity level was therefore thought worthy of study in an investigation that opened up the possibility of directly observing and measuring the child's activity in the home, as well as in an experimental situation.

Two relatively simple quantitative measures of the child's activity in the home were obtained. The child's physically active behavior was defined as locomotion, gross motor play ("rough-and-tumble"), manipulative play with toys, carrying objects, drawing, and making music. Neither eating, nor watching TV, nor listening, nor talking was included in the definition of *physically active behavior*. The percentage of observation time that the child spent in such behavior was calculated, forming the variable "percentage of time in active behavior." The second measure was the number of times during a minute of active behavior that the child shifted from one activity to another, called the *activity shift score*. These two measures were combined, via their z scores, to form the standardized *total activity score*. Details of the incidence of this behavior were presented in Chapter 3.

While the first measure represents a time measure of the child's actual activity, the second one is essentially an index of his restlessness. Each of these measures was thought of as defining a separate aspect of what is generally conceived of as "activity level." There is, indeed, evidence that the various measures of activity level have not always in past studies been closely correlated with each other (Cromwell, Baumeister, & Hawkins, 1963), and it has therefore been questioned whether activity level can be considered a unitary phenomenon. However, Buss, Block, and Block (1979), for instance, found a mechanical record and an observer rating of activity level to be correlated. Our two measures were highly correlated, too (.78, $p < .001$) and, furthermore, showed very similar correlations with other child and parent variables, the correlations always showing the same sign. As far as this investigation is concerned, therefore, activity level as observed in the home constitutes a homogeneous phenomenon, and it is sufficient to consider mainly the composite measure.

On the other hand, lack of cohesiveness of the construct "activity level" was apparent in the relation that the home-based behavior count had with the parallel experimental measure. The latter score represented a standardized composite of the number of different toys that the child picked up and the number of marked floor squares that he traversed in 10 min of exploratory play in the experimental situation. This "total activity experimental measure" had almost exactly zero correlations with the two home observation activity measures, as well as with their composite. Moreover, the only significant correlation it displayed with any other child or parent variable was with another experimental score, that of compliance. The measure will therefore not be discussed further. However, this showing suggests that some of the lack of associations between different activity measures reported in the literature (Cromwell et al., 1963) may be due more to activity's being measured in different situations—many of them being experimental—rather than to their being measured via different indices.

Is a certain activity level a characteristic that a child displays consistently across time and over age? The usual way of answering this question is to ascertain whether the rank ordering of children on this variable stays relatively stable across time, that is, whether the correlation between different occasions is significant and, possibly, strong. In fact, the evidence in the literature for such stability is somewhat conflicting. Thomas et al. (1963, 1968) found some stability for activity level from infancy to early childhood (see Thomas et al., 1968, Figure B). Maccoby and Feldman (1972) found some stability for amount of manipulative play within defined experimental situations from age 2 to 2½ and 3. But they found no significant stability coefficients between these ages for activity level, as measured by number of squares traversed. On the other hand, Buss et al. (1979) found "fair consistency" for two measures of activity level across a four-year span from age 3 to age 7. The short-term stability coefficients across two observation sessions, usually one week apart, that we noted were .671 for activity shift score and .366 for percentage of time spent in active behavior ($p < .001$ for both). Activity level was evidently a characteristic that these children displayed fairly consistently across this short time span.

Another way of looking at stability is to see to what extent the *level* of activity stays the same across situations. It can be argued (cf. Cromwell et al., 1963) that to expect this is to set up a mistaken criterion for stability, since different situations (and the observation sessions in the home were not controlled as to content or structure) may well call forth different levels of activity. However, as was noted in Chapter 2, the mean level of actions in general remained stable across the two occasions.

Past literature provides recurring evidence that activity level is subject to some genetic control (e.g., McClearn, 1970; Scarr, 1966; Willerman, 1973). Our genetic analysis, however, found no significant genetic component in this characteristic, something that will be discussed further in the next chapter.

Correlates and Determinants of Activity Level

The significant correlations that the activity measures generated with other child variables are shown in Table 57.

Activity—as assessed by our measures, which included gross motor activity, as well as toy play—evidently decreases with age, even within our narrow age range. Such a decrease over age of general motoric discharge, as measured by the number of squares entered and changes in type of toy, was

Table 57. Correlations between Activity Measures and Other Child Variables (Sig. at .05 Level or Beyond): Reduced Sample—Singletons and Even-Numbered Twins (**Maximum** N = **90**)[a]

		Activity shift score	Percentage time active behavior	Total activity score
Criteria intercorrelations				
Activity shift score	c		.78[b,c]	.94[b,c]
Percentage time active behavior	c			.95[b,c]
Child and demographic variables				
Twinship[a]		.40[b]	.43[b]	.44[b]
Vocabulary IQ		−.30[e]		−.25[f]
Age		−.27[c,f]	−.22[c,f]	−.26[c,f]
Number of child behavior units	c	.74[b,c]	.61[b,c]	−.71[b,c]
Nonverbal attachment rate	c	.57[b,c]	.34[b,c]	.48[b,c]
Attachment rating		−.23[f]	−.33[b]	−.30[e]
Instrumental independence rating		−.21[c,f]		
Rate of child speech	c		.22[f]	.22[f,g]
Frequency of child requests—%	c	−.43[b,c]	−.38[b,c]	−.43[b,c]
Expression of pleasure—%	c	.30[c,e]	.29[c,e]	.31[c,e]
Expression of displeasure—%	c	−.25[f]	−.29[e]	−.28[e]

[a] c = count.
[b] $p < .001$.
[c] Correlation significant ($p < .05$) in same direction in Sample of 46 twins.
[d] Twins coded 1, singletons 3.
[e] $p < .01$.
[f] $p < .05$.
[g] Correlation significant ($p < .05$) in opposite direction in Sample of 46 twins.

also found by Routh, Schroeder, and O'Tuama (1974) in a cross-sectional study of children ranging in age from 3 to 9 years. Maccoby and Feldman (1972), in a short-term longitudinal investigation, also found a decline of activity, measured in the same children at 2, 2½, and 3 years by number of squares crossed. However, in the same research, the amount of manipulative play and of uninterrupted play with a single toy increased over this age span. What this means is that restless activity decreases, but purposive activity and attention span increase over age at preschool and primary-school age.

Our measures of physical activity are equivalent to rate measures and hence will be affected by the level of general activity that the child exhibits. This "in-built" relationship can be seen in the very high correlations with the child's total amount of behavior, and it will also be reflected in the correlations with other rate measures. The positive correlation with the rate of child speech, however, should not be considered dependable, since the same correlation in the sample of 46 was significant and negative.

The correlations with the twin–singleton dichotomy confirm the higher level of general activity of singletons noted in Chapter 4.

The correlations with the nonverbal attachment rate must in part be interpreted as artifactual, because they are both rate measures and because of the fact that locomotion (toward mother) forms part of both the activity and the attachment measures. There is also an indication, however, that a child who is restless (as assessed by the activity shift score) tends to seek nurturance more nonverbally, and this applies particularly to the young child, since both nonverbal attachment and activity measures are inversely related to age. In other words, both are signs of immaturity, contrary to Murphy's (1962, as reported in Maccoby & Masters, 1970) view, which suggests that it is the passive child who will be slower than the active child in abandoning the less mature mother-contacting behavior. The picture of the active–restless child as being less mature is also corroborated by the fact that he is seen by observers as less instrumentally independent. At the same time, he is perceived as displaying fewer of the troublesome signs of attachment (i.e., attention seeking) that the rating captures. The more active child is also happier and less dysphoric in mood than the passive child, as indicated by behavior counts.

A high rate of activity often seems to be negatively related to indices of cognitive competence: in our case, this is evident in the negative associations with vocabulary IQ and with the relative frequency of verbal requests. In a similar vein, Schaefer and Bayley (1963) found that activity, assessed early in infancy, is negatively correlated with ratings of positive task-oriented behavior later in childhood. Kagan, Moss, and Sigel (1963) also report that inability to inhibit motoric discharge (hyperactivity) in early childhood (3–6 years) is predictive of avoidance of intellectual activities even in adulthood.

A further finding of importance is the connection between high activity in infancy and later behavior disorder (not specifically hyperactivity) reported by Thomas *et al.* (1968). In some cases, these authors suggest, high activity level presents management problems to parents that lead them to complain of behavior problems in the child.

The associations that can be considered most dependable in our study, because they have stood the test of replication in the (not fully independent) sample of 46 twins, are the positive correlations with the number of child behavior units, the nonverbal attachment rate, and the frequency of expression of pleasure, and the negative correlations with age, the frequency of child request, and instrumental independence.

In the case of activity level, it is advisable to be even more guarded than with other child characteristics in assuming that the direction of effects runs from parents to child in view of the evidence that activity level may—at least, in part—be a constitutional tendency. In speaking of "parent predictors," therefore, we have to bear in mind that the multiple-regression analysis simply demonstrates the association that exists between a set of parents' child-rearing practices, which we have arbitrarily placed in the position of predictors, and the child's activity level, viewed as the criterion.

Table 58 displays the results of the multiple-regression analysis for the sample of 90. The overall "prediction" is, in fact, rather better than for many other child characteristics: the set of predictors together explains nearly 65% of the variance, though the adjustment for shrinkage reduces the R^2 to .571. We see that father's amount of play has the highest correlation with the total activity score. Since it is play with the child that is being assessed here, and the child's play enters prominently into his activity score, this finding is hardly surprising, though we do not know whether it is an active child who persuades father to play with him constantly, or whether a play-loving father elicits a great deal of activity in the child. (We invariably adopted the convention, in coding rough-and-tumble play with mother and father, of scoring the child as the main actor, since it was usually difficult to tell who instigated it.) Maternal amount of play had a lesser, though still significant, association with the child's activity. This is understandable, as we know that she tended to play less with the child than father did during our observations.

The logic of the relationship leads us to interpret the strong association that mother's degree of command giving has with the criterion as being most probably due to the child: a highly active child, who is mobile and restless, is likely to provoke his mother into issuing many commands and prohibitions. It is much less plausible that an abundance of commands and prohibitions from her induce a high level of activity in the child. Father's command–prohibition frequency also shows a significant correlation with activity level, but has been relegated to a lower place in the regression by its high correlation with the parallel mother variable.

Table 58. Multiple-Regression Prediction of Total Activity Score (N = 90)[a]

Predictors		Multiple R² ($p < .001$)	R^2 change	Simple r
Paternal play frequency	c	.250	.250[b]	.500[c]
Maternal command–prohibition frequency	c	.374	.125[b]	.378[c]
Monitoring rating	M	.430	.056[d]	.253
Psychological rewards rating	M	.477	.047[d]	.126
Encourage mature action rating	M	.520	.043[d]	−.249[c]
Paternal affection frequency	c	.532	.012	.190
Maternal affection frequency	c	.535	.003	.214
Paternal command–prohibition frequency	c	.536	.001	.286
Maternal suggestion frequency	c	.536	.001	.099
Paternal suggestion frequency	c	.537	.001	.190
Paternal reasoning frequency	c	.537	.000	.007
Maternal reasoning frequency	c	.538	.000	.195
Twinship[e]		.590	.052[d]	.435
Maternal play frequency	c	.590	.000	.217
Mother's education		.632	.042[d]	−.123[c]
Vocabulary IQ		.648	.015[f]	−.246

[a] M = mother; c = count. Twinship, IQ, and mother's education entered separately after all other variables. No father ratings included because of number of missing cases.
[b] $p < .001$.
[c] Correlation significant ($p < .05$) in same direction in Sample of 46 twins.
[d] $p < .01$.
[e] Twins coded 1, singletons 3.
[f] $p < .10$.

The negative association of mother's encouragement of mature action with activity level (significant in both the sample of 90 and the sample of 46) reflects the fact, noted earlier, that high activity level is indicative of immaturity. It may be that a mother who fails to foster maturity in her child allows him to be highly active and therefore induces a high activity level, but this assumption of a mother-to-child effect must be somewhat speculative, since high activity—and lack of maturity—in the child may also prompt mother to be less demanding in this area. It should be noted that mother's education contributes significantly to the prediction and does so in both samples: a higher education level in the mother means less physical activity in the child.

Two studies in the literature report an aversive reaction in parents to boys' high activity. Schaefer and Bayley (1963) found that activity is associated with maternal hostility for boys (in early infancy), but not for girls. Similarly, Willerman and Plomin (1973) noted that both parents of active nursery-school boys (but not of active girls) tend to be less indulgent and protective toward them. They suggest that this may be due to parents' protectiveness in the past not having been effective in modulating their boys' activity level. Both sets of authors, at any rate, interpret parents' behavior as a reaction to the boys' activity rather than the other way round. In our investigation, however, there was no indication that high activity level in the boys aroused, or was associated with, adverse reactions by their parents, except that it evoked a succession of commands and prohibitions that might at times have been tinged with irritation. Otherwise, it is positive parental behavior—play, affection, praise, and approval—that is significantly associated with the child's activity level. In the responsiveness sample of 40 children, too, the mother's responsiveness is somewhat related to the percentage of time spent in active behavior (r: .28, $p < .10$), and father's total reactivity (i.e., his responsiveness to the child's needs and requests, as well as to speech) is slightly associated with the total activity score (r: .30, $p < .10$).

Summary

1. Activity shifts (a measure of restlessness) and the percentage of time spent in active behavior are highly interrelated. Hence, "activity level" can be considered a cohesive construct.

2. Activity level has connotations of immaturity: it decreases with age and is positively related to nonverbal attachment behavior. However, it also goes with a happy, less dysphoric mood. All these relationships have been replicated.

3. The most dependable (replicated) predictors of activity level are: father's amount of play with the child, mother's degree of command giving, a *low* degree of encouragement of maturity, and a lower education level. However, one should not think of the direction of influence as running necessarily from mother to child.

DISCUSSION

The child's positively and negatively toned actions, his instrumental independence, and his activity level are discussed together in this chapter, not because they are unimportant but because I have had to exercise some selectivity in the detailed in-depth examination of the various behavior systems encompassed in this study, and these areas have been probed somewhat less thoroughly than the other behavior systems discussed in earlier chapters.

Positively and Negatively Toned Actions

The categories of positively and negatively toned actions cut across other ways of categorizing the child's social behavior and class together those actions that parents find agreeable (including compliance) and objectionable (including noncompliance). These categories are significant in an ethological account of family interaction in that they make important contributions to the family climate in a positive or negative sense, they allow us to clarify the parents' role in producing them or reacting to them, and they illustrate the interdependence of parental and child behavior that is inherent in the family system.

Parents' responses to positive and negative actions—examined by hand analysis—follow a pattern very similar to that observed in the case of compliance–noncompliance (see Chapter 6). These actions do not activate any very clear-cut contingency system on the part of the parents; in fact, mother fails to make any response whatever to about 40% of such actions, and father to about 50% of them. The likelihood of any given response is more determined by the overall probability of the occurrence of that response in mother's repertoire of actions than it is contingent on the child's preceding act, except that the child's negative evokes more attempts at further control than one would expect from the overall probabilities.

In considering the remote effects analysis and the most plausible inferences as to the direction of effects that it generates, we must remember that this is not an analysis of events arranged in sequence along a time line; that is, we are not dealing with a conventional sequence analysis that would specify what the effects of an immediately preceding mother action is on child behavior, or vice versa. What the analysis shows are the presumed effects in the medium term (one week) of the density of a given mother action on the density of a child action, and vice versa, inferred from the correlations. The difference in the magnitudes of these correlations allows us, under favorable circumstances, to infer the preponderant direction of influence, that is, whether it is mother's behavior *tendency* that affects the child's or whether it is the other way round.

We found that mother's influence on the child's positive and negative action tendencies is in general stronger than the effect of these child actions on mother's behavior tendencies (see Figure 16). Mother's commands–prohibitions and physical control on one day produce more agreeable behavior in the child on a later occasion, but—as common sense would suggest—such agreeable behavior does not increase these modes of control by mother, nor does it decrease them. However, commands–prohibitions and physical control, on the one hand, and the child's noxious behavior, on the other, seem to feed on each other in a "coercive cycle" that suggests an interchange escalating in intensity. Mother's criticism, disapproval, or hostility, however, increase the child's tendency to annoying behavior in the medium term without a marked influence running in the reverse direction. (It does not, of course, follow that the child's negative actions have no immediate effect on mother's behavior.) Mother's criticism, etc., also tends to increase the child's more agreeable actions at a later point in time, and the latter, in turn, damp

down mother's disapproval in the long run, thus setting up a beneficial reciprocal feedback loop, well adapted to mother's purposes.

The findings of a study of sequential interactions (in the immediate
situation) of 18-month-old children with their mothers by Maccoby, Martin,
Baran, and Jacklin (1979) echo the conclusions that we have been able to
draw from the remote effects analysis. These authors, too, found that
behaviors tend to be reciprocated in kind, negatives being responded to by
negatives, positives by positives. Moreover, by separating onsets from
offsets of actions, they were able to note specifically that maternal negative
behavior influences children to stop being negative if they are engaged in
negative behavior (equivalent to our finding that mother's negative increases
the child's positive). On the other hand, maternal negative also serves to
start negative behavior in the child if it is not already under way (equivalent
to our finding that maternal negative increases child's negative). But no
such patterns were seen in the influence of the children on their mothers in
that investigation. The two sets of conclusions would appear to corroborate
and strengthen each other.

The multiple-regression analysis indicated that the most dependable
(replicated) parent predictors of the child's positive include not only warm
maternal traits but also sterner qualities, such as encouragement of independent action (the parallel ratings for fathers were not numerous enough to
be included in the analysis). The most dependable predictors of the child's
negative are mother's amount of command giving and mother's and father's
punishing, aversive actions. Generalizing from the results of the remote
effects analysis, we have some grounds for concluding that for these variables, the main effects run from parent to child.

In the separate responsiveness analysis, it was *father's* responsiveness
that was significantly related to the child's positive actions; but it was
mother's unresponsiveness that was associated with the child's negative
actions. The direction of the effects may well be reciprocal here, but the
argument is persuasive that it is the child's disagreeable actions that induce
the mother to be less responsive to, and compliant with, his wishes. It is
notable that father's responsiveness is more strongly related to the child's
positive, but mother's is more related to his negative actions. The reason
may lie in the differing relationships that mother and father have with the
child (see Chapter 3): father is the playmate, concerned mainly with the
child's entertainment and trying to make him happy, whereas mother is the
caregiver and the major disciplinarian, to whom the child turns more in his
distress, needs, and black moods.

Instrumental Independence

Fostering autonomy in the child (i.e., inducing him to let go of his
mother's apron strings) is for most parents a salient goal of the socialization

process. In this investigation, instrumental independence was defined as the degree to which the child engaged in activities independently or initiated them himself, and it was assessed by a rating. *Independence* suggests positive qualities in the child and is not the simple inverse of attachment, the latter having more emotional connotations, although a slight negative correlation between them emerged. Independence, as one would expect, increases with age, and it is related to various positive indications of competence and maturity in the child. The most important and dependable parental predictors of the child's independence are all maternal characteristics. If we assume that the direction of influence runs from parent to child, the conclusion imposes itself that it is a demanding and authoritative approach that best fosters the child's independence, but this should be coupled with the ability to see things from the child's point of view: a willingness on the part of the mother to give a rationale for her demands and to be responsive, in an appropriate way, to the child's needs. Past research has also emphasized a certain sternness in expecting and demanding mature standards of behavior as important parental antecedents of early independence. Our results are congruent with these findings. The necessary complement, according to this literature, is that the mother should also grant the child freedom to take initiatives in his own way and to make his own decisions. If this aspect of encouraging autonomy does not stand out in our results as an independence-promoting strategy, this is, no doubt, due to the young age of our children.

Physical Activity Level

The child's level of physical activity was a domain that came under scrutiny in this investigation because it was considered a basic attribute whose relationships with other characteristics of child and parents would throw light on the functioning of the child as a social being within the family system. It is through his activity that the child is exposed to a variety of stimuli, and we might therefore expect that in this way, he will experience growth, both cognitively and socially. Activity level was operationalized by a combination of the length of time spent in active behavior, including toy play, and an index of shift of activity, two aspects that turned out to be highly interrelated. Overall activity level has some negative connotations in this study. It seems to be indicative of restless, motoric discharge and immaturity: it decreases with age and, far from promoting cognitive growth, it is negatively related to intellectual competence, though it also goes with a happy, easygoing child.

No significant genetic influence on activity level was detected in this investigation. However, because of its possible constitutional basis (shown in previous research), it would seem inappropriate to speak unequivocally of parental influences on this behavior tendency. The parent characteristics that were most dependably shown to be associated with activity level are father's amount of play with the child, mother's degree of command giving, and her lack of encouragement of maturity—but the direction of influence must remain somewhat ambiguous. A hostile attitude by parents, which has sometimes been reported to be associated with high activity level (perhaps as a consequence of it?), was not related to it in this investigation. On the contrary, high activity level appears to be symptomatic of a happy child, a great deal of playful interaction with both mother and father, and an easygoing atmosphere in the home, with comparatively few cognitive and maturity demands being made.

What relationships exist between the different domains that we have been discussing in this chapter? The operational definition of positive actions—those that parents would find agreeable—did not include independent actions as such. Nevertheless, a close correspondence is noticeable between positive action and independence. The child variables that are significantly related to the child's positive actions (e.g., vocabulary IQ and compliance) show a similar relationship to independence. There is also a certain parallelism in their prediction: mother's encouragement of independence and her consistency in enforcing her rules are important predictors for both. The two domains characterize the positive social functioning of the child in the family system, within the context of cognitive competence and maturity. Activity level is a behavior system that is somewhat separate. It has a negative correlation with vocabulary IQ, and mother's encouragement of independence is an important predictor in a negative sense. The fact that mother's restrictiveness (degree of command giving) is an important predictor for both independence and activity level implies a similarity that is more apparent than real, since different kinds of restrictiveness are likely to be involved. All in all, an active child is a child who, while being relatively immature, is also functioning happily, mainly on a physical level, within a relaxed family system.

CHAPTER 9

Genetic Influences

As we observed in Chapter 1, ethological methods and outlook have recently exerted considerable attraction on behavioral scientists and have led them to look at human behavioral characteristics from an evolutionary perspective. Thus, attachment behavior has been viewed from the point of view of its evolutionary significance (e.g., Bowlby, 1969), and so has compliance with the norms of the social group (e.g., Stayton *et al.*, 1971). The emergence of sociobiology (Wilson, 1975), however embattled a theory it may be, is a pointer in the same direction. An evolutionary perspective, however, inevitably implies at least partial genetical control of behavior, as evidenced by the question: "Why does this kind of animal solve those problems of survival in this way? (What is the evolutionary history of the behavior?)" (Blurton-Jones, 1974, p. 266). In the typical ethological study, it is assumed, from a knowledge of the animal's ontogeny combined with observation, that learning plays little part in the development of certain kinds of behavior, which are then classified as innate. Both animal ethologists and those applying the ethological approach to human behavior have generally fought strangely shy of genetical studies proper (cf. Gould, 1974), though some exceptions exist (e.g., Freedman, 1974; Plomin & Rowe, 1979).

Historically, ethological investigations have concentrated on describing "typical" patterns of behavior and have tended to ignore individual differences. Although this may have been justified at the descriptive, natural-history phase of the subject, an investigation of the determinants of individual differences could lead to a more profound understanding of the biological importance and evolutionary history of the traits in question.

Human genetic studies of continuous characteristics, foremost among which has been intelligence (as opposed to single-gene, all-or-none phenomena, such as PKU), have been almost entirely based on tests and questionnaires. The present investigation employed a more direct approach to the assessment of human interactive behavior, an approach that derived from ethological methodology, and it made one of its major goals the assessment of the possible genetic basis of the social behavior thus observed; hence, twins were included in the sample. Before looking at the genetic analysis itself, let us first examine an assumption underlying such an analysis based on twins—namely, the equality of environmental treatment effects for monozygotic (MZ) and dizygotic (DZ) twins—to see if it actually holds.

AN ASSUMPTION OF THE TWIN METHOD EXAMINED: DO PARENTS CREATE, OR RESPOND TO, DIFFERENCES IN TWINS?

It is sometimes claimed (e.g., Kamin, 1974) that parents of MZ twins treat their twins more alike than do parents of DZ twins, simply because of some preconceived notion that MZ twins are more alike and therefore should receive more similar treatment. Suppose parents do accord more similar treatment to MZ twins, and suppose this treatment was due simply to their knowledge that their twins are MZ, and not a consequence of the twins' greater genetic likeness. This parental treatment effect would give rise to systematically greater similarity in various characteristics for MZ twins compared with DZ twins, and, as a result, the genetic component in these characteristics would be unduly inflated.

Some evidence has been published (e.g., Jones, 1955; Scarr, 1968) to the effect that parents do seem to treat MZ twins more alike than DZ twins. Our investigation, which obtained direct measures of parental behavior, provided the opportunity of seeking further evidence on this question and of testing the above argument via several different methods.

The first approach we can use to test the hypothesis that parents treat MZ twins more alike is to test whether the within-pair variance of parent behavioral measures is significantly smaller for MZ than for DZ pairs ($\sigma^2_{WDZ}/\sigma^2_{WMZ}$, evaluated by the F test). Table 59 displays those parent variables where this was the case and where the general condition was met that total variances for MZ and DZ twins should not differ significantly. These conditions applied to 7 out of 48 parent measures, as shown in Table 59. All the mother variables listed are ratings, because none of the mother's behavior frequency counts qualified. Father ratings are absent, because these were available for only a very small number of fathers. The definitions of behavior counts and ratings are listed in Tables 3 and 6, respectively.

If parents show greater similarity of treatment of MZ compared with DZ twins, they may, however, do so in reaction to the greater genetic simi-

Table 59. **Significant Differences in DZ/MZ Within-Pair Variances of Parental Treatment Measures**[a]

Variable	Variance within DZ pairs	Variance within MZ pairs	F
Material rewards rating (mother)	.0216	.0074	2.919[b]
Amount of play rating (mother)	.0302	.0074	4.081[c]
Support of dependence rating (mother)	.3362	.1103	3.048[c]
Encourage mature action rating (mother)	.0259	.0074	3.500[c]
Monitoring rating (mother)	.1853	.0147	12.605[d]
Use of reasoning frequency (father)	1.0817	.4680	2.311[b]
Play frequency (father)	12.7565	.9718	13.127[d]

[a] df for mother variables: 29, 17; df for father variables: 23, 15.
[b] $p < .05$.
[c] $p < .01$.
[d] $p < .001$.

larity of MZ twins rather than out of the belief that they should make their treatment more homogeneous in accordance with the MZ stereotype. In an attempt to decide between these alternatives, we made use of the fact that in the observation records information is available about the precise timing and sequence of parent and child actions. Those parent actions that were not directly elicited by a child action (defined as parent actions that were not preceded by a child action within the previous 10 sec) were separated out and called *parent-initiated actions*. It follows that if parents do not treat MZ twins more alike in such parent-initiated actions, which are freed of the influence of the child's immediate behavior, parents do not, in fact, deliberately initiate more similar treatment of MZ twins under the supposed influence of a stereotype of greater MZ likeness. While this can only be an indication, it is likely that any greater similarity that is found in parents' overall treatment of MZ, as opposed to DZ, twins (not just parent-initiated actions) is in that case due to their reacting to the MZ twins' homogeneous phenotypes, based on greater genetic similarity.

To test this hypothesis, a second approach was employed: the ratios of the within-pair variances for DZ and MZ twins were evaluated by the F test for the parent-initiated actions shown in Table 60. Individual actions were grouped together under superordinate categories, also used in the sequence analysis of the interactions, as detailed in Table 3. Superordinate categories not shown in Table 60 could not be used in the present analysis because of insufficient instances of parent-initiated actions.

The only category for which the DZ within-pair variance was significantly larger than the MZ variance was mother's suggestions. The DZ variances of mother's neutral actions and of father's commands–prohibi-

Table 60.   Within-Pair Variances of Parent-Initiated Actions for DZ and MZ Pairs

Variable	Variance within DZ pairs	Variance within MZ pairs	F
Mother (*df:* 29, 17)			
Command-prohibition	7.586	16.588	.457
Suggestion	11.845	1.794	6,603[a]
Positive action	13.121	19.853	.661
Neutral action	46.431	25.500	1.821
Father (*df:* 23, 15)			
Command-prohibition	7.283	5.133	1.419
Suggestion	4.522	5.200	.870
Positive action	10.348	13.633	.759
Neutral action	17.304	20.333	.851

[a] $p < .001$.

tions were larger, but not significantly so, and in the other cases, the DZ variances were actually smaller. In view of such random fluctuations in the within-pair variances, it would appear that parents do not, of their own accord and systematically, institute more similar treatment for MZ than for DZ twins in general, and that the greater similarity of certain kinds of parent behavior toward MZ than toward DZ twins, revealed in the comparison of overall treatment measures (Table 59), is likely to be a reaction to the MZ twins' own greater phenotypic likeness.

This conclusion received support from the third method employed for examining the question of differential treatment of MZ and DZ twins. During the interview, mothers were asked whether they made any deliberate differences between the twins, and if so, why they did this. Many mothers of both MZ and DZ twins acknowledged that they treated each twin differently, but they always attributed such differential treatment to the differing needs of the children. (Such remarks may, of course, be rationalizations.) It is noteworthy that the mothers of 6 out of 17 MZ twin pairs, but only of 3 out of 29 DZ twin pairs, did not seem to make any noticeable differences in treating their children (i.e., no differences in any of the ratings). The reasons given for any differential treatment were typically that one child needed more attention or warmth than the other or that one was more mischievous, less easygoing, and less docile than the other. In two cases (one MZ and one DZ), differences in treatment were directly related to the fact that one twin suffered respiratory distress at birth and had to be kept in an incubator for some weeks, whereas the other one did not. Some of the interviewer's notes for the MZ twin pair to whom this applied, follow:

Mother doesn't think of them as twins—J has been behind. Their personalities warrant their being treated differently. The differences that mother makes are those they demand, or events produce. J is 10 times worse than D in climbing on cupboards and tables and is usually spanked. Mother often has to spank J for things that D does not have to be spanked for. D is more sensitive—responds to a look or being sent to his room. Mother spends about half an hour holding and cuddling D, and about 15 minutes with J or as much time as he'll allow.

The fourth procedure employed to investigate possible mechanisms underlying differential treatment of twins was based on Scarr's (1968) work. She compared mothers' attitudes to and treatment of twin pairs about whose zygosity the mother was mistaken and found a strong suggestion that the mistaken pairs were treated more in accordance with their actual than their perceived zygosity. Four pairs in the present sample were thought by the mother to be DZ, when blood typing showed them to be MZ, and in another four pairs, the reverse was the case. The differences between the ratings of mothers' attitudes toward and treatment of each twin partner were calculated. (These characteristics were rated, it should be noted, before the result of the blood typing was known.) The total difference scores across 12 five-point ratings for each of these twin pairs are shown in Table 61. The total of these difference scores for the four MZ-thought-to-be-DZ pairs is 3.5, and for the four DZ-thought-to-be-MZ pairs, it is 10.5. In spite of the small sample, the difference between the group totals is significant. While

Table 61. Differences in Ratings of Mothers' Treatment of Twin Partners: MZ :Thought-to-Be- DZ and DZ Thought-to-Be MZ[a]

Twin pair	Difference score
(1) MZ thought-to-be DZ	
A	0.5
B	1.0
C	0.5
D	1.5
Total	3.5
(2) DZ thought-to-be MZ	
E	5.5
F	1.5
G	2.5
H	1.0
Total	10.5

[a] Difference between groups: $p = .029$. (Randomization test, one-tailed, Siegel, 1956.)

the low numbers must militate against any very confident generalization, the suggestion here, as in Scarr (1968), clearly is that the mothers were reacting to the twins' actual rather than their perceived zygosity.

The results of these four methods, taken together, lead to the conclusions that (1) parents do treat MZ twins more alike than DZ twins in some respects, but (2) they do not introduce systematically greater similarity of treatment for MZ twins in actions that they initiate themselves and that are not contingent on the child's immediately preceding behavior, and (3) the overall greater homogeneity of treatment of MZ twins, where it occurs, is in line with their actual, rather than their perceived, zygosity. In other words, parents respond to, rather than create, differences between the twins, something that the mother's comments also supported.

Loehlin and Nichols (1976) came to the same conclusion: "Most probably, identical twins are treated more alike because they look and act more alike—at least, we found little evidence that parental beliefs about zygosity were important per se" (p. 87). Moreover, these researchers found that within-pair differences in parental treatment correlated near zero with within-pair differences in personality; in other words, environmental differences in treatment within a family had very little effect on the twins. Other research, too (Matheny, Wilson, & Brown-Dolan, 1976; Plomin, Willerman, & Loehlin, 1976), has shown that greater resemblance in appearance in identical twins (which may elicit more similar treatment by parents) does not make the twins more similar in personality.

If the assumption of "equal environments" between MZ and DZ twins, therefore, is not always met phenotypically for overall treatment, in view of the conclusions in our, as well as other workers', research, this would not invalidate the heritability calculations. Hence, an attack on the twin method on this particular ground does not seem justified.

THE GENETIC ANALYSIS

Twins as Each Other's Environment

The means, variances, and intraclass correlations for the MZ and DZ groups of all the 28 child variables used in the major analyses of this research are shown in Table XIIA, Appendix XI. This table shows an interesting phenomenon. The difference in intraclass correlations between the MZ and DZ groups is, for the most part, not sufficiently great to allow significant genetic variance to emerge. However, the coefficients are usually moderate to very high for *both groups*, when the child characteristic was assessed in the home, but generally much lower when the measurement was derived from the laboratory playroom situation. A high correlation indicates a high degree of similarity between twin partners within the family and, conversely, significant differences between families; in the absence of significant genetic factors, the similarity must be due to very similar environmental effects influencing the twin partners.

But why should these correlations be so much lower for the laboratory situation? Apart from the artificiality of the laboratory, the outstanding difference between the home and the laboratory situations was that twins were observed together at home, but separately in the laboratory. We may speculate, therefore, that the greater similarity of the twins' behavior in the home is due to their mutual interactions. The close resemblance in twins' characteristics, by this reasoning, is not only a function of the long-term impact of similar parental treatment, similar home physical environment, similar experiences with other members of the family, etc.; it is also due to one twin's action instigating a similar action by his co-twin when they are together (with fraternals as much alike as identicals in this). In other words, in a twin or peer dyad, actions and interactions are infectious, "like begets like," and one twin acts as an environmental influence on the other. An illustration was the requests by both twins that their mother should make identical play dough figures for each, quoted in Chapter 7. That this mechanism may be an important cause in twins' similarity is often forgotten. (For similar effects in peer partners, see Cairns & Green, 1979.)

Environmental and Genetic Causes of Variation

A biometric–genetic analysis[1] was employed in order to determine the relative importance of environmental and genetic causes in the variation of the child variables. The assumptions and method required for this kind of analysis of twin data have been discussed in detail by Eaves and Eysenck (1975) and Jinks and Fulker (1970), and an outline is presented in Appendix XI.

No simple model will fit data that do not satisfy the criterion of equality of total variances for MZ and DZ groups. For this reason, variables in which the total MZ and DZ variances were different were omitted from the present genetic analysis. Individual variables that make up the linear composites "Total activity" for the home and for the playroom situation were also omitted, since the results from them are very similar to those of their composites. "Negative action" expressed as a percentage of total child actions is based on the same data as when it is expressed as a rate per minute and has also been deleted.

---

[1] The biometric–genetic analysis was designed and carried out by Nicholas G. Martin and Lindon J. Eaves at the Department of Genetics of the University of Birmingham, England. I owe them a debt of gratitude.

The results of fitting four different explanatory models to the remaining 18 variables are shown in Table 62, and further details are shown in Appendix XI, Table XIIIA.

The E_1 model tests the hypothesis that all the mean squares for a given variable are the same, that is, that all the variance is due to error or individual environmental experiences and that none is caused by systematic cultural or genetic effects. We can see that this model fits the data for four of the five playroom experimental measures and also the data for PPVT IQ, a test that was administered to nearly all subjects in the playroom. This may partly be due to the twins' being seen separately (see above). But it also confirms our suspicions aroused by the poor construct validity of the experimental measures (cf. Chapter 2) and problematic standardization of the PPVT (see Appendix XI).

In the remainder of the variables, the E_1 model fails, implying that there are sources of variance over and above error and individual experience. The other models shown test whether the addition of a between-families environmental component (E_2), or of an additive genetic component (D_R), or both, provide a better fit for the observed data.

The purely environmental model, containing only the within- and between-families environmental components, E_1E_2, fits every one of the variables. In only one case, the instrumental independence rating, does the simple genetic plus within-families-environment model (E_1D_R) give a better fit. In many cases, the latter model actually fails. The more complex genetic plus within- and between-families-environment model ($E_1E_2D_R$) also fits every variable and in each case fits better than the E_1E_2 model (see Appendix XI), as is to be expected, since we are making use of more information to explain the variance. However, only for the instrumental independence rating and the rate of speech does the $E_1E_2D_R$ model fit the data so much better that the genetic component (D_R) shows up as significant. For many variables, D_R is even slightly negative. Where the genetic component is positive, a biometric heritability estimate is given in the table, and its significance level accords with that of D_R.

The last column in the table displays heritability estimates calculated by the "classical" unweighted formula (cf., for instance, Haseman & Elston, 1970). A comparison between the two heritability estimates, arrived at via different approaches, is instructive. Both methods demonstrate a significant heritability for the same two variables. Where the heritability estimated by one method assumes an "impossible" value, it usually does the same under the other method, or else the heritability shown is near zero. The close accord of the results deriving from different methods and computations is impressive. The restriction of equality of total variances for MZ and DZ groups imposed on both methods (via selection of variables that satisfied this criterion) may explain the almost identical results. In view of

Table 62. Model Fitting and "Heritabilities" for Child Variables[a]

Variable name			Model fits			"Heritabilities"	
		E_1	E_1E_2	E_1D_R	$E_1E_2\,D_R$	Biometric $\frac{1}{2}D_R/(\frac{1}{2}D_R + E_1 + E_2)$	"Classical" $2(MS_{WDZ} - MS_{WMZ})/\sigma^2_{Tot}$
IQ–PPVT							.21
Comply ratio	C	+	+	+	+	.32 ± .38	.26
Positive action	CR	−	+	−	+	—	—
Negative action	CR	−	+	+	+	—	—
Attachment	CR	−	+	−	+	—	—
Speech	CR	−	+	+	+	.37[b] ± .21	.39[b]
Commands	CP	−	+	+	+	.11 ± .24	.10
Total activity score	COM	−	+	−	+	—	—
Compliance	HR	−	+	+	+	.07 ± .28	.07
Attachment	HR	−	+	+	+	—	—
Instrumental independence	HR	−	+	+	+	.59[c] ± .23	.58[c]
Speech maturity	HR	−	+	−	+	—	.00
Internalized standards	HR	−	+	+	+	.17 ± .29	.15
Compliance	EM	+	+	+	+	.02 ± .60	—
Attachment	EM	+	+	+	+	—	.02
Independence	EM	+	+	+	+	—	—
Total activity	EM	+	+	+	+	.90 ± .56	.75
No. form-board pieces placed	EM	−	+	+	+	—	—

[a] C = count variable; CR = rate per min.; CP = % age of child's actions; HR = home rating; EM = experimental measure; COM = composite standardized score. E_1: within-family environmental component; E_2: between-family environmental component; D_R: additive genetical component; − in heritabilities columns indicates a negative heritability.
[b] $p < .05$.
[c] $p < .01$.

the lack of a widely accepted paradigm for the estimation of genetic contribution to the variance, such concordance is reassuring.

The genetic harvest from these measures of child behavior, however, is meager: only the independence rating and the speech rate (a count variable) show a significant genetic component. The variance of the other variables can be accounted for by error and individual experiences, and by environmental differences between families.

Variance between Observers

We have found that the environmental model (E_1E_2) seems the most appropriate for nearly all the measures of child behavior. Since four different observers were employed in the data collection and interobserver reliabilities were only modest, we speculated that some of the environmental variance between twin pairs (E_2) in the count variables might be traced to variation in the coding behavior of observers. Inter*rater* agreement, however, was higher, and therefore this argument does not apply to ratings to the same extent and not at all to the experimental measures, which were all scored by the same experimenter.

To see how much of the environmental variance between families was due to observers, an analysis of variance was carried out for all twin pairs, with observers $(N = 4)$ as the independent factor. Details and results of the analysis are shown in Appendix XII.

In most of the variables that exhibit a significant between-observers component, observer variance accounts for 10%–20% of the total, whereas between-families environmental variance makes up between 49% and 88% of the total environmental variance. A figure of 10%–20% of the total due to variance between observers seems reasonable for count variables. This suggests that other causes (e.g., cultural differences) account for the greater part of the between-families variance.

Summary

1. Parents treat MZ twins more alike than DZ twins in some respects. But there is evidence that in this they react to the greater genetic similarity of MZ twins; they do not create it.

2. A significant genetic contribution to variance was found only in the instrumental independence rating and in the child's rate of speech. Our inability to detect genetic determination in most of the social characteristics studied may be due to the difficulty of identifying such factors in samples of this size.

3. For most of the present social characteristics, the largest part of the variance was explained by environmental differences between families.

DISCUSSION

We saw in the first part of this chapter that in some respects, parents do treat their MZ twins more alike than their DZ twins. Since there is evidence, however, that in this, parents respond to the greater likeness of MZ twins, such differential treatment, as far as it exists, seems to be the result of genetic similarities and dissimilarities and therefore cannot be said to invalidate the heritability calculations.

The genetic analysis showed that the only variables for which the genetic contribution was significant were instrumental independence (a rating) and speech rate (a count variable). The latter variable, which represents speech facility in a natural situation, has been shown to be an indication of competence and maturity (cf. Chapter 7) and may be a more reliable predictor of later intelligence than the PPVT score, that is, a vocabulary score obtained in a test situation that depends on motivational and attentional factors that are very variable in 2½-year-old children. In any case, we are showing here genetic determination in a cognitive, rather than a social–emotional, variable.

The difficulty of measuring interactive behavior reliably by means of behavior counts has been noted. The low reliability between observers and other anomalies may, at first sight, be thought to be the reason for the small amount of genetic determination of variation that could be found in the count variables. But the genetic contribution to ratings and experimental scores, which showed greater reliability, was no higher. (As discussed above, however, the construct validity of the experimental scores was doubtful.)

A more cogent explanation is likely to be that the probability of detecting even large amounts of genetic variation with samples of this size is rather low, as recent power calculations have shown (Martin *et al.*, 1978). yet, there are few, if any, studies involving detailed direct observation of behavior that have larger samples. (Fourty-four singletons were also included in this investigation.) This is not surprising in view of the expenditure of time involved in such a study. If an ethological approach is thought useful because it increases ecological validity, one will have to be satisfied with what, for a genetic analysis, is a small sample.

For most of the present personality characteristics, the largest part of the variance was explained by differences between families. These were partly due to interobserver differences, but they also reflected varying child-rearing situations and differences in cultural milieu. The finding of important effects arising from differences between families is at variance with some recent studies that claim that environmental differences within families are more important sources of variation than differences between families (e.g., Eaves & Eysenck, 1974; Plomin & Rowe, 1979). However, it has to be remembered that within-families differences are not all systematic; they contain error, inextricably intermingled with systematic effects. In biometric–genetic analyses, the between-families effect is often omitted deliberately from the equation, even when it is shown, as in Eaves and Eysenck (1974), that including it would improve the fit of the model. Our finding is, however, in accord with more general evidence as to the large effects produced by systematic variations between families. The differences between twin and singleton families, demonstrated in this research (cf. Chapter 4), are an instance, as are social-class differences between families, or differences between single- and two-parent families, shown in many studies.

In view of the hypotheses regarding the possible genetic basis of social characteristics, entertained at the outset of this project, the meager genetic harvest was disappointing, but it should be viewed in the context of other research in the "personality" area. What conclusions can we draw from this and other studies about the possibility of detecting genetic components in the variation of social–emotional characteristics?

General abilities, as measured by IQ or abilities tests, have repeatedly been shown to have a high heritable component (cf. Loehlin & Nichols, 1976; evidence summarized by Vernon, 1979) but studies of those psychosocial aspects of behavior that are subsumed under the term *personality* show more variable results. As far back as 1939, Portenier noted that twins were less alike on personality traits than on intellectual or physical traits. The "heritabilities" of personality variables, calculated by classical formulas or biometric methods, as well as simple differences between MZ and DZ pair correlations (Loehlin & Nichols, 1976), have been lower than for IQ measures. Moreover, they have often been inconsistent (see below).

Some researchers have abandoned computing heritabilities by any formula, because such a statistic is thought to imply a precision that the data of (usually) small samples hardly warrant (e.g., Buss & Plomin, 1975; Dworkin *et al.*, 1976; Loehlin & Nichols, 1976). Indeed, Martin *et al.* (1978) have conducted a power analysis that concludes that 600 pairs of twins (of both types together) are required, and Loehlin and Nichols (1976) even suggested that 400 pairs of each type of twins are necessary to establish an acceptable level of confidence in the relative magnitude of heritability figures. While there is force in this assertion, the alternative adopted by some authors—namely, of calculating the significance of the differences between MZ and DZ intraclass correlations—hardly escapes the same difficulty, and it suffers from the disadvantage of not permitting a significance test of the genetic component as such.[2]

On the positive side, there is converging evidence from several studies, summarized by Buss and Plomin (1975), as to a genetic contribution to "social orientation" or "sociability" (e.g., Buss & Plomin, 1975; Freedman, 1974; Scarr, 1969; Vandenberg, 1967), a disposition that has been equated with part of the extraversion–introversion dimension, itself also partly genetically controlled (e.g., Eaves & Eysenck, 1975; Gottesman, 1966; Vandenberg, 1967), or with "conversational poise" (Horn, Plomin, & Rosenman, 1976).

Genetic factors also seem to make at least a moderate contribution to the phenotypic expression of activity motivation, as demonstrated in studies by Buss and Plomin (1975), Rutter, Korn, and Birch (1963), Scarr (1966), and Willerman (1973). All these studies showed heritability in children's activity motivation assessed by ratings, but no significant heritability could be detected in Scarr's (1966) experimental measures, nor in our count measures of activity. Ratings, it has been noted (cf. Loehlin & Nichols, 1976), may sharpen the differences between MZ and DZ twins through raters' stereotypes of MZ likeness.

Further, there is an intriguing convergence of evidence on a genetic contribution for dominance in *males*, but not females. This evidence comes mainly from two laboratories, and it has been confirmed in several subsamples. Dworkin *et al.* (1976) showed significant genetic variance in dominance, assessed by the California Psychological Inventory, with both sexes pooled, at adolescence and at a repeated testing in adulthood. Analyzing separately males and females of an enlarged sample, Dworkin (1977), demonstrated genetic variance in males, but not females, in adulthood. Loehlin and Nichols (1976) also found consistent, large differences between MZ and DZ correlations for dominance in two subsamples of male, but not female, adolescents. Such a finding of genetic determination for males, but not females, would accord well with the fact that dominant behavior has usually been found to be more marked in males than in females (Maccoby & Jacklin, 1974; Jacklin & Maccoby, 1978).

While it is possible to show *some* genetic control in certain defined personality characteristics across samples, there has been a distressing failure to find consistency in the relative amount of genetic control (1) across sexes;

[2] The convergence of two different methods in producing virtually identical heritability estimates, demonstrated above, provides some reassurance about the validity of the calculations, once certain restrictive assumptions are made, although the estimates may, of course, differ for a different sample. Compare also Loehlin's (1978) reconciliation between the genetic findings on intelligence of the Hawaiian and the Birmingham schools, achieved by equating their respective assumptions.

(2) across different samples or subsamples; and (3) over age. Such consistency has been sought by correlating actual heritability (h^2) values, or the rank orders of the differences between MZ and DZ intraclass correlations, or the rank orders of the F ratios (within-pair DZ variance/within-pair MZ variance) between different samples across the various subscales of *the same tests*, for example, the California Psychological Inventory (CPI) or the Minnesota Multiphasic Personality Inventory (MMPI). Thus, Nichols (1969) demonstrated a lack of consistency in h^2 values between the sexes across the 18 subscales of the CPI within his own sample, as well as within Gottesman's (1966), and a similar lack of consistency between these two samples. This demonstration, however, is not very damaging to a genetic theory, since correlations (the measure of consistency) depend on the actual magnitude of the heritability figures. A mixed bag of subscales (in terms of genetic control) would not be expected to contain many with numerically stable genetic components and thus would produce a near-zero correlation of heritabilities, particularly as Gottesman's (1966) sample was relatively small. The same can be said of the lack of correlation for the F ratios across the subscales of the MMPI and of Cattell's Junior Personality Questionnaire (JPQ) between three different samples, reported by Vandenberg (1967), or of the lack of consistency in the differences between MZ and DZ correlations across the CPI subscales found between two subsamples in Loehlin and Nichols's (1976) study, although in this latter case, the subsamples were fairly substantial (ranging from 54 to 153 pairs). Consistency in genetic determination between the sexes is not to be expected on a further ground, namely, obvious gene-based sex differences (cf. the example of dominance cited above).

What might be considered more damaging for the genetic hypothesis is the fact that no variable in the MMPI and JPQ scales had a *significant F* ratio across all three studies summarized by Vandenberg (1967). Dworkin *et al.* (1976) also assessed the *significance* of MZ–DZ correlation differences and of the F ratios for the subscales of the MMPI and of the CPI in a longitudinal study of the "Harvard sample," who were first seen at adolescence and about a quarter of whom were retested 12 years later as adults. (The retested subsample was shown to be representative of the full sample.) Only the dependency and anxiety subscales of the MMPI, and only the dominance subscale of the CPI, showed significant genetic variance at both ages. This means that only for these traits could a "real" and stable genetic component be said to exist. The genetic variances of the other subscales displayed either an increasing trend (so that they became significant only in adulthood) or, on the contrary and more frequently, a decreasing trend (so that they lost their previous significance in adulthood). It can plausibly be argued that a trait may manifest diminished genetic variance at a later age because environmental differences between twins tend to accumulate and become wider with age, especially when the twins live apart. Some heritable diseases, due to a single dominant gene (e.g., Huntington's chorea), on the other hand, manifest themselves only in adulthood. Other arguments have been put forward to explain the conflicting phenomena of emerging and disappearing genetic components over age (e.g., a change from an expressive to a suppressive environment, or vice versa) or the fact that regulator genes may activate structural genes to produce proteins for limited periods only (Gottesman, 1974). It is far from clear how far such explanations are applicable to human personality traits with a presumed polygenic basis.[3]

Nichols (1969) believed that some of the difficulty in obtaining replicable results in genetic analyses may derive from the nature of the self-report inventories used, because they are subject not only to random error but also to bias due to systematic distortions by respondents. However, our direct observation measures, which can be said to possess ecological validity, did no better, and it is a moot question whether our results would be replicated.

When batteries of personality scales are administered to different twin samples (though not differing in race), or the same sample at different ages, it is difficult to demonstrate consistently greater similarity for MZ twin on some traits than on others, when such consistency is sought by *correlating the heritabilities of samples across all traits of the battery*. However, it is possible to identify *some* characteristics for which a significant genetic component emerges consistently across different samples and at different times, as illustrated above. It may well be that we have to select more carefully the traits (and the indices we use to measure them) in which we hope to demonstrate replicable genetic components.

There is a paradox here: many human traits can be presumed to be "adaptive"; that is, they have evolved because they increase the Darwinian fitness and survival chances of the population and therefore must have a genetic base for their expression. (For a discussion of the relation between the continued transmission of a characteristic and its adaptive value, see Gottesman, 1965.) Yet, this genetic base is very difficult to pin down for most of them, as we have seen. It has been argued that selection for adaptive traits occurs in a directional sense toward the high expression of the trait which would be associated with high reproductive fitness. High directional selection will, however, reduce additive genetic variance because the relevant genes will be universally built into the species with resultant *low* heritability for the trait. Such a mechanism has been demonstrated for nest building in mice (cf. McClearn & DeFries, 1973) and it might apply to, say, compliance

---

[3] It should also be noted that a tendency of the genetic variance of a trait to increase or decrease with age is different in principle from the unpredictable occurrence of schizophrenic episodes (discussed in Gottesman, 1974), which, within the framework of genetic predisposition, may flare up differentially in one twin or the other in response to transient internal or environmental stressors.

in humans. Unfortunately for this argument, however, speech is surely adaptive in humans in that it is instrumental in securing a mate and, therefore, improves the reproductive fitness of the individual possessing it to a high degree; yet speech is one of the two variables that has here been found to be under genetic control. Hence it is difficult to accept this theory as an *ex post facto* explanation whenever heritability is absent in a trait.

Possible environmental influences, on the other hand, also do not easily bear the burden of explaining the development of personality characteristics: they seem to act almost in a random fashion within families, and treatment differences between twins (ascertained from parents' reports) are not very predictive of later personality differences, as Loehlin and Nichols (1976) have shown with a very large twin sample. The fact that environmental factors operate in such complex ways in itself points to the importance of person–situation interaction in explaining the variance of personality traits (Endler, 1975; Endler & Magnusson, 1976). A significant genetic component has been found in the person–situation interaction for at least one such trait–anxiety (Dworkin, 1977)—and this implies the existence of genotype–environment interaction for this characteristic.

The search for the biological foundations of social behavior is a very popular topic nowadays, made fashionable by the emerging alliance of disciplines called *sociobiology* (Wilson, 1975). The hard fact is that genetic factors, particularly in human social characteristics, are extremely elusive and hard to demonstrate in replicable form in empirical genetic investigations. It may be that the genes for these characteristics are so universally built into the species that no genetic variability is left, or the fault may lie with the unreliable instruments with which we measure the traits. Wilson (1975) speculates about the possibility of "conformer genes" benefiting both society and the individual; so far, however, conformer genes, or similar precisely defined genes for social behavior, must be regarded as being more in the nature of a metaphor than an empirical fact, supported by evidence.

CHAPTER 10

Conclusions and Implications

We have come to the end of a long journey. This book has presented a natural-history account of child rearing, with all the details of family interchanges observed in the home. But beyond the descriptive account, we identified, by means of analysis of behavior sequences, the parental contingencies that facilitated (or inhibited) certain child actions, particularly in the area of attachment and compliance behavior; further, looking at the process through the other end of the telescope, we identified the effects that the child's attachment and compliance behavior had on certain parental actions. We also examined some of the factors affecting parent–child communication. For a complementary view of more long-term socialization effects, we employed regression analyses, which indicated how well parental practices and attitudes predicted some major child characteristics, viewed as traits.

In all this, I have endeavored to stay close to the data—perhaps too microscopically close for many readers—so as to demonstrate that these are empirical findings and to show precisely how they were derived from the data. It is time now to bring the pieces of the jigsaw together to examine parent–child relations in the socialization process from a larger point of view and to allow a little freer rein to personal views and speculation. I will here draw together the threads of some findings scattered over several chapters, particularly on the family system, so as to look at the family in the round. I will also place the major behavior systems of attachment and compliance in the wider perspective of their implications for human development. But for the actual findings on each of the behavioral areas that we examined, the reader is referred to the summaries and the discussion sections in each chapter.

THE FAMILY SYSTEM AND MATERNAL
AND PATERNAL ROLES

The family can be viewed as a system in which each member influences, and is influenced by, every other member, such influences operating both in a direct and an indirect manner. This "microsystem" (Bronfenbrenner, 1977) is itself nested within broader systems, such as neighborhood, class, region, and country. The impact on the family of two such systems (the mother's education—a categorization related to social class—and twinship or nontwinship) have been examined in this report.

However, our main interest is focused on systematic relationships within the family. Going beyond the traditional concentration on the mother–child dyad, I have included the father as an integral member of the family system. To make the work manageable, I have concentrated for formal–analytical purposes, on two subsystems, namely, the mother–child and the father–child dyads, which in twin families immediately become four subsystems, since mother and father each relate to two twins. Father's effects on mother–child relations have also been analyzed and will be summarized here, and other influences, such as sibling interactions, have been brought in tangentially.

Mother's and father's influences have been considered and compared for each of the child behavior systems in their respective chapters, and the differences in incidence of certain major behaviors have been reported in Chapter 3. (For an overview see Table 9.) My task now is to bring together the several strands of evidence in order to consider how mothers and fathers share out and adjust their roles in the North American family of today.

Our detailed recording of interactions enabled us to discover how mother's communication and discipline encounters with the child were affected by father's presence, as compared to when she and the child were alone together. These are the indirect or so-called second-order effects exerted by father on mother–child relations. Because of the short time that father was alone with the child, an analysis of mother's effects on father–child relations was possible only for general speech.

Mother was in the child's company for an average of 238 minutes of observation time, 97 of them alone; father was in the child's company for an average of 153 minutes altogether, 12 of them alone, so that both parents were present together for 141 minutes during the two observation periods. Single-parent families and families where father was by force of circumstance absent from both observations have been disregarded for all these comparisons. The much shorter average time that father was present was due to his being out at work for part of the observation, or to his going out again for a variety of purposes (we did not attempt to control such comings and goings), or, in a few cases, to his being entirely absent from one of the observation sessions. Some of the differences between mother and father behavior that we found can no doubt be traced to the scarcity value of father's presence in most families.

Let us now discuss the roles that mother and father play in the various areas of social interaction that have been the topic of this book. (For the detailed evidence, refer to the relevant chapters and also to Table 9.)

Attachment, Nurturance, and Play

When it comes to seeking nurturance—seeking either proximity or attention or help—the child clearly turns to mother on the whole rather more than to father. This applies to the overall average, and it also applies individually to 70% of the children. Since the child in general communicates his needs and demands, as well as his signals of distress, more to mother than to father, it seems that he directs his attachment behavior preferentially to mother in most situations and not only when he is under special stress. A larger proportion of twins than of singletons concentrate their attachment behavior on father, and the reason may well lie in the great demands on, and competition for, a twin mother's time and attention, so that she may often simply be unavailable. Apart from this, however, it is what the child perceives as mother's less friendly and engaging characteristics, rather than father's outstandingly positive ones, that prompt the "father-attached" children to attach themselves more closely to him. Although mother is the prime recipient of the child's expressions of needs, distresses, or demands, both parents, when addressed, respond equally—and to very high degree—to such bids.

When it comes to play, however, the situation is reversed: father engages in far more play, and particularly rough-and-tumble play, with the child than mother does, both absolutely and relative to his time in the home and his total actions. Play occupies a more salient place in father's interactions with the child than in mother's, no doubt because our observations took place round suppertime, when father comes home and mother, after a long day's dealings with the child, is glad to let him take over and to retire from "play duty," often to prepare supper. Margaret Mead might have been speaking of our fathers when she once said that nowadays, it is no longer the tired businessman who returns home to relax amid the family circle, but it is rather a tired father who recovers in the office!

That father exhibits more affection and positively toned actions generally than mother, whereas mother issues more negatively toned actions, is very probably also an artifact of the time of day when we carried out the observations, and also a result of the preeminent position that play occupied in father's interactions with the child. Nevertheless, the overall higher level of negative actions by mother than by father does not stop the

child from seeing her as the appropriate person for giving him comfort and
attention in the majority of cases. On the other hand, clearly, 2-year-old
boys mark father out as the proper—and willing—partner for romping. It
should be noted that our findings are consonant with popular belief and with
the conclusions of the majority of research studies, which agree that mother
is the preferred attachment object for most young children, as might be
expected on theoretical grounds. In only a minority of cases does the child
go against the prevailing trend, for the reasons outlined above.

Changing the Child's Behavior

Mother plays a far more prominent role than father in attempting to
change the child's ongoing behavior. Her absolute number of commands–prohibitions far exceeds his (87:37, on average), and allowing for his
shorter time with the child, the rate of her command giving (about one command every 2½ min) is also greater than the rate of his command giving
(about one command every 4 min during his presence). Conversely, the child
complies relatively more with father's directions than with mother's.
Mother evidently feels more responsible for the child's behavior and welfare
and hence intervenes more in his doings—on his behalf, as well as to restrain
and change his behavior. The consequent plethora of directions by her may
result in the child's turning a selectively deaf ear to her, whereas father's
fewer directions stand out as having greater force. But we must also bear in
mind that father shows greater willingness to comply with the fewer
requests that the child makes of him than mother does with the greater
number of requests addressed to her. A certain reciprocity thus governs
these relationships.

Mother and father also differ somewhat in the means of control they
use to redirect the child's change-worthy behavior: mother provides significantly more rational explanations and justifications for her orders than
father, thus enabling the child to develop a cognitive base in which moral
behavior can be grounded and from which moral rules can be generalized.
The average relative frequency of physical punishment is very slightly higher
for father than for mother, but *more* fathers than mothers (about two-thirds
as against one half) never employ physical punishment at all. This means
that *some* fathers use it very much more than mothers.

We also observed some fathers to be much harsher and more authoritarian than mothers. One rather peremptory father, for example, rapidly
repeated an order before the child had a chance to comply with it, and then
father added: "Hurry up, hurry up!" Mother: 'Why should he hurry?"
Father: "Because I told him to. Or I'll give him a licking when he gets
back!" This mother sometimes repeated father's order, adding the "please"
that he had omitted.

What are the second-order effects of father's presence on mother–child relations in this area? When father is present, mother intervenes less and issues fewer directives, but is obeyed more often, compared with when she is on her own with the child. However, even in father's presence, she makes more attempts than he does to change the child's behavior.

Mother's greater tendency toward command giving is also reflected in the fact that she issues several directions in succession concerning the same matter more frequently than father. Moreover, when father issues a request or command, she backs it up with a reinforcing command of her own more frequently than the other way round. The consequences are notable: father's reinforcing mother's directions increases the chances of the child's complying, but mother's reinforcing father's directions decreases this probability!

In sum, father, in general, intervenes less frequently to change the direction of the child's behavior, but when he does so, he is more effective than mother in having his wishes carried out. It seems that his simple presence, as well as his backing, add authority to her requests. However, he is less intent on rewarding the child for good deeds, which he seems to take more for granted than mother, but he is more alert to the child's bad deeds. Indeed, when father is about, mother is willing and glad to let him deal with the child's disobedience on many occasions. Moreover, his presence changes the quantity and quality of mother's responses to the child. These second-order effects are markedly beneficial; for example, they spur mother on to respond more positively to the child's compliance (which father tends to leave to her); above all, father assumes some of the responsibility for the child, and especially his misdeeds, and relieves some of the strain on mother. These effects extend to the child, since he, in his father's presence, is more responsive to his mother, too.

Parent–Child Communication

Verbal communication between parents and children touches almost everything in the daily round of family life: information giving and asking, requests, explanations, affectionate expressions, criticism, seeking attention, etc.. All this is subsumed under the umbrella variable speech. Here, too, there are some significant mother–father differences. Mother's rate of speech per minute of her presence exceeds father's speech, calculated in a similar way, both overall and under the "one parent present" and "both parents present" conditions. Mother also initiates more dialogues and is more responsive to the child's utterances.

The effects of having both mother and father present in the home is to increase the amount of communication all round, but to reduce the level of speech within both the mother–child and father–child dyads, compared with the one-parent condition (we did not systematically record mother–father

speech). A twofold process is operating here: there is greater stimulation
and more to say between two parents and one child than between one parent
and one child, but, on the other hand, the topics of conversation will be
shared out among the two dyads, thus reducing the amount of speech within
each of them.

Apart from differences in the quantity of speech, there were some
interesting differences in the way some speech measures were related to
each other. It appears from these relationships that the child's initiations of
dialogues with father are influenced to some extent by the latter's interest in
the child, but initiations to mother are more dictated by the child's needs of
the moment than by her initiating conversations. This reflects again the
greater involvement on day-to-day affairs between mother and child and his
greater reliance on her for the satisfaction of his needs.

Moreover, it seems that mother exerts greater influence on the quantity
of the child's speech, while father's influence is felt more in the quality of
the child's speech. This intriguing difference may come about because
father, in his shorter time with the child, may insist more on coherent, relatively "correct" speech, whereas for mother, who is constantly exposed to
the child's speech, this is of lesser concern, while she enhances the child's
willingness to talk and his fluency by her own conversations and her
attitudes.

Family Climate

We have noted systematic differences in the amount and quality of the
mutual interactions that mothers and fathers engage in with their children.
But while the levels of these social interactive behaviors differ in meaningful
ways and show an asymmetric distribution among family members, there
invariably also exist significant positive correlations among the members of
the system, indicating that the rank orders of mother and father across different families are fairly similar. In other words, any given family system is
marked by characteristics that single it out from others: more or less attachment behavior by the child to both mother and father; more verbal communication within one family than within another; more control, or more
nagging, by both mother and father within one family than another, etc. In
this way, over and above their differences, mother, father, and children
together create a common and distinct climate that characterizes and distinguishes the family.

Mothers' and Fathers' Complementary Roles

The clear differences between mothers' and fathers' roles in the
socialization process that have emerged from our overview of the evidence

should not make us forget the great variability that mothers—and even more so, fathers—display in their behavior. In trying to sum up their respective roles, I am very conscious of the oversimplification that is inherent in any such attempt. We must also remember that we are here talking about relationships of 2- to 3-year-old boys in intact North American families, observed in the early evening, around suppertime.

Bearing in mind these limitations, however, we can arrive at some generalizations:

1. Father engages much more in rough-and-tumble physical contact with the boy than mother does. But some fathers also resort to somewhat more physical contact of a negative kind (physical punishment) than mothers. Mother, on the other hand, is involved in far more verbal interchanges of all kinds with the child. Exaggerating somewhat, we might say that father interacts by doing and mother by speech.

2. Father's interactions with the child at this time of day are largely positive. It is clear that, as he then takes over from mother, worn out by the day's ructions, he fulfills an important child-rearing role through play; he is the playmate. It should be noted, however, that the fathers we observed did not disdain involvement in other caregiving tasks, such as bathing, undressing, and feeding.

3. Mother intervenes more in the child's doings, often in what is bound to be a restraining, negative way. Her interventions are chiefly verbal, and she particularly employs explanations, a cognitive method of control, much more than father. Nowadays, mother no longer holds over the child the threat of father as the bogeyman and executioner. She is willing to take the major responsibility for the child's welfare and behavior, both when she is on her own with him and when father is present. At this time, he takes a part in guiding the child's behavior—and chiefly in dealing with his misdemeanors. However, father attempts to direct the child less than mother does and, on the whole, assumes a supportive role in shaping the child's conduct. When he does intervene, he is more effective than mother in achieving his wishes and less repetitious in making them known.

4. Finally, despite father's role as playmate, the child, in the great majority of cases, looks to mother as the main source of comfort and nurturance. Father as the main object of attachment represents the exception and, in this society, an atypical situation.

Overall, it is mother who is not only the primary caregiver and comforter but who, in addition, fills the role of primary agent of socialization. Therefore, at this age, she combines in her person the "instrumental" and "expressive" roles in the sense in which Talcott Parsons has defined these terms.

It is of interest that the Newsons (1978) in their study of family relationships in Nottingham, England, come to conclusions as regards 7-year-olds that are very similar to mine about 2-year-olds. They sum up the main trends in family relations as (1) mother is the more familiar figure; hence, children tend to be more amenable to father's authority; (2) mother is the nurturant, cherishing parent; in illness or hurt, the child turns to her; and (3) father, because of his masculinity, is better fitted to cope with the rumbustious side of the male child, which is not often considered the mother's job (p. 302). It appears that my findings are not isolated ones and have been replicated across age levels and in other parts of the English-speaking world.

The evidence as regards the degree of participation of fathers in child rearing and child care is somewhat conflicting. Kotelchuck (1972) reports that only 25% of fathers interviewed said that they took any regular part in caregiving for their 1-year-old children. On the other hand, the Newsons (1965, 1970)—in Britain—interviewed *mothers* and on the basis of their reports concluded that just over 50% of the fathers of 1-year-olds and 4-year-olds were "highly participant" in caring for their infants, including bathing, changing diapers, etc. In general, the participation rate increased with higher social status, reflecting greater equality in the division of labor at higher social-class levels. The Newsons also report that 99% of fathers played with their infants, and therefore play ceased to be a distinguishing mark.

I have no accurate information on the extent to which fathers participated in physical caregiving in our sample, since we did not analyze the data for this aspect. Our impression, however, was that a great many fathers took an active part in these tasks, too, insofar as help was required. On the other hand, there was also the father who hid behind his newspaper throughout the whole of the observation period.

Certainly, our evidence suggests extensive and positive social interaction between father and child—in addition to play—rather more than he has been given credit for in some of the literature about infants, apart from the Newsons' studies. If fathers come out of this rather well, it should be said that this is not because of the male gender of the author, since all the observers, who recorded and coded the detailed behavior were women. Nor can fathers' participation in child rearing be explained by the presence of twins in the sample, since the number of actions of twin fathers was never significantly higher than that of singleton fathers, except that twins sat on father's knees more than singletons. Fathers' involvement with their children was no doubt enhanced because of the time of our observations, as noted earlier. Partly, their participation may be due also to the fact that by age two what was a semihuman creature has turned into a human being who can be talked to, played with, and teased.

Each of the different types of experience that the male child has with mother and father is important in its own way. Mother's emphasis on verbal interchanges will have a formative influence on the child's verbal competence, which is basic to his whole cognitive development. He will derive a sense of the ways of his family and of the world from her endeavors to direct his behavior and her explicit rationales. Through commerce with her, he will affirm his identity as a member of his family and of society.

The frequent and intense physical play interactions that the child engages in with father will also have a significant formative influence on his development. Such interactions will add another dimension to the child's experience. It may be thought that they will influence particularly his cognitive development in the spatial sphere and also the development of interpersonal skills with equals outside the family circle. The rough rumbustiousness of his interaction with father will, moreover, help him to form a self-concept as a male human being. Father's indirect influence, by the effect he has on mother's behavior vis-à-vis the child, may be as important as his direct influence. The indirect influence appears to be generally beneficial, since by his presence and by taking a share in the responsibility for the child, father smooths out mother–child relations.

Part of the indirect effect on the child also arise from the quality of the marital relationship. Several researchers have found this to be important; Feiring (1976), for instance, found that a strong positive association existed between mother's assessment of support from father and ratings of maternal involvement and responsivity to the child.

In interactions with the child, mother and father play complementary roles, but they adjust their roles to the other's presence and personality, thus setting up a self-balancing family system. So long as the system contains such variety and flexibility while maintaining itself in a steady state, it will be adaptive to the needs of its members, particularly the child, and remain viable.

Mother's and father's roles, as I outlined them, are, however, not God-given and immutable. For instance, they must be seen in the context of the fact that almost all our mothers were not working outside the home, and in part, they will be due to social convention and an accepted division of labor. In fact, a shift toward greater participation in child rearing by fathers has been in progress probably throughout the postwar period. It was noted by the Newsons (1965) in Britain as long ago as the early 1960s, and it was no doubt helped on by an increase in leisure time that employed fathers had at their disposal. The postwar shift in traditional task allocation has, of course, been accelerated by an increasing trend toward women's taking paid jobs (cf. Aldous, 1977). As Gronseth (1975) and others have found, when task division is more egalitarian, fathers tend to participate more in child rearing, but they leave washing, cleaning, and mending clothes to the wives, while wives leave house and car repairs to their husbands. However, we should not delude ourselves that this development is entirely new and due to the inexorable march of progress in the late 20th century; John Locke's "Some Thoughts Concerning Education," published nearly 300 years ago, addressed advice on child rearing, originally in letter form, to one particular father, and then when published, to fathers in general. Locke believed that mothers only spoil children by "cockering and tenderness." But the fathers he addressed were leisured English gentry.

Thus, "traditional" notions of what is considered men's and what women's work are constantly shifting.[1] With women's increasing participation in the labor force, the respective roles of men and women in the family may well change further. The patterns of parental interaction with their children that I have described may not be bound up inescapably with maleness and femaleness but may be patterns determined by who is the major and who the minor caregiver. Situations may arise where mother and father exchange these roles, for example, where mother takes a full-time job and father turns his talents to being a "house-husband." How far will they then go in reversing the patterns of interaction that I have here identified as "maternal" or "paternal"? We may find that some of mothers' and fathers' present roles are, indeed, constrained by biological necessities, though, beyond nursing at the breast, it is difficult to say which ones. Indeed, there might well be a move back to traditional roles before such a reversal of roles has gone too far. Such a move back has, in fact, already occurred in one society: the Israeli kibbutz prided itself on establishing complete equality between men and women; women were originally given every opportunity and encouragement to take up any position whatever in the kibbutz economy and to shed most of the responsibilities of motherhood. A new generation of women, however—many of them themselves raised on the kibbutz—have in recent times shown a marked desire to return to the baby cot and the kitchen stove. There may be a lesson for us here.

SOCIALIZATION EFFECTS: WHO SHAPES WHOM?

That parent–child relations consist of a constant two-way flow of influence processes, the child adapting to the parents and they, in turn, adapting to him, is in a sense a truism. However, for many years, social scientists consigned this view to a scientific limbo in favor of the opposite assumption of unidirectional influences running from parents to child. Recent work—and particularly the books by Bell and Harper (1977) and Lerner and Spanier (1978)—rehabilitated the reciprocity theory scientifi-

---

[1] An illustration of this—as reflected in a child's mind—is the conversation reported by the Newsons (1965): their 5-year-old, exasperated by his mother's being busy with examination papers, complained, "Marking exam papers isn't women's work." "What is women's work, then?" "Oh, painting ceilings and all that sort of thing!"

cally, and there is some empirical evidence for the existence of reciprocal influences between parents and child (cited in Chapter 1). Nevertheless, I there characterized reciprocal effects as the neglected aspect of socialization—neglected as a scientific problem that would seek answers to such questions as: How does this mechanism operate in detail? Which child behavior affects which parent behavior? Do reciprocal effects operate differently in some areas of interaction from others? Where does the balance of power lie for any given behavior? Cairns (1979b) put it as follows:

> Left unanswered is the critical theoretical question of how the equation of influence is balanced in specific adult–child . . . relationships. It is also unclear how the weights of influence may shift as a function of situational and ontogenetic constraints. (p. 354)

In an attempt to formulate some answers to these questions (tentative though they must be, since none of the evidence is very strong), this section draws together the strands of evidence concerning this topic that are scattered through various chapters of this book. Let me first discuss the *immediate* effects of parents' on children's actions, and vice versa, in the areas of attachment and compliance behavior, for which we carried out detailed analyses of parent–child behavior sequences (see Chapters 5 and 6).

The analysis of parent-control–child-compliance sequences (Chapter 6) indicated that all modes of control—commands–prohibitions, milder suggestions, and commands coupled with explanations—increase the probability of both compliance and noncompliance considerably, compared with the ordinary occurrence of compliance–noncompliance during the observation generally (the base rate). This is not surprising: a parental command or request usually compels the child either to comply or not to comply. Suggestions, it was found, particularly facilitate compliance. We also analyzed whether other parental actions, preceding the control statements, have an additional effect on compliance–noncompliance over and above that of the control statement by itself. Such second-order antecedents (to be distinguished from the "second-order effect" of father on mother–child interaction) do, indeed, have an effect in certain cases: physical control, for instance, joined to a command, lessens the probability of compliance. Positive actions, on the other hand—such as smiling, hugging, or praise—coupled with a command, enhance the probability of compliance.

On the other hand, the effects of children's compliance–noncompliance on parents' subsequent actions seem to be much smaller. One-third of the time, parents make no response to either compliance or noncompliance. Noncompliance increases the likelihood of some modes of control somewhat, but the probabilities of the differing parent behavior categories (e.g., commands and positive or negative actions) keep the same rank order after compliance that they have in the observation as a whole (i.e., the rank order of their base rates).

While children's compliance–noncompliance influences parental reactions to some extent, these responses, it seems, are much more a function of the parents' own predispositions and attitudes, although these have, in part, been shaped by previous experiences with their children. In disciplinary encounters, then, the immediate impact of parent on child is much greater than the other way round.

However, when we looked at attachment behavior (Chapter 5), the situation was rather different. The child's attachment behavior, it was noted, generated more significant effects on parents' immediately following actions than the other way round, though often the influences are two-way, or reciprocal. Maternal negative actions (disapproval and criticism), for instance, motivate the child to seek her attention or help, and this behavior, in turn, often tends to increase mother's negative actions above their base rate. But mother's positive actions (e.g., praise and approval) and child's attention-seeking also are mutually facilitative, and attention seeking increases mother's positive actions rather more strongly and frequently than it does negative actions. Moreover, child's attention seeking has a stronger influence on mother's actions overall than the other way round.

So it seems that in the area of attachment behavior, the immediate influences between parents and child are much more balanced, and even weighted on the child's side, than in the area of compliance. Here mother is reacting to the child's needs and wishes (though not always in compliance with them). While mother's negative and critical attitude spurs the child on to seek her attention or approval in order to propitiate her, this behavior then in most cases tends to evoke, even more strongly, warm and positive responses from mother—which is what the child wanted to achieve.

We will now consider the *medium-term* effects of parents and children on each other. These were examined by means of a cross-lagged panel analysis that correlated mother and child behavior over two points in time (see Figure 12). Time 1 and Time 2 were the two observations we conducted in each home, about one week apart; hence, any effects we may note will be medium- rather than long-term. We can reasonably assume that instances of mother (or child) behavior tendencies, when accumulated over longer periods, as they are during childhood, would show stronger effects. The correlations are based on rates of action per minute, that is, on the density of behavior.

In the area of attachment behavior, the cross-lagged panel analysis allowed us to draw inferences about the direction of effects only for mother's use of suggestions—a matter of lesser interest. We were able to identify complementary influences operating as a feedback loop, with mother's influence, however, being the stronger one in the medium term.

A similar cross-lagged panel analysis for compliance and various parental modes of control produced one significant relationship, namely, between mother's use of reasoning and child's compliance (see Figure 15). The operation of a feedback loop mechanism is even more evident here: the tendency to reason increases compliance, and, in turn, compliance reduces the need for reasoning over time. While the interrelations generally are not very strong, mother's influence somewhat outweighs the child's. For the other modes of control used by mother or father, no clear direction of effects could be assigned for the medium time-span, but the signs of the correlations are the same as for reasoning, and hence, similar kinds of effects are at least plausible.

The child's positive actions (e.g., expressing affection, smiling, and compliance) and his negative actions (e.g., whining, crying, and noncompliance) were also submitted to cross-lagged correlations with various parental action categories. (Figure 16 shows a summary of the effects.) Whenever a definite direction of effects could be identified, the preponderant influence runs from mother to child, though sometimes a secondary effect in the opposite direction is also noticeable. Mother's commands–prohibitions and physical control, on the one hand, and child's negative actions, on the other, are embroiled in a mutually reinforcing and escalating relationship, a kind of "coercive cycle." However, mother's negative actions increased child's positive ones over time, and child's positive actions eventually tend to reduce mother's negative ones, thus demonstrating another feedback loop. Overall, mother's influence again outweighs the child's.

In sum, the analyses demonstrate that although reciprocity and complementarity of effects are noticeable in some cases, in no instance in any of these behavior systems does the child exert a unilateral influence on his parents.

We now come to the effects that parents' or children's actions have on each other's *long-term* behavior tendencies. Here, the correlational analyses, as is well known, permit us no more than to make plausible guesses as to the direction in which these effects are likely to flow. The fact that we had twins in the sample, however, enabled us to examine the question whether parents' treatment of twins was influenced by a stereotypic belief that identical twins should be treated alike, or whether it was influenced by the actual greater similarity of identical twins. We were able to ascertain (see Chapter 9) that parents do *not* treat their identical twins more alike simply because of a fixed belief in the appropriateness of doing so. Parents do here and there make greater differences between fraternal than between identical twins. However, we found that in doing so, parents react to their children's genetic makeup and respond to differences between the twins, rather than create them.

A genetic analysis was undertaken in the hope of demonstrating an important genetic component in these child characteristics, for the formation of which parents have so often been held responsible. Such a demonstration would obviously strengthen the case for *child* effects in parent–child interactions, since we would know where the child characteristics originate. In any event, the genetic analysis showed only two child behavior systems to be under significant genetic control: instrumental independence and amount of speech (see Chapter 9). It is therefore arguable that these characteristics, at any rate, will have an influence on parents' treatment of their child.

The analysis of the differential treatment of twins, and the genetic analysis to a limited degree, therefore suggest that over the very long term, mother's attitudes and reactions to the child may also be responsive to the child's own genetic makeup. Her behavior tendencies, in other words, would then be modulated by his nature, as well as being determined by her own predispositions.

We see, then, that the answer to the question "Who shapes whom?" is anything but simple. Differing effects arise from the three waves of influence that we can distinguish: (1) effects by one person on another's immediate actions in the here-and-now; (2) effects on a person's action tendencies in the medium term; and (3) effects on a person's long-term behavior tendencies.

Hoffman (1975) presents a persuasive theoretical argument to the effect that in the area of moral internalization, the direction of influence runs preponderantly from parent to child. This argument rests on the fact of overwhelming parental power that enables parents to place far greater constraints on the child than the other way round, and that, in fact, determines the degree of freedom left to the child. When examined closely, this position is easily reconcilable with the notion that child effects operate, too, since Hoffman agrees that some factors in the child (e.g., his readiness to comply with certain discipline techniques rather than others) or his person orientation (the latter probably of congenital origin) may influence parental discipline patterns. Moral internalization, under this view, is thus not one of the child's congenital characteristics but is mediated by the disciplinary experiences that the child has had. What is left unresolved is whether readiness to comply in itself is a contributor to, or a product of, parental disciplinary practices.

Our empirical data do, in fact, support Hoffman's contention that in disciplinary encounters, mother's influence far outweighs that of the child. In general, the date impel me to the conclusion that *while the child shapes his own immediate environment to some extent, he has little power to mold his parents' enduring characteristics.*

Our genetic analysis indicated that genetic factors played only a relatively minor role in the development of the child's social characteristics, as we measured them, though the limitations of the sample size and of the data should be borne in mind. Yet the adaptive value and the evolutionary history of many of these traits make some genetic contribution to their variation very probable. This paradox, discussed in Chapter 9, remains unresolved.

IMPLICATIONS FOR PRACTICE

This book is obviously not intended as a child-rearing manual. Readers will, I hope, be able to gain illumination from it about the dynamics of parent–child interactions as they actually proceed in North American families of this day and age. In this way, the book forms a complement, as it were, to the studies by the Newsons (1965, 1970, 1978), who looked at the socialization process through the eyes of mothers who reported on their practices, attitudes, and feelings in interviews. The book documents the effects that parents have on children, and those of children on parents. This evidence will form *part* of the background knowledge that professionals have at their disposal in guiding parents to gain a perspective on the reciprocal effects that they actually achieve and receive. In this way, the information in this book should assist professionals in helping a given set of parents to discover what may be effective for them. Parents who read this book will, I hope, be able to draw similar inferences for their own practice. What are desirable and what undesirable effects, professionals and parents will decide in the light of their own philosophies and goals. With the Newsons (1978), I believe that "In the long-term perspective, [parents'] intentions are to provide a protected and positive social environment in which the child's autonomous personality development can take place," though I am acutely aware that such a goal is very much embedded in our particular culture.

A few words of caution are appropriate at this juncture. First, we all realize that the character of the complex web of relationships that parents and children are enmeshed in is a function of a great many interacting factors, arising from the wider context, from personality tendencies and from situations. As I noted before, the child's contribution is an important ingredient in the relationship, and parents very often adjust their actions to the child's predispositions. (That they can do so consciously is a reflection of their greater control over the mutual interactions that we discussed in the previous section.) Hence, it is futile for anyone to hope to produce an ideal "prescription" that is valid for everybody. What I can do is to show the balance of the general contingencies and effects, as they apply on average. The breakdowns for individual children in Chapters 5 and 6 demonstrate directly how the general balance is inapplicable to some children, who buck the trend.

Second, the direction of effects, as is well known, is often ambiguous in a correlation linking Parent Action A with Child Action B. (This does not, however, apply to the sequence analyses of immediate effects.) Moreover, even significant correlations often fail to be replicated across different samples, as could be seen in the discussion of replications of the regression analyses in earlier chapters. Clarke-Stewart *et al.* (1979) studied the replicability of parent–child relations across four small samples (*N*s of 30 or less) and discovered that about one-third of the significant correlations were replicated in three, or all four, of the samples. They investigated which kind of relations were replicated and found that nearly all the highly replicated relations were predictable from the literature and general psychological theory, but very few of the nonreplicated ones were. This demonstrates the advisability of applying informed judgment and the context of related literature in interpreting correlations from one study. One must be wary of a new trend or relationship, however intriguing and fascinating, discovered in only a single study. We might be tempted to conclude that we can, in principle, only rediscover what is already known. Yet, new advances in knowledge must start in one study; but we should accept a finding as part of an established knowledge base only when we can have confidence in its robustness and stability as a result of several successful replications. Hence, conclusions as to practice are insecure unless some corroboration is available.

Third, we should remember that although certain practices on balance seem to have what present-day enlightened opinion would consider adverse effects, children's resilience often allows them to survive adverse circumstances unscathed (see below for a more detailed discussion of this point).

The following are some more wide-ranging remarks on larger perspectives and issues related to the areas of social behavior that we have examined.

Attachment and Dependence

I remarked in Chapter 5 that in perusing the research literature, we find that the terms *attachment* and *dependence* refer essentially to the same clusters of social behavior. Two distinctions between these terms, however, emerge in the literature: first, research dealing with this behavior in infants has named it *attachment* and has been influenced by an ethological approach, whereas research dealing with the same behavior in preschool children has labeled it *dependence* and has often stood under the aegis of social learning theory; second, *attachment* has been used to refer to a bond to one or a few persons, while *dependence* has been used to refer to a generalized response tendency (Ainsworth, 1972).

However, there also exists a distinction residing in normal linguistic usage, which attaches different value connotations to the two terms. Very simply, parents want to see their children attached, but not dependent. Indeed, the value difference between attachment and dependence parallels the value difference between liberty and license, or between order and repression; that is, in each case, extremity makes the characteristic undesirable. When I stress the similarity of the shorthand terms, I am really referring to the *behavior* expressing attachment or dependence. We can conceptually distinguish between attachment behavior and attachment itself (i.e., the feeling of being close to a person—the bond) that inspires it, but attachment can be measured only by attachment behavior. The bond persists into adulthood and old age, but it will express itself in different ways. The attachment behavior of young children—and this is what the literature is invariably about—follows a typical developmental pattern of waxing and waning, so that with increasing age, the young spend less time in close proximity to their parents. Outwardly, therefore, but only outwardly, a process of "detachment" succeeds attachment.

In this research, we measured attachment by the frequency of such behavior (indicating its strength), and this turned out empirically—as one would expect on theoretical grounds—to be a measure of insecurity. Our highly attached children are equivalent to what the Ainsworth typology calls "ambivalently attached" children (cf. Ainsworth, Blehar, Waters, & Wall, 1978, for the criteria employed). As pointed out earlier, a high degree of attachment had negative connotations for the competence and maturity of these children. The later consequences of varying degrees of early attachment (and of other characteristics and experiences) are being investigated in a follow-up study of the twins of this sample in middle childhood, to be published at some later date. That a high degree of attachment (which some prefer to call *overdependence*) is prognostic of poor social adjustment, both concurrently and later, is by no means an isolated finding—some such associations were cited in Chapter 5. Further, Tizard and Hodges (1978) found that institutionalized children who displayed characteristically excessive clinging (but no selective bond) in the preschool years also showed impaired relationships with adults and other children in middle childhood. The association seems quite well established.

It follows that a high degree of attachment behavior—and particularly of the verbal kind, such as attention seeking—is an undesirable characteristic. This does not, it should be stressed, apply to attachment behavior within the normal range, typical of a given age. A high intensity of attachment behavior, especially if it is diffusely and indiscriminately addressed to many people, is, in fact, antithetical to the formation of a selective, secure bond with one or a few persons, a process that is universal and, it is thought, of psychological importance.

We have repeated evidence that maternal responsiveness and sensitivity to the child facilitates secure relationships with mother or sociability with mother in infancy (e.g., Ainsworth, 1973; Clarke-Stewart, 1973). By contrast, there is cumulative evidence that parental rejection is associated with high intensity of attachment (cf. Maccoby & Masters, 1970), and similar associations between parental negative actions and unresponsiveness, on the one hand, and child's attachment behavior, on the other, found in this study, can be interpreted in the same vein. The analysis of behavior sequences suggested that parental negative actions lead to an increase in attachment behavior in the child, which, in turn, mostly leads to an increase in parental positive actions. How complexly intertwined such parent and child behaviors are—something of which mere correlations give one no inkling—is illustrated by the following description of a pattern observed in one of our families:

> There seems to be a pattern of: (1) child makes repeated requests; (2) mother gets angry; (3) child becomes upset (and will, very likely, seek mother's proximity and affection); (4) mother loves him up and he calms down—until the next round.

Theorists who write about the "securely attached" child attribute many different positive social qualities to him (e.g., Waters, Wippman, & Sroufe, 1979) and thus equate "securely attached" and "well adjusted." Such an equation may well be correct. Taking this wider view, we must realize, however, that we do not know whether it is completely within the power of parents to engender security of attachment, or a healthy personality, in their children, or to ward off all insecurities, since endogenous forces in the child may here interact with the environment that the parents create (cf. Rutter, 1979).

Compliance and Moral Development

Parents cannot avoid imposing some demands on their child or escape the responsibility of inducting him into the norms of society. However, in doing so, parents are working not against the child but with his natural proclivities, since from an evolutionary point of view, it is reasonable to assume that the child's native tendencies are adapted to the needs of group living. Hence "conformity is normal and deviancy must be explained" (Hogan, Johnson, & Emler, 1978, p. 6). However, the ultimate goal of socialization is not compliance with external commands but "autonomous moral behavior" that operates independently of external compulsion, although the importance that we attach to the goal of "autonomy" no doubt derives from the value system of Western society, which places a premium on self-direction.

If we examine this question closely, we can, in fact, speak only of "relatively autonomous morality," since the values we adhere to are still part of the culture we live in, even though very broadly defined. As Hogan et al. (1978) put it: "Autonomous moral behavior is not autonomous with regard to collective rules and values. It is, rather, the autonomous defense of what one sees as highest in one's culture, despite the demands of family, peers, and conventional authority."

Compliance at an early age need not be the enemy of autonomy in later childhood and adulthood. Like Baumrind (1973), we found compliance to be an indication of maturity, competence, and independence, and hence, it may well be the precursor of later autonomy, and autonomous moral behavior, too. The developmental processes and parental practices that ensure that compliance develops in the direction of autonomous morality are not as yet very clear. In part, its development goes hand in hand with the greater complexity of thought that comes about with increasing age. There is some evidence (Hoffman & Saltzstein, 1967) that it is the parents' rationality and cognitive orientation that help to promote the development of advanced moral judgment. But the evidence is not so strong as to provide us with firm guidelines for action, particularly since, as we have seen, the child's own disposition also has a part to play in these reciprocal interchanges. If we go beyond the evidence, it seems reasonable to suggest not only that parents can help the process of generalization and of building cognitive structure by giving reasons and explanations for their actions but that such explanations can also assist the child toward greater insight into others' feelings and reactions to his own behavior (i.e., empathy). But, as we can infer from our findings, such empathy may also be nurtured by the parents' own accommodating and responsive attitude to the child, which serves as a model to him. It is the fusion of empathy with a cognitive awareness of the effects of one's actions that, according to one theory (Hoffman, 1970), ultimately generates prosocial morality. Hogan *et al.* (1978) also believe that, in addition to modeling, experiences that encourage introspection and perspective on oneself—and this would include parents' explanations or discussions of issues—are important in this respect.

One way of building cognitive structure in the moral area is for parents to distinguish between commands that are grounded in moral imperatives (e.g., not to hammer baby brother) and those whose purpose it is to safeguard the parents' or the family's convenience (e.g., not to pester Mother while she is talking on the telephone). The extent to which a command appears reasonable in the child's eyes in itself has a positive effect on his ability to build a cognitive inner code that will control his conduct. On the other hand, emotional intensity in insisting on a command is likely to evoke a high degree of anxiety in the child and thereby to affect adversely the development of rational structures.

Reasoning was used quite widely in our families. The following is an observer's comment on a particularly rationally oriented family in which even the 2-year-olds "reasoned":

> The twins were observed to express disagreement with mother and even to reason with her. If the reasons seemed valid, mother would allow the objection, but if not, mother explained and insisted they comply. Mother appears to view the twins more as individuals than most mothers do.

If reasoning in this investigation nevertheless seemed to have very little effect on the establishment of internalized standards, this may be because rational explanations assume greater importance with older than with younger children. At any rate, evidence from a number of studies points to a link between the use of reasoning (particularly explaining the effects of his actions to the child) and the establishment of an internalized conscience (Hoffman, 1970).

However, parents who would invariably carefully explain the reasons for all their actions, or for the inadvisability of the child's actions, would soon talk the child into the ground and themselves to a standstill, with the result that the child would cease to listen. Moreover, there are many situations in which parents see a clear and present danger to the child or to others, and that do not allow time for a lengthy: "The reason I am not allowing you to do so and so is. . . ." Many professional parents, as the Newsons (1970) point out, have learned the psychological lesson that reasoning is the best policy only too well. If they are somewhat inexperienced and idealistic, they may expect that sweet reason on their part will always be met by reasonable cooperativeness on the part of the toddler, only to find that their reasoning meets with prolonged stubborn resistance; they may then feel very guilty when they are driven to a very peremptory and authoritarian yell: "DO as I TELL you." Yet parents are only human, and there is a time and a season for everything!

Consistency, too, has been recommended in the literature—with great consistency—over many years. In this study, it has also been shown to be an important determinant of compliance. What is meant by *consistency* here is consistency in insisting that a rule, once laid down, be followed, not necessarily consistently carrying out every threat of punishment. Indeed, total consistency is probably not feasible in the hurly-burly of family life. Moreover, some inconsistency may actually be desirable in disciplinary matters: occasional forgiveness may be just as effective as applying punishment ruthlessly for every violation, provided the general principle is upheld (cf. Leff, 1969), and it is also more humane. While total inconsistency is unsettling for the child's expectations of regularity, situations alter cases, and if his parents are not always consistent, the child will learn that they react differently according to the situation or according to their mood. Such experiences may help him to adapt more flexibly to the needs and moods of others, and they may also teach him something about human frailty.

That variation in discipline practices may have beneficial effects is suggested by a study by Hoffman (1970). He found that the parents of 12-year-old children who gave humanistic responses to moral judgment questions (i.e., showing particular sensitivity to the human consequences of actions) used discipline techniques that were more varied, ranging from permissiveness to power assertion, depending on the situation, but they also focused on precipitating issues in conflict situations and suggested reparation where possible. On the other hand, the parents of children who provided conventional answers (i.e., showing mainly guilt over impulses) made frequent use of love withdrawal and often responded to misdemeanors by highlighting the harm done to the parents by the child's action.

Modern parents—particularly in the higher social classes—see themselves in a dual role: they wish to be their children's friends, and they feel the need to be figures of authority, as well. This is not a dilemma that is unresolvable, as many teachers and youth leaders will testify. However, it is probably easier to keep the balance with adolescents, when friendship can be based on authentic egalitarian relationships, and authority is respected when—and only when—its claims are well-founded.

With younger children, the balance will tilt toward the authority role, as the imbalance in power, skills, and competence is too great to allow genuine equality of relationships to emerge. The "friendship" is more a condescending one, from stronger to weaker, from protector to protégé. If complete permissiveness ever existed with younger children, it has long since flown out of the window; its abandonment was signaled, for instance, in the 1957 revision of Benjamin Spock's *Baby and Child Care*. Nevertheless, feeling that the democratic principle of self-determination that governs society at large must also—*mutatis mutandis*—apply to the child, the parent will want to respect the child's wishes, whenever these are consonant with his long-term interests and needs.

We can nowadays accept both that compliance up to a point has positive value and that it is a two-way process. The evidence does suggest that in the attempt to foster the development of both autonomy and morality in their child, parents need not abdicate the authority role that is their lot, provided it is linked to a positively toned, sensitive approach to the child.

Language and Competence

Parent–child communication is the most important vehicle of socialization for cognitive competence, since the child's linguistic proficiency will determine to a large extent complexity and structure of thought, and hence, it will also be the foundation for school achievement. Language level and intellectual competence are, indeed, highly interrelated.

The literature is unanimous regarding the effectiveness of maternal stimulation in fostering language and intellectual development (see Clarke-Stewart & Apfel, 1978, for a review). Stimulation can take many forms: provision of play materials, playing with the child, social contacts, or responsiveness to verbal and social initiatives by the child. Mother's warmth and affection, too, have been found to have an effect, but they probably operate indirectly, by generating social contacts. The link in all this is, no doubt, the amount of language directed at the child: the more mother and father talk to him, particularly about objects, persons, or events (as opposed to giving directions), the greater will be his intellectual competence later. A study of preschool children (White, Kaban, & Attanucci, 1979) that focused mainly on parental practices conducive to the development of competence came to essentially the same conclusion.

Twins

A unique contribution of this research project has been to advance our knowledge of the development of twins by a firsthand account of their experiences and relationships in the family circle. It has always been known that twins have slightly below-average scores on *verbal* intelligence and achievement measures, though not necessarily on nonverbal measures. This research has been able to clarify this finding by separating out possible causes: prenatal and perinatal environment versus postnatal family environment, explanations that I have, for short, called *biological* and *environmental*, respectively. The upshot is that the latter seems to be more responsible than the former for the twins' slight language inferiority.

Twin parents do, of course, face special difficulties, which start with mother's having to feed and physically care for two infants at one time, rather than just one. Given the greater pressures on parents' time and resources and the greater stress on them when two children of the same age demand care and help, there is a limit to the amount of attention that their parents can pay to each of them. The strain that twins can mean to a mother is illustrated by the following notes on a twin family:

> During the initial interview, mother volunteered the information that the only way she was able to cope with the twins was to leave them with baby-sitters and give herself a rest from them. During the observation periods, she often chose to separate herself from them by sending them to another room. Being sent to another room was used both as a form of reward and as punishment. Mother also kept herself apart from the twins by reading for considerable periods of time when in their presence. Mother's role in playing with the twins was mainly that of a passive observer.

This was an extreme case. But because of the pressures I mentioned, with the best will in the world, parents address less speech of all kinds to each twin, though, if we added speech to the two twin partners together it would, no doubt, exceed the amount of speech to a singleton. (I explained in Chapter 4 why this could not, in practice, be done.) Nevertheless, each twin receives less verbal stimulation personally than a singleton does.

Parents also display less affection to the twins than singleton parents do to their children. This does not, however, imply that they love them less. Often, we noted competition between the twins for parental nurturance:

each twin would appropriate one parent as his own and would seek greater closeness and affectionate interaction with her or him.

Similar phenomena to those we noted apply more generally to closely spaced siblings. The hard fact is that the closer children are in age, the harder it is for their parents to give them all the attention they would like to devote to them.

Twins are, however, not generally "handicapped" persons, in the usual sense of this word. Most twins make a good adjustment in later life and are perfectly competent adults. Nevertheless, their somewhat lower linguistic facility, on average, as compared with nontwins, is a matter of importance to them. The weight of the evidence also indicates that the average deficit continues into adolescence. Twin parents are sometimes upset at hearing that research suggests that they may contribute to this lowered ability. However, parents may benefit from being made aware of what they may be doing unwittingly, as this knowledge will enable them to take counter-measures, as far as these lie within their power.

Do Parents Make a Difference?

In the end, we are left with the question: What difference do parents' practices or their attitudes toward their children really make? It is a common observation—and all research bears it out—that some children, even from the most terrible homes, or children of psychotic parents, turn into healthy, well-adjusted adults. Why do these children seem invulnerable? Our knowledge in this area is as yet sketchy, but there is evidence that certain trends and modifying variables may act as protective factors against the ill effects of discordant and disrupted homes (summarized by Rutter, 1979).

If there is stress in a home, but family circumstances and climate change for the better in later childhood, this can mean a reduction in disorders, such as attention or behavioral difficulties, in the child. Temperamental factors in the child will also have an effect—sometimes beneficial—on his parents' treatment of him. Further, heredity and environment will interact and modify each other. A study of adoptive children, for instance, suggested that a criminal environment will leave children who have no genetic predisposition to criminality relatively untouched, whereas it will make children with such a susceptibility more vulnerable (Hutchings & Mednick, 1974). A good relationship with at least one parent may also have an ameliorating effect, in that children with such a relationship in a discordant home are less likely to develop conduct disorders than children who have no good rapport with either parent. Finally, schools have effects, too: children from discordant homes are less likely to develop problems in a better-functioning school.

Some children, we see, overcome considerable handicaps. On the other hand, children whose parents bring them up "by the book" and genuinely care for them may have difficulties of one sort or another. However, the fact that benign and loving parental treatment is no guarantee against later pathology and the obverse fact that children often survive a disastrous environment unscathed do not mean that adverse circumstances are of no consequence. It would be equally valid to argue that it does not matter if people are starving, because some persons with an abundance of food also fall victim to disease, or because the effects of malnutrition can be overcome.

According to Kagan, Kearsley, and Zelazo (1978), what matters for healthy psychological development is not so much parents' actual early affection but whether the child perceives himself to be valued at any particular time of life. There must be a high correlation, however, between the child's sense of being valued and parental treatment and affection at the time. The child is not likely to misconstrue consistently his parents' feelings toward him. Further, there is evidence that later good adjustment and social development are dependent on the formation of an affectionate bond early in life (Rutter, 1979; Tizard & Hodges, 1978), though other factors, such as genetic ones, may play a buffering role.

Single, isolated parental practices are of little significance in the child's social development, since their effects will be embedded in, and, if detrimental, can be redeemed by, the general climate that envelops the child. But whether this climate is a caring one or not does matter; and caring includes being sensitive to the child's own nature. Such sensitivity will guide parents in intuitively adjusting their actions to the child's dispositions and needs, while realizing that there are limitations to their powers to form the child's personality.

APPENDIX I

Table IA. PACIC: Parent–Child Interaction Code (Adapted from B. M. Caldwell's APPROACH Scheme)

I *Subject of behavioral sentence* (1st place)

O Observer
C Central figure (CF)
T Twin
M Female adult
F Male adult
G Female child
B Male child
W Family as a whole
E Environment
I Item
N Food, nourishment
R Relative, Friend
P Pair (of twins)
Z Setting alert

II, III *Behavioral predicates* (2nd and 3rd Place)

Environmental contact (00–09)
00 Ignores
01 Attends
02 Locomotes (towards)
03 Establishes, seeks or maintains contact
04 Terminates contact
07 Seeks approval, attention
08 Seeks help

Information processing (10–19)
11 Shows (to) or demonstrates (for), reads to
12 Communicates or converses
13 Writes or draws (for)
18 Informs about culture (rules)

Caretaking procedures (20–24)
20 Feeds
21 Gives food (to)
22 Dresses
23 Washes, wipes, combs

Manual Activities (25–29)
25 Transfers item (to or from)
27 Manipulates
28 Transports, holds

Negative reinforcement (30–39)
30 Contradicts, refuses
32 Expresses displeasure, discomfort (to)
33 Criticizes or derogates
34 Expresses hostility
35 Interferes or restricts
36 Resists or rejects
37 Threatens or frightens
38 Assaults
39 Withdraws privileges

Positive reinforcement (40–49)
40 Permits or sanctions
42 Shows pleasure
43 Approves, encourages
44 Expresses affection, solicitude (vbly)
45 Facilitates
47 Bargains, promises
49 Rewards tangibly

Body activities (50–59)
51 Sits, lies, stands inactively
53 Sits on knee (of)
54 Strokes, comforts

Continued

293

Table IA   (*continued*)

55 Perioralizes
56 Acts *in situ*
57 Plays—large muscle (with),
    dances

Miscellaneous (60–69)
60 Acts or occurs
61 Tidies up
64 Disorganizes
65 Disintegrates emotionally
66 Makes music (with)
67 Eliminates

Control techniques (70–79)
70 Suggests
71 Requests, orders
72 Requests permission
73 Inhibits
75 Offers
77 Reasons

99 Unsatisfactory record

IV *Object of behavioral sentence*
    (4th place)

    Same as 1st place
—No information

V *Adverbs describing action* (5th
   place)

1 Playfully
2 With irritation
3 Quietly, gently, carefully

4 With intensity
5 Quickly
6 Slowly, with reluctance
7 Ineptly
8 Imitatively
—No information

VI *Supplementary information*
    (6th place)

O Negative
V Accompanied by verbalization
P Involving interpersonal
   physical contact
P (with 37) With physical punish-
   ment
C In a specified manner, place, or
   time (comply)
N In a manner, place, or time
   other than that specified (non-
   comply)
T In continuation
S Simultaneously
H With adult help
I Interchange of conversation
D (with 37) With deprivation of
   privileges
L (with 37) With deprivation of
   love
—No information

Sample Fragment of Coded Interaction

Father romps with child, but in gentle manner.
    F57C3-
Child giggles.   Child shows father a book and talks about it.
    C42---   C11F-V
Grandma enters the room.   Child sits on father's knee.
    R02E--   C53F--
Child laughs.
    C42-4S
Child sits on chesterfield and handles book.
    C51E--   C27I-S
Child hits father with book.   Father says, "Ouch."
    C38F--   F32C--
Father hits child with book.   Father: "Does that hurt?"
    F38C--   F12C--
Child: "Yes, it does."
    C12F--
Child romps with father.   Child laughs.
    C57F--   C42-4-
Father: "You know you shouldn't hit."
    F18C--
Father: "Go open the door."   Child goes to open the door.
    F71C--   C02I-C
Child returns to father.   Child continues playing with father.
    C02F--   C57F-T

APPENDIX II

PARENT INTERVIEW I

Date _____

Interviewer _____

I. Demographic Information

1. Name of child _____ 2. Male/Female ____
   Surname   Given Names
3. Date of birth _____
4. Address of child _____
5. Name of father _____
6. Name of mother _____
7. Date of birth: father _____ 8. mother _____
9. Other children in family:

Name	Sex	Date of Birth
_____	___	_____
_____	___	_____
_____	___	_____

10. Present occupation of father _____
11. Previous occupation of mother _____
12. Highest academic level - father: _____
    special training _____
13. Highest academic level - mother: _____
    special training _____
14. Country of birth: father _____ 15. mother _____
16. Description of home: single/duplex/apartment _____
17. Other persons living in the home: none _____
    relatives _____
    non-relatives _____

II. Birth Information

1. Any complications in pregnancy (high blood pressure, anaemia, German measles, nerves): _____

2. Child was: full term/premature by _____ weeks/overdue by _____
    weeks/doesn't know _____.
3. Birth induced: because overdue/for other reasons _____
4. (If induced) By drug/by rupturing membrane (using anaesthetic) _____
5. Presentation was: normal/breech/otherwise abnormal _____
6. Caesarean: pre-arranged/during labour _____
7. Any other complications _____
8. Weight of child at birth _____
9. Birth was: at home/in hospital _____
10. (If twins) This child was born: first/second _____
11. Shared one placenta/separate placentas _____
12. Other twin living/born alive but died at _____
13. Born: macerated/stillborn/malformed _____
14. Other twin's sex _____. 15.   Birth weight _____
16. The twins are: Identical/definitely not/doubtful _____
17. Condition at birth was: normal (shown to m soon after delivery and
    given to fee in first 12 hours and regularly thereafter)/baby was
    normal but not brought to m owing to her own condition/not given to
    m until the _____ th day/special treatment (fed through tube; kept in
    incubator; blood transfusion) _____
18. Black or blue (cyanosed) immediately after birth but soon recovered/
    blue later _____
    (Only score if diagnosed blue, etc., by doctor).
19. Jaundiced (skin and whites of eyes yellow): first noticed on _____ th
    day; definitely faded by _____ th day; no treatment given/given blood
    transfusion/exchange of blood _____
20. Respiratory trouble (slow to cry or breathe): immediately after birth
    but responded within a few minutes/serious difficulty in getting
    breathing going, needed a lot of reviving/respiratory distress (breath-
    ing difficulties after 1st day) _____
21. Other poor condition _____

Additional Information about Mother and Child

1. Illnesses of child since birth: serious _____
    baby illnesses (colds & teething) _____
2. Have you started toilet training the child? _____
3. How do/did you carry out the training? _____
4. When did you train the child? _____
    Is bowel training complete? _____
    Has he any accidents as regards soiling? _____
    How often? _____
    Is X sometimes wet during the day or at night? _____

How often during the day? (per week)_____
How often at night? (per week) _____
5. Does the child still get his bottle?_____
6. If not, when did he stop getting it? _____
7. Did the child ever have a soother? _____
8. Does he still have it? _____
9. Have you felt quite well since the child was born, or have you frequently felt tired and upset?_____
10. Have you worked since the child was born? _____
11. Do you plan to go back to work?_____

MOTHER INTERVIEW II

Twins

C Twin's Name _____ Date Seen _____
T Twin's Name _____ Interviewer _____

1. Does C usually do as you ask him right away, or do you have to ask him several times before he does it?_____
   What about T? _____
2. Does C do many things that you feel he should know better than to do? _____
   What about T? _____
3. Does C play with his own toys most of the time, or does he frequently get into things that don't belong to him?_____
   What about T? _____
4. At what time is C most difficult to deal with: at mealtimes, bedtime, bathing? _____
   What about T? _____
5. Does C play in your yard, or does he wander away when he is not closely watched?_____
   What about T? _____
6. Does C follow you around and hang on to you?_____
   Does T? _____
7. Does C want you to notice everything he does? _____
   Does T? _____
8. How does C react when you go out and leave him with someone else?
   T?_____
9. (a) Does C go to sleep easily? _____
   T?_____
   (b) Does C sleep right through the night? What happens? _____
   T?_____

10. How often do you take C into your bed or sleep in his bed because he is upset? _____
    T?_____

11. Does C help with dressing himself? _____
    T?_____

12. How does C help to dress himself? _____
    T?_____

13. Does C wash himself? _____
    T?_____

14. Does C clear away his own toys? _____
    T?_____

15. Does C feed himself? _____
    T?_____

16. How does C feed himself? _____
    T?_____

17. Does C play at activities without your suggestion? _____
    T?_____

18. Does C go to the toilet by himself? _____
    T?_____

19. When C has difficulties solving some problems, does he usually come to you for help? _____
    T?_____

20. Is C an active child compared with other children in the family?_____
    T?_____

21. At what times during the day or night is C most active? _____
    T?_____

22. Does C play at one activity for long periods of time, or does he change activities often? _____
    What is the longest period he will play at one thing?_____
    T?_____
    What is the longest period T will play at one thing? _____

23. Does C ever climb up on the tables, cupboards, etc.? _____
    T?_____
    What do you say or do?_____

24. Some parents expect their children to obey immediately when they tell them to be quiet, to pick up something, and so on; others don't think it's terribly important for the child to obey right away. How do you feel about this? _____

25. How does you husband feel about strict obedience? _____

26. How do you react to either of the twins when they jump up and do what you have asked them to do?_____

27. If they don't do what you asked, do you ever just drop the subject, or do you always see to it that they do it? _____

28. What are the things that you insist they must *not* do? _____
29. If they do something that you very much disapprove of, what do you do? Give examples. _____
30. How often do you tell the twins (or one of them) that you're going to punish them and then for some reason not follow through? _____
31. Do you insist that the twins try to do certain things that you feel they are old enough to do? _____
32. Do you often use a promise of candy, toys, etc., to get the twins to do as you want them to?_____
    Do you give them candy or a gift after good behavior as a reward? __
33. How much time do you spend dressing, bathing, or washing both twins together per day? _____
34. How much time do you spend playing with both twins amusing them per day? _____
35. Would you describe C as an affectionate child? _____
    T?_____
36. How do you react to C when he clings to you or follows you around?
    T?_____
37. Do you keep track of exactly where C is and what he is doing most of the time, or can you let him watch out for himself quite a bit?_____
    T?_____
38. Is your yard enclosed? _____
    Do you allow C to play in the yard alone for quite long periods of time without checking him? _____
    For how long?_____
    T?_____
    On the street? _____
39. How much time do you spend holding C or cuddling him? _____
    T?_____
40. Do you try to treat both twins alike, or do you make deliberate differences? _____
41. If you make differences, what are they and why? _____
42. Which twin is the more dominant one? _____
43. Does it upset the twins to be separated? _____

Children often take a long while to learn to do the things their parents want them to do. You have already told me about some of the things you are at present insisting on. We are also interested in the things you have insisted on in the past, things that, in the past, you have reminded him to do or *not* to do but that he now does without your telling him (or with only the occasional reminder).

I would like to go through a list of things you may insist on and ask you whether each twin has learned to do them without your telling him. We

may have mentioned some of these already. Tell me if you don't bother
about some of these things. Some families insist on some and not on others,
and we are interested in the things that you have insisted on.

I will always ask about C first, and then about T.

Example (*negative*).   Climbing on furniture: Do you insist that C must not
do this? (If yes:) Does he never have to be reminded about this, does he have
to be reminded sometimes, or does he always have to be reminded? And T?

Example (*positive*).   Tidying up toys: Do you insist that C must do this on
his own? (If yes:) Does he never do it without being told, does he sometimes
do it, or does he always do it? And T?

	C TWIN				T TWIN		
	M has not insisted	Conforms mostly without being told	Conforms sometimes without being told	Never conforms	Conforms mostly without being told	Conforms sometimes without being told	Never conforms
1. Climbing on furniture.							
2. Playing with food.							
3. Leaving food on plate.							
4. Leaving table in middle of meal.							
5. Going into road.							
6. Playing with things that you don't want him to play with or that are dangerous.							
7. Tearing up books.							
8. Getting into drawers or rooms where you do not want him.							
9. Coloring on walls or furniture.							
10. Taking toys away from younger siblings (or twin).							
11. Being too rough with younger child (or twin) (including biting).							
12. Helping with chores where you want him to.							

Continued

13. Tidying up toys (do not count if with M/F's help.)

14. Playing in the place where you want him to play, rather than somewhere else.

15. Saying "please."

16. Saying "thank you."

17. What about when you take him out, are there any things you don't want him to do? Has he learned not to do them? (Specify) ....
....
....
....

18. Other ....
....
....
....

APPENDIX III

Table IIA. Means, Standard Deviations, Minima, and Maxima of Variables (Discussed in Chapter 3)

Variable		Mean	SD	Min.	Max.
Duration of observation		246.79	16.63	196.00	316.17
Time present	M[a]	230.92	22.61	172.67	310.33
Time present	F[b]	151.11	59.37	20.83	259.00
Behavior units	Child	1040.63	256.01	586.00	1828.00
Behavior units	M	636.43	279.29	222.00	1941.00
Behavior units	F	290.24	173.96	17.00	848.00
	Child actions				
Rough-and-tumble play	% of actions	4.35	2.76	0.00	13.17
Rough-and-tumble play	% of time	6.44	4.40	0.00	23.32
Manipulative play	% of actions	9.98	3.30	2.26	23.11
Manipulative play	% of time	16.90	6.49	4.01	38.46
Walking	% of actions	10.31	4.05	2.61	24.23
Walking	% of time	7.63	3.51	1.85	20.51
Total physically active behavior	% of time	34.98	9.38	13.84	60.51
Activity shift score		3.45	0.83	1.65	5.35
Speech	% of actions	41.95	12.96	11.76	69.43
Speech rate per min		1.80	0.78	0.39	4.05
Demands—frequency		43.29	24.36	1.00	150.00
Demands	% of actions	4.25	2.16	0.10	10.35
Comply—frequency		114.49	45.82	25.00	238.00
Comply ratio		0.65	0.10	0.38	0.89
Expression of pleasure	% of actions	4.30	2.80	0.08	16.30
All positive actions	% of actions	16.63	4.37	7.2	28.2
Expression of displeasure	% of actions	2.75	1.99	0.26	10.87
Disorganized behavior	% of actions	1.18	0.97	0.00	5.20
All negative actions	% of actions	19.76	5.98	8.5	36.6
Approaching M	% of actions	1.59	0.77	0.0	3.67
Approaching F	% of actions	0.75	0.57	0.0	3.16
Touching M	% of actions	0.18	0.23	0.0	1.30
Touching F	% of actions	0.16	0.23	0.0	0.92
Seeking attention M	% of actions	0.53	0.64	0.0	3.62

Continued

305

Table IIA　(*continued*)

Child actions						
Seeking attention F	% of actions		0.19	0.30	0.0	1.57
Seeking help M	% of actions		0.26	0.30	0.0	1.50
Seeking help F	% of actions		0.10	0.16	0.0	0.81
Seeking permission M	% of actions		0.32	0.42	0.0	2.53
Seeking permission F	% of actions		0.10	0.15	0.0	0.88
Sitting on knee M	% of actions		0.28	0.34	0.0	1.85
Sitting on knee F	% of actions		0.29	0.43	0.0	2.66
Romping with M	% of actions		0.45	0.66	0.0	3.35
Romping with F	% of actions		0.72	0.90	0.0	5.26
Total of 14 above actions	% of actions		5.62	2.40	0.96	14.00
Attachment rate (narrow) to M			0.11	0.06	0.01	0.32
Attachment rate (narrow) to F			0.08	0.05	0.00	0.23
Nonverbal attachment rate			0.13	0.07	0.03	0.37
Verbal attachment rate			0.06	0.06	0.00	0.40

Father and Mother actions						
Rate of F–C speech per min.			1.07	0.66	0.03	3.57
Rate of F–C interchange per min.			1.74	1.13	0.03	6.36
Rate of M–C speech per min.			1.49	0.79	0.22	4.11
Rate of M–C interchange per min.			2.37	1.34	0.33	6.70
Commands—frequency M			65.27	35.34	6.0	185.0
Commands—frequency F			27.01	21.41	0.0	119.0
Commands	% of actions	M	10.70	5.07	2.28	26.95
Commands	% of actions	F	9.93	6.44	0.0	41.18
Prohibitions	% of actions	M	3.58	2.24	0.64	12.99
Prohibitions	% of actions	F	3.88	3.18	0.0	20.79
Suggestion	% of actions	M	5.40	3.43	0.41	17.60
Suggestion	% of actions	F	5.66	4.27	0.0	17.77
Reasoning	% of actions	M	3.11	1.73	0.00	10.40
Reasoning	% of actions	F	2.19	1.71	0.00	9.00
Comply ratio—M			0.62	0.13	0.31	0.95
Comply ratio—F			0.69	0.15	0.33	1.0
Helping	% of actions	M	1.09	0.89	0.0	5.79
Helping	% of actions	F	1.02	1.03	0.0	4.44
Affectionate behavior	% of actions	M	5.63	2.84	1.35	15.43
Affectionate behavior	% of actions	F	6.59	4.55	0.00	30.21
All positive actions	% of actions	M	16.50	4.44	8.4	30.7
All positive actions	% of actions	F	17.93	6.62	0.00	40.2
Refusing	% of actions	M	1.01	1.10	0.0	7.84
Refusing	% of actions	F	0.70	0.94	0.0	6.82
Criticizing	% of actions	M	0.59	0.57	0.0	4.03
Criticizing	% of actions	F	0.54	0.66	0.0	3.39
Threatening	% of actions	M	0.85	0.88	0.0	4.35
Threatening	% of actions	F	0.70	1.08	0.0	5.52
All negative actions	% of actions	M	5.74	3.10	0.8	19.3

Table IIA (*continued*)

Father and Mother actions						
All negative actions	% of actions	F	4.53	2.95	0.00	17.9
Hitting	% of actions	M	0.25	0.39	0.0	2.20
Hitting	% of actions	F	0.29	0.74	0.0	5.88
Restricting, interfering	% of actions	M	0.99	0.89	0.0	5.02
Restricting, interfering	% of actions	F	0.96	1.37	0.0	8.03

[a] M = Mother.
[b] F = Father.

Factor Analysis of Child and Parent Interactive Behavior

Because of the nonindependence of data from twin partners, the correlational analysis was carried out on a reduced sample, consisting of all singletons and one randomly selected partner from each twin pair. The eight twin pairs whose fathers were absent were also omitted from the analysis, and the resulting N for all analyses was 82.

Product–moment correlations were calculated for the relative frequencies of the most important behavior counts, that is, the raw frequencies expressed as percentages of total actions of the given agent. There were 23 variables for children and 18 each for mothers and fathers. Each variable is based on an individual verb in the code, except for "Speech," which represents the sum of all speech verbs, including, for instance, approving and commands, but only a small percentage of the speech total is listed as separate verbs as well. The comply ratio, though not representing an action itself, was also included as an important attribute of children's and parents' behavior. The verbs included sum to 79% of all child actions, 60% of mother actions, and 62% of father actions. Since less than 100% of all actions are included and since no variable is a complete linear combination of other variables, the problem of linear dependence has been avoided. Following a preliminary factor analysis, certain variables were eliminated because of unsatisfactory sampling adequacy (Dziuban & Shirkey, 1974) and low communalities.

An eight-factor model best fitted the data for child and mother variables, as determined by chi square derived from a J factor analysis (Nie et al., 1975). For the father variables, the six factors that had an eigenvalue of 1.0 or more were retained for rotation. A principal-axes factor analysis with Varimax rotation was then applied to the three data sets separately. Finally, the domains of child, mother, and father actions were intercorrelated by means of factor scores derived from the analyses.

CHILD BEHAVIOR

The rotated factors of child action frequencies are shown in Table IIIA, and I will now briefly characterize the nature of the factors.

Factor 1 essentially represents rough-and-tumble play, with the father in particular. It accounts for 31% of the *common* variance represented by the eight factors, and its importance in the factor model demonstrates the significance of this behavior for the child. Factor 2 can be interpreted as verbal attachment behavior to both mother and father, with the exclusion of attention seeking directed to mother. Factor 3 consists of variables indicating nonverbal attachment behavior addressed to mother. Factor 4, a bipolar fac-

Table IIIA. Rotated Factors—Child Actions[a]

Variables	1	2	3	4	5	6	7	8	Commonalities
Comply ratio							65		52
Sitting on M's[b] lap			64						47
Approaching M						60			45
Touching M			56	40	29				57
Seeking M's attention								90	96
Seeking M's help		73							59
Seeking M's permission		33		−32					38
Romping with M			69						67
Sitting on F's[c] lap				43					33
Approaching F	47			36					53
Touching F				85					81
Seeking F's attention		41						48	54
Seeking F's help		72		37					71
Seeking F's permission		54							41
Romping with F	83								73
Requests, orders				−69					52
Expression of pleasure	48			46					49
Expression of displeasure						−85			78
Locomotion				39	86				96
Drawing	−38								25
Transporting				45					30
Rough-and-tumble play	58				38				63
Speech				−46	−47	49			81
Eigenvalues	4.16	2.42	1.58	1.48	1.32	1.09	0.77	0.60	

[a] Only loadings of > .28 shown. Decimal points omitted.
[b] M = Mother.
[c] F = Father.

tor, contrasts physical activity with speech and suggests that such physical activity is pleasurable for the child. Factor 5 mainly represents nonverbal attachment behavior directed toward father, but it seems that this tendency is opposed to seeking mother's permission or that it makes the latter unnecessary. Factor 6 contrasts movement—and rough-and-tumble play—with speech. Factor 7 suggests that compliance and speech go together, but both are incompatible with a dysphoric mood. Factor 8 brackets together attention-seeking tendencies toward mother and father.

The eight factors together account for 71.7% of the variance of child actions and thus explain a considerable part of this domain. One noteworthy aspect is that physical activity and movement, on the one hand, and speech, on the other, seem to be categorized as incompatible with each other; this finding parallels the contrast between the lower education group, which tends to be more active physically, and the higher education group, which leans toward greater verbal facility. It is also interesting to note that compliance and negative affect, or dysphoric mood, are at opposite poles and evidently mutually incompatible. These are all plausible and psychologically meaningful relationships. Actions that are generally classed as attachment behavior, when directed to father, fall fairly neatly into two categories—verbal and nonverbal—clustered on two factors. Attachment behavior addressed to mother, however, is somewhat more diffuse.

MOTHER BEHAVIOR

Table IVA displays the rotated factors of mother actions addressed to the child. Factor 1 can be interpreted as positive reinforcement by the mother, and it accounts for 32% of the *common* variance of the eight factors. Factor 2, a bipolar factor, represents negative psychological control versus a compliant attitude. Factor 3 expresses affection, both physical and verbal. Factor 4, where the accent is more on control than in Factor 1, can be characterized as positive psychological control. Factor 5 contrasts reasoned restrictions with a compliant, accommodating tendency. Factor 6 epitomizes what can be called *power assertion*. Factor 7 places physical restraint at one pole and autonomy granting at the other, and Factor 8 indicates a helpful, accommodating attitude.

The eight factors together account for 79.2% of the variance of the mother's actions, and thus together they explain a high proportion of her behavior. Positively and negatively toned psychological control, power assertion, and affection are important dimensions of socialization behavior, and the contrasts within the factors are meaningful in psychological terms (e.g., an accommodating attitude as the negation of aversive psychological procedures).

Table IVA.   Rotated Factors—Mother Actions[a]

Variables	1	2	3	4	5	6	7	8	Commonalities
Commands						60			55
Prohibitions					80	34			91
Suggestions	67			35					73
Use of reasoning				80	31				82
Approval	85								75
Verbal affection	33		67						68
Physical affection	30		29						31
Carrying child			85						87
Giving permission	35			34			−31		43
Helping								50	28
Promising				76					67
Refusal		85							79
Criticizing		50							37
Physical intervention							82		77
Threats		51				54			67
Physical punishment						60			40
Mother–child speech	54			53					73
Comply ratio		−52			−35			48	78
Eigenvalues	3.68	2.20	1.44	1.22	1.01	0.80	0.66	0.50	

[a] Only loadings of > .28 are shown. Decimal points omitted.

FATHER BEHAVIOR

The rotated factors of father behavior directed to the child are shown in Table VA. Factor 1 represents positive psychological control and is equivalent to mother Factor 4. Carrying 30.6% of the *common* variance, it is the most important factor in this domain. Factor 2 clearly epitomizes power assertion and corresponds to mother Factor 6. It is interesting to note that power assertion is a more important factor in father's than in mother's behavior. Factor 3 can be interpreted as reasoned restrictions and corresponds in part to mother Factor 5. Factor 4 loads on only one variable and therefore does not help to simplify the structure of the inter-relations. The variable *helping* immediately describes the nature of the factor; it is the equivalent of part of mother Factor 8. Factor 5—like mother Factor 2—can be characterized as negative psychological control versus a compliant attitude. Factor 6 incorporates variables indicative of affection and autonomy versus restraint. The loading of threat here is somewhat incongruous and makes the interpretation of this least important factor somewhat hazardous.

The six factors together account for 62.9% of the variance of the father's actions, and they explain rather less of this domain than do the factors structuring child's and mother's behavior. The factors are in content very largely parallel to mother's factors, and although they do not cover the domain as exhaustively as mother's factors do, they reflect its most important dimensions.

INTERCORRELATIONS OF CHILD, MOTHER, AND FATHER BEHAVIOR

The factors within one factor solution are, of course, by reason of the principal-axes method exployed, forced into orthogonal positions and are therefore uncorrelated with one another. However, using factor scores derived from the rotated factors, product–moment correlations were calculated between factors in the different domains of child, mother, and father behavior. The resulting network of relationships between child, mother, and father factors appears in Table VIA, showing the reciprocal influences at work in this triadic system.

Any inference as to causality based on correlations must perforce be very speculative, and conclusions have to be treated warily. Cause-effect relationships were discussed in Chapter 5 (see also Appendix VI) dealing with the sequence analysis of behavior where such discussion was on firmer ground.

Table VA.   Rotated Factors—Father Actions[a]

Variables	1	2	3	4	5	6	Commonalities
Commands		75			33		75
Prohibitions		62	54				70
Suggestions	78						66
Use of reasoning	41		58				59
Approval	65						48
Verbal affection						38	23
Physical affection						33	25
Carrying child			40				19
Giving permission	60					28	51
Helping				99			1.00
Promising			38			52	49
Refusal					69		50
Criticizing					36		20
Physical Intervention						−41	19
Threat		32			47	36	48
Physical punishment		70					52
Father–child speech	70						59
Comply ratio					−36		27
Eigenvalues	2.63	2.25	1.13	1.10	0.80	0.68	

[a] Only loadings of > .28 shown. Decimal points omitted.

Table VIA. Intercorrelations between Child, Mother, and Father Factors (Action Relative Frequencies)
(N = 82)[a]

	M1	M2	M3	M4	M5	M6	M7	M8	F1	F2	F3	F4	F5	F6
C1														
C2					327^b									
C3									234^c					
C4				-339^d		-314^b								
C5								356^b						
C6	-331^b			-400^d			-212^e		-454^d					
C7	221^c		-445^d	227^c				287^b	268^b	196^e				
C8	233^c						-192^e			-234^c				
F1	502^d			472^d										
F2		298^b				245^c								
F3			246^c		310^b									
F4				209^e		-184^e								
F5		638^d		207^e		192^e								
F6							-241^c						-286^b	

[a] Only correlations significant at the .10 level or beyond are shown. Decimal points omitted.
[b] $p < .01$.
[c] $p < .05$.
[d] $p < .001$.
[e] $p < .10$.

Child Factors

C1 Play with father
C2 Verbal attachment behavior—to father and mother
C3 Nonverbal attachment behavior—to mother
C4 Physical activity versus speech
C5 Nonverbal attachment behavior—to father
C6 Movement versus speech
C7 Compliance versus negative affect
C8 Attention seeking—mother and father

Mother Factors

M1 Positive reinforcement
M2 Negative psychological control versus compliance
M3 Affection
M4 Positive psychological control
M5 Reasoned restrictions versus compliance
M6 Power assertion
M7 Physical restraint versus autonomy granting
M8 Helpful attitude

Father Factors

F1 Positive psychological control
F2 Power assertion
F3 Reasoned restrictions
F4 Helpful attitude
F5 Negative psychological control versus compliance
F6 Affection and autonomy granting versus restraint

Some of the relationships are best understood by focusing on the negative pole of a factor and reversing the sign of the correlation; for example, looked at in this way, speech (the negative pole of child Factors 4 and 6) is seen to have positive relationships with mother's and father's positive approaches to the child (Factors M1, M4, and F6). These data, however, do not give us grounds for deciding whether the parents' positive verbal approach facilitates the child's speech, or whether the direction of effect is the reverse.

Positive approaches to discipline (i.e., the use of reasoning, suggestion and approval—(M1, M4, and F1) also appear to facilitate compliance (C7) in the child. Moreover, the child's compliance has a reciprocal, positive relationship with the mother's showing an accommodating attitude to the child's wishes (M8).

Physical restraint, on the other hand, is related to noncompliance and a dysphoric mood on the part of the child (relationships between M7 and C7). The dysphoric mood is expressed largely through crying and whining, through which the child gives vent to his discomfort, and it is likely and natural that such expressions of unhappiness and discomfort will give rise to comforting behavior by the mother—hence the otherwise surprising positive relationship between negative affect (C7—signs reversed) and mother's affection (M3).

Parents' use of physical restraint and power assertion (M7 and F2), it seems, tend to discourage the child from seeking their attention and approval (C8). The fact that the mother's reasoned restriction (M5) has a strong positive association with child's joyful play, mainly with the father (C1), suggests that a compensatory mechanism is at work here: greater severity by the mother drives the child to more interaction with the father.

In considering the interrelations between the domains of mother and father actions, we see that factors with similar content are positively related to one another, so that four father factors have significant positive correlations with the parallel mother factors bearing the same name. The other two—"Helpful attitude" (F4) and "Affection–autonomy–granting" (F6)—have negative correlations with the mother factors denoting the opposite tendencies.

APPENDIX V

This appendix displays the percentage of variance in the criteria accounted for by mother's education and the additional percentage accounted for by the fact of twinship, scored as a "dummy variable." The probability values of the F statistics for mother's education, entered as the first predictor, have been omitted as not of central interest here.

Table VIIA. **Multivariate Analysis of Criterion Variables with Mother's Education and Twinship as Predictors[a]**

	% of variance accounted for by		Univariate F^b for twinship P	Step-down F^c for twinship P
	Mother's education	Twinship additionally		
Child variables				
Vocabulary IQ	3.19	2.23	.0787	.0787
Number of actions	.20	52.74	.0001	.0001[d]
Rate child speech	9.15	40.99	.0001	.0001[d]
Comply ratio	5.70	2.59	.0549	.8202
Attachment behavior % of actions	.05	5.51	.0062	.0131[d]
Instrumental independence (rating)	.23	2.76	.0538	.2465
Total activity score	3.63	19.69	.0001	.3710
Mother variables				
Consistency of enforcement (rating)	2.41	4.00	.0186	.0186
Rate mother–child speech	8.18	16.64	.0001	.0001[d]
Use of reasoning— % of actions	3.19	18.96	.0001	.0002[d]
Command–prohibition %	.00	17.42	.0001	.0001[d]
Affection %	.01	7.77	.0011	.0023[d]

Continued

Table VIIA   (*continued*)

Mother variables				
Positive action %	.02	10.41	.0002	.0001[d]
Suggestion %	1.32	23.47	.0001	.0001[d]

Father variables				
Rate father–child speech	3.00	11.18	.0002	.0002[d]
Use of reasoning— % of actions	3.71	4.70	.0158	.0007[d]
Command–prohibition %	.16	7.42	.0028	.0030[d]
Affection %	.00	11.36	.0002	.0007[d]
Positive action %	.00	6.82	.0042	.0302
Suggestion %	1.19	22.54	.0001	.0002[d]

[a] The F statistics for mother's education have been omitted, as not of central interest here.

"% of actions" and "%" denote percentage of the given agent's total actions. Multivariate analysis carried out on arcsin transformations.

[b] Univariate F evaluates the additional percentage of variance accounted for by twinship for each criterion independently of other criteria, allowance having been made for mother's education.

[c] Step-down F evaluates the additional percentage of variance accounted for by twinship for each criterion, having allowed for criteria placed higher, as well as mother's education.

[d] These step-down F values remain significant when individual α levels of .014 have been assigned so that the overall α level for the seven criteria is $<.01$ in simultaneous confidence testing.

APPENDIX VI

Sequence Analysis

The program computed the unconditional probability or base rate of each attachment indicator as a successor $[p(R_j)]$, the base rate being the variable's frequency divided by the total frequency of mother–(father)–child dyads recorded. The program also computed the conditional probability, that is, the probability of a child attachment response R_j occurring, given that a particular parent antecedent action, A_i, had occurred within the two preceding time intervals: $p(R_j|A_i)$. When a search was made in the reverse direction (see above), child and parent variables changed places in the probability formula. The complete algorithm and program are described in Taerum, Ferris, Lytton, and Zwirner (1976).

To decide whether a given parent behavior was a significant facilitator (inhibitor) of a given attachment indicator, the probability of the difference between the conditional probability and the base rate was evaluated. This was done independently for each successor, using the binomial test of proportions, as suggested by Goodman (1965) and used by Bobbitt, Gourevitch, Miller, and Jensen (1969).

We adapted the Goodman formula, intended for simultaneous confidence testing, to one for independent tests:

$$z = \frac{UP - CP}{\sqrt{CP\,(1 - CP)/N}}$$

where N is the frequency of a given antecedent, UP is the unconditional probability, and CP the conditional probability (the "sample probability," in Goodman's terms) of a given successor. The formula is a conservative one, minimizing Type I errors. To assess which differences would remain significant when all successors are evaluated simultaneously, one can then apply the formula: overall $\alpha = 1 - (1 - \alpha_1)(1 - \alpha_2)\ldots(1 - \alpha_n)$, which

Table VIIIA. Patterns of Facilitation and Inhibition of Child Attachment Behavior (Parents' Single Actions)[a]

Mother (N = 136)

Child attachment behavior (consequents)

Mother antecedents	N	Approaching		Touching		Sitting on lap		Seeking attention		Seeking help		Seeking permission	
N:		2218		260		421		750		360		482	
Base rate:		.011		.001		.002		.004		.002		.002	
	N	CP	FP	CP	FP	CP	FP	CP	FP	CP	FP	CP	FP
Ignoring child	620	.026[b,c]	1.38	.011[b,c]	7.90	.006	2.14	.060[d]	15.31	.019[d]	10.02	.011[b,c]	3.80
Talking to child	16606	.012	.06	.003[a]	1.33	.005[a]	1.20	.008[a]	1.09	.003[b,c]	.51	.008[a]	2.43
Suggesting	4707	.026[a]	1.38	.003	1.01	.004[b,c]	1.07	.007[e]	.92	.008[a]	3.84	.006[e]	1.35
Command	8862	.041[d]	2.79	.002	.69	.004[e]	.87	.003	-.14	.004[d]	1.44	.005[d]	1.16
Approval	1377	.012	.07	.001	.15	.002	.06	.013[e]	2.57	.008[e]	3.55	.009[b]	2.71
Reasoning	2609	.017[b]	.59	.002	.51	.004	1.05	.003	-.27	.003	.53	.011[d]	3.56
Prohibition	3019	.014	.29	.001	.05	.003	.45	.005	.27	.002	.13	.008[d]	2.24
Leaving child	179	.095[a]	7.78	.006	3.40	.006	1.72	.017	3.58	.000	-1.00	.000	-1.00
Threatening	790	.013	.17	.001	-.00	.009[b,c]	3.31	.005	.38	.003	.44	.008	2.23
Expressing pleasure	1316	.013	.19	.005	2.59	.007[b,c]	2.33	.005	.45	.005	1.60	.002	-.35
Giving object to child	1051	.010	-.03	.001	-.25	.001	-.54	.005	.30	.008[b,c]	3.33	.006	1.43
Physical affection	997	.006[b,c]	-.44	.002	.58	.013[e]	5.35	.006	.65	.003	.71	.005	1.13
Holding child	781	.004[d]	-.65	.000	-1.00	.044[d]	20.20	.000	-1.00	.000	-1.00	.006	1.72
Dressing child	610	.005[b,c]	-.55	.002	.29	.010[b,c]	3.79	.005	.34	.000	-1.00	.005	1.09
Feeding child	424	.000[b,c]	-1.0	.002	.86	.000	-1.00	.005	.29	.005	1.69	.005	1.01
Helping	910	.005[b,c]	-.49	.001	-.13	.005	1.68	.003	-.10	.003	.88	.003	.40
Providing food	1596	.003[d]	-.71	.001	-.01	.001[b,c]	-.70	.003	-.32	.003	.78	.004	.87
Showing, reading to child	2176	.005[d]	-.58	.002	.81	.000[d]	-.78	.003	-.12	.001	-.22	.003	.17

Father (N = 120)

Father antecedents	N	940 .005 CP	940 FP	193 .001 CP	193 FP	427 .002 CP	427 FP	220 .001 CP	220 FP	119 .001 CP	119 FP	126 .001 CP	126 FP
Talking to child	7779	.010[a]	.75	.005[a]	3.25	.009[a]	2.79	.004[a]	1.82	.003[a]	3.48	.003[a]	3.40
Command	3232	.041[a]	6.50	.003	1.49	.007[a]	2.00	.002	.70	.005[a]	6.63	.004[e]	4.09
Suggesting	2126	.021[a]	2.80	.001	.26	.007[b,c]	1.66	.006[e]	3.43	.007[a]	9.24	.002	2.22
Expressing pleasure	671	.016[b,c]	2.01	.003	1.67	.010[b,c]	3.22	.009[b,c]	6.02	.000	-1.00	.003	3.08
Prohibition	1245	.015[e]	1.80	.004	2.59	.009[b]	2.57	.002	.26	.002	1.33	.002	1.20
Physical affection	609	.011	1.11	.008[b,c]	6.34	.030[a]	10.95	.002	.29	.000	-1.00	.005	5.75
Reasoning	736	.015[b,c]	1.75	.000	-1.00	.003	.10	.003	1.13	.001	.97	.008[b,c]	10.17
Holding child	391	.005	-.06	.003	1.29	.064[a]	24.85	.003	1.01	.000	-1.00	.005	6.01
Ignoring child	195	.026	3.71	.010	8.17	.005	1.07	.046[e]	35.22	.010	13.88	.000	-1.00
Leaving child	54	.130[e]	22.81	.000	-1.00	.000	-1.00	.019	13.531	.000	-1.00	.000	-1.00
Showing, reading to child	673	.001[e]	-.73	.000	-1.00	.003	.20	.001	.17	.003	3.31	.003	3.07

[a] CP = conditional probability. FP = facilitating power. Minus sign for FP indicates antecedent acts as inhibitor. The p values refer to the difference between conditional probability and base rate of consequent. Total mother–child dyads: 204974; total father–child dyads: 172627.

[b] p < .05.
[c] This difference has a p > .017 and is not significant when all consequents combined are taken into account, with $\alpha = .10$.
[d] p < .001.
[e] p < .01.

Table IXA.   Patterns of Facilitation and Inhibition of Child Attachment Behavior (Grouped Parent Actions)[a]

		Mother (N = 136)											
		Child attachment behavior											
		Approaching		Touching		Sitting on lap		Seeking attention		Seeking help		Seeking permission	
		.010		.001		.002		.003		.002		.002	
Mother antecedents	Base rate:	CP	FP	CP	FP	CP	FP	CP	FP	CP	FP	CP	FP
		(Consequents)											
Command–prohibition		.034[a]	2.41	.002[b]	.98	.004[e]	.91	.003	-.15	.003[a]	1.12	.006[a]	1.73
Suggestion		.024[a]	1.37	.002	.79	.004[b,c]	1.10	.007[e]	1.11	.008[a]	3.92	.005[e]	1.22
Reasoning control		.021[e]	1.07	.002	1.04	.002	-.16	.002	-.29	.005	1.95	.006	1.57
Negative action		.010	.04	.001	.24	.003	.53	.011[a]	2.32	.006[a]	2.85	.006[a]	1.87
Positive action		.009	-.07	.002	.51	.006[a]	2.16	.006[a]	.65	.003[e]	.91	.005[a]	1.27
Neutral action		.013[a]	.25	.002[a]	.59	.003[a]	.49	.005[a]	.55	.002	.20	.004[a]	.75
Mother consequents	Base rate					(Antecedents)							
Command–prohibition	.111	.065[a]	-.41	.046[a]	-.59	.055[a]	-.51	.047[a]	-.58	.094	-.15	.039[a]	-.65
Suggestion	.049	.027[a]	-.46	.050	.02	.067	.35	.024[a]	-.51	.042	-.15	.023[a]	-.54
Reasoning control	.013	.008[e]	-.41	.000	-1.00	.010	-.27	.008	-.38	.008	-.36	.025	.92
Physical control	.012	.007[e]	-.43	.012	-.03	.017	.40	.005[b]	-.55	.000[b]	-1.0	.004[e]	-.65
Negative action	.050	.009[a]	-.81	.019[a]	-.61	.033	-.33	.164[a]	2.31	.214[a]	3.31	.398[a]	7.03
Positive action	.142	.093[a]	-.34	.092[e]	-.35	.124	-.13	.631[a]	3.44	.447[a]	2.15	.407[a]	1.86
Neutral action	.515	.225[a]	-.56	.292[a]	-.43	.268[a]	-.48	.032[a]	-.94	.128[a]	-.75	.091[a]	-.82

Father (N = 120)

Father antecedents	Base rate:	.005		.001		.002		.001		.001		.001	
		CP	FP	CP	FP	CP	FP	CP	FP	CP	FP	CP	FP
(Consequents)													
Command–prohibition		.034[b]	5.49	.003[b]	2.07	.008[b]	2.17	.002	.54	.004[e]	4.34	.003[e]	3.37
Suggestion		.019[b]	2.63	.001	.29	.006[b,c]	1.53	.005[b]	3.16	.007[d]	9.48	.002	2.30
Reasoning control		.023[b,c]	3.27	.000	−1.00	.003	.34	.003	1.61	.003	3.82	.003	3.55
Negative action		.010	.82	.004	2.54	.005	1.13	.010[b]	7.28	.003	2.83	.006[e]	7.13
Positive action		.007	.35	.002	.81	.010[b]	3.31	.005[d]	2.73	.001	1.09	.003[d]	3.35
Neutral action		.014[b]	1.65	.003[d]	1.77	.007[b]	1.76	.002[e]	.86	.002[d]	1.90	.002[d]	1.88
Father consequents	**Base rate**												
(Antecedents)													
Command–prohibition	.101	.066[b]	−.35	.062[b,c]	−.39	.037[b]	−.63	.018[b]	−.82	.059[b,c]	−.42	.040[d]	−.61
Suggestion	.052	.030[b]	−.42	.026[b,c]	−.50	.044	−.14	.005[b]	−.91	.017[e]	−.68	.016[d]	−.69
Negative action	.038	.006[b]	−.83	.026	−.31	.014[b]	−.63	.177[b]	3.70	.202[d]	4.34	.310[b]	7.20
Positive action	.153	.079[b]	−.48	.104[b,c]	−.32	.112[e]	−.26	.650[b]	3.26	.487[d]	2.19	.532[b]	2.48
Neutral action	.474	.200[b]	−.58	.197[d]	−.59	.248[b]	−.48	.027[b]	−.94	.118[d]	−.75	.087[d]	−.82

[a] CP = conditional probability. FP = facilitating power. Minus sign for FP indicates antecedent acts as inhibitor. In the top part of both mother and father sections of the table, child attachment behavior is the consequent; in the bottom part, it is the antecedent. The p values refer to the difference between conditional probability and base rate of consequent.

[b] p < .05.

[c] This difference has a p > .017 and is not significant when all consequents combined are taken into account, with α = .10.

[d] p < .001.

[e] p < .01.

gives the overall probability of a chance finding being accepted as significant when n tests are carried out (Bock and Haggard, 1968). Significance under this condition has been indicated on the relevant tables.

The significance levels provide information on the relative rarity of such a difference's occurring under the null hypothesis. However, it is also important to know the proportional power of a given antecedent to boost a successor's occurrence above, or depress it below, its base rate. As an index of the relative strength of facilitation or inhibition the "facilitating power" was therefore calculated: $FP = [p(R_j | A_i) - p(R_j)]/p(R_j)$. This index shows the proportional increase in the occurrence of a successor, in multiples of its base rate, given that a specified antecedent has occurred. A negative value of the index means that the frequency of the successor has been decreased, following that antecedent. It is then an "inhibitory power." By the nature of the formula, the maximum value that the inhibitory power can take is -1.0. The sampling distribution of FP is not known; hence, we cannot test the hypothesis of $EP = 0$ or compare two different observed FP values for significance.

Facilitation of Attachment Behavior in Twins' and Singletons' Subgroups

Table XA. Significant Facilitation (Inhibition) Effects in Twins' and Singletons' Subgroups, Not Present in Total Sample (Pooled Data)[a]

	Antecedent			Successor	Effect in total sample
			Twins		
M	Suggestions	Facilitates	C	Touching	N.S.
M	Promise	Facilitates	C	Approach	N.S.
M	Approval	Inhibits	C	Approach	N.S. in reverse direction
M	Commands–prohibitions	Inhibits	C	Seeking attention	N.S.
F	Restricting	Facilitates	C	Approach	N.S.
F	Threatening	Facilitates	C	·Approach	N.S.
C	Approach	Inhibits	F	Reasoning	N.S.
			Singletons		
F	Giving object to child	Facilitates	C	Seeking permission	N.S.
C	Touching	Inhibits	M	Suggestions	N.S.
C	Sitting on lap	Inhibits	M	Negative actions	N.S.
C	Seeking attention	Inhibits	M	Reasoning	N.S.
C	Seeking help	Inhibits	M	Commands–prohibitions	N.S.

[a] C = Child; M = Mother; F = Father. N.S. = Not significant.

Remote Effects or Cross-Lagged Panel Analysis for Attachment Behavior

DETAILED DISCUSSION

The obvious conclusion from the cross-lagged differential (see Figure 12) is that mother's suggestion increases the child's attachment behavior over time. However, it is also possible that mother's suggestions increase attachment behavior during the same observation and that attachment T1 in turn has a positive effect on attachment T2. Under this hypothesis, suggestion T1 operates in a circuitous way on attachment T2. To test this hypothesis, the partial correlation between suggestion T1 and attachment T2, holding constant attachment T1, was calculated and found to be .204 (shown in parentheses on the diagram), which is very nearly significant. This manipulation has the effect of equalizing for attachment behavior T1 by removing the variance that it has in common with the other two variables; that is, it shows us what the correlation between suggestion T1 and attachment T2 would be, if attachment behavior T1 was equal for all children. Put differently, the partial correlation shows what long-term effects suggestion has, over and above its immediate effect on attachment—and, indeed, over and above the immediate effects that attachment behavior might have on suggestion. Since this partial correlation, though reduced, is still very nearly significant and, moreover, is much larger than the opposite cross-lagged correlation (.063), the most plausible interpretation of the relationships is that suggestion increases attachment behavior both immediately and over time.

However, there are other, rival explanations. Rozelle and Campbell (1969) have suggested that the explanation for a cross-lagged differential may not only be that X increases Y, but also that Y decreases X. For the immediate facilitating effects of mother's suggestions on the child's attachment behavior and vice versa, this is indeed the case (see pooled data, Figure 11); that is, mother's suggestions tend to increase the child's attachment behavior, which in turn decreases her suggestions. That a similar mechanism operates in the case of the delayed effects we are now considering is strongly suggested by the fact that the partial correlation between attachment T1 and suggestion T2, holding constant suggestion T1, is -0.238 (shown in brackets on the diagram). This means that once the positive effect of suggestion T1 is removed, it can be seen that attachment decreases suggestion over time. The positive correlations between suggestion and attachment, then, reflect the strong positive influence of suggestion on attachment, which is, however, partly counterbalanced by the opposite, or negative, pull of attachment on suggestion, resulting particularly in a reduced correlation between attachment T1 and suggestion T2.

It will be noted that the correlation between suggestion and attachment at Time 2 is much lower than the parallel correlation at Time 1. Kenny (1975) has suggested that such a lower synchronous correlation may be due to a decreased reliability of one or both variables at Time 2 and that such decreases in reliability over time may produce spurious cross-lagged differentials. According to this suggestion, variables that decrease in reliability over time would appear to be causes. This hypothesis could not be tested in our case, as I had no same-time internal reliability estimates available separately for Time 1 and Time 2. It must also be remembered that rate measures are influenced by the overall level of activity of the agent, and hence, correlations may contain an element due to similar activity levels by the two partners. In view of these possibilities, the causal interpretation advanced above must be considered somewhat tentative.

APPENDIX IX

Table XIA. **Stepwise Discriminant Function Analysis between Twins and Singletons Mother Control (N = 136)**[a]

| Mother antecedents | Child successors | FP means | | Univariate F ratio | Contributed significantly to stepwise discrimination[b] |
		Singletons (N = 44)	Twins (N = 92)		
Command–pro-hibition	Comply	10.751	11.044	.062	No
	Noncomply	10.828	12.051	.525	Yes
	Neither	−.195	−.579	22.471[c]	Yes
Suggestion	Comply	11.406	11.941	.103	No
	Noncomply	10.923	11.079	.009	No
	Neither	−.223	−.649	13.595[c]	No
Reasoning	Comply	7.898	7.722	.024	No
	Noncomply	12.390	7.659	9.962[d]	Yes
	Neither	.280	−.360	16.225[c]	Yes
No verbal control	Comply	−.268	−.583	22.342[c]	Yes
	Noncomply	−.309	−.649	16.446[c]	No

Discriminant function Wilk's lambda = .709
$df = 11 \ p < .0001$

[a] FP = Facilitating Power.
[b] Determined by change in Rao's V.
[c] $p < .001$.
[d] $p < .01$.

Remote Effects or Cross-Lagged Panel Analysis for Positive and Negative Actions

DETAILED DISCUSSION

Significant cross-lagged differentials are displayed in diagram form in Figure IA. Let us first consider the relation of mother's commands–prohibitions and her physical control with the child's positive actions (diagrams a and b). The significantly larger cross-lagged correlations between these mother forms of control T1 and the child's positive T2 suggest in the first place that the influence runs from mother to child. The synchronous correlations are moderate and positive, and a rival hypothesis therefore might be that the child's positive action increases mother's commands–prohibitions and physical control during the same observation and that positive actions T1 also influence positive actions T2. This reasoning would suggest that the child's positive action is the causative factor that is also responsible, in a roundabout way, for the high cross-lagged correlation. Effects in this direction are rather implausible, but to test this hypothesis, the partial correlations between mother behavior T1 and child action T2, holding constant child action T1, were computed (they are shown in parentheses beneath the right-hand cross-lagged correlations). (The reasoning underlying partial correlations is set out in detail in Appendix VIII.) These partial correlations indicate what remote effects mother's behavior has, ruling out the effects arising from the child's positive T1, and also over and above the immediate effects of mother's behavior on the child's positive actions. Since the two partial correlations for commands–prohibitions T1 and physical control T1 with child positive T2 (.346 and .294, respectively), though reduced, are still

331

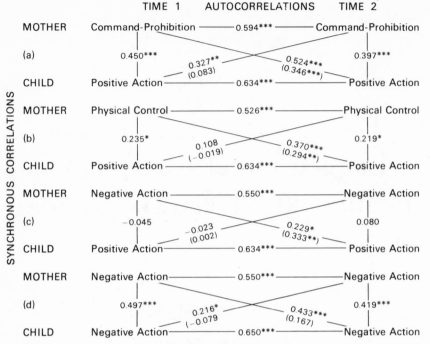

Figure IA. Cross-lagged panel for child positive–negative actions and various mother action categories. (Figures in parentheses are partial correlations, holding constant the appropriate Time 1 variable.)

significant, the most plausible interpretation would be that the direction of effects runs from the mother's modes of control to the child's positive action (among which acts of compliance were counted). In other words, the greater the rate at which the mother engages in these forms of control, the greater will be the rate at which the child displays behavior acceptable to her at a later point in time, though part of the effects can be accounted for by the immediate influence that mother's control behavior has on the child's positive action. This finding shows, of course, psychologically an entirely meaningful cause–effect relationship, whereas the reverse would be highly implausible.

If we consider the association between mother's negative action and the child's negative action (diagram d), we note that similar relationships hold for the cross-lagged correlations. However, here, when we hold constant the child's negative actions T1 by partialing out this variable, the partial correlation is reduced to nonsignificance (.167). This finding suggests that the mother's negative action T1 exercises its influence on the child's negative actions T2 to a large extent by increasing the child's negative actions T1 first. This lowered partial correlation also leaves the possibility that the child's negative action is the causative factor that increases mother's negative action contemporaneously (as well as affecting the child's negative T2), and hence the child's negative T1 would be responsible for both significant cross-lagged correlations, for one directly and for the other indirectly. To test this hypothesis, the partial cross-lagged correlation child negative T1:mother negative T2 was computed, holding constant mother negative T1. Since this partial correlation is near zero ($-.079$), it follows that when we equalize for mother negative T1, child negative seems to have lost its influence on mother negative. Hence, the most plausible interpretation is still that the mother's negative action increases the child's negative action both immediately and over time.

Fitting Genotype–Environment Models to the Data[1]

The means, variances, and intraclass correlations for the MZ and DZ groups of all the 28 child variables used in the major analyses of this research are shown in Table XIIA.

The starting point for an analysis of the causes of variation is the between- and within-pairs mean squares obtained from an analysis of variance on pairs of twin scores:

	df	Expected mean squares
Between pairs	$n - 1$	$\sigma_w^2 + 2\sigma_b^2$
Within pairs	n	σ_w^2

The opportunity for partitioning genetical and environmental contributions to the total variance arises from the fact that the genetic expectations for σ_w^2 and σ_b^2 are different for MZ and DZ twins. We define E_1 as a variance component due to individual environmental experiences within a twin pair (this includes systematic variation, as well as chance environmental experiences and errors of measurement); E_2 is variance due to environmental differences between pairs and includes cultural and class differences; D_R represents additive genetic variance and is defined in detail in Mather and Jinks (1971), as are the other terms.

---

[1] The biometric–genetic analysis was designed and carried out by Nicholas G. Martin and Lindon J. Eaves at the Department of Genetics of the University of Birmingham, England. This appendix is based to a large extent on Nicholas Martin's account of the method.

From the following equations:

$$\sigma^2_{bMZ} = E_2 + \tfrac{1}{2}D_R$$

$$\sigma^2_{wMZ} = E_1$$

$$\sigma^2_{bDZ} = E_2 + \tfrac{1}{4}D_R$$

$$\sigma^2_{wDZ} = E_1 + \tfrac{1}{4}D_R$$

we can write our model for MZ and DZ mean squares in terms of the parameters E_1, E_2, and D_R in the following matrix form:

Mean square	E_1	E_2	D_R
MZ_b	1	2	1
MZ_w	1	0	0
DZ_b	1	2	$\tfrac{3}{4}$
DZ_w	1	0	$\tfrac{1}{4}$

We have four observed statistics (mean squares) and are restricted to estimating a maximum of three parameters by the method of weighted least squares (see Eaves & Eysenck, 1975).

If we have s observed mean squares and estimate $s - 1$ parameters, then we are left with a residual sum of squares, which, for large numbers, is distributed approximately as χ^2 on one degree of freedom with which to test the fit of the model. We may fit other models that are subsets of the three parameter model given above, and we did fit models, including the E_1 parameter alone, and two two-parameter models, E_1E_2 and E_1D_R.

If numbers are sufficiently large, the method of weighted least squares provides maximum likelihood estimates of genetic and enviromental parameters and subsumes less efficient ratios such as those of Falconer (1960), Holzinger (1929), and others that attempt to provide "heritability" estimates with no test of the implied model (Jinks & Fulker, 1970).

Which parameters to include in the model is largely a matter of choice to be decided in the light of theory and the importance the investigator attaches to various factors. Any three-parameter model that constrains the total variances to be equal will give identical residuals. Estimates are given for D_R, E_1, and E_2 as the most basic and theoretically important environmental and genetic sources of variation, but it would be possible to reparameterize the model in a number of other ways, for example, by including nonadditive genetic variation in the place of one of the environmental factors. In every case, the contribution of each parameter can be tested for significance and the model for fit.

The general criteria to be satisfied before fitting models in which no covariance between genotype and environment is assumed have been stated by Jinks and Fulker (1970). Basically, one should see whether the MZ and DZ groups have been sampled from the same population by testing whether the total means and variances are equal, and one should do what one can to test for genotype × environment interaction. With a classical twin study such as this, we are able to test only for interaction between within-pairs environmental effects (E_1) (measured by MZ absolute pair differences) and genotype (G) and/or between-families environmental effects (E_2) (measured by MZ pair sums).

Significant differences in means between the MZ and DZ groups were in fact found, as shown in Table XIIA. Analysis of covariance showed that none of these could be accounted for by different age compositions of the groups. However, the differences might possibly be explained by variations between the groups in mothers' education, nonsignificant though the latter were. Multiple-regression analyses were therefore performed, with the child variables as the dependent variables and (a) the mother's education and (b) the twin type (MZ versus DZ) as the independent variables, entered in this order. The results showed that the mother's education did, indeed, predict these variables, and once this effect had been allowed for, no significant difference between MZ and DZ groups remained in any variable, save variable 23. In other words, the original differences in these variables between the twin groups could be accounted for by differing distributions of the mothers' education. (For further details see Chapter 4.) Table XIIA also indicates where significant differences exist between the total variances of the MZ and DZ groups.

The variable showing one of the largest differences between groups is the Peabody Picture Vocabulary Test (PPVT). The differences probably reflect inequalities of sampling and possible dependence of means and variances. The large day-to-day fluctuations in attention and motivation usually encountered in children of this age (cf. the seeming unreliability of the test reported in Chapter 2) would also have led to difficulties in standardization for this age range (cf. Lyman, in Buros, 1965, p. 820). All this suggests that in this study the PPVT is probably an unsatisfactory measure.

A test for $G \times E$ interaction in twin pairs (Jinks & Fulker, 1970), regression of absolute MZ pair differences on their pair sums, was also carried out for each variable. Genotype–environment interactions detected like this produce distortions in the distribution of the variable that are a reflection of particular patterns of individual differences. Factors that produce linear regressions also tend to yield skewed distributions, while kurtosis may reflect factors producing quadratic regression terms.

The worst distortions in scale are found in the count variables where the preponderance of very low scores, either rates per minute or percentages, produces strong positive skewness and often positive kurtosis as well. Consequently, it is not surprising to find most of the sum–difference

Table XIIA. Means, Variances, and Intraclass Correlations for MZ and DZ Groups[a]

Number	Variable	Type	Means			Variances			Intraclass r	
			MZ	DZ	p	MZ	DZ	p	MZ	DZ
6	IQ-PPVT	C	78.27	87.93	0.003[b]	175.170	225.539	0.439	0.224	0.291
10	Comply ratio	C	0.66	0.62	0.059	0.010	0.009	0.713	0.619	0.444
18	Positive action	CR	0.63	0.62	0.851	0.050	0.032	0.138	0.903	0.848
19	Negative action	CR	0.71	0.77	0.305	0.073	0.061	0.543	0.510	0.532
14	Attachment	CR	0.15	0.15	0.880	0.005	0.003	0.089	0.600	0.714
30	Child speech	CR	1.24	1.52	0.012[b]	0.193	0.302	0.168	0.793	0.686
31	Child–mother speech	CR	0.55	0.74	0.034[b]	0.077	0.205	0.003	0.646	0.812
32	Child–father speech	CR	0.40	0.57	0.032[b]	0.068	0.146	0.032	0.741	0.684
86	Positive action	CP	0.17	0.17	0.901	0.002	0.001	0.021	0.900	0.800
87	Negative action	CP	0.19	0.21	0.178	0.004	0.003	0.336	0.500	0.429
92	Attachment	CP	3.87	4.01	0.653	3.328	1.662	0.021	0.556	0.586
28	Child command	CP	3.94	4.50	0.229	4.849	4.481	0.778	0.755	0.681
24	Activity shift	C	1.21	1.01	0.020[b]	0.196	0.126	0.142	0.906	0.867

25	Active Behavior	CPT	33.45	31.91	0.387	71.360	64.597	0.727	0.878	0.811
26	Total activity	COM	49.26	46.28	0.085	77.533	53.382	0.214	0.894	0.850
9	Compliance	HR	2.78	3.03	0.199	0.821	0.841	0.960	0.675	0.645
13	Attachment	HR	2.74	2.74	1.000	0.401	0.356	0.680	0.434	0.510
16	Instrumental independence	HR	2.94	3.13	0.137	0.376	0.341	0.732	0.899	0.586
27	Speech maturity	HR	2.44	2.97	0.016[b]	0.709	1.122	0.158	0.858	0.910
17	Internalized standards	HR	3.02	2.84	0.343	0.654	0.523	0.518	0.782	0.642
8	Compliance	EM	3.97	4.17	0.189	0.511	0.380	0.353	0.276	0.198
12	Attachment	EM	2.79	2.56	0.191	0.496	0.555	0.760	0.192	0.267
15	Instrumental independence	EM	3.20	3.44	0.176	0.587	0.605	0.945	0.422	0.443
20	Toys	EM	20.19	20.35	0.934	57.125	89.383	0.190	0.333	0.118
21	Movement	EM	38.53	39.85	0.812	674.193	529.70	0.447	0.349	0.240
22	Total activity	EM	50.03	50.40	0.843	71.345	62.262	0.662	0.470	0.000
23	No. form-board pieces placed	EM	3.61	6.72	0.005	17.581	21.407	0.593	0.560	0.713
11	Proximity	EM	2.90	2.64	0.261	1.320	0.679	0.054	0.591	0.200

[a] C = a count variable; CR = rate per minute; CP = percentage of child's actions; CPT = percent of time; COM = composite of activity shift and active behavior, standardized score; HR = home rating; EM = experimental measures.

[b] Difference is nonsignificant after adjusting for regression on the mother's education level.

Table XIIIA. Results of Model Fitting for Child Variables[a]

Variable	Type	$E_1(\chi_3^2)$	$p<$	$E_1E_2(\chi_2^2)$	$E_1D_R(\chi_2^2)$	$p<$	$E_1E_2D_R(\chi_1^2)$	$\hat{E}_2$ $p<$	$\hat{D}_R$ $p<$	$\hat{h}_2^2$	$p<$
IQ-PPVT[b,c,d]		4.11	NS	0.60	1.02	NS	0.60	NS	– NS	—	—
Comply ratio[c]	C	13.31	0.01	0.94	0.96	NS	0.23	NS	NS	0.32 ± 0.38	NS
Positive action[c,d]	CR	40.52	0.001	1.33	12.72	0.01	1.27	0.001	– NS	—	—
Negative action	CR	13.10	0.01	0.45	3.17	NS	0.27	0.05	– NS	—	—
Attachment	CR	21.88	0.001	3.45	8.07	0.05	1.40	0.001	– NS	—	—
Child speech[b]	CR	26.05	0.001	3.50	4.84	NS	1.24	0.05	0.05	0.37 ± 0.21	0.05
Child command	CP	23.68	0.001	0.25	4.59	NS	0.06	0.01	NS	0.11 ± 0.24	NS
Total activity	COM	38.80	0.001	0.94	11.76	0.01	0.94	0.001	– NS	—	—
Compliance[c,d]	HR	19.96	0.001	0.06	3.98	NS	0.00	0.05	NS	0.07 ± 0.28	NS
Attachment[c]	HR	10.76	0.05	0.46	2.93	NS	0.14	0.05	– NS	—	—
Instrumental independence	HR	25.28	0.001	5.79	1.42	NS	0.09	NS	0.01	0.59 ± 0.23	0.01
Speech maturity[b]	HR	41.24	0.001	1.22	17.90	0.001	1.22	0.001	– NS	—	—
Internalized standards	HR	17.84	0.001	0.63	3.07	NS	0.32	0.05	NS	0.17 ± 0.29	NS
Compliance[c]	EM	3.27	NS	0.84	1.02	NS	0.84	NS	NS	0.02 ± 0.60	NS
Attachment	EM	2.27	NS	0.13	0.58	NS	0.10	NS	NS	—	—
Instrumental independence	EM	7.55	NS	0.01	1.48	NS	0.00	NS	NS	—	—
Total activity	EM	4.32	NS	2.47	1.13	NS	0.20	NS	NS	0.90 ± 0.56	NS
No. form-board pieces placed[b]	EM	17.30	0.001	0.60	5.77	NS	0.22	0.01	– NS	—	—

[a] Residual chi-squares shown test the fit of the model. A model fits when the associated chi-square is not significant. – Indicates that a parameter takes a negative value. C = a count variable; CR = rate per minute; CP = percentage of child's actions; CPT = percentage of time; HR = home rating; EM = experimental measure; COM = composite of activity shift and active behavior, standardized score; NS = nonsignificant; χ^2 = nonsignificant for all variables under E_1E_2 model.

[b] Indicates MZ and DZ means are significantly different (before correction for regression on mother's education).

[c] Indicates significant regression of MZ absolute pair differences on pair sums.

[d] Indicates that a square-root transformation removed the MZ sum–difference regression and that the results of model fitting to the transformed data were substantially the same.

regressions among these variables. Significant ($p < .05$) linear regression was found for variables 6, 8, and 13; significant quadratic regression for variables 9, 10, and 18; both linear and quadratic regression for variable 92.

It is well known that nonadditivity, which produces, for example, sum–difference regressions for twin pairs, can often be removed by transformation of scale (see Mather & Jinks, 1971). However, it was found in the analysis of twin–singleton differences (cf. Chapter 4) and in a genetic analysis of questionnaire personality data (Martin & Eysenck, 1976) that transformations of scale often made very little difference to the results of the analysis of second-degree statistics in small samples. It was therefore decided to carry out the initial genetic analyses on untransformed data in the belief that the extra refinement would not substantially affect the conclusions. Inspection of the distributions of variables displaying sum–difference regressions (6, 8, 9, 10, 13, 18) suggested that a square root transformation might remove the nonnormality of the distributions and the regressions. The transformation was successful for variables 6, 9, and 18 but made little difference to the results of the genetic analysis of these variables.

The detailed results of fitting the E_1, E_1E_2, E_1D_R, and $E_1E_2D_R$ models to the variables are shown in Table XIIIA. The table shows the residual chi squares after fitting these four models by the method of weighted least squares. A model fits when the associated chi square is not significant. The significance of the parameters $\hat{E}_2$ and $\hat{D}_R$ from the fit of the $E_1E_2D_R$ model is also given.

APPENDIX XII

Analysis of Variance between Observers

A hierarchical analysis of variance was carried out for all twin pairs, with observers ($N = 4$) as the first factor and twin pairs as the second factor, nested within observers. Since inspection of the distribution of mother's education between observers suggested differences between them as regards this measure, mother's education was used as a covariate to correct for these differences. The following table shows the results for those variables for which (1) $\hat{D}_R$ was not significant and (2) the observer mean square was significantly larger (10% level) than the pairs-within-observers mean square. The table permits a comparison of the proportion of total variance due to observers (SS_O/SS_T), after covarying the mother's education, and that due to between-families differences, $\hat{E}_2/(\hat{E}_1 + \hat{E}_2)$.

All the variables where a significant between-observers component is found are count variables. Child ratings, as expected, were less affected. Some of the differences originally noted between observers in the activity variables (variables 24, 25, and 26) were evidently due to differences in mothers' education, since taking out the effect of mothers' education reduced the proportion of observer variance from their original higher levels, but other variables were not affected.

Table XIVA.   **Proportion of Total Variance due to Variance between Observers and to E_2[a]**

Variable number		Type	SS_O^b/SS_T	$\hat{E}_2/\hat{E}_1 + \hat{E}_2$
14	Attachment	CR	.17	.65
86	Positive action	CP	.14	.85
87	Negative action	CP	.15	.49
28	Child command	CP	.17	.71
24	Activity shift	C	.39	.88
26	Total activity	COM	.21	.87

[a] CR = rate per minute; CP = percentage of child's actions; C = a count variable; COM = composite of activity shift and active behavior, standardized score; SS_O = sum of squares due to observers; SS_T = total sum of squares.

[b] ^{SS}Observer has been adjusted by covariance for mother's education.

References

Ainsworth, M. D. S. Attachment and dependency: A comparison. In J. L. Gewirtz (Ed.), *Attachment and dependency*. Washington: V. H. Winston & Sons, 1972.

Ainsworth, M. D. S. The development of infant–mother attachment. In B. Caldwell & H. Riccinti (Eds.), *Review of child development research*, Vol. 3. Chicago: University of Chicago Press, 1973.

Ainsworth, M. D. S., & Bell, S. M. Attachment, exploration and separation: Illustrated by the behavior of one-year-olds in a strange situation. *Child Development*, 1970, *41*, 49–67.

Ainsworth, M. D. S., & Wittig, B. A. Attachment and exploratory behavior of one-year olds in a strange situation. In B. M. Foss (Ed.) *Determinants of Infant Behavior*, Vol. 4. London: Methuen, 1969.

Ainsworth, M. D. S., Bell, S. M., & Stayton, D. J. Individual differences in the development of some attachment behaviors. *Merrill-Palmer Quarterly*, 1972, *18*, 123–143.

Ainsworth, M. D. S., Blehar, M., Waters, E., & Wall, S. *Patterns of attachment*. Hillsdale, N.J.: Erlbaum, 1978.

Aldous, J. Family interaction patterns. *Annual Review of Sociology*, 1977, *3*, 105–135.

Allen, G. Comments on the analysis of twin samples. *Acta Geneticae Medicae et Gemellogogiae*, 1955, *4*, 143–159.

Altmann, N. Naturalistic studies of maternal care in moose and elk. In H. L. Rheingold (Ed.), *Maternal behavior in mammals*. New York: Wiley, 1963.

Antonovsky, H. F. A contribution to research in the area of the mother–child relationship. *Child Development*, 1959, *30*, 37–51.

Apgar, V. A. A proposal for a new method of evaluation of the newborn infant. *Anesthesia and Analgesia*, 1953, *32*, 260.

Aronfreed, J. *Conduct and conscience: the socialization of internalized control over behavior.* New York: Academic Press, 1968.

Baldwin, A. L., & Baldwin, C. P. The study of mother–child interaction. *American Scientist*, 1973, *61*. 714–721.

Baldwin, A. L., Kalhorn, J., & Breese, F. H. The appraisal of parent behavior. *Psychological Monographs*, 1949, *63*(4), Whole No. 299.

Ban, P. L., & Lewis, M. Mothers and fathers, girls and boys: Attachment behavior in the one-year-old. *Merrill-Palmer Quarterly*, 1974, *20*, 195–204.

Bandura, A., & Walters, R. H. *Social learning and personality development*. New York: Holt, Rinehart and Winston, 1963.

Barker, R. G., & Wright, H. R. *Midwest and its children: The psychological ecology of an American town*. Evanston, Ill.: Row, Peterson, 1955.

Baumrind, D. Child care practices anteceding three patterns of preschool behavior. *Genetic Psychology Monographs*, 1967, *75*, 43–88.

Baumrind, D. Current patterns of parent authority. *Developmental Psychology Monograph*, 1971, *4*, No. 1, Pt. 2.

Baumrind, D. The development of instrumental competence through socialization. In A. D. Pick (Ed.), *Minnesota Symposia on Child Psychology*, Vol. 7. Minneapolis: University of Minnesota Press, 1973.

Baumrind, D., & Black, A. E. Socialization practices associated with dimensions of competence in pre-school boys and girls. *Child Development*, 1967, *38*, 291–327.

Bayley, N., & Schaefer, E. S. Relationships between socioeconomic variables and the behavior of mother toward young children. *Journal of Genetic Psychology*, 1960, *96*, 61–77.

Bee, H. L, Van Egeren, L. F., Streissguth, A. P., Nyman, B. A., & Leckie, M. S. Social class differences in maternal teaching strategies and speech patterns. *Developmental Psychology*, 1969, *1*, 726–734.

Bell, R. Q. A re-interpretation of the direction of effects in studies of socialization. *Psychological Review*, 1968, *75*, 81–95.

Bell, R. Q. Socialization findings reexamined. In R. Q. Bell & L. V. Harper (Eds.), *Child effects on adults*. Hillsdale, N.J.: Lawrence Erlbaum, 1977.

Bell, R. Q., & Harper, L. V. (Eds.), *Child effects on adults*. Hillsdale, N. J.: Lawrence Erlbaum, 1977.

Bell, S. M., & Ainsworth, M. D. S. Infant crying and maternal responsiveness. *Child Development*, 1972, *43*, 1171–1190.

Beller, E. K. Dependency and independence in young children. *Journal of Genetic Psychology*, 1955, *87*, 25–35.

Beller, E. K. Dependency and autonomous achievement striving related to orality and anality in early childhood. *Child Development*, 1957, *28*, 289–315.

Belsky, J. Mother–father–infant interaction: A naturalistic observational study. *Develop-* at the Meeting of the Society for Research in Child Development, New Orleans, March 1977.

Belsky, J. Mother–father–infant interactions: A naturalistic observational study. *Developmental Psychology*, 1979, *15*, 601–607.

Benirschke, K., & Kim, C. K. Multiple pregnancy (Part 1). *New England Journal of Medicine*, 1973, *288*, 1276–1284.

Bernstein, B. B. Language and socialization. In S. Rogers (Ed.), *Children and language: Readings in early language and socialization*. London: Oxford Unviersity Press, 1975.

Blishen, B. R. A socio-economic index for occupations in Canada. *Canadian Review of Sociology and Anthropology*, 1967, *4*, 41–53.

Bloom, L. Language development. In F. D. Horowitz (Ed.), *Review of Child Development Research*, Vol. 4. Chicago: University of Chicago Press, 1975. (a)

Bloom, L. Language in a context. In S. Rogers (Ed.), *Children and language: Readings in early language and socialization*. London: Oxford University Press, 1975. (b)

Bloom, L., Lightbown, P., & Hood, L. Structure and variation in child language. *Monographs of the society for Research in Child Development*, 1975, *40*(2, Serial No. 160).

Blunden, D., Spring, C., & Greenberg, L. M. Validation of the classroom behavior inventory. *Journal of Consulting and Clinical Psychology*, 1974. *42*, 84–88.

Blurton-Jones, N. Ethology and early socialization. In M. P. M. Richards (Ed.), *The integration of a child into a social world*. London: Cambridge University Press, 1974.

Blurton-Jones, N. G. Categories of child–child interaction. In N. G. Blurton-Jones (Ed.), *Ethological studies of child behavior*. London: Cambridge University Press, 1972.

Bobbitt, R. A., Gourevitch, V. P., Miller, L. E., & Jensen, G. D. Dynamics of social interaction behavior: A computerized procedure for analyzing trends, patterns, and sequences. *Psychological Bulletin*, 1969, *71*, 110–121.

Bock, R. D., & Haggard, E. A. The use of multivariate analysis of variance in research. In D. K. Whitla (Ed.), *Handbook of measurement and assessment in behavioral sciences*. Reading, Mass.: Addison-Wesley, 1968.

Bower, T. G. R. *Development in infancy*. San Francisco: W. H. Freeman, 1974.

Bowlby, J. *Attachment and Loss*, Vol. 1: *Attachment*. London: Hogarth Press, 1969.

Brazelton, T. B., Koslowski, B., & Main, M. The origins of reciprocity: The early mother–infant interaction. In M. Lewis & L. A. Rosenblum (Eds.), *The effect of the infant on its caregiver*. New York: Wiley, 1974.

Breland, H. M. Birth order, family configuration and verbal achievement. *Child Development*. 1974, *45*, 1011–1019.

Brody, G. F. Socioeconomic differences in stated maternal child rearing practises and in observed maternal behavior. *Journal of Marriage and the Family*, 1968, *30*, 656–660.

Broman, S. H., Nichols, P. L., & Kennedy, W. A. *Preschool IQ: Prenatal and early developmental correlates*. Hillsdale, N.J.: Lawrence Erlbaum, 1975.

Bronfenbrenner, U. Socialization and social class through time and space. In E. E. Maccoby, T. M. Newcomb, & E. L. Hartley (Eds.), *Readings in social psychology*. New York: Holt, 1958.

Bronfenbrenner, U. Toward an experimental ecology of human development. *American Psychologist*, 1977, *32*, 513–531.

Brown, R. *A first language: The early stages*. Cambridge, Mass.: Harvard University Press, 1973.

Bruner, J. Learning how to do things with words. In J. S. Bruner & A. Garton (Eds.), *Human growth and development*. London: Oxford University Press, 1978.

Buros, O. K. *The sixth mental measurements yearbook*. Highlands Park, N.J.: Gryphon Press, 1965.

Burton, R. V., Maccoby, E. E., & Allinsmith, W. Antecedents of resistance to tempatation in four-year-old children. *Child Development*, 1961, *32*, 689–710.

Buss, A. H., & Plomin, R. *A temperament theory of personality development*. New York: Wiley, 1975.

Buss, D. M., Block, J., & Block, J. H. *Activity level: Personality correlates, sex differences, and developmental implications*. Paper read at the Meeting of the Society for Research in Child Development, San Francisco, March 1979.

Butler, N. R., & Alberman, E. D. *Perinatal problems*. London: E. and S. Livingstone, 1969.

Cairns, R. B. (Ed.). *The analysis of social interactions: Methods, issues and illustrations*. Hillsdale, N.J.: Lawrence Erlbaum, 1979. (a)

Cairns, R. B. Review of R. Q. Bell and L. V. Harper: Child effects on adults. *Contemporary Psychology*, 1979, *24*, 353–354. (b)

Cairns, R. B., & Green, J. A. How to assess personality and social patterns: observations or ratings? In R. B. Cairns (Ed.), *The analysis of social interactions: Methods, issues and illustrations*. Hillsdale, N.J.: Lawrence Erlbaum, 1979.

Caldwell, B. M. A new "APPROACH" to behavioral ecology. In J. P. Hill (Ed.), *Minnesota Symposia on Child Psychology*, Vol. 2. Minneapolis: University of Minnesota Press, 1969.

Campbell, R., & Wales, R. The study of language acquisition. In S. Rogers (Ed.), *Children and language: Readings in early language and socialization*. London: Oxford University Press, 1975.

Carlsmith, G. M., Lepper, M., & Landauer, T. K. Children's obedience to adult requests: Interactive effects of anxiety arousal and apparent punitiveness of the adult. *Journal of Personality and Social Psychology*, 1974, *30*, 822–828.

Chance, J. E. Independence training and first graders' achievement. *Journal of Consulting Psychology*, 1961, *25*, 149–154.

Chomsky, N. *Aspects of the theory of syntax*. Cambridge, Mass.: MIT Press, 1965.

Clarke-Stewart, K. A. Interactions between mothers and their young children: Characteristics and consequences. *Monographs of the Society for Research in Child Development*, 1973, *38*(6–7, Serial No. 153).

Clarke-Stewart, K. A. And daddy makes three: The father's impact on mother and young child. *Child Development*, 1978, *49*, 466–478.

Clarke-Stewart, K. A., & Apfel, N. Evaluating parental effects on child development. In L. S. Shulman (Ed.), *Review of Research in Education*, 1978, *6*, 49–119.

Clarke-Stewart, K. A., Vanderstoep, L., & Killian, G. A. Analysis and replication of mother–child relations at two years of age. *Child Development*, 1979, *50*, 777–793.

Cohen, L. J., & Campos, J. J. Father, mother and stranger as elicitors of attachment behaviors in infancy. *Developmental Psychology*, 1974, *10*, 146–154.

Conway, D. *Language complexity in twins and singletons, related to specified biological, developmental and maternal speech measures*. Unpublished doctoral dissertation, University of Calgary, 1974.

Conway, D., Lytton, H., & Pysh, F. Twin–singleton language differences. *Canadian Journal of Behavioural Science*, 1980, (in press).

Crandall, V. J., Preston, A., & Rabson, A. Maternal reactions and the development of independence and achievement behavior in young children. *Child Development*, 1960, *31*, 243–251.

Cromwell, R. L., Baumeister, A., & Hawkins, W. F., Research in activity level. In N. R. Ellis (Ed.), *Handbook of mental deficiency*. New York: McGraw-Hill, 1963.

Cronbach, L., & Meehl, P. Construct validity in psychological tests. *Psychological Bulletin*, 1955, *52*, 281–302.

Darlington, R. B. Multiple regression in psychological research and practice. *Psychological Bulletin*, 1968, *69*, 161–182.

Davis, E. A. The development of linguistic skill in twins, singletons and sibs, and only children from five to ten. *University of Minnesota Institute of Child Welfare Monograph*, 1937, *14*.

Day, E. The development of language in twins: A comparison of twins and single children. *Child Development*, 1932, *3*, 179–199.

Denhoff, E., Hainsworth, P., & Hainsworth, M. L. The child at risk for learning disorder. *Clinical Pediatrics*, 1972, *11*, 164–170.

Deutsch, M. *Report on compensatory Education program*. New York: Institute of Developmental Studies, New York University, 1969.

de Villiers, J. G., & de Villiers, P. A. A cross-sectional study of the development of grammatical morphemes in child speech. *Journal of Psycholinguistic Research*, 1973, *2*.

Douglas, J. W. B., Lawson, A., & Cooper, J. E. Family interaction and the activities of young children. *Journal of Child Psychology and Psychiatry*, 1968, *9*, 157–171.

Drews, E., & Teahan, J. Parental attitudes and academic achievement. *Journal of Clinical Psychology*, 1957, *13*, 328–332.

Dworkin, R. H. Genetic and environmental influences on personsituation interactions. Paper presented at meeting of Behavior Genetics Association, Louisville, Kentucky, 1977.

Dworkin, R. H., Burke, B. W., Maher, B. A., & Gottesman, I. I. A longitudinal study of the genetics of personality. *Journal of Personality and Social Psychology*, 1976, *34*, 510–518.

Dziuban, C. D., & Shirkey, E. C. When is a correlation matrix appropriate for factor analysis? *Psychological Bulletin*, 1974, *81*, 358–361.

Eaves, L. J., & Eysenck, H. J. Genetics and the development of social attitudes. *Nature*, 1974, *249*, 288–289.

Eaves, L. J., & Eysenck, H. J. The nature of extraversion: A genetical analysis. *Journal of Personality and Social Psychology*, 1975, *32*, 102–112.

Elardo, R., Bradley, R., & Caldwell, B. M. A longitudinal study of the relation of infants' home environments to language development at age three. *Child Development*, 1977, *48*, 595–603.

Emmerich, W. Continuity stability in early social development. *Child Development*, 1964, *35*, 311–332.

Emmerich, W. Continuity and stability in early social development, II: Teacher's ratings. *Child Development*, 1966, *37*, 17–27.

Endler, N. S. The case for person–situation interaction. *Canadian Psychological Review*, 1975, *16*, 12–21.

Endler, N. S., & Magnusson, D. Toward an interactional psychology of personality. *Psychological Bulletin*, 1976, *83*, 956–974.

Ervin-Tripp, S. M. Imitation and structural change in children's language. In C. A. Ferguson & D. I. Slobin (Eds.), *Studies of child language development*. New York: Holt, 1973.

Escalona, S. K. Basic modes of social interaction: Their emergence and patterning during the first two years of life. *Merrill-Palmer Quarterly*, 1973, *19*, 205–232.

Falconer, D. E. *Introduction to quantitative genetics*. New York: Ronald Press, 1960.

Feiring, C. *The preliminary development of a social systems model of early infant–mother attachment*. Paper presented at the Eastern Psychological Association Convention, New York, April 1976.

Feiring, C. & Lewis, M. The child as a member of the family system. *Behavioral Science*, 1978, *23*, 225–233.

Freedman, D. G. *Human infancy: An evolutionary perspective*. New York: Wiley, 1974.

Gewirtz, J. L. Three determinants of attention-seeking in young children. *Monographs of the Society for Research in Child Development*, 1954, *19*, (2, Serial No. 59).

Gewirtz, J. L. Attachment, dependence, and a distinction in terms of stimulus control. In J. L. Gewirtz (Ed.), *Attachment and dependency*. Washington: V. H. Winston, 1972.

Gewirtz, J. L., & Baer, D. M. Deprivation and satiation of social reinforcers as drive conditions. *Journal of Abnormal and Social Psychology*, 1958, *56*, 49–56.

Goodman, L. A. On simultaneous confidence intervals for multinomial proportions. *Technometrics*, 1965, *7*, 247–254.

Gosher-Gottstein, E. R. Families of twins: A longitudinal study in coping. *Twins: Newsletter of the International Society for Twin Studies*, 1979, No. *4–5*, 2.

Gottesman, I. I. Personality and natural selection. In S. G. Vandenberg (Ed.), *Methods and goals in human behavior genetics*. New York: Academic Press, 1965.

Gottesman, I. I. Genetic variance in adaptive personality traits. *Journal of Child Psychology and Psychiatry*, 1966, *7*, 199–308.

Gottesman, I. I. Developmental genetics and ontogenetic psychology: Overdue détente and propositions from a matchmaker. In A. D. Pick (Ed.), *Minnesota Symposia on Child Psychology*, Vol. 8. Minneapolis: University of Minnesota Press, 1974.

Gould, J. L. Genetics and molecular ethology. *Zeitschrift für Tierpsychologie*, 1974, *36*, 267–292.

Greenberg, S., & Formanek, R. Social class differences in spontaneous verbal interaction. *Child Study Journal*, 1974, *4*, 145–153.

Grinder, R. E. Parental child rearing practices, conscience, and resistance of temptation of sixth grade children. *Child Development*, 1962, *33*, 803–820.

Gronseth, E. Worksharing families: Adaptations of pioneering families with husband and wife in part-time employment. *Acta Sociologica*, 1975, *18*, 202–221.

Gump, P. V., & Sutton-Smith, B. The "it" role in children's games. *The Group*, 1955, *17*, 3–8.

Hanson, R. A. Consistency and stability of home environmental measures related to IQ. *Child Development*, 1975, *46*, 470–480.

Harding, D. W. *Social psychology and individual values*. London: Hutchinson University Library, 1953.

Harris, A. Observer effect on family interaction. Unpublished doctoral dissertation, University of Oregon, 1969.

Hartup, W. W. Dependence and independence. In H. W. Stevenson (Ed.), *Child Psychology*, 62nd Yearbook, Part I. Chicago: National Society for the Study of Education, 1963.

Haseman, J. K., & Elston, R. C. The estimation of genetic variance from twin data. *Behavior Genetics*, 1970, *1*, 11–19.

Hatfield, J. S., Ferguson, L. R., & Alpert, R. Mother–child interaction and the socialization process. *Child Development*, 1967, *38*, 365–414.

Heathers, G. Emotional dependence and independence in a physical threat situation. *Child Development*, 1953, *24*, 169–179.

Heathers, G. Emotional dependence and independence in nursery school play. *Journal of Genetic Psychology*, 1955, *87*, 37–57.

Hess, R. D. Social class and ethnic influences on socialization. In P. H. Mussen (Ed.), *Carmichael's Manual of Child Psychology*, Vol. 2. New York: Wiley, 1970.

Hess, R. D., & Shipman, V. C. Cognitive elements in maternal behavior. In J. P. Hill (Ed.), *Minnesota Symposia on Child Psychology*, Vol. 1. Minneapolis: University of Minnesota Press, 1967.

Hetherington, E. M., & McIntyre, C. W. Developmental psychology. *Annual Review of Psychology*, 1975, *26*, 97–136.

Hetherington, E. M., Cox, M., & Cox, R. The aftermath of divorce. In J. H. Stevens, Jr., & Marilyn Matthews (Eds.), *Mother–child, father–child relations*. Washington: NAEYC, 1978.

Hinde, R. A. *Biological bases of human social behavior*. New York: McGraw-Hill, 1974.

Hinde, R. A. On describing relationships. *Journal of Child Psychology and Psychiatry*, 1976, *17*, 1–19.

Hoffman, L. W., Rosen, S., & Lippitt, R. Parental coerciveness, child autonomy, and child's role at school. *Sociometry*, 1960, *23*, 15–22.

Hoffman, M. L. Moral development. In P. H. Mussen (Ed.), *Carmichael's Manual of Child Psychology*, Vol. 2. New York: Wiley, 1970.

Hoffman, M. L. Moral internalization, parental power, and the nature of parent–child interaction. *Developmental Psychology*, 1975, *11*, 228–239.

Hoffman, M. L., & Saltzstein, H. D. Parent discipline and the child's moral development. *Journal of Personality and Social Psychology*, 1967, *5*, 45–57.

Hogan, R. Moral conduct and moral character: A psychological perspective. *Psychological Bulletin*, 1973, *79*, 217–232.

Hogan, R., Johnson, J. A., & Emler, N. P. A socioanalytic theory of moral development. In W. Damon (Ed.), *Moral development*. San Francisco: Jossey-Bass, 1978.

Holzinger, K. J. The relative effect of nature and nurture influences on twin differences. *Journal of Educational Psychology*, 1929, *20*, 245–248.

Horn, J. M., Plomin, R., & Rosenman, R. Heritability of personality traits in adult male twins. *Behavior Genetics*, 1976, *6*, 17–30.

Hughes, M., Carmichael, H., Pinkerton, G., & Tizard, B. Recording children's conversations at home and at nursery school: A technique and some methodological considerations. *Journal of Child Psychology and Psychiatry*, 1979, *20*, 225–232.

Husen, T. *Psychological twin research*. Stockholm: Almquist & Wiksell, 1959.

Hutchings, B., & Mednick, S. A. Registered criminality in the adoptive and biological parents of registered male adoptees. In S. A. Mednick, F. Schulsinger, J. Higgins, & B. Bell (Eds.), *Genetics, environment and psychopathology*. Amsterdam: North-Holland, 1974.

Hutt, S. J., & Hutt, C. *Direct observation and measurement of behavior*. Springfield, Ill.: Charles C Thomas, 1970.

Jacklin, C. N., & Maccoby, E. E. Social behavior at 33 months in same-sex and mixed sex dyads. *Child Development*, 1978, *49*, 557–569.

Jeffree, D. M., & McConkey, R. An observation scheme for recording children's imaginative doll play. *Journal of Child Psychology and Psychiatry*, 1976, *17*, 189–197.

Jinks, J. L., & Fulker, D. W. Comparison of the biometrical genetical, MAVA, and classical approaches to the analysis of human behavior. *Psychological Bulletin*, 1970, *73*, 311–349.

Jones, H. E. Perceived differences among twins. *Eugenics Quarterly*, 1955, *5*, 98–102.

Jones, R. R., Reid, J. B., & Patterson, G. R. Naturalistic observations in clinical assessment. In R. McReynolds (Ed.), *Advances in Psychological Assessment*, Vol. 3. San Francisco: Jossey-Bass, 1975.

Kagan, J., & Moss, H. A. *Birth to Maturity: The Fels study of psychological development.* New York: Wiley, 1962.

Kagan, J., Moss, H., & Sigel, I. E. Psychological significance of styles of conceptualization. In J. C. Wright & J. Kagan (Eds.), Basic cognitive processes in children. *Monographs of the Society for Research in Child Development*, 1963, *28*(2, Serial No. 86).

Kagan, J., Kearsley, R. B., & Zelazo, P. R. *Infancy: Its place in human development.* Cambridge, Mass.: Harvard University Press, 1978.

Kalnins, I. V., & Bruner, J. S. Infant sucking used to change the clarity of a visual display. In L. J. Stone, H. T. Smith, & L. B. Murphy (Eds.), *The competent infant.* New York: Basic Books, 1973.

Kamii, C. K., & Radin, N. L. Class differences in the socialization practises of Negro mothers. *Journal of Marriage and the Family*, 1967, *24*, 302–310.

Kamin, L. G. *The science and politics of IQ.* Potomac, Md.: Erlbaum, 1974.

Keenan, E. O. Conversational competence in children. *Journal of Child Language*, 1974, *1*, 163–183.

Kenny, D. A. Cross-lagged panel correlation: A test for spuriousness. *Psychological Bulletin*, 1975, *82*, 887–903.

Kim, C. C., Dales, R. J., Connor, R., Walters, J., & Witherspoon, R. Social interaction of like-sex twins and singletons in relation to intelligence, language, and physical development. *Journal of Genetic Psychology*, 1969, *114*, 203–214.

Klima, E. S., & Bellugi, U. Syntactic regularities in the speech of children. In C. A. Ferguson & D. I. Slobin (Eds.), *Studies of child language development.* New York: Holt, 1973.

Koch, H. L. *Twins and twin relations.* Chicago: University Chicago Press, 1966.

Kogan, K. L., & Wimberger, H. C. Interaction patterns in disadvantaged families. *Journal of Clinical Psychology*, 1969, *25*, 347–352.

Kohlberg, L. Stage and sequence: The cognitive–developmental approach to socialization. In D. A. Goslin (Ed.), *Handbook of socialization theory and research.* Chicago: Rand McNally, 1969.

Kohn, M. L., & Carroll, E. E. Social class and the allocation of parental responsibilities. *Sociometry*, 1960, *23*, 372–392.

Kotelchuck, M. *The nature of the child's tie to his father.* Unpublished doctoral dissertation, Harvard University, 1972.

Lamb, M. E. Twelve-month-olds and their parents: Interactions in a laboratory playroom. *Developmental Psychology*, 1976, *12*, 237–244.

Lamb, M. E. Father–infant and mother–infant interaction in the first year of life. *Child Development*, 1977, *47*, 167–181.

Leff, R. Effects of punishment intensity and consistency on the internalization of behavioral suppression in children. *Developmental Psychology*, 1969, *1*, 345–356.

Lerner, R. M., & Spanier, G. B. (Eds.). *Child influences on marital and family interaction—A life-span perspective.* New York: Academic Press, 1978.

Lewis, M. State as an infant–environment interaction: An analysis of mother–infant interactions as a function of sex. *Merrill-Palmer Quarterly*, 1972, *18*, 95–121.

Lewis, M., & Weinraub, M. The father's role in the child's social network. In M. E. Lamb (Ed.), *The role of the father in child development*. New York: Wiley, 1976.

Lewis, M., Weinraub, M. & Ban, P. Mothers and fathers, girls and boys: Attachment behavior in the first two years of life. Paper presented at the meeting of the Society for Research in Child Development. Philadelphia, March 1973.

Lobitz, W. C., & Johnson, S. M. Parental manipulation of the behavior of normal and deviant children. *Child Development*, 1975, *46*, 719–726.

Loehlin, J. C. Identical twins reared apart and other routes to the same destination. In W. E. Nance (Ed.), *Twin research* Part A: *Psychology and methodology*. New York: Alan R. Liss, 1978.

Loehlin, J. C., & Nichols, R. C. *Heredity, environment and personality: A study of 850 sets of twins*. Austin: University of Texas Press, 1976.

Lytton, H. Observation studies of parent–child interaction: A methodological review. *Child Development*, 1971, *42*, 651–684.

Lytton, H. Three approaches to the study of parent–child interaction: Ethological, interview and experimental. *Journal of Child Psychology and Psychiatry*, 1973, *14*, 1–17.

Lytton, H. Comparative yield of three data sources in the study of parent-child interaction. *Merrill-Palmer Quarterly*, 1974, *20*, 53–64.

Lytton, H. The socialization of two-year-old boys: Ecological findings. *Journal of Child Psychology and Psychiatry*, 1976, *17*, 287–304.

Lytton, H. Correlates of compliance and the rudiments of consicence in two-year-old boys. *Canadian Journal of Behavioral Science*, 1977, *9*, 242–251 (a)

Lytton, H. Do parents create, or respond to, differences in twins? *Developmental Psychology*, 1977, *13*, 456–459. (b)

Lytton, H. A genetic analysis of twins' naturalistically observed behavior. In W. E. Nance (Ed.), *Twin research*. Proceedings of the second International Congress on Twin Studies, Part A, Psychology and Methodology. New York: Alan R. Liss, 1978.

Lytton, H., & Zwirner, W. Compliance and its controlling stimuli observed in a natural setting. *Developmental Psychology*, 1975, *11*, 769–779.

Lytton, H., Conway, D., & Sauvé, R. The impact of twinship on parent–child interaction. *Journal of Personality and Social Psychology*, 1977, *35*, 97–107. (a)

Lytton, H., Martin, N. G., & Eaves, L. J. Environmental and genetical causes of variation in ethological aspects of behavior in two-year-old boys, *Social Biology*, 1977, *24*, 200–211. (b)

Maccoby, E. E. The taking of adult roles in middle childhood. *Journal of Abnormal and Social Psychology*, 1961, *63*, 493–503.

Maccoby, E. E. Moral values and behavior in childhood. In J. A. Clausen (Ed.), *Socialization and society*. Boston: Little Brown, 1968.

Maccoby, E. E., & Feldman, S. S. Mother-attachment and stranger-reactions in the third year of life. *Monographs of the Society for Research in Child Development*, 1972, *37*(1, Serial No. 146).

Maccoby, E. E., & Jacklin, C. N. *The psychology of sex differences*. Stanford, Calif.: Stanford University Press, 1974.

Maccoby, E. E., & Masters, J. C. Attachment and dependency. In P. H. Mussen (Ed.), *Carmichael's Manual of Child Psychology*, Vol. 2 New York: Wiley, 1970.

Maccoby, E. E., Martin, J. A., Baran, K., & Jacklin, C. N. *Sequential analysis of mother–child interaction at 18 months: A comparison of several analytic methods*. Unpublished manuscript, 1979.

Martin, N. G., & Eysenck, H. J. The genetics of sexual behavior. Chapter 6 in H. J. Eysenck (Ed.), *Sex and personality*. London: Open Books, 1976.

Martin, N. G., Eaves, L. J., Kearsey, M. J., & Davies, P. The power of the classical twin study. *Heredity*, 1978, *40*, 97–116.

Mash, E. J., & McElwee, J. D. Situational effects on observer accuracy: Behavioral predictability, Prior experience and number of coding categories. *Child Development*, 1974, *45*, 367–377.

Masters, J. C., & Wellman, H. M. The study of human infant attachment: A procedural critique. *Psychological Bulletin*, 1974, *81*, 218–237.

Matheny, A. P., Wilson, R. S., & Brown-Dolan, A. Relations between twins' similarity of appearance and behavioral similarity: Testing an assumption. *Behavior Genetics*, 1976, *6*, 343–351.

Mather, K., & Jinks, J. L. *Biometrical genetics*. London: Chapman & Hall, 1971.

McCall, R. B., Applebaum, M. I., & Hogarty, P. S. Developmental changes in mental performance. *Monographs of the Society for Research in Child Development*, 1973, *38*(3, Serial No. 150).

McCann, L. J. Ecology of the mountain sheep. *American Midland Naturalist*, 1956, *56*, 297–324.

McClearn, G. E. Genetic influences on behavior and development. In P. H. Mussen (Ed.), *Carmichael's Manual of Child Psychology*. New York: Wiley, 1970.

McClearn, G. E., & De Fries, J. C. *Introduction to behavior genetics*. San Francisco: W. H. Freeman, 1973.

McClelland, D. C., Atkinson, J. W., Clark, R. A., & Lowell, E. L. *The achievement motive*. New York: Appleton-Century, 1953.

McGrew, W. C. *An ethological study of children's behavior*. New York: Academic Press, 1972.

McNeill, D. The contribution of experience. In S. Rogers (Ed.), *Children and language: Readings in early language and socialization*. London: Oxford University Press, 1975.

Mead, M. Socialization and enculturation. *Current Anthropology*, 1963, *4*, 184–188.

Messer, S. B., & Lewis, M. Social class and sex differences in the attachment and play behavior of the year-old infant. *Merrill-Palmer Quarterly*, 1972, *18*, 295–306.

Milgram, S. *Obedience to authority: An experimental view*. New York: Harper & Row, 1974.

Miller, W. R., & Ervin-Tripp, S. M. The development of grammar in child language. In C. A. Ferguson & D. I. Slobin (Eds.), *Studies of child language development*. New York: Holt, 1973.

Minton, C., Kagan, J., & Levine, J. A. Maternal control and obedience in the two-year-old. *Child Development*, 1971, *42*, 1873–1894.

Mittler, P. Biological and social aspects of language development in twins. *Developmental Medicine and Child Neurology*, 1970, *12*, 741–757. (a)

Mittler, P. *A study of twins*. London: Penguin, 1970.(b)

Moss, H. A. Methodological issues in studying mother–infant interactions. *American Journal of Orthopsychiatry*, 1965, *35*, 482–486.

Murphy, L. B. *The widening world of childhood*. New York: Basic Books, 1962.

Nakamura, C. Y., & Rogers, M. M. Parents' expectations of autonomous behavior and children's autonomy. *Developmental Psychology*, 1969, *1*, 613–617.

Nelson, K. Structure and stratey in learning to talk. *Monographs of the Society for Research in Child Development*, 1973, *38*(1–2, Serial No. 149).

Newson, J., & Newson, E. *Patterns of infant care in an urban community*. London: Penguin, 1965.

Newson, J., & Newson, E. *Four years old in an urban community*. London: Penguin, 1970.

Newson, J., & Newson, E. *Seven years old in the home environment.* London: Penguin, 1978.

Nichols, R. C. The resemblance of twins in personality and interests. In M. Manosevitz, G. Lindzey, & D. D. Thiessen (Eds.), *Behavioral genetics: Method and research.* New York: Appleton-Century, 1969.

Nie, N. H., Hull, C. H., Jenkins, J. G., Steinbrenner, K., & Bent, D. H. *Statistical package for the social sciences* (2nd ed.). New York: McGraw-Hill, 1975.

Olim, E. G. Maternal language styles and cognitive development. In S. Rogers (Ed.), *Children and language: Readings in early language and socialization.* London: Oxford University Press, 1975.

O'Rourke, J. F. Field and laboratory: The decision-making behavior of family groups in two experimental conditions. *Sociometry,* 1963, *26,* 422–435.

Osofsky, J., & O'Connell, E. J. Parent–child interaction: Daughters' effects upon mothers' and fathers' behaviors. *Developmental Psychology,* 1972, *7,* 157–168.

Parke, R. D. (Ed.). *Readings in social development.* New York: Holt, Rinehart & Winston, 1969.

Parke, R. D. Interactional design. In R. B. Cairns (Ed.), *The analysis of social interactions: Methods, issues and illustrations.* Hillsdale, N.J.: Lawrence Erlbaum, 1979.

Parke, R. D., & O'Leary, S. Father–mother–infant interaction in the newborn period: Some findings, some observations, and some unresolved issues. In K. Riegel & J. Meacham (Eds.), *The developing individual in a changing world,* Vol. 2: *Social and environmental issues.* The Hauge: Mouton, 1975.

Patterson, G. R. A performance theory for coercive family interaction. In R. B. Cairns (Ed.), *The analysis of social interaction.* Hillsdale, N.J.: Lawrence Erlbaum, 1979.

Patterson, G. R., & Cobb, J. A. A dyadic analysis of "aggressive" behaviors. In J. P. Hill (Ed.), *Minnesota Symposia on Child Psychology,* Vol. 5. Minneapolis: University of Minnesota Press, 1971.

Patterson, G. R., & Cobb, J. A. Stimulus control for classes of noxious behaviors. In J. F. Knutson (Ed.), *The control of aggression: Implications from Basic Research.* Chicago: Aldine, 1973.

Patterson, G. R., & Reid, J. B. Reciprocity and coercion: Two facets of social systems. Unpublished manuscript. Oregon Research Institute, University of Oregon, 1969.

Plomin, R., & Rowe, D. C. Genetic and environmental etiology of social behavior in infancy. *Developmental Psychology,* 1979, *15,* 62–72.

Plomin, R., Willerman, L., & Loehlin, J. C. Resemblance in appearance and the equal environments assumption in twin studies of personality traits. *Behavior Genetics,* 1976, *6,* 43–52.

Portenier, L. Twinning vs. a factor influencing personality. *Journal of Educational Psychology,* 1939, *30,* 542–547.

Radin, N. Maternal warmth, achievement motivation, and cognitive functioning in lower-class preschool children. *Child Development,* 1971, *42,* 1560–1565.

Radin, N. Observed maternal behavior with 4-year-old boys and girls in lower-class families. *Child Development,* 1974, *45,* 1126–1131.

Ragozin, A. S. A laboratory assessment of attachment behavior in day-care children. In Helen Bee (Ed.), *Social issues in developmental psychology* (2nd ed.). New York: Harper & Row, 1978.

Randall, M. An analysis of observer influence on sex and social class differences in mother–infant interaction. Paper read at the Biennial Meeting of the Society of Research in Child Development, Denver, 1975.

Record, R. G., McKeown, T., & Edwards, J. H. An investigation of the difference in measured intelligence between twins and single births. *Annals of Human Genetics,* 1970, *34,* 11–20.

Richards, M. P. M. *The integration of a child into a social world.* London: Cambridge University Press, 1974.

Routh, D. K., Schroeder, C. S., & O'Tuama, L. A. Development of activity level in children. *Developmental Psychology*, 1974, *10*, 163–168.

Rozelle, R. M., & Campbell, D. T. More plausible rival hypotheses in the cross-lagged panel correlation technique. *Psychological Bulletin*, 1969, *71*, 74–80.

Rutter, M. Maternal deprivation, 1972–1978: New findings, new concepts, new approaches. *Child Development*, 1979, *50*, 283–305.

Rutter, M., & Brown, G. W. The reliability and validity of measures of family life and relationships in families containing a psychiatric patient. *Social Psychiatry*, 1966, *1*, 38–53.

Rutter, M. Korn, S., & Birch, H. G. Genetic and environmental factors in the development of "primary reaction patterns." *British Journal of Social and Clinical Psychology*, 1963, *2*, 161–173.

Scarr, S. Genetic factors in activity motivation. *Child Development*, 1966, *37*, 663–673.

Scarr, S. Environmental bias in twin studies. *Eugenics Quarterly*, 1968, *15*, 34–40.

Scarr, S. Social introversion–extraversion as a heritable response. *Child Development*, 1969, *40*, 823–832.

Schaefer, E. S. A configurational analysis of children's reports of parent behavior. *Journal of Consulting Psychology*, 1965, *29*, 552–557.

Schaefer, E. S., & Bayley, N. Maternal behavior, child behavior, and their intercorrelations from infancy through adolescence. *Monographs of the society for Research in Child Development*, 1963, *28*, (3, Serial No. 87).

Schaffer, H. R. Early social behavior and the study of reciprocity. *Bulletin, British Psychological Society*, 1974, *27*, 209–216.

Schaffer, H. R., & Emerson, P. E. The development of social attachments in infancy. *Monographs of the Society for Research in Child Development*, 1964, *29*(3, Serial No. 94).

Schalock, H. *Observation of mother–child interaction in the laboratory and in the home.* Unpublished doctoral dissertation, University of Nebraska, 1965.

Schmalt, H. D. Selbstaendigkeitserziehung und verschiedene Aspekte des Leistungs-motives. (Independence training and various aspects of achievement motivation.) *Zeitschrift für Entwicklungspsychologie und Paedagogische Psychologie*, 1975, *7*, 24–37.

Sears, R., Maccoby, E., & Levin, H. *Patterns of child rearing.* Evanston, Ill.: Row, Peterson, 1957.

Sears, R. R., Rau, L., & Alpert, R. *Indentification and child rearing.* Stanford, Calif.: Stanford University Press, 1965.

Shapira, A., & Madsen, M. C. Co-operative and competitive behavior of kibbutz and urban children in Israel. *Child Development*, 1969, *40*, 609–617.

Shaw, M. C., & Dutton, B. E. The use of the parent attitude research inventory with the parents of bright academic underachievers. *Journal of Educational Psychology*, 1962, *53*, 203–208.

Siegel, S. *Nonparametric statistics for the behavioral sciences.* New York: McGraw-Hill, 1956.

Smith, H. T. A comparison of interview and observation methods of maternal behavior. *Journal of Abnormal and Social psychology*, 1958, *57*, 278–282.

Smith, P. K., & Connolly, K. Patterns of play and social interaction in pre-school children. In N. G. Blurton-Jones (Ed.), *Ethological studies of child behavior.* London: Cambridge University Press, 1972.

Sroufe, L. A., & Waters, E. Attachment as an organizational construct. *Child Development*, 1977, *48*, 1184–1199.

Stayton, D. J., Hogan, R., & Ainsworth, M. D. S. Infant obedience and maternal behavior: The origins of socialization reconsidered. *Child Development*, 1971, *42*, 1057–1069.

Stern, D. Mother and infant at play: The dyadic interaction involving facial, vocal, and gaze behaviors. In M. Lewis & L. A. Rosenblum (Eds.), *The effect of the infant on its caregiver.* New York: Wiley, 1974.

Streissguth, A. P., & Bee, H. L Mother–child interaction and cognitive development in children. *Young Children,* 1972, *2,* 154–173.

Taerum, T., Ferris, C., Lytton, H., & Zwirner, W. Programs for the analysis of dependencies in parent–child interaction sequences. *Behavior Research Methods and Instrumentation,* 1976, *8,* 517–519.

Thomas, A., Chess, S., Birch, H. G., Hertzig, M., Korn, S. *Behavioral individuality in early childhood.* New York: New York University Press, 1963.

Thomas, A., Chess, S., & Birch, H. G. *Temperament and behavior disorders in childhood.* New York: New York University Press, 1968.

Tinbergen, N. On aims and methods of ethology. *Zeitschrift für Tierpsychologie,* 1963, *20,* 410–433.

Tizard, B., & Hodges, J. The effect of early instituational rearing on the development of eight-year-old children. *Journal of Child Psychology and Psychiatry,* 1978, *19,* 99–118.

Tracy, R. L., Lamb, M. E., & Ainsworth, M. D. S. Infant approach behavior as related to attachment. *Child Development,* 1976, *47,* 571–578.

Tulkin, S. R. Social class differences in attachment behaviors of ten-month-old infants. *Child Development,* 1973, *44,* 171–174.

Tulkin, S. R., & Kagan, J. Mother–child interaction in the first year of life. *Child Development,* 1972, *43,* 31–41.

Tunnell, G. B. Three dimensions of naturalness: An expanded definition of field research. *Psychological Bulletin,* 1977, *84,* 426–437.

Vandenberg, S. G. Hereditary factors in normal personality traits (as measured by inventories). *Recent Advances in Biological Psychiatry,* 1967, *9,* 65–104.

Vernon, P. *Personality assessment.* London: Methuen, 1964.

Vernon, P. E. *Intelligence: Heredity and environment.* San Francisco: W. H. Freeman, 1979.

Waddington, C. H. *The ethical animal.* Chicago: University of Chicago Press, 1967.

Wainer, H. On the sensitivity of regression and regressor. *Psychological Bulletin,* 1978, *85,* 267–273.

Walters, R. H. & Parke, R. D. Influence of the response consequences to a social model on resistance to deviation. *Journal of Experimental Child Psychology,* 1964, *1,* 269–280.

Waters, E., Wippman, J., & Sroufe, L. A. Attachment, positive affect and competence in the peer group: Two studies in construct validation. *Child Development,* 1979, *50,* 821–829.

Watson, G. A comparison of the effects of lax versus strict home training. *Journal of Social Psychology,* 1934, *5,* 102–105.

Watts, D. *Mother–child interaction at home and in the laboratory: The effect of setting.* Unpublished master's thesis, University of Calgary, 1978.

Weick, K. E. Systematic observational methods. In G. Lindzey & F. Aronson (Eds.), *Handbook of social psychology* (2nd ed.), Vol. 2. Reading, Mass.: Addison-Wesley, 1968.

Weir, R. *Language in the crib.* The Hague: Mouton, 1962.

White, B. L., Kaban, B. T., & Attanucci, J. S. *The origins of human competence.* Lexington, Mass.: D. C. Heath, 1979.

White, S. H. The learning theory approach. In P. H. Mussen (Ed.), *Carmichael's Manual of Child Psychology, Vol. 1. New York: Wiley, 1970.*

Willerman, L. *Activity level hyperactivity in twins. Child Development,* 1973, *44,* 288–293.

Willerman, L, & Plomin, R. Activity level in children and their parents. *Child Development,* 1973, *44,* 854–858.

Wilson E. *Sociobiology: A new synthesis.* Cambridge, Mass.: Harvard University Press, 1975.

Wilson, R. S. Twins: Patterns of cognitive development as measured on the Wechsler Preschool and Primary Scale of Intelligence. *Developmental Psychology*, 1975, *11*, 126–134.

Winer, B. J. *Statistical principles in experimental design*. New York: McGraw-Hill, 1962.

Winterbottom, M. R. The relation of need for achievement to learning experiences in independence and mastery. In J. Atkinson (Ed.), *Motives in fantasy, action and society*. Princeton, N.J.: Van Nostrand, 1958.

Witkin, H. A., Dyk, R. B., Faterson, H. F., Goodenough, D. R., & Karp, S. A. *Psychological differentiation*. New York: Wiley, 1962.

Yarrow, L. J. Research in dimensions of early maternal care. *Merrill-Palmer Quarterly*, 1963, *9*, 101–114.

Yarrow, M. R. Problems of methods in parent–child research. *Child Development*, 1963, 34, 215–226.

Yarrow, M. R., & Scott, P. M. Imitation of nurturant and nonurturant models. *Journal of Personality and Social Psychology*, 1972, *23*, 259–270.

Yarrow, M. R., Campbell, J. D., & Burton, R. V. *Child rearing: An inquiry into research and methods*. San Francisco: Jossey-Bass, 1968.

Yarrow, M. R., Waxler, C. Z., & Scott, P. M. Child effects on adult behavior. *Developmental Psychology*, 1971, *5*, 300–311.

Young, J. Z. *An introduction to the study of man*. London: Oxford University Press, 1971.

Yuzwak, W. J. *The effect of setting and mother's education on mother-child interaction*. Unpublished master's thesis, University of Calgary, 1979.

Zajonc, R. B., & Markus, G. B. Birth order and intellectual development. *Psychological Review*, 1975, *82*, 74–88.

Zazzo, R. *Les jumeaux: Le couple et la personne*. Paris: Presses Universitaires de France, 1960.

Zegiob, L. E., & Forehand, R. Maternal interactive behavior as a function of rare, socioeconomic status and sex of the child. *Child Development*, 1975, *46*, 564–568.

Zigler, E. F., & Child, I. L. (Eds.), *Socialization and personality development*. Reading, Mass.: Addison-Wesley, 1973.

Zunich, M. A study of relationships between child rearing attitudes and maternal behavior. *Journal of Experimental Education*, 1961, *30*, 231–241.

Zussman, J. U. Relationship of demographic factors to parental discipline techniques. *Developmental Psychology*, 1978, *14*, 685–686.

Index